QUANTITATIVE TOOLKIT FOR ECONOMICS AND FINANCE

STEPHEN MATHIS
Shippensburg University

LEE SIEGEL
Pennsylvania Department of Treasury

Kolb Publishing Company
4705 S.W. 72 Ave. Miami, Florida 33155
(305) 663-0550   FAX (305) 663-6579

To my mother, Allene, my special friend, Bertha, and in memory of my father, Virgil.

Stephen Mathis

To my parents, Minerva and Jack, my wife, Eva, my children, Michael and Traci, and in memory of my niece, Eve Renee Friedman.

Lee Siegel

Library of Congress Catalog Card Number 92-72578

ISBN: 1-878975-14-5

Kolb Publishing Company
4705 S.W. 72 Ave. Miami, Florida 33155
(305) 663-0550   FAX (305) 663-6579

Preface

The purpose of this book is to provide a concise source of basic methodological and technical skills for undergraduate and Masters level graduate economics and MBA students. It is designed to serve as a supplement or handbook for principles and intermediate level students. However, it could be treated as a lower level Mathematical Economics text. The book begins by describing the purpose and techniques, both algebraic and geometric, associated with basic economic model building and interpretation. Building upon this background, the later chapters develop and discuss the calculus–based tools relevant to economic analysis at a higher level. The book concludes with a chapter devoted to basic statistical techniques used for estimating and interpreting simple models. It should be stressed that the authors' intent is to develop a book which serves to bridge the gap between mathematical tools and economic theory.

The primary audience for this book is at the principles and intermediate level. However, it is flexible enough to be a reference book and/or toolbook for a wide variety of courses and levels of student background including those at the MBA level. More specifically, the book is applicable to both noncalculus– and calculus–based courses. In the latter event, although those chapters containing calculus review some of the basic theory, they are most useful and are intended primarily for students who have previously been introduced to calculus. In a similar vein, the statistics chapter is primarily intended for students already familiar with basic statistical techniques. In both cases, these chapters demonstrate the application of such tools to economic analysis.

In addition to providing some theoretical insight on a more intuitive level, the book contains numerous applications to economics. As an aid to student comprehension, glossaries, problem sets, and references are included.

The authors feel there is a strong need for a book of this nature. These contentions are based on a number of observations:

1) Much of the difficulty faced by students enrolled in economics courses is related to understanding the methodology and mathematics associated with economics. Even students familiar with quantitative tools often have difficulty applying and interpreting those tools in an economic context.

2) There are no recent books addressing this problem. Most economic textbooks are primarily devoted to developing economic concepts and ignore the problems. The few books in Mathematical Economics are overdeveloped from the standpoint of the target audience of this text.

3) A book of the this type should have a broad appeal. Most of the fundamental methodology and mathematical tools covered are common to macroeconomic and microeconomic areas. In addition, this material remains applicable to upper-level economics courses, enabling the book to serve as a reference source.

This text is not designed to compete against theory textbooks nor, as currently written, against fully developed mathematical economics texts. Instead, the book addresses two of the major problems faced by economics students. For students with a weaker background in mathematics, the book provides an intuitive explanation of the basic mathematical tools utilized in economics. For students with a stronger background, the book facilitates the application of those tools through numerous economic examples. These attributes make the book ideal as either a supplementary text or as a reference source for many economics courses.

We are grateful to a number of people who have aided in the preparation of this book. We would like to thank Karen Kelley and Joyce Yocum for their considerable efforts in word processing this manuscript. We are also very appreciative to the helpful reviews and comments made by Professors Jan Koscianski and Frank Dangello of Shippensburg University. Also, we are indebted to the staff of Kolb Publishing Company, particularly Kateri Davis, Evelyn Gosnell, and Andrea Coens for reviewing and editing the manuscript. Finally, we would like to thank several of our research assistants, including Robert King, Nadine Celone, Jennifer Walz, Andrew Speer, and A. Srinivasa for their various contributions to this project.

Contents

Chapter 3
Multivariate Functions 67

Chapter 4
Marginal Functions and Their Applications 88

Chapter 5
Average Functions and Elasticities 148

Chapter 6
Simultaneous Equation Models   192

Chapter 7
Derivatives: Univariate Functions   218

Chapter 8
Derivatives: Multivariate Functions   275

Chapter 9
Estimation of Simple Models   **319**

Solutions to Excercises   **367**

1

Introduction to Model Building

Introduction

The science of economics is concerned with the basic dilemma of how to allocate scarce resources among various uses in a society. Solving this allocation problem involves making rational choices. Although the particular choices selected often depend on the values and ideologies embedded in a particular society, many of the techniques for examining the rational choice process remain common to all. Thus, regardless of ideology, the student of economics must become familiar with the basic techniques and tools used in the process of formally analyzing economic problems. The purpose of this book is to develop a set of such tools and show how they can be applied to economic problems. The first part of this chapter discusses a general methodology within which economic problems are analyzed. Within this context, the characteristics, assumptions, and specification techniques associated with economic models are discussed. The remainder of the chapter contains a brief description of the material covered in subsequent chapters.

Characteristics of Models

The general approach to solving economic problems is one of constructing models. It is within this framework that we can analyze the process of making rational choices. A **model** can be defined as a formal framework expressing the relationship between certain facts, and the model can be used to analyze a variety of problems. More specifically, models are constructed to explain and/or predict the behavior of some variable, or group of variables, on the basis of another variable or group of variables. Such models are representations of causal theories. A **variable** is some quantity or attribute that can take a set of values. Given the goals of explanation and/or prediction, it is necessary when constructing a model to postulate which variables are to be explained and which are to be used to provide the explanation. The variables designated to be explained are called **dependent variables** and those providing the explanation are **independent variables**. Dependent variables are sometimes referred to as **endogenous variables**, while independent variables are often termed **exogenous variables**. This designation process is based on logic and intuition. It establishes a clear purpose for the model, and it also sets up the model in a way that makes it testable and potentially refutable. This is necessary because it is possible to construct a multitude of models to explain the same event. Some of these models, however, may be incorrect, and some may be better than others. Since not even the brightest of researchers is omniscient, models must be constructed in a way that allows them to be tested against real-world events in order to determine their validity. Ultimately, with all else equal, we want to choose the model that does the best job of explaining and predicting real-world events.

Most relationships between variables are functional relationships. A **function** is a relationship such that for every admissible value assigned to the independent variable or variables, there will exist a unique value corresponding to the dependent variable. Some models are quite simple, containing one functional relationship between just two variables, one dependent and one independent. This type of relationship is defined as a **univariate function**. Other models are more complex, containing functional relationships which have several independent variables. These relationships are defined as **multivariate functions**. The most complex models contain more than one functional relationship, and thus they are not only multivariate, but multiequation as well. The complexity of a model depends on a number of factors: the complexity of the problem to be analyzed, the degree of precision desired, and the amount of resources available to the researcher.

As stated earlier, models are designed to explain and/or predict events. It should be noted, however, that these two goals do not always coincide, and as a result, the researcher must sometimes settle for one or the other. For example, a simple model, containing only one independent variable, might provide some explanation regarding the dependent variable. Due to its lack of comprehensiveness, however, it may fail to reliably predict its behavior. On the other hand, a more comprehensive model, containing several independent variables, may as a package provide reliable predictions about the dependent variable's behavior, but it may fail to separate out the effects attributed to each independent variable. As another example, economists sometimes specify a dependent variable to be a function of past values of itself, i.e., its own past values represent the independent variable. This type of model often predicts well but provides no explanation or insight as to why the dependent variable behaves as it does. A model which neither explains nor predicts very well is not deemed to be of much use. It should be pointed out, however, that the process of determining these results is not worthless. The fact that a model has been constructed, tested, and rejected helps refine the body of knowledge.

Another important characteristic associated with models is that they are by their very nature abstractions. In an attempt to explain reality, which is complex, we form a theory that captures the essence of reality while ignoring complicating factors that are deemed unimportant. In this way, a theory might be compared to a road map that contains the vital information necessary to a traveler while leaving out some details. The omission of these details, rather than making the map less useful, actually increases its usefulness. Could you imagine a roadmap that depicted every curve in the road or the positions and contents of every sign? Such a map would be either too large or too cluttered and would detract from its main function. Judgments have to be made, both in developing maps and in constructing theories, with regard to what is considered essential and important, as opposed to mere trivial details.

Underlying Assumptions

Before constructing a model, we must specify the underlying assumptions on which it is based. These assumptions help focus the model on the problem being analyzed. By doing so, complicating factors considered unessential to understanding the problem are eliminated from the analysis. This process enables the model to be a manageable abstraction from the real world, and it also outlines the scope within which the model can be applied. We must bear in mind, however, that assumptions do provide limitations regarding the conclusions and predictions that can ultimately be made from the model. Underlying assumptions are necessary for any type of research; however, we will develop them within the context of economic research.

The first type of major assumption necessary for building an economic model is that of **rationality**. This means all economic agents, (e.g., consumers, firms, owners of factors of production) will act in a manner to better themselves. Another way to view this is that economic agents will not intentionally act in a manner that makes themselves worse. This assumption almost sounds trivial, but it is essential if a model is to be used to predict outcomes. If agents behaved in an irrational and unpredictable manner, the applicability of any conventional economic model would be in jeopardy.

A second category of assumptions underlying an economic model is that of the **environmental assumptions**. These assumptions describe the factors which circumscribe the model and hence influence its results. Some examples of these types of assumptions are the amount of information available to economic agents, the type of market within which agents operate, and the influence of government on the decision-making process. Clearly all of these factors will affect the outcomes predicted by an economic model, and as a result, making assumptions about their nature is essential.

Construction and Testing of Models

Once the assumptions underlying a model have been established, it is possible to construct the actual model. Building a model is essentially a constrained maximization problem, i.e., getting the most for least. We want a model that explains and predicts as accurately as possible, but at the same time we want to keep the model as simple as possible, bearing in mind its manageability and cost. First we must establish the goal of the model which, within our context, is likely to explain and/or predict some economic phenomena. With this thought in mind, it is then necessary to designate the variables, as the dependent variables, that are to represent this phenomenon. Since the goal is to explain and predict the behavior of these variables, the next step is to establish those variables, designated as independent variables, which are postulated to affect the dependent variables. This process is essentially governed by logic and intuition, while also keeping in mind the ultimate measurability of the included variables. In other words, it makes little practical sense to include variables that cannot be accurately measured.

At this point, the researcher must decide how many independent variables to include. Although not always the case, we can generally say that the inclusion of more independent variables increases the comprehensiveness or explanatory power of a model. Technically, there may be thousands of independent variables affecting a dependent variable. Recall, however, that for a model to be useful, it must be a manageable abstraction. Thus, using good intuition, we include in a model only those independent variables that make a significant contribution. The number of independent variables to be included also depends on the degree of precision or accuracy desired for the project at hand. In some instances a general ballpark estimate of the relationship between variables may suffice, and a simple univariate function, containing only one independent variable, may be appropriate. In other cases, where a greater degree of precision is desired, a more complex multivariate model containing several independent variables may be necessary. For example, we might build a model to explain and predict the quantity demanded of some product. A simple model, which might accomplish this task to a certain degree, would be a univariate function expressing the quantity demanded of a good as a function of its own price. We are postulating that the price of a good can be used to explain and predict the quantity demanded of that good. Hence, price is designated as the independent variable. However, if deemed desirable, the model can be made more comprehensive by including additional independent variables such as income of consumers, tastes, and prices of related goods. This multivariate version will probably provide a higher degree of precision with regard to explanation and prediction, but it also becomes somewhat more cumbersome to use.

Multivariate models are designed to show how changes in each independent variable in isolation affect the dependent variable, even though several independent variables may be included in the model. Recall that for a functional relationship to exist between variables, there must be a unique value pertaining to the dependent variable for each chosen value of the independent one. In order for this functional relationship to hold, all independent variables, other than the one in question, must be held constant. This procedure is known as the **ceteris paribus assumption,** which means "all else constant." Implicitly, this assumption is also made for the factors not specifically included in a model. Without this assumption it would be impossible to generate unique outcomes for dependent variables.

Once the variables to be included in a model have been defined, it is necessary to specify the form of the model, i.e., we must establish the manner in which the variables are linked. Different forms are used to represent types of relationships between variables. The form specified is, again, postulated by the researcher using logic, intuition, and convenience.

A researcher, of course, is not omniscient. Thus he or she has no way of knowing if the theoretical model is an accurate depiction of reality unless it can be tested. Accordingly, models are constructed in a way that allows them to be tested with real-world data to see how well they perform. Generally speaking, a model can be expressed in several forms, e.g., verbal, tabular, graphical, or mathematical. The mathematical version, while representing only one way of investigating economic problems, is the approach which best facilitates the process of testing a model. Furthermore, a model must be set up in a way that allows it to be rejected if it does not perform adequately. A rejection does not mean the research has been wasted, because it enables the researcher to move on and construct a new or alternative model, which will also be tested. Models that are set up too broadly, allowing for too many possible outcomes, are of little use. For example, a fortune teller predicts that a "big" event will happen in the world, sometime in the next year. This "model," and associated prediction, is so encompassing that it provides no insight. There is really no way to test it and possibly reject it because it allows for too many outcomes. The odds are virtually 100 percent that some big event will happen in the world next year. Due to a lack of specificity of the nature of a "big" event, the fortune teller after the fact can always claim that some event that occurred was a "big" event. As such, this "model" can never be rejected. Technically this approach is an application of what most relevant literature defines as the **scientific method**. In other words, a theory is generally accepted until it can be proven false. But for a model to be tested for its falsifiability, and ultimately deemed useful, it must "stick its neck out somewhat."

Pitfalls to Avoid in Model Building

In specifying a theory or model, attention should be paid to the underlying assumptions. The predictions of a theory can generally be deduced directly from these assumptions, although it is often easier to derive these predictions by manipulating the formal model. Therefore, always choose assumptions carefully.

The purpose of theory is both to explain and predict. However, due to the complexity of reality, it is often useful for the theorist to employ simplifying assumptions. The theorist hopes that these assumptions capture the essence of the phenomena under consideration without causing major distractions. Though some distortion will occur, we can determine a tolerable level of distortion by the use to which the model is put and the cost of that distortion. In other words, a theory only approximates reality. How close an approximation is depends on the costs of making an error relative to the costs of improving the approximation. The magnitude of both types of costs depends on the specific application.

In elementary physics, for example, it is common when describing the motion of an object to assume that friction is nonexistent. This simplifying assumption, though unrealistic, is useful. Although friction is present, the prediction of the theory in many applications is close enough for all practical purposes. Although the use of the assumption causes a distortion, its impact is considered negligible. On the other hand, when the theory is used to put a rocket on the moon, it is no longer reasonable to ignore the effects of friction.

A similar example from economics can also illustrate this point. When predicting the quantity and price of a good that will be transacted, it is common to utilize a model of supply and demand. The supply and demand model implicitly assumes that the market is perfectly competitive, though the conditions necessary for perfect competition are unlikely to be met in any particular market. However, for most applications the theory predicts reasonably well and thus represents a close enough approximation to reality. In other cases it may be fruitful to use a model approximate to a different market structure, i.e., monopoly, oligopoly, or monopolistic competition.

The previous discussion of recognizing the limitations of a model due to its underlying assumptions indicates the first pitfall to avoid. While it is common and useful to extrapolate the results of a model to cases where the assumptions are not fulfilled, we must be careful in doing so. Some assumptions are critical to the results, while others have a negligible impact. When a critical assumption is violated, a large distortion is likely. Therefore, we should choose a theory with a sufficient degree of realism, based upon the type of problem the theory is supposed to solve.

The remaining pitfalls are logical errors frequently encountered in constructing a theory. While they are easy to describe, they are often difficult to detect. As a group they constitute fallacies in reasoning. The three fallacies that will be discussed are the fallacy of false cause or the post hoc fallacy, the fallacy of composition, and the fallacy of division. While other fallacies exist, these are probably most often encountered.

First is the **fallacy of false cause**. Economic theories describe a causal relationship between variables. A causal relationship can be expressed by an *if–then* statement. For example, suppose that we believe that some set of causal or independent factors, A, cause some phenomenon, B, to occur. We can express this as: *if* A occurs, *then* B will occur. In that case A represents the cause, and B represents the effect. It should be clear that in order for A to cause B, A must occur first, and B then follows. The time difference between A and B might be large or very small. If A is the act of conception and B is the birth of a child, the time difference is large—approximately nine months. When A is the striking of a match and B is the match lighting, the time difference is very small—a fraction of a second. In any event, in order to state that A causes B, A must precede B, if only by some infinitesimal amount. When A and B occur simultaneously, or if B precedes A, there is no way that we can claim that A caused B. Therefore, the assumed cause should always precede the assumed effect.

Time causal relationships obviously have this property. However, it is improper to assume that just because A preceded B, that, in fact, A caused B to occur. It is possible that A and B are not causally related, and yet still observe that B follows A. One might even observe that situation numerous times. It might occur by random chance (dumb luck) or because there is some third factor, C, that is causing both A and B. In either event we could state that A and B are correlated or related, but not in a causal manner. In order for A and B to be causally related, they must be correlated. However, correlation alone is not sufficient to guarantee causality.

Consider the following hypothetical observation. In some Scandinavian country after World War II, the following was noticed. Shortly after the war, people in that country observed many more storks overhead. Soon thereafter, the number of births in that country was observed to increase. A naive theorist observing these phenomena might be led to the theory that storks (or the observation of them) cause babies to be born. This theory would exemplify the post hoc fallacy. The name of this fallacy derives from the latin expression, "post hoc ergo propter hoc" which means, after this, therefore, because of this. Notice that just because the storks were observed first and then the babies were born does not imply that the storks caused the babies to be born.

An explanation for this observed correlation might be as follows. When the soldiers returned from the war, many new households were established and new homes were built. The homes contained chimneys, which is where storks like to build nests. This explains why more storks were observed. Why the return of soldiers from war might lead to more babies being born, we leave up to the reader's imagination.

One way to avoid this causal pitfall is to start with a leading example of our theory. This leading example should be almost like a story, where the variables under consideration are defined and classified as causal (independent) or explained (dependent). The story should explain why and how we expect the independent variable(s) to affect the dependent variable. In other words, the reason we expect a causal link should be included. This rationale should be plausible and not contrived. While it is still possible that our plausible explanation is wrong, we at least have reason to believe that a causal link exists and that the correlation observed is not spurious.

Another commonly encountered fallacy is the **fallacy of composition**. This fallacy is most likely encountered in constructing a macroeconomic theory. This occurs because macroeconomics deals with the behavior of aggregates, i.e., the aggregate level of consumption expenditures. To explain the behavior of an aggregate it seems reasonable to look at factors affecting the individual and generalize that to the aggregate. For example, in explaining the aggregate level of consumption expenditures, we might start by looking at factors that affect the consumption expenditures of an individual household. We might postulate that the household's consumption expenditure level depends upon its disposable income, wealth, interest rates, and the like. We might then generalize from this and assume that the same factors aggregated affect the aggregate level of consumption expenditures.

This process of generalizing from the part (individual) to the whole (society) is in most cases legitimate and fruitful. However, care must be exercised in doing so, since what is true for the part might not be true for the whole. The fallacy of composition occurs when one generalizes in this manner, in a situation where it is not legitimate to do so. The fallacy occurs because the situation faced by the part is not analogous to that faced by the whole.

The following noneconomic example provides a good illustration of the fallacy of composition. Assume that you are at a football stadium in the back row and cannot see clearly. You stand up and find that you can see better. Generalizing from your specific circumstance you might reason as follows. Since when I stand up I can see better, if everyone stood up then everyone would see better. This reasoning, however, is obviously flawed. The reason you can see better when you stand up is that if you alone do so, you have a better vantage point. However, if everyone stood up, no one's vantage point, including your own, would be improved.

Another example from economics might further clarify this fallacy. Assume that you sell a product whose price is determined by the market, and the price of your product increased. If nothing else had changed, this price increase would increase your purchasing power and therefore make you better off. Again, you might be led to generalize from your personal experience to the impact of price increases for society overall. You might reason as follows: "Since when the price of my product increased, I was better off; if all prices increased by the same percent, everyone would be better off." Again, the fallacy of composition has been committed since what is true for the part is not true for the whole. The flaw in reasoning is that when only your price increases, it is true that your purchasing power has risen. This occurs because your income rises, and with all other prices unchanged, this increase in income represents an increase in purchasing power. However, when all prices rise proportionately, all incomes will rise proportionately as well, but the purchasing power represented by this higher income is unchanged. Therefore with purchasing power unchanged, no one would be better off.

In theorizing about the behavior of the whole, it is common to generalize from the behavior of a part. When the situation of the part and the whole is analogous, it is legitimate to do so. However, we should always check that the situations are truly analogous. When they are not, we run the risk of committing the fallacy of composition.

The last fallacy to be discussed is the **fallacy of division**. It can occur when we reason that what is true for the whole must also be true for each part. Sometimes such reasoning can lead to correct conclusions. However, it is not universally valid.

The fallacy of division is not as common as the other two fallacies. Again we shall demonstrate this fallacy by means of an economic example. Under suitable conditions, it can be shown that free trade between countries, i.e., no trade barriers, is preferable from society's standpoint to no trade. Since society overall is better off with free trade, one might reason that everyone in society must also benefit from free trade. This is generally not the case. Some individuals who produce and sell goods domestically might be better off if no trade took place when the same goods are imported under free trade. For example, domestic car manufacturers might benefit if they didn't have to compete with foreign manufacturers. The increased competition might lower their prices and profits. While other segments of society, i.e., car consumers, gain as does the society overall, not everyone benefits from free trade.

The purpose of this section was to sensitize the reader to the pitfalls encountered in developing and interpreting theories. When evaluating a theory, we should check that these errors in logic have not been committed. While these pitfalls are easy to describe, they may be difficult to detect, since the logical processes that give rise to them are sometimes legitimate and sometimes illegitimate. In addition, the fallacies often occur in a subtle manner, and, by following the suggestions in this section, they can often be detected or avoided.

An Overview of the Book

As can be seen from this first chapter, the focus of this book is the development of tools necessary for constructing and interpretating economic models. Two types of tools will be developed: methodological tools and mathematical tools. Wherever possible, the relationship between these two types of tools will be discussed and interpreted. This is true both in terms of the models considered as well as the tools necessary for those models.

The simplest economic models are relationships between one independent variable and one dependent variable. Some such relationships are termed univariate functions and are the focus of Chapter 2. Starting with the elementary concept of Cartesian coordinates, methods of graphing such relationships are presented. Particular attention is paid to determining and interpreting the intercept and the slope. Different functional forms are examined, starting with linear relationships (the simplest) and proceeding to more complex nonlinear functional forms.

As a first approximation of reality, it is common to express theories as univariate functions. However, most dependent variables in economics depend upon more than one independent variable. When univariate functions do not possess sufficient explanatory or predictive power, the first step in generalizing a theory is to add more independent variables. Theories containing one dependent variable and more than one independent variable can be expressed as multivariate functions. In Chapter 3, the concept of a function is extended to the multivariate case. In addition, tools for graphing and interpreting multivariate functions are provided, with particular focus on the partial slope and intercept. In this context the relation of the "ceteris paribus" assumption to the mathematical tools is explored.

The focus on the slope in Chapters 2 and 3 is not coincidental. Many economic concepts are related to, if not represented by, the slope of some function. Chapter 4 presents many examples from both microeconomics and macroeconomics where this is indeed the case. In addition, the relationship between the slope and optimization problems in economics is explored. In this context the slope is referred to as the "marginal function" and conditions for maximizing or minimizing some function are expressed in terms of the properties of these marginal functions. Both univariate as well as multivariate functions are utilized, and the concepts of concavity are developed.

While marginal functions are the primary application of the slope, average functions and elasticities are related to the slope as well. In Chapter 5, average functions are initially developed, and the relationship between average and total functions is explored with applications from economics. Both graphical and algebraic techniques are utilized in discussing this relationship. The marginal–average relationship is also developed. The concept of an elasticity is then investigated and is found to be the ratio of the marginal function to the average function. Methods of calculation, of both point and arc elasticities, are provided. The significance and interpretation of various elasticities is discussed.

The models and tools utilized up to this point will have been of the "simple" variety. That is, that the model contains only one equation and, therefore, only one dependent variable. It is often the case that two or more variables are simultaneously determined by a set of independent variables. In that event the model would be represented by a set of equations whose solution values must satisfy each equation. This is known as a simultaneous equation model and is the focus of Chapter 6. This chapter includes a discussion of equilibrium along with its application to supply and demand, monopoly pricing, and national income determination.

Chapters 7 and 8 deal with much of the material covered in Chapters 4 and 5. The difference in treatment of these concepts is the level of mathematical sophistication. Prior to these chapters only algebraic or geometrical tools are utilized. These last two chapters employ tools from calculus. Chapter 7 develops calculus techniques applicable to univariate functions, while Chapter 8 does the same for multivariate functions. In Chapter 7 the concept of a limit and its relation to the derivative is developed, followed by methods of differentiation. It is shown that the derivative is another name for the marginal function, and applications of marginal functions, including optimization problems, are discussed. In addition, the concept of an elasticity is redefined in terms of the derivative. Chapter 8 generalizes the concept of the derivative (total and partial) to multivariate functions. In that context, elasticities and optimization problems are revisited. The chapter culminates with techniques for handling a constrained optimization problem, including the Lagrangean method.

In general, theory alone does not inform us of the exact relationship between variables. Instead researchers collect and analyze data in an effort to estimate what the true relationships are. Techniques for estimation, interpretation, and testing of models are presented in Chapter 9.

Over time the field of economics has become more mathematical. Today a student of economics must master both economic concepts and mathematical tools. The goal of this book is to remove mathematics as an obstacle to understanding economics. Towards this end, mathematical tools are developed first and are then followed by numerous economic applications. In this way, students will see the relationship between the economic and mathematical concepts. They can then see the graphical and mathematical expositions of a theory as being identical to the verbal exposition.

Important Terms in this Chapter

Ceteris paribus assumption – "all else constant."

Dependent variable – a variable whose behavior is affected by another variable(s).

Fallacy of composition – process of generalizing from the part (individual) to the whole (society), where the situation faced by the part is not analogous to that faced by the whole.

Fallacy of division - process of extending a conclusion which is true for the whole to each of its component parts when the situations faced by each are not analogous.

Fallacy of false cause (post hoc fallacy) – a fallacy which states that if two events are in sequence, the first causes the second.

Function – a relationship such that for every admissible value assigned to the causal (independent) variable or variables, there will exist a unique value corresponding to the explained (dependent) variable.

Independent variable – a variable used to explain the behavior of another variable.

Model - a formal framework expressing the relationship between certain facts that can be used to analyze a variety of problems.

Multivariate function - a function containing more than one independent variable.

Scientific method - a method of analysis which involves forming a model, collecting data, and forming and testing hypotheses.

Variable - some quantity that can take on a set of values or attributes.

Exercises

1. Explain why you agree or disagree with the following statements.
   a) If a model is based upon unrealistic assumptions, it is necessarily a bad model.
   b) A model whose predictions encompass *all potential* outcomes is a good model.
   c) A model that does a good job of explaining phenomena will automatically predict well. Similarly, a model that predicts well will automatically provide a good explanation of the relevant phenomena.

2. Explain the significance and relationship of the following within the context of a causal theory.
   a) independent variables
   b) dependent variables
   c) mathematical functions

3. Identify the fallacy in reasoning present in the following arguments. Explain the logical error leading to that fallacy.
   a) I observe that inflationary periods are also periods of prosperity. I therefore conclude that inflation causes prosperity.
   b) The government through fiscal policy may stimulate the economy and cause the level of national income to increase. This increased prosperity for the economy will be beneficial to all members of society.
   c) What's good for General Motors is good for the U.S. economy.

4. If two variables are causally related, they will also be correlated. Therefore, any time I observe a correlation between variables, I can infer that they are causally related. Comment.

Univariate Functions

Introduction

As discussed in Chapter 1, an economic model can be expressed in a number of forms: verbal, tabular, graphical, or mathematical. The initial construction of a model is based on basic economic intuition. For example, it might be plausible that the quantity demanded of a good can, at least in part, be explained by its price level. Once a model has been conceived, it is generally desirable to express it in some testable form so that its validity can be determined. It is the mathematical version of a model that usually facilitates meeting this criterion.

These mathematical models are often presented graphically as well, in order to provide a clear concise picture of what is being described. The purpose of this chapter is to establish some of the basic mathematical and graphical tools used in model building. In addition, this chapter describes how these basic tools can be used to construct some simple models that are useful to economists.

Basic Mathematical Conceptualization

The science of economics, or, for that matter, any science, is concerned with determining the nature and the magnitude of relationships between variables. A **variable** is some quantity or attribute that can take on a set of values. The simplest relationship is one between only two variables, where the goal is to explain the behavior of one variable on the basis of values assigned to the other. When stating a theory or model, it is necessary to postulate the direction of the relationship between the variables by designating which is the independent and which is the dependent variable. This process is determined by economic intuition. In the example here, if we feel that the quantity demanded of a product is determined by its price, then it is logical to treat the quantity demanded as the dependent variable and the price as the independent variable.

Most relationships used in economics are functional relationships. A **function** is a relationship such that, for every admissible value assigned to the independent variable, there will exist a unique value corresponding to the dependent variable. The set of values from which the independent variable is drawn is defined as the **domain** of the function, while the set of values that can be assigned to the dependent variable is referred to as the **range**. The simplest type of function is one containing only one independent variable, as well as one dependent variable, and is defined as a **univariate function**. Thus the term univariate, meaning *one variable*, refers to the number of independent variables in an equation. This can easily be expressed in terms of a mathematical equation, where by convention, the dependent variable is placed on the left side of the equation and the independent variable is placed on the right. Returning to the above example, let Q represent the dependent variable, quantity demanded, and P represent the independent variable, price. This is a type of univariate function and can be expressed in general functional form as $Q = f(P)$. This is read as "Q is equal to some function of P." It is a mathematical representation of a theory and is designed not only to demonstrate that a relationship exists between two variables, but also to predict the effect that a change in an independent variable has on the dependent variable.

Cartesian Coordinates

Before discussing any specific forms of univariate functions and their associated graphics, it is useful to review some of the basics underlying graphical analyses. Since the concern of this chapter is with univariate or two variable functions, it is necessary to define an **ordered pair** (two numbers) and demonstrate how to plot them. A pair of numbers is an ordered pair if the order in which they are listed has some type of significance. This ordered pair can be plotted graphically provided a two-dimensional space is used, one dimension for each number, and provided each dimension has a scale that is sequentially numbered. This can be done by establishing a plane containing two perpendicularly intersecting number lines. The first, usually horizontal, is generally referred to as the x axis, while the other, usually vertical, is referred to as the y axis. The point of intersection is where x and y are assigned values of zero and is called the **origin**. The values of x increase in the positive direction moving rightward from the origin and increase negatively moving leftward from the origin. The values of y increase positively moving upward from the origin and negatively moving downward from the origin. This system of ordering is demonstrated in Figure 2.1.

The scales used in this scheme are known as **Cartesian coordinates**, and they provide a systematic way to plot ordered pairs of numbers. For

Figure 2.1
Cartesian Coordinates

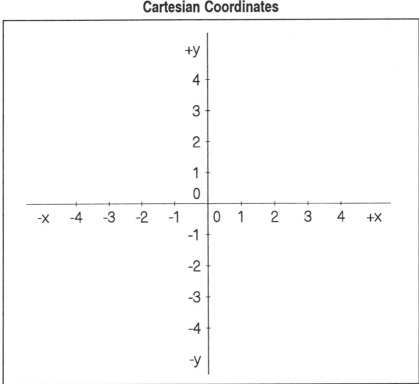

example the following x, y pairs (1,2), (2,3), (–1,1), (–2,–3) and (2,–2) can be plotted as in Figure 2.2.

Note that the first number in each ordered pair refers to the x value and the second to the y value. Although negative numbers are occasionally used in economics, most economic variables are of positive values. As a consequence, most of our attention is focused on the northeast quadrant (quadrant I) of the graph for which the values of the plotted variables x and y are positive. In addition to simply plotting groups of ordered pairs of numbers, a graphical analysis also provides a useful tool for depicting functional relationships.

Figure 2.2
Plots of Ordered Pairs

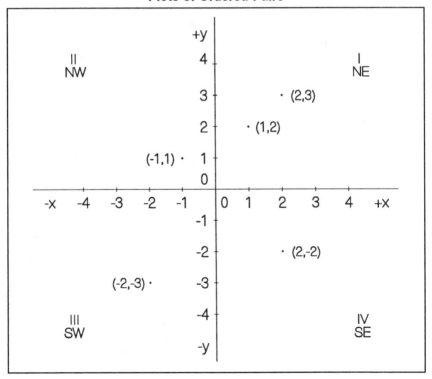

Linear Functions

The analysis developed up to this point has referred only to general functional forms such as Q = f(P) or y = f(x). These are examples of univariate functions in that each contains only one independent variable, or just two variables in total. In each case, it is theorized that the value of the variable on the left-hand side of the equation (the dependent variable) is determined by the value of the variable on the right-hand side (the independent variable). The exact nature of the functional relationships have yet to be specified. In order to make a model more specific and ultimately testable, it is necessary to specify the mathematical nature of the functional relationship between the variables. One of the most basic, yet frequently used, is the linear functional relationship. A **linear function** is one containing variables raised to only the first power. Some examples of linear functions are: y = 2x, y = .5x, y = 2 + 4x or y = 10 − 5x. In each case, the variables y and x are raised only to the first power. More generally, any linear function can be expressed as $y = b_0 + b_1 x$, where y and x are the variables as defined previously and b_0 and b_1 represent values known as either **coefficients** or **parameters**. These coefficients are not variables but are instead givens. In most basic economics courses, they are simply specified. Some information about how these coefficients are actually estimated is presented in Chapter 9. What is important for our present purposes is how to interpret these coefficients. Students may recognize that the general linear function $y = b_0 + b_1 x$ is the same as the expression y = mx + b presented in many algebra textbooks. In our version we are letting $b = b_0$ and $m = b_1$.

The Intercept Coefficient

The term b_0 in the above equation is defined as the **intercept** coefficient and represents the value of the left hand or dependent variable, y, when the right hand or independent variable, x, is equal to zero. In a sense, it represents that part of y not explained by the variable x. Substituting x = 0 into the general linear function, $y = b_0 + b_1 x_1$, yields $y = b_0$. For the specific functions y = 2x, y = .5x, y = 2 + 4x, and y = 10 − 5x, we can substitute x = 0 in each case and obtain intercept values of 0, 0, 2, and 10 respectively.

When graphing a function in x - y space, the intercept represents the y value at which x = 0, or where the function "intercepts" the y axis. Before graphing some linear functions, it is necessary to interpret the other coefficient, b_1.

The Slope Coefficient

The term b_1 is the value by which the right hand or independent variable is multiplied, and for linear functions, is defined as the **slope coefficient** or simply the **slope**. This term is very important both in terms of its sign and magnitude. It represents in which direction, and by how much, the dependent variable y changes when there is some change in the independent variable x. Symbolically, the slope is expressed as $\Delta y/\Delta x$, which reads as "the change in y caused by a change in x" or as "the rate of change in y caused by a change in x." It can be demonstrated that the slope of a linear function is equal to the constant coefficient b_1, associated with the independent variable. This is done by calculating $\Delta y/\Delta x$ over any interval of the function $y = b_0 + b_1x$. For any two values of x, say x_0 and x_1, the corresponding values of y are $y_0 = b_0 + b_1x_0$ and $y_1 = b_0 + b_1x_1$ respectively. Therefore:

$$\frac{\Delta y}{\Delta x} = \frac{y_1 - y_0}{x_1 - x_0} = \frac{b_0 + b_1x_1 - b_0 - b_1x_0}{x_1 - x_0} = \frac{b_1(x_1 - x_0)}{x_1 - x_0} = b_1$$

Since any values for x_0 and x_1 can be assigned, the slope will be the same throughout the entire function. It will always turn out to be the coefficient b_1, and as a result will not change as x varies. The overall sign associated with this term can be either positive, negative, or zero. If it is positive, then both the numerator, Δy, and the denominator, Δx, must have the same sign, reflecting that the two variables move in the same direction. If x goes up, then y will go up, or if x goes down, then y will go down. This type of relationship is referred to as a **direct relationship** between variables, and it is always reflected by a positive slope coefficient.

If the sign of b_1 is negative, then one of the terms, Δy or Δx, must be positive and the other negative. This means the two variables change in opposite directions, and reflects what is defined as an **inverse relationship**—if one goes up the other goes down and vice versa.

If b_1 is equal to zero, this indicates that any change in the independent variable provokes no response at all in the dependent variable. Technically, this reflects a special case known as a **constant function**. This is a function for which the dependent variable takes on only one value, equal to the intercept, for any number of values assigned to the independent variable.

The magnitude of the slope coefficient is also of considerable significance. For example, the function $y = 2 + 4x$ contains a slope coefficient of +4. As described earlier, the positive sign indicates that the variables x and y are directly related. Furthermore, its value of +4 indicates that if the variable x changes by one unit, the variable y will change in the same direction by four times the one unit change in x. For each one unit increase in x, y rises by four units, while for each one unit decrease in x, y will fall by four units. As another example, the function $y = 10 - 5x$ has a slope coefficient of –5, indicating that a one unit change for x will lead to a five unit change for y in the opposite direction. If x rises by one unit, y will fall by five units. Should x fall by one unit, y will rise by five units. Clearly, a very large slope value means that a small change in the independent variable leads to very large absolute change in the dependent variable.

The importance of the slope coefficient cannot be overstated. It is the term which reflects the direction and the magnitude of any relationship between the independent variable and the dependent variable in a function. A good theory not only tells us which variables are independent and which are dependent and that a function exists between them, it also should inform us of the nature of that relationship. This is done by specifying the sign (and sometimes the magnitude) of the slope. It is no wonder that the estimation and interpretation of this term constitutes the central thrust of most research in the social sciences.

Graphing Linear Univariate Functions

At this point it is possible to put together the previously discussed concepts of Cartesian coordinates, linear functions, intercepts, and slopes to create graphical representations of univariate linear functions. A graphical analysis does not represent anything new conceptually speaking, but it does provide a technique for depicting and often clarifying mathematical representations, i.e., "a picture is worth a thousand words." We will first discuss and graph a general linear univariate function. Then the remainder of this section will demonstrate the use of graphical analyses within the context of some linear univariate functions commonly encountered in the study of economics.

The general form of a linear univariate function is $y = b_0 + b_1 x$, where y is the dependent variable, x is the independent variable, b_0 is the intercept coefficient, and b_1 is the slope coefficient. This form is so general that we must make some assumptions about the signs of the coefficients before we can graph the function. If we assume that b_0 and b_1 are positive, it is implied that the intercept will be above the origin on the y axis and that the relationship between x and y will be direct. Also, the slope coefficient b_1 being a constant reflects the fact that this is a linear function, i.e., the slope does not change as x changes. The task of plotting this function can be accomplished by simply substituting values for x into the equation, solving for the corresponding values of y, and then plotting the x, y combinations using the system of Cartesian coordinates. It should be noted that it is conventional to plot the values of the explained or dependent variable on the vertical axis and the causal or independent variable on the horizontal. Also, since the values of most economic variables are positive, the focus of our graphical analysis will be confined to the northeast quadrant, also called quadrant I, of the broader coordinate system. The function $y = b_0 + b_1 x$ is plotted in Figure 2.3.

x	y
$x_0 = 0$	$y_0 = b_0 + b_1(0) = b_0$
$x_1 = 1$	$y_1 = b_0 + b_1(1) = b_0 + b_1$
$x_2 = 2$	$y_2 = b_0 + b_1(2) = b_0 + 2b_1$

In order to connect the points and generate a smooth line, it is necessary to assume that all points in the domain of x are included in the function. In other words, the domain of x contains not only the three specified values, but *all* values between them. Three points have been chosen for plotting, although, since the function is linear, two points would suffice. (Recall the old adage "two points make a line"). Actually, any points can be chosen, although it is often convenient to include the intercept. In a graphical sense the intercept determines the position of the plotted function. As a consequence, a change in the intercept value,

Figure 2.3
Graph of a Linear Function

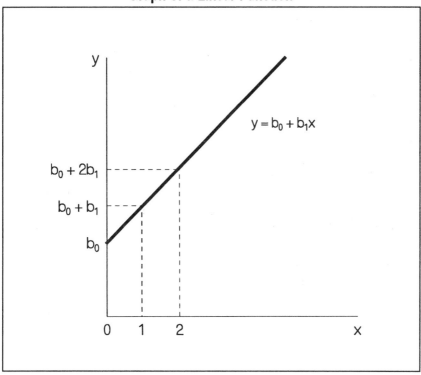

holding the slope coefficient constant, will lead to a repositioning of the function. This is sometimes referred to as a parallel "shift" in the function. As an example, suppose the intercept is of a higher value b_0', i.e., $b_0' > b_0$. The function becomes $y = b_0' + b_1x$ and is contrasted with the previous function $y = b_0 + b_1x$ in Figure 2.4.

x	y
$x_0 = 0$	$y_0' = b_0$
$x_1 = 1$	$y_1' = b_0' + b_1$
$x_2 = 2$	$y_2' = b_0' + 2b_1$

Figure 2.4
Linear Functions with Different Intercept Coefficients

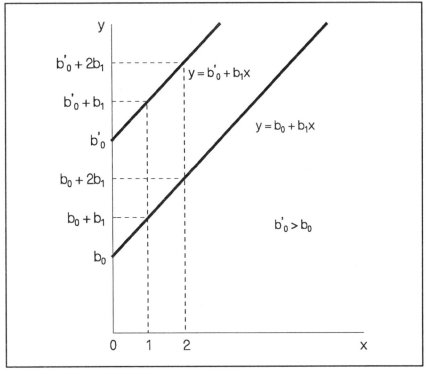

The second function, $y = b_0' + b_1 x$, parallels the first because it has the same slope b_1 but lies everywhere above, reflecting the higher intercept value b_0'. Intuitively, this means that for any given value of x, the value for y will be greater for the function containing the larger intercept. This topic of "shifting" functions will be treated in further detail in the next chapter.

A few comments should be made about the slope coefficient b_1 as it relates to the graphical analysis. Since the convention is to place the dependent variable on the vertical or rising axis, and the independent variable on the horizontal or running axis, the slope $\Delta y / \Delta x$ is often defined generally as $\Delta \text{rise}/\Delta \text{run}$. It is the rate of increase (decrease) associated with a function depending on whether the variables are directly (inversely) related. Graphically, the slope determines the tilt of the function. Should the slope value be changed, the plotted function will rotate or change its tilt. For example, if the slope is increased such that $b_1^* > b_1$, holding the intercept b_0 constant, the plotted curve will rotate counterclockwise, or become steeper. This reflects the fact that changes in the independent variable x now have a greater impact on the dependent variable y. Using the same values for x as before this change in the relationship between x and y is demonstrated in Figure 2.5.

x	y
$x_0 = 0$	$y_0^* = b_0$
$x_1 = 1$	$y_1^* = b_0 + b_1^*$
$x_2 = 2$	$y_2^* = b_0 + 2b_1^*$

Figure 2.5
Linear Functions with Different Slope Coefficients

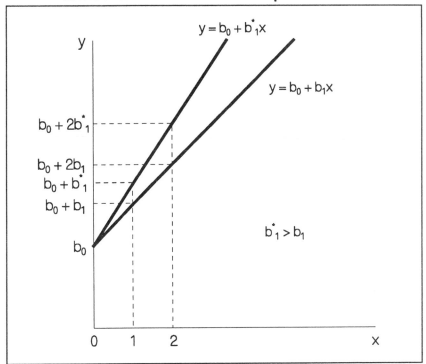

It might be helpful to include some numerical examples. The function y = 2 + 4x has an intercept value of 2 (b_0 = 2) and a slope value of +4 (b_1 = +4). The variables x and y are directly related, and for every one unit change in x, there will be a corresponding four unit change in y. This relationship is shown in Figure 2.6.

Point	x	y	Δy	Δx	$\Delta y / \Delta x = b_1$
A	0	2 + 4(0) = 2	–	–	–
B	1	2 + 4(1) = 6	4	1	4
C	2	2 + 4(2) = 10	4	1	4

Figure 2.6
Linear Functions for b_0 = 2 and b_1 = 4

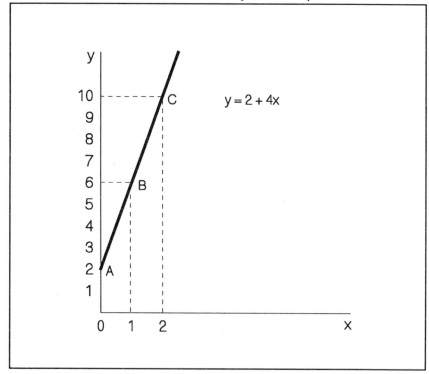

As another numerical example, y = 10 – 5x represents a function for which the relationship between x and y is inverse. This relationship is shown in Figure 2.7.

Point	x	y	Δy	Δx	$\Delta y/\Delta x = b_1$
A	0	10 – 5(0) = 10	–	–	–
B	1	10 – 5(1) = 5	–5	1	–5
C	2	10 – 5(2) = 0	–5	1	–5

Figure 2.7
Linear Function for b_0 = 10 and b_1 = –5

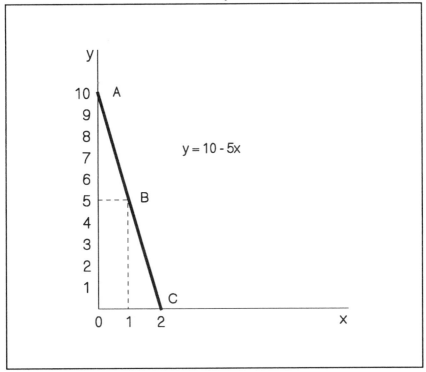

Example 2.1 Demand Functions

Many economic concepts can be analyzed using linear functions. In this section we discuss some of the linear functions most commonly encountered in economics. One such function is the demand function presented at the beginning of this chapter. Many demand functions encountered are assumed to be linear and can be expressed as:

$$Q^d = b_0 + b_1 P$$

where:

Q^d = quantity demanded in units per period of time
P = price in dollars per unit

Rather than using the general coefficients b_0 and b_1, it may be more clear to assign them numerical values. Letting $b_0 = 10$ and $b_1 = -2$, the function becomes $Q^d = 10 - 2P$. The negative sign on the slope coefficient indicates that quantity and price are inversely related. More specifically if P changes by one dollar per unit, Q^d will change in the opposite direction by two units per period of time. This demand function is depicted in Figure 2.8.

Q^d	P	$\Delta Q^d / \Delta P = b_1$
10	0	–
6	2	-2
2	4	-2
0	5	-2

The function has been plotted by simply substituting arbitrary values for the independent variable P into the equation and calculating the corresponding values for the dependent variable Q^d. Note that one of the points chosen is the intercept, 10, or the value of Q^d when P is equal to zero. Should the intercept be assigned a different value, say 12, then the function becomes $Q^d = 12 - 2P$, which is plotted in Figure 2.9.

Q^d	P	$\Delta Q^d/\Delta P$
12	0	–
8	2	–2
4	4	–2
2	5	–2
0	6	–2

Figure 2.8
Demand Curve with Q on Vertical Axis

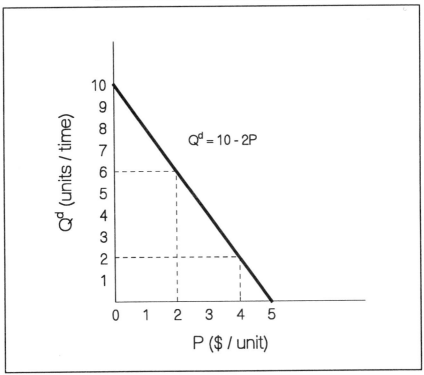

Figure 2.9
Demand Curves with Different Intercepts

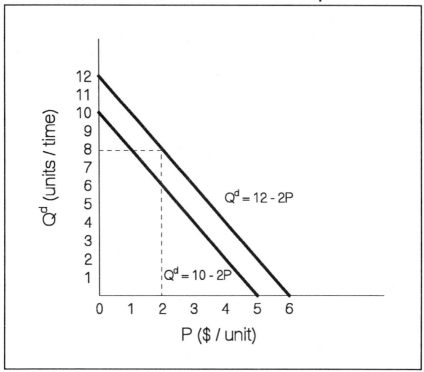

The two functions have been plotted on the same graph and are parallel because they have the same slope coefficient. The function with the greater intercept, 12, lies everywhere above the function with the intercept of 10, demonstrating that any chosen value of P will yield a greater value for Q^d. Specifically, in this case any calculated value of Q^d will always be 12-10, or 2 units greater. Intuitively, a different intercept reflects different levels of variables that have not been included in the function. For example, quantity demanded logically depends on variables other than price, such as income. Since income has not been included in the function, its influence is through the intercept. Often a higher income, for any given level of price, will lead to a greater level of quantity demanded. The resulting change in the intercept is sometimes referred to as a "shift" in the curve. This concept has greater meaning when applied to functions with more than one causal variable, and it will be treated in more detail in the next chapter.

This function can also be used to demonstrate how a change in the slope coefficient causes a rotation of the plotted curve. If the slope coefficient is assigned a value of −3 rather than −2, then a one unit change in P leads to a 3 unit change in Q^d in the opposite direction, rather than a 2 unit change. Keeping the original intercept of 10, the function can now be expressed as $Q^d = 10 - 3P$ and, graphically speaking, becomes a steeper curve. This is plotted in Figure 2.10.

Q^d	P	$\Delta Q^d / \Delta P$
10	0	−
4	2	−3
1	3	−3

All of the graphical analysis pertaining to demand functions has been conducted placing Q^d on the vertical axis and P on the horizontal. This procedure is quite valid and seems logical since P is expressed as the causal or independent variable and Q^d as the explained or dependent variable. Unfortunately, in the field of economics the convention is to reverse the axes labels, placing P on the vertical axis and Q^d on the horizontal. Conceptually, we can still think of Q^d as the dependent variable and P as the independent variable, only the axis labels have been reversed. Returning to the general expression for a linear demand function, $Q^d = b_0 - b_1 P$, we can plot the curve in this manner by simply solving for P and isolating it on the left-hand side of the equation. This is called an **inverse demand function** and in our example becomes: $P = (b_0 / b_1) - (1/b_1)Q^d$. For the specific demand example, $Q^d = 10 - 2P$, the inverse demand function is:

$$P = 10/2 - Q^d/2$$

or

$$P = 5 - .5Q^d$$

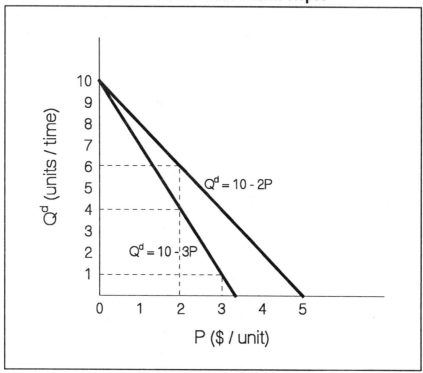

Figure 2.10
Demand Curves with Different Slopes

This is plotted in Figure 2.11.

P	Q^d	$\Delta P/\Delta Q^d$
5	0	–
4	2	–.5
2	6	–.5
0	10	–.5

Note that this is a rearrangement of the original function. The inverse demand function expresses P as a function of Q^d, while in the original

Figure 2.11
Demand Curve Plotted in Inverse Form (More Conventional Form)

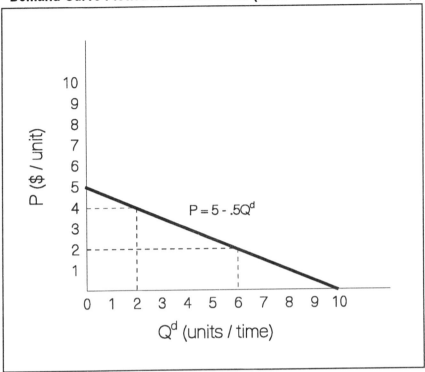

demand function Q^d is a function of P. Although technically these represent different functions, the combinations of values for P and Q^d that satisfy one function also satisfy the other. Since by convention P is placed on the vertical axis, the inverse demand function is more convenient for plotting purposes. For this reason demand functions are often originally expressed in the inverse form, $P = f^{-1}(Q^d)$, where f^{-1} is the inverse function of f. In these instances, however, we may often want to mathematically solve them in the form $Q^d = f(P)$ so as to place proper intuition on the slope and intercept terms.

Example 2.2 Supply Functions

Another economic concept which is frequently expressed as a linear function is the **supply function**. This is defined as a curve which expresses the quantity supplied of some good as a function of the price of that same good, ceteris paribus. A numerical example of such a function might be of the form:

$$Q^s = -200 + 10P$$

where:

Q^s = quantity supplied in units per period of time
P = price in dollars per unit

Intuitively, a supply function is constructed from the producers' perspective. This is reflected by the direct relationship between Q and P which demonstrates that as price increases by one dollar per unit, producers are willing and able to supply 10 x 1 = 10 more units of the product. Although price is the causal variable, the convention is to plot it on the vertical axis and plot quantity supplied on the horizontal. Thus, for graphing purposes it is helpful to solve the equation in terms of P to get:

$$P = 20 + .1Q^s$$

This function is plotted in Figure 2.12.

P	Q^s	$\Delta P/\Delta Q^s$
20	0	–
21	10	.1
22	20	.1

Example 2.3 Budget Constraints

Another economic concept usually expressed in linear form is the **budget constraint**. This represents a locus or set of combinations of two goods that some economic agent, usually an individual consumer, can choose to purchase given his or her income, prices of the goods, and the assumption that all income is spent on the two goods. A typical budget constraint is of the form:

$$P_x x + P_y y = I$$

Figure 2.12
Supply Curve Plotted in Inverse or Conventional Form

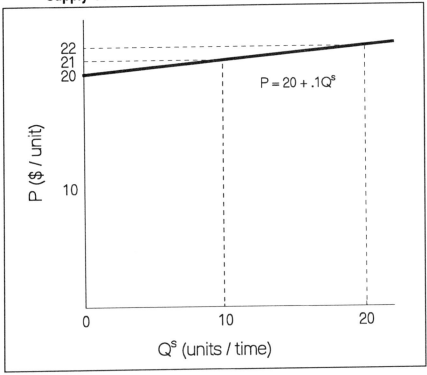

where:
- x = amount of good x purchased in units per period of time
- y = amount of good y purchased in units per period of time
- P_x = price of good x in dollars per unit
- P_y = price of good y in dollars per unit
- I = income in dollars per period of time

Since income and the two prices are given (exogenous to the analysis), the only two variables in a budget constraint are the quantities of the two goods x and y. Suppose the given values for P_x, P_y, and I are \$1/unit, \$2/unit, and \$100 respectively. The budget constraint now becomes:

$$x + 2y = 100$$

Since a budget constraint represents the combinations of goods that an individual is able to purchase, the only cause-effect between x and y is that the individual must forego some of one good in order to purchase more of the other. This is one of the few examples where the direction of causality is not particularly important. In this case the amount of y that can be bought depends on the amount of x purchased. However, it is also true that the amount of x that is bought depends on the amount of y purchased. As a consequence, it really doesn't matter which variable is placed on the vertical axis; however, by convention, y is generally chosen. This being the case, we can now solve the function for y, so as to facilitate graphing the function:

$$2y = 100 - x$$
or
$$y = 50 - .5x$$

The slope coefficient of -.5 indicates that if an individual chooses to purchase one more unit of x, he or she must reduce consumption of y by half a unit. The function is graphed in Figure 2.13.

x	y	$\Delta y/\Delta x$
0	50	–
50	25	-.5
100	0	-.5

Example 2.4 Consumption Functions

As a final example, let's turn our attention to a macroeconomic concept known as the **consumption function**. This is a concept which expresses:

$$C = b_0 + b_1 y_d$$
where:
    C = consumption expenditures in billions of dollars per year
    y_d = disposable income in billions of dollars per year

If b_0 is given to be 1000 and b_1 is .6, the function becomes:

$$C = 1000 + .6y_d$$

Figure 2.13
Budget Constraint

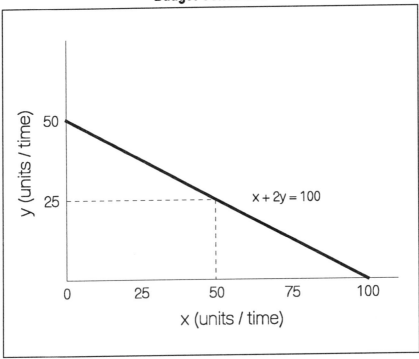

The first coefficient b_0, or 1000 in this case, is the intercept and represents the level of consumption expenditures when disposable income is equal to zero. Another way of viewing it is as the level of consumption that does not vary with disposable income. This coefficient has a particular name in economic theory, and it is defined as **autonomous consumption**. The second coefficient b_1, or .6 in this case, is the slope or the amount by which consumption expenditures change in response to a change in disposable income. The particular name given to this slope coefficient in a consumption function is the **marginal propensity to consume**, or MPC for short. In this example, the MPC of .6 indicates that for every extra billion dollars of disposable income, consumption expenditures increase by .6 X $1 billion = $600 million. The graphical plot of this function is shown in Figure 2.14.

C	y_d	$\Delta C / \Delta y_d$
1000	0	–
4000	5000	.6
4600	6000	.6

Developing a thorough understanding of univariate linear functions enables us to analyze many of the basic concepts associated with the study of economics. In addition, this understanding provides a good foundation for the more complex tools to be encountered—such as nonlinear functions and multivariate functions. The remaining section of this chapter shall provide an introduction to nonlinear functions, while a more detailed discussion of their interpretation and application will be treated in Chapter 4. Multivariate functions will be treated in the next chapter.

Figure 2.14
Consumption Function

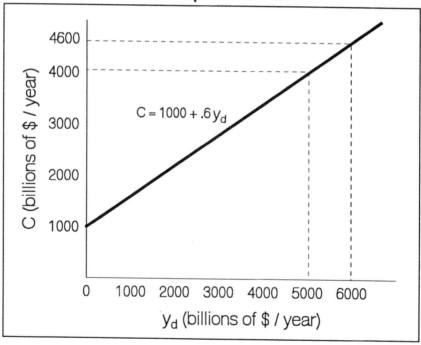

Exercise Set 2.1

1. A function has the form $y = 20 + 5x$.
   a) What type of function is this? How do you know? How are the variables x and y related?
   b) Identify the slope and intercept coefficients. How can these terms be interpreted?
   c) Using graph paper, plot the function.

2. A function has the form $y = 10 - .8x$.
   a) What does the negative sign associated with the coefficient of x indicate?
   b) Plot the function.
   c) Suppose the coefficient of x is changed to -1.0, so that the function is expressed as $y = 10 - 1.0x$. Now plot the function on the same graph. How do the two plotted curves differ?

3. A linear demand function has the form $Q^d = 6 - 2P$, where:

   Q^d = quantity demanded in units per period of time
   P = price of the good in dollars per unit

   a) Plot the demand curve. How would you interpret the intercept and slope terms?
   b) Solve for the inverse function and plot it.

4. An individual faces a budget constraint of the form $P_x x + P_y y = I$, where:

   x = amount of good x purchased in units per period of time
   y = amount of good y purchased in units per period of time
   P_x = price of good x in dollars per unit
   P_y = price of good y in dollars per unit
   I = money income in dollars per period of time

   a) Suppose P_x = $2/unit, P_y = $3/unit, and I = $10/time. Plot the curve.
   b) If P_x = $1/unit, and the other terms are the same as in Part a, how is the plotted curve changed?
   c) Suppose I = $20/time and the other terms are the same as in Part a. How does this affect the plotted curve?

Nonlinear Functions

Not all relationships behave in a linear manner. As a consequence, we must expand our box of tools in order to analyze other types of functions as well. Nonlinear functions are often called **curvilinear functions**. There are so many different types of such functions that the easiest approach to discussing them is to start with a general picture and describe some of the related properties. Some of the specific types will then be discussed as they relate to economic examples.

Suppose we have a univariate function $y = f(x)$, which is considered to be curvilinear. This means that the exponent on the independent variable x is something other than one. When graphed, this function will

Figure 2.15
Curvilinear Function

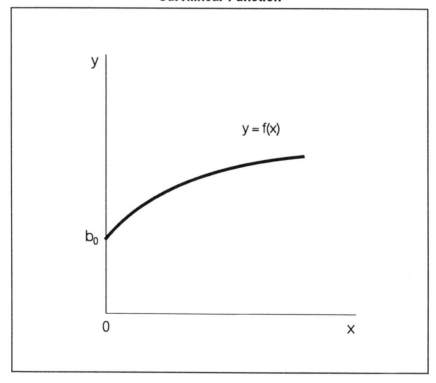

not be a straight line, but instead will exhibit some type of curvature. One example is shown in Figure 2.15.

Again, the exact nature of this function has not been specified, but it has been constructed exhibiting an intercept, as do most linear or curvilinear functions. In fact, the intercept concept is the same in either case and needs no further explanation. The slope concept, however, is another matter. In the linear case, the slope was defined as the change in the dependent variable caused by a change in the independent variable, $\Delta y/\Delta x$, and it was found to be constant throughout the function. This does not hold, however, for curvilinear functions. The slope is still defined as $\Delta y/\Delta x$, but it takes on different values for different movements along the curve. Due to this variation, it becomes necessary to distinguish between the **average slope** and the **instantaneous slope** of a curve. The average slope is determined by the Δrise/Δrun formula and represents what we have been using up to this point for our calculations. What distinguishes this term as an average slope is that it uses discrete changes in the rise and run variables ($\Delta y, \Delta x$). Therefore, in this case, the slope pertains to a segment or arc of the curve. The instantaneous slope, on the other hand, is still the rate of change of a curve, or the change in rise divided by the change in run, but it refers to infinitesimally small changes in x and y. Thus, the instantaneous slope pertains to a point on a curve and in general represents a more precise measure of slope.

This distinction between average and instantaneous slopes is unnecessary for the linear cases, because the slope does not change for different movements along the curve. It doesn't matter if different points or different arcs are chosen as the basis for calculation, because the slope is always the same. But in the curvilinear case, the slope is different for different points on the curve. The mathematical calculation of instantaneous slopes involves calculus and is presented in Chapter 8, but it can be described conceptually by looking at some graphical analyses.

The different slope values pertaining to different points on the curve, such as A and B, can be demonstrated by constructing tangents to the curve at those points and finding the slope of these tangents. A **tangent** to a curve is a straight line touching a curve at some point and possessing the same slope as the curve at that point. It is easy to observe from the graph in Figure 2.16 that the two tangents drawn to the curve at points A and B have different slopes. The tangent at point B is flatter than the tangent at point A, reflecting that the change in y due to a change in x is smaller at point B than at point A. Thus the calculated slope coeffi-

Figure 2.16
Instantaneous Slopes for Curvilinear Function

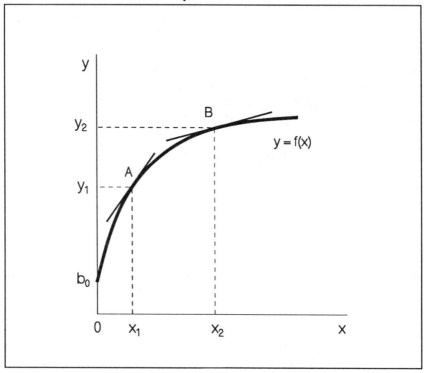

cient, in absolute value terms, will be smaller at point B than it is at A. The preferability of the instantaneous slope over the average slope as applied to curvilinear functions is demonstrated graphically in Figure 2.17.

In order to find the average slope, finite changes in x and y must be allowed, cutting out an arc on the curve such as AC. The average slope over this distance can be calculated by the formula $\Delta y/\Delta x$ or:

$$\frac{y_2 - y_1}{x_2 - x_1}$$

Geometrically, this is actually the slope of a straight line drawn between the two points A and C known as a **secant**. The slope of this secant is the

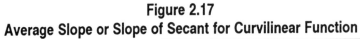

Figure 2.17
Average Slope or Slope of Secant for Curvilinear Function

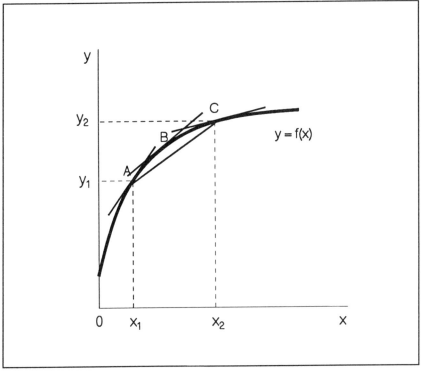

average for the entire related arc AC. As can be seen by examining the tangents to the curve at points A and C, and any points in between such as B, the slopes are different for different points along this arc. An average slope tends to be too general. Of course, the shorter the arcs selected for slope calculation, the more precise the average slope will be.

The difference between an average and an instantaneous slope can perhaps be clarified by an everyday example. Imagine that you are driving cross country and that your distance traveled, D, is a function of time, t, spent driving, i.e., $D = f(t)$. The average slope of this function, $\Delta D/\Delta t$, tells of your average speed over some interval, say 1 hour. Assume that you check your odometer, and that after one hour you have covered 50 miles. Your average speed (velocity) over this interval is 50 miles/hour. This does not imply that over this hour you continuously traveled at that rate. Your instantaneous speed can continuously be read from your speedometer. It measures your speed at any instant and essentially measures your average speed over an infinitesimally small time interval. Your instantaneous speed exactly one hour after you start driving can differ radically from your average speed over that hour. However, as the time interval between checks of the odometer gets very small, the average speed over this small interval of time ending at one hour will approach your instantaneous speed.

The slopes calculated in the rest of this chapter will be average slopes. This is done because they are easy to calculate and require only the use of simple arithmetic. In order to minimize the aforementioned shortcomings associated with average slopes, we will calculate them over very short arcs.

The curves shown in Figures 2.15–2.17 represent only one of the many different shapes which may be assumed by curvilinear functions. In fact, there are so many that we are going to dwell on only those few that are frequently encountered in the study of economics.

Functions with Positive Fractional Exponents

In general, this type of function is of the form $y = b_0 + b_1 x^{b_2}$, where $0 < b_2 < 1$. In other words, b_2 represents some fractional power to which x is raised. The denominator in the exponent b_2 represents some root to which the variable x is taken. For example, if $b_2 = 1/2$, then the second root, commonly called the square root, of x is taken. If $b = 1/3$, the third root, known as the cube root, is found. The numerator could be something other than 1, as long as $0 < b_2 < 1$, e.g., $b_2 = 2/3$. The procedure in this case is to take the cube root of x and then square the result. The term b_0 is the intercept and has the usual implications, i.e., it is the value of y when $x = 0$. The term b_1, however, can no longer be interpreted as the slope of the function. As the coefficient on the independent variable, it plays a role in determining the slope, but the exponent b_2 must also be taken into account. The variable y is calculated by taking b_1 times the b_2th power of x and adding this amount to the intercept. For successive equal changes in x, y will vary by differing amounts because of the different power values associated with different values of x. In other words, the rate at which y changes as x changes (the slope) depends on the value of x and is therefore variable.

Example 2.5 Production Functions

One economic concept which is often represented by such a function is the **production function**. This is a function which shows the maximum quantity of output that can be produced, given different combinations of inputs. An example of such a function is:

$$Q = L^{1/2}$$

where:

Q = units of output produced per period of time
L = labor-hours used per period of time

This is a simplified example of the more general root function expressed above. The intercept b_0 has been set equal to zero, so when plotted the curve will emanate from the origin. The coefficient b_1 is equal to one in this case. Intuitively, this could be interpreted as representing the impact of some fixed amount of some other input such as capital. The exponent b_2 has been assigned the value 1/2, and consequently this type of function is more specifically referred to as a square root function. Figure 2.18 contains the graphical representation.

L	Q	$\Delta Q/\Delta L$
0	0	–
1	1.00	1.00
2	1.41	.41
3	1.73	.32
4	2.00	.27

Figure 2.18
Quadratic Production Function

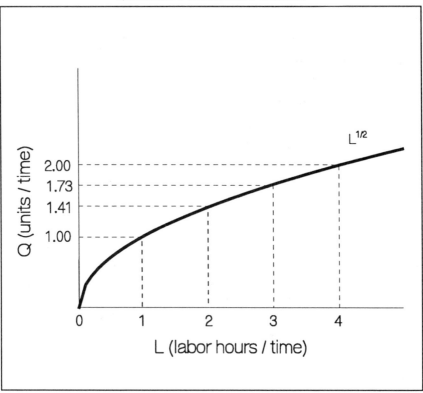

Notice that for successive equal increases in L, the corresponding increases in Q get smaller and smaller. Thus, the slope gets smaller as L increases. As applied to a production function, this property is defined as the **law of diminishing marginal productivity**.

Quadratic Functions

Another curvilinear function often encountered in economics is the **quadratic function**. This is a special type of **polynomial function**. A polynomial is a multiterm function, for which each term is the product of a constant coefficient times the single independent variable which is raised to a power that is a nonnegative integer. The linear functions discussed previously in this chapter are polynomials for which the independent variable is raised to the first power. A quadratic function is another type of polynomial for which the highest power associated with the independent variable is raised to the value two. A general example of such a function is $y = b_0 + b_1x + b_2x^2$. The intercept in this equation is the term b_0, and the slope is some changing value which depends on the value of x. In other words, as with all curvilinear functions, the slope varies along the curve.

Example 2.6 Production Possibilities Curves

An economic concept frequently represented by quadratic functions is the **production possibilities curve**. This is a curve which shows the maximum quantities of two goods a society can choose to produce, given a fixed level of resources and technology. A typical example of a production possibilities curve is the function:

$$y = 9 - x^2$$

where:

y = quantity of good y in billions of units per period of time
x = quantity of good x in billions of units per period of time

This curve is plotted in Figure 2.19.

x	y	$\Delta y/\Delta x$
0	9	–
1	8	-1
2	5	-3
3	0	-5

The downward sloping nature of the curve reflects a negative slope or a trade-off between the two variables. More x can be produced if some y is foregone. The fact that the curve is bowed out away from the origin demonstrates that the slope rises in absolute value terms for increasing values of x; that is, in terms of the amount of y foregone, it becomes increasingly more expensive for this society to produce more and more amounts of x.

Figure 2.19
Quadratic Production Possibilities Curve

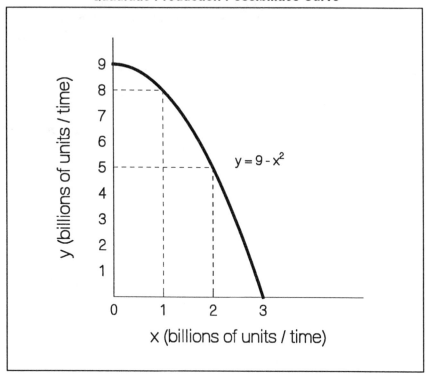

Example 2.7 Total Revenue Functions

Another frequently encountered application of quadratic functions is in **total revenue functions**. This is a function which expresses the value of a firm's sales in terms of the amount of output it sells. A typical example is:

$$R = 8Q - 2Q^2$$

where:

R = the value of a firm's sales in thousands of dollars per period of time

Q = units of output sold per period of time

This total revenue function is plotted in Figure 2.20.

R	Q	ΔR/ΔQ
0	0	–
6	1	6
8	2	2
6	3	–2
0	4	–6

Figure 2.20
Quadratic Total Revenue Function

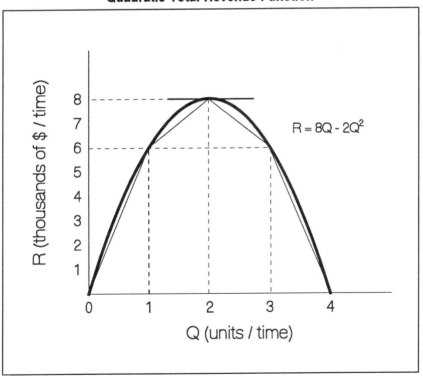

This quadratic revenue function exhibits a number of interesting properties. First, the function has a vertical intercept of zero. This is logical because if a firm sells no output, it cannot earn any revenue. Also note that the slope is positive but decreasing for greater values of Q until Q = 2. At this point the instantaneous slope is equal to zero. The slope then becomes negative as Q is increased beyond this point. Finally as Q = 4, revenue becomes zero and there is no point continuing the graph. Why does a revenue function often behave in this manner, rising with increases in Q, hitting a peak at some point, then falling as Q is increased further? The answer lies in the underlying economic theory. It is assumed here that for a firm to sell more output, it must lower its price. In this example, as the price is lowered, quantity sold increases by a proportionally greater amount up to the second unit sold. As a consequence total revenue, which is calculated by taking the price of a product times the number of units sold, will increase. However, as price is lowered even more, the quantity sold while still increasing does so by a proportionally smaller amount. Thus, total revenues will eventually fall.

Cubic Functions

Another curvilinear function useful to economists is the **cubic function**. This is a polynomial function for which the highest exponent associated with the causal or independent variable is three. A general representation of such a function is $y = b_0 + b_1x + b_2x^2 + b_3x^3$, where b_0 is the vertical intercept, and b_1, b_2, and b_3 are coefficients which enter into the slope calculation. As with all curvilinear functions, the slope of a cubic function varies along the curve, thereby depending on the value of x.

Example 2.8 Cost Functions

The most prevalent application of cubic functions to economic theory is with **total cost functions**. A total cost function expresses a firm's total costs in terms of the level of output it produces. A typical cost function facing a firm might be of the form:

$$C = 10 + 3Q - 1.5Q^2 + .25Q^3$$

where:

C = total costs in thousands of dollars per period of time
Q = units of output produced in thousands per period of time

The function is plotted in Figure 2.21.

C	Q	$\Delta C/\Delta Q$
10.00	0	–
11.75	1	1.75
12.00	2	.25
12.25	3	.25
14.00	4	1.75
18.75	5	4.75

There are several important points regarding this curve. First, it has a vertical intercept of 10. This means the firm incurs ten thousand dollars in costs even though it produces no output. In economic jargon, these are defined as **fixed costs**. As a consequence, the function can be identified as a short run total cost function, since fixed costs are a short run phenomenon. A long run total cost curve might have a similar shape, but the vertical intercept would have to occur at the origin since there are no fixed costs in the long run. Another point to note about this function has to do with its slope. Total cost, C, is everywhere an increasing function of output Q, and as a result, the function always has a positive slope. The manner in which the slope changes reflects the interesting nature of cubic functions. The slope in this case decreases as Q increases up to point A where Q = 2, then increases as Q increases beyond this value. In other words, the slope achieves its minimum value at the turning point A, which is technically defined as the **inflection point**. The economic implication of this example is that costs increase at a decreasing rate up to the inflection point, then increase at an increasing rate for further increases in the quantity produced. Intuitively, this reflects the law of diminishing marginal productivity; it becomes increasingly expensive to produce more units of a product varying only some inputs while holding others constant.

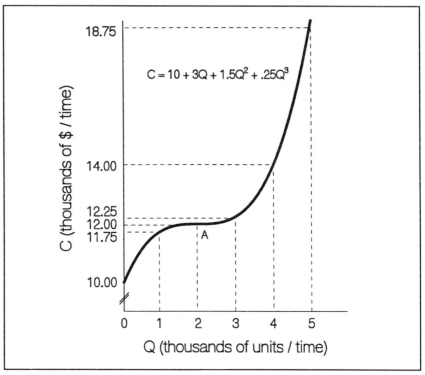

Figure 2.21
Cubic Short Run Total Cost Function

$C = 10 + 3Q + 1.5Q^2 + .25Q^3$

C (thousands of $ / time)

Q (thousands of units / time)

Hyperbolic Functions

The final curvilinear function to be discussed is the **hyperbolic function**. This is a function for which the product of the two included variables is a constant. Generally, a hyperbolic function has the form $y = b/x$. Multiplying the explained variable y by the independent variable x yields the constant b. Since a hyperbolic function is not defined for either $x = 0$ or $y = 0$, it is not possible to define intercepts. Instead the function is said to be asymptotic to each axis; that is, it approaches the x axis and y axis as x and y increase respectively.

Example 2.9 Demand Functions Revisited

Some demand functions are of a hyperbolic form. Such an example is the function:

$$P = 10/Q^d$$

where:

P = price in dollars per unit
Q^d = quantity demanded in units per period of time

This demand function has been expressed in the inverse form so that it is easy to see how P can be plotted on the vertical axis and Q^d on the horizontal. The curve is shown in Figure 2.22.

P	Q^d	$\Delta P/\Delta Q^d$
10	1	–
5	2	–5
3.67	3	–1.33
2.5	4	–1.17

Observe that the slope, while always negative, decreases in absolute value for greater values of Q^d. These types of demand functions are particularly applicable to those products for which some percentage change in price always generates an equivalent percentage change in quantity demanded. Notice also that $P \times Q^d$, the total expenditure on the good, is a constant = 10. In other words, consumers always spend $10/period of time on this good, irrespective of the good's price.

Conclusion

This chapter has been an introduction to many of the basic functions and their associated properties that are fundamental to studying economics. More specific applications of these functions to economic analysis will be developed as we proceed into the more advanced chapters of this book. Remember also that everything discussed in this chapter has been

Figure 2.22
Hyperbolic Demand Function

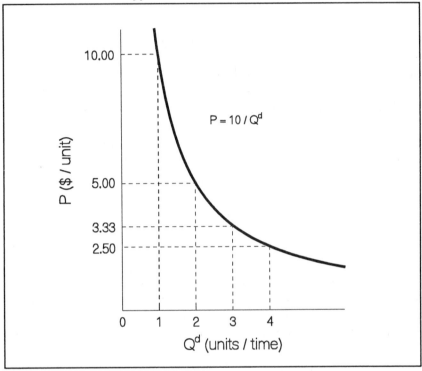

done within the context of univariate functions. As explained, these are functions containing only one independent variable or just two variables in total. In many instances, univariate functions may be sufficient for accomplishing the task at hand. In other situations, however, they may not be comprehensive enough to provide adequate explanations about how certain variables are determined. Many times a dependent variable will be determined by more than just one independent variable. Functions containing two or more independent variables are defined as multivariate functions and are the subject of the next chapter.

Appendix

Numbers

Economic theories deal with relationships between variables. The variables considered are at least potentially measurable, and the values that they take are usually represented by numbers. These theories are usually represented as functional relationships that associate one, and only one, value from the range with each value in the domain. It is generally assumed, but infrequently mentioned, that these functions are **continuous** and have **real numbers** for their domains and ranges. The purpose of this appendix is to explain these two concepts and the relationship between them. Towards this end, different types of numbers and their relevance to economic problems are discussed.

The first encounter with mathematics for most children is learning how to count. Starting with the number 1, we construct a series of numbers by adding 1 to the previous number. This results in a sequence 1, 2, 3, 4, 5, 6, 7, 8, 9, 10, 11, . . . , where the three dots mean that we continue this process indefinitely. The numbers generated by this process are the **natural numbers**. While the addition of any two or more natural numbers always results in a natural number, the same cannot be said for subtraction. The following example demonstrates why this is a problem.

Consider three variables; profits, revenues, and costs that are related by the equation, profits = revenues minus costs. Assume for argument's sake that revenues and costs can each be represented by a natural number. Can the same be said for profits? When revenues exceed costs, the answer is yes. However, when revenues exactly equal costs, no natural number exists that could represent profits. A new number, zero (0), needs to be created to measure profits. The addition of zero to the natural numbers is still inadequate to measure profits, when costs exceed revenues. We would have to add a series of negative numbers to our list of numbers to take care of that eventuality.

The previous example demonstrates the need to have at least the natural numbers, 0, and the negative of each natural number. The numbers contained in these three groups together are called the **integers**. Further, the natural numbers can now be called positive integers, while the negative of each natural number is a negative integer. The integers have the property that the addition or subtraction of any two integers is an integer. However, even the integers are incapable of measuring all economic variables.

The variable "average profit" is simply the profit per unit of output. It is related to two variables, total profits and total output by the equation, average profit = total profits divided by total output. Even when these two variables can be represented by integers, average profit will not necessarily follow suit. For example, if total profits are $100 per day and total output is 40 units per day, then average profit is $2.50 per unit. Notice that the number 2.50, or 2 1/2, is not an integer. To alleviate this problem we have to create a bigger set of numbers called **rational numbers**. The rational numbers include any number that can be expressed in the form p/q where p and q are integers and q is not equal to zero. The term rational stems from the word ratio, and has nothing to do with rationality. Notice that all the integers are rational numbers (let q = 1), but the rationals also include any fractions between the integers. Rational numbers can always be expressed in decimal form by dividing the numerator by the denominator. The decimal representation of 1/2 = 0.5, while that of 5/3 = 1.666. . . . The decimal representation of any rational number either terminates, i.e., consists of only zero to the right of some digit, or else repeats in regular cycles forever. Conversely, any terminating or repeating decimal is a rational number.

There are magnitudes, however, that are not captured by the rational numbers. In this chapter the square root function, $y = \sqrt{x}$, was introduced. When x = 2, $y = \sqrt{2}$, while for x = 3, $y = \sqrt{3}$. Neither $\sqrt{2}$ nor $\sqrt{3}$ can be represented as the quotient of two integers, and, consequently, neither is rational. In decimal form, these two numbers neither terminate nor repeat and are examples of **irrational numbers**. All numbers that can be expressed in decimal form as nonterminating and nonrepeating are irrational numbers. In fact, there are an infinite number of irrationals between any two rational numbers. The number pi, π = 3.14159 . . . is another example of an irrational number. Recently two mathematicians have calculated the value of π to over 400 million decimal places!

It is probably uncommon for an economics student to solve a problem for which the solution is an irrational number. However, irrational numbers are important when graphing a function. Just as fractions fill in gaps between integers, irrational numbers fill in the gaps between the rationals. The **real numbers** consist of all the rational and all the irrational numbers. Every point on a number line or on either axis of the Cartesian coordinates is a real number. It is generally assumed that the values of economic variables are real numbers. Consequently, both the domain and range of economic functions are the real numbers or some interval thereof. Imagine the problem of graphing a function if both the domain and range were restricted to be rational numbers. Consider the aforementioned square root function. First we would eliminate all irrational numbers from the domain. There are still values of x that have to be eliminated (such as 2) since the corresponding values of y are irrational. We would end up with a curve that had an infinite number of spaces between points. Letting the domain and range be real numbers enables us to work with **continuous functions**. A continuous function is one whose graph is unbroken. Therefore, the graph of a continuous function can be drawn without lifting a pencil off the paper. The functions considered throughout this book are continuous over the whole domain, or at least over some interval thereof.

It should be noted that, whereas in mathematics the domain of a function is generally all the reals from negative to plus infinity, the domain of functions in economics typically is restricted. That is due to the fact that many economic variables can only take on nonnegative values. It is generally assumed, for example, that the only economically meaningful values of the price of a good and its quantity are positive or zero. Consequently, the domain of a demand function must be restricted so that the demand curve lies in the first quadrant. The demand function given by $Q^d = 100 - 2P$ (where Q^d is the dependent variable representing the quantity demanded in units/day, and P is the independent variable representing price in dollars/unit) is only relevant for values of P between 0 and 50, inclusive. When a domain is restricted and does not contain all of the reals, values that lie in the restricted domain are termed **admissible values**. In a similar fashion we can talk about admissible values of a range, when it is restricted.

For completeness it should be mentioned that there are numbers that are not contained in the reals. Since the domains and ranges of economic functions are generally the reals, or some interval of them, these numbers are less important to us. They may inadvertently crop up as solutions to problems and should therefore be mentioned. The numbers we are speaking about are called **imaginary numbers**. An imaginary number includes a term with the even root of a negative number. Every imaginary number can be expressed as a + bi, where a and b are real numbers, b ≠ 0, and $i = \sqrt{-1}$. The term bi is referred to as purely imaginary. Finally, the **complex numbers** include all the real and all the imaginary numbers.

The expression a + bi where a and b are real and i = $\sqrt{-1}$ represents all the complex numbers. Recall that when b ≠ 0, all of the imaginary numbers are indicated. When b = 0 all of the reals are represented.

In summary, the broadest category of numbers are complex. They include both the real and imaginary numbers. The real numbers in turn include both rational and irrational numbers. The rational numbers include the integers and fractions. The integers are divided into three groups: positive integers, negative integers, and zero. Lastly, the positive integers are also called natural numbers.

Important Terms in this Chapter

Admissible values – values of the independent or dependent variable respectively for which the domain or range of a function is restricted and does not contain all the real numbers.

Autonomous consumption – the level of consumption expenditures when disposable income is equal to zero (the intercept of a consumption function).

Average slope – a method of calculating a slope using discrete increments in the dependent and independent variables.

Budget constraint – a locus or set of combinations of two goods that some economic agent can choose to purchase, given his or her income, prices of the goods, and the assumption that all income is spent on the two goods.

Cartesian coordinates – two perpendicularly intersecting lines, each having scales that are sequentially numbered from the point of intersection.

Coefficients (parameters) – the "given" factors in an equation.

Complex numbers – all numbers that can be represented as either a real or an imaginary number.

Constant function – a function for which the dependent variable takes on only one value for any number of values assigned to the independent variable.

Consumption function – a function which expresses consumption expenditures as a function of disposable income.

Continuous function – a function for which the graph is unbroken over some interval in the domain.

Cubic function – a polynomial function for which the highest exponent associated with the causal independent variable is three.

Curvilinear function – a nonlinear function, or (in most cases) a function for which the independent variable is raised to some power other than one.

Demand function – a function which expresses the quantity demanded of some good as a function of its own price, ceteris paribus.

Direct relationship (between variables) – a relationship reflecting that two variables move in the same direction.

Domain – set of values from which the independent variable is drawn.

Function – a relationship such that for every admissible value assigned to the independent variable, there will exist a unique value corresponding to the dependent variable.

Hyperbolic function – a function for which the product of the two included variables is a constant.

Imaginary numbers – all numbers that include a term with an even root of a negative number. Every imaginary number can be represented by a + bi, where a and b are real numbers with b ≠ 0 and $i = \sqrt{-1}$.

Instantaneous slope – a method of calculating a slope, using infinitesimally small changes in the dependent and independent variables.

Integers – numbers that can be formed by the addition or subtraction of two natural numbers. They include the natural numbers, their negatives, and zero.

Intercept coefficient – the value of the dependent variable when the independent variable is equal to zero.

Inverse demand function – a demand function which represents a rearrangement of some original demand function so that the variables assigned as dependent and independent are reversed, i.e., if a function is Q = f(P), there is an inverse function such that P = f^{-1}(Q).

Inverse relationship (between variables) – a relationship reflecting that two variables move in opposite directions.

Irrational numbers – numbers for which the decimal representation is a nonterminating and nonrepeating decimal.

Law of diminishing marginal productivity – as additional increments of an input are used, holding other inputs constant, the resulting increments to output tend to diminish beyond some point.

Linear function – a polynomial function containing variables raised, at most, to the first power.

Marginal propensity to consume – the rate of change in consumption expenditures due to a change in disposable income.

Natural numbers – the counting numbers represented by the sequence 1, 2, 3, 4, 5, . . . , where the three dots indicate that the process of adding 1 to the previous number continues indefinitely.

Ordered pair – a pair of numbers for which the order in which they are listed is significant.

Polynomial function – a multiterm function for which each term is the product of a constant coefficient times the single independent variable raised to a power that is a nonnegative integer.

Production function – a function which shows the maximum quantity of output that can be produced, given different combinations of inputs.

Production possibilities curve (frontier) – a curve which shows the maximum quantities of two goods a society can choose to produce, given a fixed level of resources and technology.

Quadratic function – a polynomial function for which the highest power associated with the independent variable is raised to the value two.

Range – set of values from which the dependent variable is drawn.

Rational numbers – numbers formed as the quotient of two integers where the divisor is nonzero. These include all of the integers as well as any fraction between two integers. The decimal representation of a rational number either terminates or repeats.

Real numbers – any number that is either rational or irrational. Real numbers have a decimal representation which terminates, or repeats, or neither.

Secant – a straight line connecting two points on a curve.

Supply function – a function which expresses the quantity supplied of a good as a function of its own price, ceteris paribus.

Tangent (to a curve) – a straight line touching a curve at some point and possessing the same slope as the curve at that point.

Total cost function – a function which expresses a firm's total costs in terms of the level of output it produces.

Total revenue function – a function which expresses the value of a firm's sales in terms of the amount of output it sells.

Slope coefficient – the rate of change in a dependent variable due to a change in an independent variable.

Univariate function – type of function containing only one independent variable.

Variable – some quantity that can take on a set of values.

Exercise Set 2.2

1. A function has the form $y = 2x^{1/2}$.
    a) What is the value of its intercept?
    b) What general form describes this function?
    c) What can be said about the slope associated with this type of function?
    d) Using graph paper, plot this function, incrementing x by (only) one unit up to where x = 4.

2. Using the function given in Problem 1, calculate the average slope for each one unit increment in x up to where x = 4. What are the shortcomings associated with using average slopes? Suppose we know the instantaneous slope related to this function is $1/\sqrt{x}$. Calculate the instantaneous slope values for x = 1, x = 2, x = 3, and x = 4. How do these results compare with the average slopes you have already calculated? Why are they different?

3. Assume a society faces a production possibilities curve of the form:

$$y = 8 - 2x^2$$

    where:
       y = quantity of good y in billions of units per year
       x = quantity of good x in billions of units per year

    a) What type of function is this?
    b) How are the two goods, x and y, related?
    c) Using graph paper, plot the function. What shape does it exhibit?
    d) If this society decides to produce all y and no x, how much y can they produce? Alternatively, if it decides to produce all x and no y, how much x can they produce?
    e) Calculate the average slope over increments of x from 0 to 1 and 1 to 2. What do these two slope values tell you about the relationship between x and y?

4. A demand function can be of different forms depending on the nature of the price–quantity demanded relationship. One such form is the linear function:

$$P = 10 - 5Q^d$$

    where:
       P = price in dollars per unit
       Q^d = quantity demanded in units per period of time

    Another type of demand curve is the hyperbolic function:

$$P = 8/Q^d$$

where P and Q^d are defined as here. (Note these demand functions are already expressed in the inverse form).

a) Plot the two functions, using two different graphs.
b) Looking at the graphs, contrast the two functions. How are they different?
c) Total expenditures on a good equals price times quantity demanded. Calculate this value for several P, Q^d combinations on each demand curve. How do total expenditures change as we move along each demand curve?

5. Sketch a general cubic cost function, assuming it has a positive intercept. What does this intercept represent from an economic perspective? Does this curve represent a short run or long run cost function? What does the cubic shape reflect about the nature of a firm's costs?

6. A function familiar to most students of finance is the yield curve. It is a curve which shows the various interest rates that exist at a point in time for various issues of credit instruments differing by maturity. Suppose a yield curve has the form:

$$R = 10 + T^{1/2}$$

where:
  R = nominal interest rate in percentage points
  T = time in years

What is the current interest rate? What is the general form of this yield curve? Plot the curve. At the point in time to which the curve pertains, what is the relationship between short- and long-term interest rates? Do you have an explanation for this relationship?

References

Gobran, A., *Intermediate Algebra,* Boston: Prindle, Weber, and Schmidt, 1984.

Kelly, T. J., R. H. Balomenos, and J. T. Anderson, *College Algebra,* Boston: Houghton Mifflin, 1986.

Miller, C. D. and M. Lial, *Fundamentals of College Algebra,* Glenview, IL: Scott, Foresman, 1986.

Swokowski, E. W., *Fundamentals of Algebra and Trigonometry,* Boston: Prindle, Weber, and Schmidt, 1986.

Multivariate Functions

Introduction

In constructing theories, it is usual to begin with the simple and build in more complexity by increasing the level of realism. We would like a theory that is both simple and easy to comprehend, while at the same time one that predicts well and/or has great explanatory power. These goals are often in conflict, and a trade-off exists. It is for this reason that, initially, simple theories are exposited. When these theories don't possess sufficient explanatory power, possibly because variables that have been omitted are important and not trivial, the next step is to include these other explanatory variables.

The simplest theories are those that contain one independent variable and one dependent variable. These theories can be represented mathematically as univariate functions which were discussed in the previous chapter. One example that was utilized was that quantity demanded of a good was a function of the good's price. As a first approximation to reality, this is satisfactory. It highlights the idea that a good's price is the prime determinant of how much would be demanded. However, it was based on the *ceteris paribus* assumption that all other variables that could influence the quantity demanded were held constant. It had nothing to say (no explanatory power) about the impact of changes in the prices of substitutes or complements, population, or income. A more complete theory of demand would include these factors as independent variables as well as the good's price. The same idea can be expressed in mathematical terminology by, "the quantity demanded of a good is a **function** of its own price, the prices of substitute goods, the prices of complementary goods, population, and income."

This chapter generalizes the tools and concepts developed previously for the univariate case. Particular attention is paid to graphical techniques and interpretations of the slope and intercept in the multivariate case. How can a relationship between three or more variables be represented on a two dimensional graph? How can we measure the rate of change of a dependent variable with respect to an independent variable, if other independent variables are present? These are just two of the questions that we should be able to answer after reading this chapter.

Functions: The Multivariate Case

In the univariate case a function is defined notationally as $Y = f(X)$. This expression demonstrates a relationship between Y and X, such that for each admissible value of X there is one and only one corresponding value of Y. If Y is a multivariate function, then the concept of a function can be generalized and expressed as $Y = f(X_1, X_2, \ldots, X_n)$, where Y is still the dependent variable, and $X_1, X_2, \ldots, X_n$ represent a set of independent variables. In this case, for each set of admissible values, one for each of the Xs, there is one and only one corresponding value of Y. An important implication of the multivariate analysis is that if Y is a function of $X_1, X_2, \ldots, X_n$, then Y can be expressed as a function of any one of the X variables only if the values of the remaining Xs are specified. This is due to the fact that a multiplicity of Y values would correspond to each value of any one of the Xs if the others are allowed to vary. As such, no function would exist between Y and any one of the Xs, unless the others are held constant. For example, Y can be expressed as a function of X_1 in the following manner:

$$Y = f(X_1, X_{2,0}, \ldots, X_{n,0})$$

The second subscripts on those Xs other than X_1 denote that their values have been specified at some particular level. If Y is expressed as a function of X_2, then the equation can be written as:

$$Y = f(X_{1,0}, X_2, \ldots, X_{n,0})$$

In this case, all of the X variables other than X_2 have been specified.

A specific example should provide some clarification. Since linear functions are frequently encountered in the study of economics, it is useful to expand the general univariate linear example, given in the previous chapter, to include more variables. Such a multivariate linear function is of the form:

$$Y = b_0 + b_1 X_1 + b_2 X_2 + \ldots + b_n X_n$$

where b_0 represents the intercept, and $b_1, b_2, \ldots, b_n$ represent the slope coefficients, more specifically known as **partial slope coefficients**. This concept will be explained in the next section.

Interpretation of the Slope and Intercept for the Multivariate Case

Slope in the univariate case was defined in Chapter 2 as the change in the dependent variable due to a change in the independent variable. Geometrically, the average slope is the slope of a line drawn between two points on a curve, and the instantaneous slope at a point on a curve is the slope of the tangent to the curve at that point. These simple definitions hold at all times in this case because the dependent variable Y depends only on the value of the independent variable X and upon no other variables.

In the case of the multivariate function, account must be taken of the other variables under consideration. Again, consider the general case:

$$Y = f(X_1, X_2, \ldots, X_n)$$

It is meaningful to talk about the slope or rate of change of Y with respect to X_1 or the rate of change of Y with respect to X_2, and so on, only with one important qualification. Recall that for Y to be a function of any one of the Xs, it is necessary that the values of all remaining Xs be specified. Therefore, the slope of Y with respect to any of the Xs can be defined only when the levels of the remaining Xs are known. For example, the slope of Y with respect to X_1, when all other Xs are specified at some level, can be written as:

$$\frac{\Delta Y}{\Delta X_1} \mid X_{2,0}, \ldots, X_{n,0}$$

The vertical slash simply indicates that those variables following it are held constant. The second subscript represents the level at which the other independent variables are specified. Similarly, the slope of Y with respect to X_2, with all other Xs held constant, can be written as:

$$\frac{\Delta Y}{\Delta X_2} \mid X_{1,0}, X_{3,0}, \ldots, X_{n,0}$$

A more specific name for these expressions is that of partial slope coefficients, which in the case of the instantaneous slope is termed the partial derivative, which will be examined in Chapter 8.

Regarding the linear example of a multivariate function:

$$Y = b_0 + b_1 X_1 + b_2 X_2 + \ldots + b_n X_n$$

it can be seen that the coefficients b_1, b_2, $\ldots$, b_n on the independent variables represent the respective partial slope coefficients that have just been discussed. Recall from Chapter 2 that the coefficients pertaining to the independent variables represent the respective slope coefficients. The intuitive significance of these partial slope coefficients cannot be overstated. In an equation that may contain a number of independent variables, it is these values that indicate the degree of impact that each respective independent variable, by itself, has on the dependent variable. To a large extent, this is what economic research, or any research for that matter, is primarily intended to accomplish. That goal is finding the direction and the degree to which one variable affects another.

The intercept also plays an important role. Mathematically, the multivariate intercept (b_0) represents the value of a dependent variable (Y) when all of the independent variables (the Xs) are equal to zero. An alternative interpretation of the intercept is to think of it as incorporating all those factors which affect the dependent variable (Y), but are not explicitly treated as variables in the equation, i.e., b_0 is a function of the omitted variables. The interpretations placed on the slope and intercept are very important when graphing a multivariate function in two dimensional space.

Graphing Multivariate Functions

The problem of graphing a multivariate function in two dimensional space amounts to "squashing" a multidimensional relationship into two dimensions. In other words, for graphing purposes, there must be a method of treating a multivariate function as if were a univariate function. In fact, this method has already been described here both mathematically and verbally, and it is simply an application of the *ceteris paribus* assumption described in Chapter 1. Specifically, a multidimensional relationship can be depicted in two dimensions as long as the values of all but one independent variable are specified. This, of course, leaves only two variables left to plot: the dependent variable and the one independent variable being examined. As an example, in order to graph Y vs. X_1 from the multivariate function, $Y = f(X_1, X_2, \ldots, X_n)$, or more specifically a linear example of such a function, $Y = b_0 + b_1X_1 + b_2X_2 + \ldots + b_nX_n$, it is necessary to specify the other independent variables $X_2, \ldots, X_n$ at some level. This yields:

$$Y = f(X_1, X_{2,0}, \ldots, X_{n,0})$$

or

$$Y = b_0 + b_1X_1 + b_2X_{2,0} + \ldots + b_nX_{n,0}$$

It is now possible to plot the relationship between the two variables Y and X_1. The inclusion of the specified X levels, $X_{2,0}, \ldots, X_{n,0}$, is necessary to distinguish this relationship from one which would reflect some different set of specification levels, e.g., $X_{2,1}, \ldots, X_{n,0}$. In this latter case, note that the level of the variable $X_{2,1}$ has been set at some value different from its previous value of $X_{2,0}$. This representation can be referred to as parameterizing the graph. Parameterization of graphs is necessary whenever a multivariate function is graphed in two dimensional space.

Figure 3.1
Multivariate Function Graphed in Two Dimensions

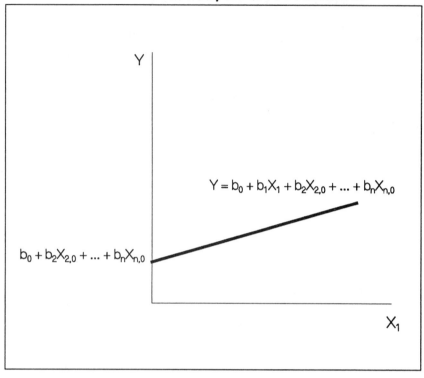

Based on the graph in Figure 3.1, what can be said about the sign of b_1? What are the associated implications?

The exact slope and position of the curve depends on the numerical values assigned to the coefficients b_0, b_1, . . . , b_n, and the numerical levels at which the other independent variables X_2, . . . , X_n are fixed. Suppose X_2 is now fixed at some level $X_{2,1}$ which is greater than $X_{2,0}$, and everything else remains the same as before. The equations take the form:

$$Y = f(X_1, X_{2,1}, . . . , X_{n,0})$$

or in the linear example:

$$Y = b_0 + b_1X_1 + b_2X_{2,1} + . . . + b_nX_{n,0}$$

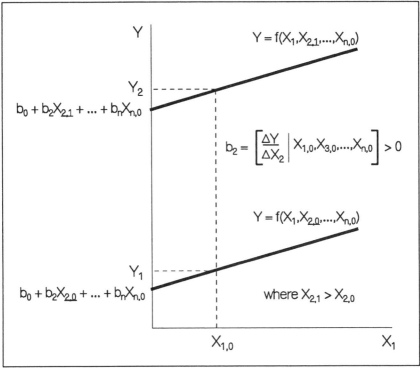

Figure 3.2
Multivariate Functions with Different Intercepts

There now exists a different functional relationship between Y and X_1, and the result can be added to the preceding graph (see Figure 3.2).

Notice that the new function has the same slope, b_1, as the old but lies above it at every value of X_1, due to the higher specified value of X_2. This implies that b_2 is positive. Specifically, the vertical distance between the two curves, at any chosen value for X_1, say $X_{1,0}$ is equal to b_2 multiplied by the change in X_2 or:

$$\left(\frac{\Delta Y}{\Delta X_2} \,|\, X_{1,0},\, X_{3,0},\, \ldots,\, X_{n,0} \right) \cdot \Delta X_2$$

What would be the result if $b_2 < 0$? What implication would this condition have regarding the relationship between Y and X_2? It is important at this point to emphasize the significance of understanding the intercept concept. It can easily be seen in the preceding functions and graphs that when the level of a specified variable is changed, the impact is manifested through a change in the intercept. This is to be expected, because once independent variables are specified, they become part of the univariate intercept. For example, if the general linear form:

$$Y = b_0 + b_1 X_1 + b_2 X_2 + \ldots + b_n X_n$$

has $X_2, \ldots, X_n$ fixed at some level 0, the function becomes:

$$Y = b_0 + b_1 X_1 + b_2 X_{2,0} + \ldots + b_n X_{n,0}$$

The intercept is now $b_0 + b_2 X_{2,0} + \ldots + b_n X_{n,0}$. Therefore, a change in any of the $X_2, \ldots, X_n$ terms from level 0 to some other level will alter the value of the intercept.[1] This results in what is often referred to as a "shift" in the plotted curve.

Exercise Set 3.1

1. A function has the form:

    $$Y = 5 + 2X_1 + 4X_2$$

    where Y is the dependent variable and X_1 and X_2 represent independent variables.

    a) What are the values for the partial slope coefficients?
    b) Plot Y vs. X_1 when $X_2 = 1$. What is the value of the Y intercept pertaining to this curve?
    c) Plot Y vs. X_1 when $X_2 = 2$. How has the intercept value changed?

2. Using the same function in Problem 1, plot the curve relating Y to X_2 when $X_1 = 1$. What is the value of the Y intercept in this case? If $X_1 = 2$, what is the new intercept value?

Applications to Economics

It is useful at this point to apply the procedures described previously to some economic analysis.

Example 3.1 Demand and Engel Curves

Suppose a demand function takes the form:

$$Q^d = 100 - 2P + .2I$$

where:
    Q^d = quantity demanded in units per period of time
    P = price in dollars per unit
    I = income in dollars per period of time

This is a multivariate function containing two independent variables P and I. If the goal is to plot this as a function of Q^d and P, it is necessary to specify the value of I. If I is set at some value, say \$100/week, then the demand function becomes:

$$Q^d = 100 - 2P + .2(100)$$

or

$$Q^d = 120 - 2P$$

Suppose I is set at some other value, say \$200/week. The function then becomes:

$$Q^d = 100 - 2P + .2(200)$$

or

$$Q^d = 140 - 2P$$

The two functions are graphed in Figure 3.3.
    Note that the different values for I change the intercept values but do not affect the slope value of:

$$\frac{-2 \ \text{units/week}}{\$/\text{unit}}$$

Figure 3.3
Multivariate Demand Functions with Different Intercepts

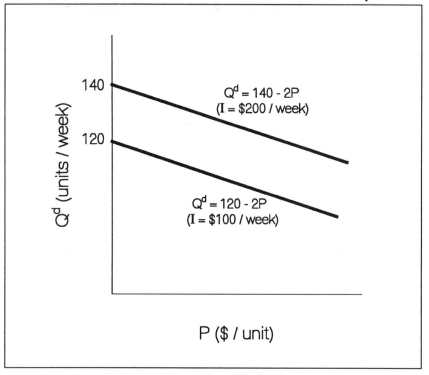

As stated in Chapter 2, the convention in economics is to plot supply and demand functions in the inverse form. This requires only a slight modification of the demand functions. Solving for P as a function of Q^d, respectively, yields $P = 60 - .5Q^d$ and $P = 70 - .5Q^d$. The labels on the axes can now be reversed and the graphs take the form as shown in Figure 3.4.

The analysis just presented shows how to generate a two–dimensional demand function from a function containing more than two variables. Economists tend to view "demand" as the relationship between the quantity demanded of a good and its price, *ceteris paribus,* and, therefore, all but these two variables were held constant. However, if we choose, it is possible to take the same equation, specify the value of

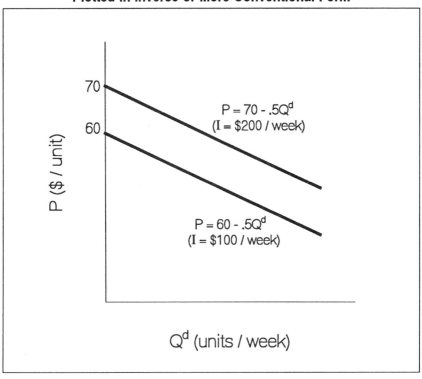

Figure 3.4
Multivariate Demand Functions with Different Intercepts,
Plotted in Inverse or More Conventional Form

$P = 70 - .5Q^d$
$(I = \$200 / \text{week})$

$P = 60 - .5Q^d$
$(I = \$100 / \text{week})$

P ($ / unit)

Q^d (units / week)

price, and let income be the independent variable to be plotted. Suppose price is set at $10/unit. Then the equation becomes:

$$Q^d = 100 - 2(10) + .2I$$

or

$$Q^d = 80 + .2I$$

This relationship is graphed in Figure 3.5 and is referred to as an Engel curve. An **Engel curve** relates the quantity demanded of some good to money income, holding other independent variables constant.

Figure 3.5
Engel Curve

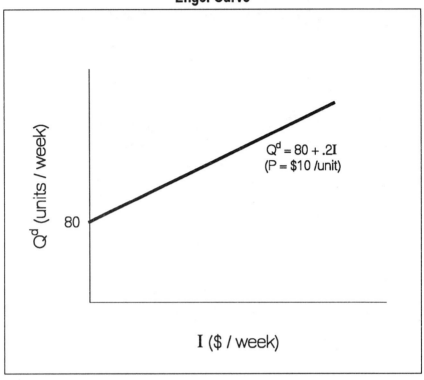

Now suppose price is set at \$20. The function becomes:

$$Q^d = 100 - 2(20) + .2I$$

or

$$Q^d = 60 + .2I$$

This function is added to the previous graph to get Figure 3.6.

Example 3.2 Supply Curves

The same basic principles utilized in these prior illustrations can be applied to other economic examples. A supply function may take the following form:

Figure 3.6
Engel Curves with Different Intercepts

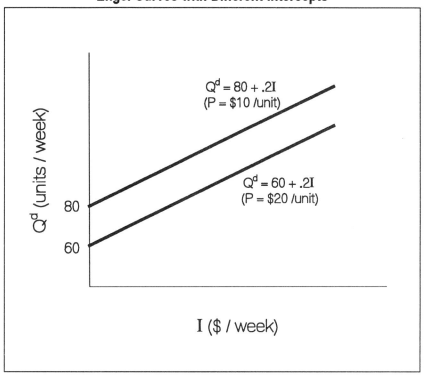

$$Q^s = -200 + 10P - 4W$$

where:

Q^s = quantity supplied in units per period of time
P = price in dollars per unit
W = wage rate in dollars per hour per worker

As with demand functions, the convention is to plot price on the vertical axis and quantity on the horizontal. Therefore, it is useful to solve the supply function in terms of P and generate the following inverse supply function:

$$P = 20 + .1Q^s + .4W$$

If the goal is to plot the function in terms of Q^s and P, it becomes necessary to specify the value of W. If W is set equal to \$5 per hour, the function becomes:

$$P = 20 + .1Q^s + .4(5)$$

or

$$P = 22 + .1Q^s$$

The function can also be examined for a different value of W, say \$10 per hour. It now becomes:

$$P = 20 + .1Q^s + .4(10)$$

or

$$P = 24 + .1Q^s$$

Both functions are presented graphically in Figure 3.7.

Figure 3.7
Inverse Supply Curves with Different Intercepts

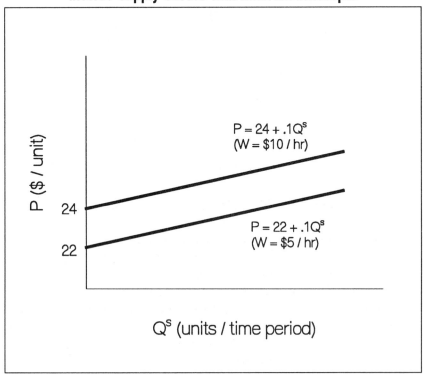

Example 3.3 Consumption Functions

As a final example, this analysis can be applied to a consumption function. Recall that this type of function is a macroeconomic concept which relates consumption expenditures to disposable, or after tax, income. In order to make this a more comprehensive function, other independent variables such as interest rates may be included as well. An example of a consumption function might take the form:

$$C = 1000 + .6Y_d - 1.0R$$

where:
   C = consumption expenditures in billions of dollars per year
   Y_d = disposable income in billions of dollars per year
   R = interest rate in percentage points

This consumption function can be plotted in terms of consumption expenditures and disposable income, provided the interest rate is set at some level. If the interest rate is specified to be 10 percent, then the function becomes:

$$C = 1000 + .6Y_d - 1.0 (10)$$

or

$$C = 990 + .6Y_d$$

If instead the interest rate is set at 20 percent, the function becomes:

$$C = 1000 + .6Y_d - 1.0 (20)$$

or

$$C = 980 + .6Y_d$$

These two functions are plotted in Figure 3.8.

Notice that the slope of the consumption function, .6, is unaltered by the different interest rate levels. This slope has an economic interpretation defined as the marginal propensity to consume (MPC), which represents the fraction of the extra dollar of disposable income that is spent for consumption purposes. The general rule to be followed is that the level(s) of the fixed factor(s) determine the position of the plotted curve.

Figure 3.8
Consumption Function

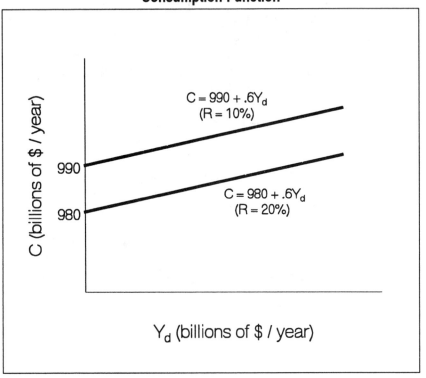

$C = 990 + .6Y_d$
$(R = 10\%)$

$C = 980 + .6Y_d$
$(R = 20\%)$

C (billions of \$ / year)

990

980

Y_d (billions of \$ / year)

Are Curves Really Shifted?

The demand examples just depicted can be used to avoid the common mistake of confusing changes in demand with changes in quantity demanded. It is typically explained that a movement along the curve represents a change in the quantity demanded, while a "shift" of the curve represents a change in demand. Since demand relationships are presented in the price–quantity space, it should be recognized that a change in the price causes a change in the quantity demanded, while a change in any independent variable that is being held constant represents a change in demand. This is because demand to an economist is not some particular quantity but rather a relationship between price and quantity. The implication is that if any of the variables which position the demand curve were to change, the relationship between price and quantity would be altered. This different valued function represents a change in demand. However, is it correct to say that the curves have shifted?

The answer unfortunately is no, and the problem this creates is as follows. When we talk about shifting curves, it seems to imply that some dynamic process is taking place, or that these changes are occurring over time. However, the analysis that is typically presented is static, i.e., timeless in nature. Taking the demand function presented earlier, $Q^d = 100 - 2P + .2I$, it can be seen that time does not enter as an independent variable. As shown previously, the function simply demonstrates that a different relationship between price and quantity demanded exists when income is at one level, i.e., 100, as opposed to being at another level, i.e., 200. However, these relationships always existed for the specified levels of income. It is merely our focus that has shifted, from one demand relationship to another, rather than the curves themselves.

Conclusion

This chapter has enabled us to progress beyond the simple univariate functions developed in Chapter 2, thus making it possible for us to construct more comprehensive models. In Chapter 4, we will discuss how the slope concept associated with both univariate and multivariate functions can be interpreted as an important economic concept known as the **marginal function**.

Important Terms in this Chapter

Engel curve – A curve which relates the quantity demanded of some good to money income, holding other independent variables constant.

Multivariate function – A function containing more than one independent variable.

Partial slope coefficient – The change in a dependent variable due to a change in some respective independent variable, while other independent variables are held constant.

Exercise Set 3.2

1. A demand function might be expressed as:

    $$Q^d = 5000 - 50P + .1I + 80POP$$

    where:

    $\quad\quad Q^d$ = quantity demanded in thousands of units per year
    $\quad\quad\; P$ = price in dollars per unit
    $\quad\quad\;\; I$ = income per capita in thousands of dollars per year
    $\quad POP$ = population in millions

    a) Express this multivariate demand function as simply a function of P when I = 20 and POP = 200.
    b) Determine and interpret the slope and intercept associated with the function in Part a.
    c) Graph the function, being sure to appropriately parameterize the curve.

2. Using the function given in Problem 1, find the resulting demand function, slope, and intercept if I = 40 and POP = 200. Graph the function and compare the results to that of Problem 1. Has the curve shifted? Be careful in your explanation.

3. Using this same function from Problem 1, determine the Engel curve, along with its related slope and intercept if P = $50 and POP = 200. What happens to this Engel curve if P is changed to equal $75?

4. If a supply function takes the form:

    $$Q^s = -500 + 20P - 5W$$

    where:

    $\quad Q^s$ = quantity supplied in thousands of units per year
    $\quad\; P$ = price in dollars per unit
    $\quad W$ = wage rate in dollars per day per worker

a) Determine the supply function if W = $25. What are the associated slope and intercept? How do you interpret this negative intercept? What is the lowest price at which anything will be supplied?

b) If P = $50 and W = $25, what is the corresponding value of Q^s? Suppose P = $60 and W = $25, now what is the value of Q^s? Does this represent a change in supply or a change in the quantity supplied? Explain your answer.

5. If consumption expenditures are given by the following function:

$$C = 600 + .8Y_d$$

where:

C = consumption expenditures in billions of dollars per year
Y_d = disposable (after tax) income in billions of dollars per year

also

$$Y_d = Y - T \quad \text{and} \quad T = tY$$

where:

Y = national income in billions of dollars per year
T = total tax revenues in billions of dollars per year
t = average tax rate

Consumption expenditures can now be expressed as a function of national income and the tax rate by the function:

$$C = 600 + .8(1 - t)Y$$

a) If t is treated as a constant, then consumption expenditures can be expressed as a linear function of Y. What are the resulting slope and intercept terms? Economically, what do these terms represent? [Hint: the value of .8 represents the marginal propensity to consume (MPC) out of disposable income.]

b) Plot the consumption function for the following values of t:

$$t = 0$$
$$t = .10$$
$$t = .20$$

c) What effects do the different t values have on the slope and intercept terms? What is different about this example as compared to those presented in the chapter?

6. A yield curve of the form, $R = 10 + T^{1/2}$, was discussed in the exercises at the end of Chapter 2, where:

R = nominal interest rate in percentage points
T = time in years

Suppose the interest rate pertaining to maturing securities is 12 percent rather than 10. Plot the yield curve under these new conditions. Given these new circumstances, has the relationship between the time to maturity and the interest rate on maturing securities been altered?

7. Assume a two time period model, for which an individual must decide how to allocate his or her consumption levels between the two time periods. The constraint facing the individual is:

$$C_2 = Y_2 + (Y_1 - C_1) + R(Y_1 - C_1)$$

where:
C_1 = consumption expenditures for period one, in dollars
C_2 = consumption expenditures for period two, in dollars
Y_1 = income for period one, in dollars
Y_2 = income for period two, in dollars
R = interest rate, in percentage points

The term $(Y_1 - C_1)$ represents the amount saved in period one. This individual can transfer income between the two periods by either lending or borrowing at the rate of interest R. Suppose $Y_1 = \$10,000$, $Y_2 = \$20,000$, and $R = 10$ percent.

Compute the C_1 and C_2 intercepts. Can you interpret these intercepts by incorporating the present and future value concepts? Compute the slope. Suppose R increases to 20 percent. How does this affect the intercepts and slope?

Note

1. The analysis conducted here is based on the assumption that the function is separable in its arguments. This assumption perhaps oversimplifies the results, but it is consistent with the analysis presented in most principles and intermediate economics texts.

4

Marginal Functions and Their Applications

Introduction

The attention focused on the slope in the previous chapters was not accidental. The slope is one of the most used and useful mathematical tools in the economist's repertoire. Many important economic concepts can be interpreted as slopes of various functions. This relationship is not always apparent, as it is sometimes masked by the terminology (economic jargon) employed. The astute reader may wonder why economists find it desirable to develop a set of new terms that then have to be deciphered by others, in particular, students of economics. The explanation is based on efficiency grounds, something with which economists are particularly concerned. All professions and disciplines establish a unique jargon to facilitate communication among their members. A basic concept may take a sentence, paragraph, or even a page to explain when it is initially introduced. After its initial introduction, a phrase consisting of a few words can be substituted for a lengthy explanation of the concept. This represents an economy of language and is therefore efficient.

Economics, which focuses on efficiency, is certainly no exception to this. The terminology employed is simply a shorthand method of expressing concepts. It is therefore important for the student of economics to be familiar with the meanings of the terms utilized. The remainder of this chapter is devoted to economic terms (and the concepts they represent) that are in some way related to the mathematical concept of the slope and the nature of that relationship.

Marginal Functions and Their Relationship to Total Functions

A key assumption in economic theory is that individuals make decisions "on the margin." That is, that given an individual's initial situation, he or she considers the impact on net benefits of altering variables under his or her control by small amounts. For example, consider a producer whose goal is to maximize total profits, which depend upon the quantity produced. The producer would consider small incremental changes in quantity and their effect on total profits. If by increasing quantity by 1 unit/year (or some other small amount), profits would be increased, such a change should be undertaken. The process is then repeated starting from this new quantity. This is done successively until the change in profits is zero. The process would be analogous for small decreases in quantity. In either event, the producer is considering small changes, rather than large ones, in the decision-making process. These small changes are referred to as marginal changes, hence the phrase "deciding on the margin."[1]

Typically, it is the value of the *total* of some variable that is to be explained. The effect of a marginal change of an independent variable on this total variable is simply the rate of change of the dependent variable with respect to the independent variable. It should be recognized that this rate of change is simply the *slope*. When total "something" is the dependent variable, its slope is typically called marginal "something."

In mathematics the most common representation of a univariate function is y = f(x). In that form, y represents the dependent variable, and f is the "name" of the function relating y to the independent variable, x. In economics it is common to use the same symbol to represent both the dependent variable and the name of the function. The symbol chosen usually serves as a reminder of what the dependent variable is. Assume that y is the total of some variable which is a function of another variable x. It would be convenient to denote the dependent variable, and the function's name, as T (brief for total). The relationship would then be expressed as $T = T(x)$. The slope of the function T with respect to x is usually referred to as the marginal of T (with respect to x). It is convenient to denote this slope as M (for marginal), where M is also a function of x. This relationship is expressed as $M = M(x)$, where again M represents both the variable as well as function name.[2] As a convention, whenever marginals and totals in general are discussed, they will be denoted by M and T respectively.

When T is a multivariate function, it may be represented as $T = T(x_1, x_2)$. In that event, two marginals can be formed: the marginal of T with respect to x_1, and the marginal of T with respect to x_2. In general, one marginal can be formed for each independent variable. The marginals in this case are partial slopes, i.e., the slope of T with respect to one independent variable, when the values of all other independent variables are held constant. In a multivariate context, it is necessary to distinguish which marginal is being used. Towards this end, subscripts will be utilized, so that:

$$M_{x_1}$$

would denote the marginal of T with respect to x_1 (holding x_2 and other independent variables constant), while:

$$M_{x_2}$$

denotes the marginal of T with respect to x_2 (with all other independent variables constant). Again, it is generally the case that if $T = T(x_1, x_2)$, then the marginal functions are multivariate as well:

$$M_{x_1} = M_{x_1}(x_1, x_2) \quad \text{and} \quad M_{x_2} = M_{x_2}(x_1, x_2)$$

The above total–marginal principle is useful in interpreting many economic terms. Whenever the word marginal is used to describe an economic concept, it should signal the reader that what is being discussed can be interpreted as the slope of some function. The number of examples that could be provided is quite large, and, therefore, only a sample of such examples is cited here.

Example 4.1 Marginal Propensity to Save (MPS) and Marginal Propensity to Consume (MPC)

There are only two things that a household can do with its disposable income, Y_d: consume (spend), or save. In other words:

$$Y_d = C + S$$

where:

C = consumption expenditures
S = saving

Given some level of Y_d, the household will choose the level of C and whatever remains is S. Alternatively, given Y_d the household could choose S and the residual is then C. Therefore, the choice of C also determines S. There is only one independent decision being made since the choice of either C or S determines the other. Since in essence only one decision is being made, whatever independent variables affect C also affect S. In particular, given that $C = C(Y_d)$, we also have $S = S(Y_d)$. In other words, since consumption expenditures, C, are a function of disposable income, so is saving, S. The relationship between C and Y_d is the consumption function, while that between S and Y_d is the **saving function**. The slope of the consumption function is the rate of change of C with respect to Y_d, and it is called the **marginal propensity to consume** or **MPC**. Similarly, the slope of the saving function is the rate of change of S with respect to Y_d, and it is referred to as the **marginal propensity to save, or MPS**. When C and S are univariate functions of Y_d, the MPC = $\Delta C / \Delta Y_d$ while the MPS = $\Delta S / \Delta Y_d$. When consumption expenditures depend on other independent variables in addition to Y_d, the consumption function is multivariate. In that event, the saving function is multivariate as well. If consumption expenditures depend upon the interest rate, i, as well as disposable income, the consumption function is $C = C(Y_d, i)$, while the saving function is $S = S(Y_d, i)$. In that event the MPC and the MPS have to be interpreted as partial slopes, that is, the rate of change of C and S respectively with respect to Y_d, when i is held constant. In general, both the MPC and MPS would be multivariate functions of Y_d and i.

The MPC and MPS are related by the equation, MPC + MPS = 1. This relationship is derived from the fact that $Y_d = C + S$. Assume that initially, $Y_d = Y_{d_0}$, $C = C_0$, and $S = S_0$. It follows that $Y_{d_0} = C_0 + S_0$. If disposable income now changes by ΔY_d, its new level is $Y_{d_0} + \Delta Y_d$. In response to this change in Y_d, C and S will change as well. Their new levels are $C_0 + \Delta C$, and $S_0 + \Delta S$, respectively, where Δ means the "change in." The new level of disposable income must equal the new level of C plus the new level of S. Thus, $Y_{d_0} + \Delta Y_d = C_0 + \Delta C + S_0 + \Delta S$. Subtracting Y_{d_0} from both sides yields $\Delta Y_d = \Delta C + \Delta S$, since $C_0 + S_0 = Y_{d_0}$. This implies that the sum of the changes of C and S equals the change in Y_d. Dividing this relationship by ΔYd yields:

$$\frac{\Delta Y_d}{\Delta Y_d} = \frac{\Delta C}{\Delta Y_d} + \frac{\Delta S}{\Delta Y_d} \quad \text{or} \quad 1 = MPC + MPS$$

This implies that for each *additional* dollar in disposable income, the *extra* consumption expenditures plus the *extra* savings generated must sum to an extra dollar. This relationship is sometimes expressed as MPS = 1 − MPC. Knowledge of either the MPC or the MPS is sufficient to derive the other.

Consider the following data generated from the linear saving function given by:

$$S = -100 + .2Y_d$$

where:

S = savings in billions of dollars per year
Y_d = disposable income in billions of dollars per year

From the saving function equation and the fact that it is linear, we can tell that the S intercept = −100 and its slope $(\Delta S/\Delta Y_d)$ = +.2. The S intercept indicates what the level of saving will be when Y_d = 0. Since it is equal to −100, it tells us the consumers are **dissaving** $100 billion/year, at that income level. In other words, they are consuming $100 billion/year more than their disposable income. Since Y_d = 0, total consumption must be $100 billion/year at that income level, indicating that autonomous consumption = $100 billion/year. The S intercept then represents the negative of autonomous consumption. More important for our current purposes is the value of the slope, which is .2. This represents our marginal propensity to save and indicates that out of *every additional dollar* of disposable income received, households will save an *additional* twenty cents. Using the data from the table, the same result is obtained.

Figure 4.1
A Univariate Linear Saving Function

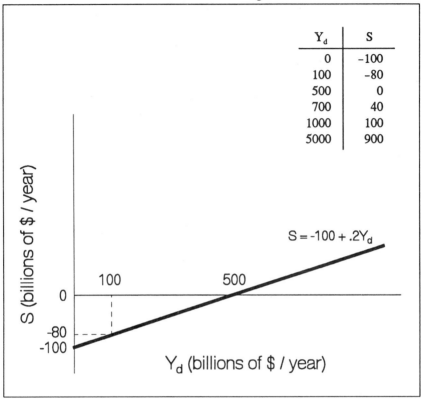

Y_d	S
0	-100
100	-80
500	0
700	40
1000	100
5000	900

$S = -100 + .2Y_d$

In addition, given that the MPC = 1 – MPS, it is clear that the MPC = .8 and is constant (for all levels of Y_d, ceteris paribus) as well. This implies that out of each additional dollar of disposable income, households will consume an additional eighty cents.

Example 4.2 Marginal Revenue

The total revenue, R, of a producer (in dollars/year) is dependent on the quantity, Q, (in units/year) produced. In other words R = R(Q), where R is also the name of the function. The rate of change of R with respect to Q is simply the slope of R with respect to Q and is given the name

marginal revenue, MR. Notice that since R is a univariate function, it is unnecessary to call the slope the marginal revenue with respect to Q. Since Q is the only causal variable, it is understood that it is "with respect to Q" and it is simply termed marginal revenue. Before computing marginal revenue from total revenue, it is helpful to show how a total revenue function is constructed. Total revenue is simply the value of total sales and therefore represents the product of the price of a good times the quantity of the good sold, i.e., $R = P \times Q$. It is usually assumed that producers choose the value of Q and, consequently, we want R to be expressed as a function of Q. That will only be the case when P is a function of Q. Generally, however, P and Q are inversely related, where the relationship is given by the demand function, $Q = f(P)$, or by the inverse demand function, $P = f^{-1}(Q)$. Since we desire P to be a function of Q, use of the inverse demand function is indicated.[3] Substituting it for P in the total revenue function yields:

$$R = f^{-1}(Q) \times Q$$

This construction of a total revenue function and the resulting calculation of marginal revenue can best be clarified by use of a specific example. Assume that a producer faces a demand curve given by:

$$Q = 10 - .1P$$

where:

Q = quantity demanded per unit of time
P = price in dollars per unit

The inverse demand function (treating price rather than quantity as the dependent variable) can be expressed as $P = 100 - 10Q$. Economic theory tells us that the only relevant combinations satisfying this equation take place where both P and Q are nonnegative. Therefore, the domain of Q is such that $0 \leq Q \leq 10$. The relevant range of P is $0 \leq P \leq 100$. Multiplying the inverse demand function by Q yields $PQ = 100Q - 10Q^2$, where by definition, PQ is simply total revenue, R. Therefore, R is a nonlinear quadratic function of Q. The slope of this function is the marginal revenue, which is also a function of Q. Since R is a nonlinear function, its slope varies as Q varies. Using techniques developed in Chapter 7, it can be shown that the MR at any Q in this domain is given by, $MR = 100 - 20Q$. However, barring those techniques (which are calculating the instantaneous slope), the MR can be calculated using the average slope method. When only discrete points on the function are known, only the average slope method can be utilized. As seen in Chapter 2, when a function is nonlinear, the two methods generate different values, while for a linear function they yield identical results. Therefore, it is necessary in this example to demonstrate both methods, which was not the case in Example 4.1, where the function was linear. Consider the following data and its corresponding graph in Figure 4.2.

When the only data available is the discrete data of the table in Figure 4.2, we assume that the revenue function can be approximated by a series of straight lines between each pair of consecutive points.

Figure 4.2
A Quadratic Total Revenue Function

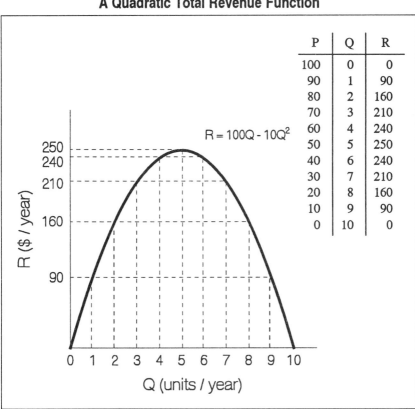

P	Q	R
100	0	0
90	1	90
80	2	160
70	3	210
60	4	240
50	5	250
40	6	240
30	7	210
20	8	160
10	9	90
0	10	0

$R = 100Q - 10Q^2$

Therefore, the marginal revenue *over each interval* is represented by the average slope over the interval, $\Delta R/\Delta Q$. When more information and better techniques are available, it is desirable to represent the marginal revenue by its instantaneous slope, given by MR = 100 - 20Q. The latter gives us the MR *exactly* at that point, while the former gives us the "average" MR over the interval.

Since Q is continuously variable, it may be appropriate to ask at what rate revenue is changing when we increase quantity by some arbitrarily small amount. The answer would be given by the instantaneous slope. Alternatively, the average slopes from the data in the table indicate the average rate at which revenue is changing per unit of output over the interval of 1 unit. In Table 4.1 a comparison of the values of MR, computed by the two alternative methods, is presented. Since using the

Table 4.1
Computed Values of MR Using the Average and Instantaneous Slope Methods, for the Total Revenue Function $R = 100Q - 10Q^2$

Q	MR = $\Delta R/\Delta Q$ (Average Slope)	MR = 100 - 20Q (Instantaneous Slope)
0		100
	90	
1		80
	70	
2		60
	50	
3		40
	30	
4		20
	10	
5		0
	-10	
6		-20
	-30	
7		-40
	-50	
8		-60
	-70	
9		-80
	-90	
10	-90	-100

average slope method would refer to the interval between 2 units, that data is recorded between the lines. Using the instantaneous slope method gives the MR exactly at that quantity, and that data is recorded on the lines.

When the true revenue function is unknown or is known but techniques for computing the instantaneous slope (for a nonlinear function) are not, the average slope method should be utilized. It generally provides a good approximation for the instantaneous slope, especially when the interval (here 1 unit) is small. When larger intervals are utilized, the approximation is not as good. For example, consider the MR from 4-6 units (a two unit interval) computed by the average slope method. Since R is the same (240) at Q = 4 as it is at Q = 6, MR over this interval is zero. This implies that, on average, all the units and parts thereof contribute no additional revenue to the firm. However, as can be readily seen from the graph, this result is due to the fact that all increments to Q from 4-5 units contribute positively to revenue, while those increments from 5-6 detract from revenue by an equal amount.

Example 4.3 Marginal Cost

The total cost of production, C (in dollars/year), may depend upon the quantity, Q (in units/year) produced. This can be represented as C = C(Q). The slope of the total cost function (with respect to Q) is the rate at which total cost changes as Q changes. This is referred to as **marginal cost** and is usually denoted **MC**.

Example 4.4 Marginal Profit

Total profit, π, is defined as total revenue minus total cost, i.e., $\pi = R - C$. Given the assumptions in Examples 4.2 and 4.3 that R and C are both univariate functions of Q, π will follow suit. In other words, $\pi = \pi(Q) = R(Q) - C(Q)$. **Marginal profits, M$\pi$**, is the slope of the total profit function with respect to Q and indicates the **rate** at which total profit changes in response to changes in Q. As Q changes, both R and C change in response. The rate of change of π with respect to Q is equal to the rate at which R changes minus the rate at which C changes.

Example 4.5 Marginal Utility

Early economists assumed that total utility (satisfaction) was cardinal. By that was meant that we could measure (quantify) the amount of utility a person received from any consumption bundle. This measurement could be in terms of a standardized unit called a **util**. If total utility, U (in utils), depends only on the amounts of two goods, food, F, and clothing, C, (both measured in some appropriate manner) per year, then $U = U(F,C)$. In this event U is a multivariate function. The rate that total utility changes as F changes (holding C constant) is referred to as the **marginal utility** of food and could be denoted MU_F. Similarly, the marginal utility of clothing, MU_C, is the rate at which total utility changes in response to changes in C (when F is held constant). Both MU_F and MU_C are simply partial slopes of the total utility function with respect to the amounts of the respective goods. Notice that it would be reasonable to suspect that the marginal utility of one good depends not only on the amount of that good (consumed) but on the amount of the other good as well.

Example 4.6 Marginal Product

The amount of total product (output), Q, produced per year depends on the amounts of each input used per year. Assume that there are only two inputs, capital, K, and labor, L. This relationship is known as a production function and could be expressed as $Q = f(K,L)$. If the level of K is held constant, then the rate of change of total product with respect to the labor input is known as the **marginal product of labor** or MP_L. This is simply the slope of the production function with respect to L, when K is constant. The **marginal product of capital, MP_K** is defined analogously.

Example 4.7 Marginal Propensity to Invest (out of National Income), MPI

The level of total investment expenditures/year, I, may be dependent on the interest rate, i, and the level of national income, Y. (Of course, other causal variables might be included as well.) The investment function can be expressed as $I = I(i, Y)$. For a given level of i, the slope of the investment function (with respect to Y) is referred to as the **marginal propensity to invest** or **MPI**. The MPI represents the rate of change of total investment expenditures caused by a change in national income.

Exercise Set 4.1

1. Using the data in Example 4.1 on page 93:
   a) Calculate the values of C (consumption expenditures in billions of dollars per year) that correspond to the values of Y_d in the table alongside Figure 4.1.
   b) Derive the consumption function from the saving function.
   c) Graph this function and interpret its slope.

2. The investment expenditure function is given by:

   $$I = 100 + .05Y$$

   where:
   I = investment expenditures in billions of dollars per year
   Y = national income in billions of dollars per year

   Graph this function and interpret its slope. What does the intercept represent?

3. A consumption function is given by:

   $$C = 1000 + .75Y_d$$

   where:
   C = consumption expenditures in billions of dollars per year
   Y_d = disposable income in billions of dollars per year

   Graph this function and interpret its slope. Given that S (saving) = Y_d - C, graph it, and interpret its slope. What is the relationship between the two slopes? Explain why this is so.

4. In Example 4.1 it was proven that 1 = MPC + MPS. Use a similar proof to show that $M\pi$ = MR - MC, where $M\pi$ = marginal profit, MR = marginal revenue, and MC = marginal cost. [Hint: Review Examples 4.2-4.4.] Explain intuitively why this relationship is true.

5. Given the total cost function:

   $$C = 10 + Q^2$$

where:

C = total cost in dollars per year

Q = total output in units per year

a) Calculate the values of C for integer values of Q between 0 and 10, inclusive.

b) Use the average slope method to calculate the marginal cost, MC, over each unit interval.

c) The MC (using the instantaneous slope) is given by MC = 2Q. Calculate the values of MC for integer values of Q between 0 and 10 inclusive.

d) Compare the values derived in Parts b and c above and explain why they differ.

6. Using the total cost function given in Problem 5 and the total revenue function from Example 4.2:

a) Derive the total profit function.

b) Derive the marginal profit function, $M\pi$, a function of Q. Use the equations for the instantaneous MR and MC, and the relationship:

$$M\pi = MR - MC$$

c) Graph the $M\pi$ function derived above. For what values of Q is $M\pi$ positive? Negative? Zero? Interpret these results.

Sketching Marginal Curves from Knowledge of Total Functions

Marginal functions may be of more interest (due to the assumption that decisions are made on the margin), but generally it is the total function that is known. It is then necessary to construct the marginal function from knowledge of its total counterpart. To do so, it should be recalled that the marginal function is simply the slope of the total. In addition, it is generally true that the marginal will be a function of the same independent variables as the total. Therefore, a slope of the marginal function can also be derived, which we call M'. M' is a function and generally has a slope (the same is true for its slope, and so on). For purposes of curve sketching, it is usually sufficient to focus on the signs of M and M'.

The sign of M can take on three classes of values being: positive (+), negative (-), or zero (0). Since M is the value of the slope of the total function $T = T(x)$, the sign of M indicates, in a gross sense, what the relationship between T and x is. A direct relationship between T and x indicates that M is positive, while an inverse one would indicate that M is negative. When x has no effect on T (either over an interval or at some point), the slope of T with respect to x would be zero and, therefore, M would be zero as well. Using the instantaneous slope method, we could construct tangents to the T function at points of concern to ascertain the sign of M. If at a point the tangent is upward sloping, then $M > 0$, while if it is downward sloping, then $M < 0$. When the tangent is horizontal, M = 0. This latter case is of the utmost importance, since as will be demonstrated later, when that occurs, T will either be at its maximum or minimum value, or at an inflection point.

The slope of the total function provides much information about the marginal function. In addition to telling us about the sign of the marginal, it also can convey information about its rate of change (i.e., whether M is increasing, decreasing, or constant). This rate of change is the slope of the marginal function. Knowledge of this slope facilitates the sketching of the marginal function. Since M is a function of x, that is, $M = M(x)$, its slope, M', generally will be as well. M' is simply the rate of change of M with respect to x, or in discrete terms $M' = \Delta M/\Delta x$. When T is a multivariate function, M and M' will follow suit. In that event, they would be interpreted as partial slopes, where the ceteris paribus assumption (all other independent variables held constant) is binding. The sign of M' informs us of the relationship between M and x. A direct relationship between M and x would mean that $M' > 0$, while an inverse relationship would indicate that $M' < 0$. A constant relationship (i.e., x has no effect on M) would take place when $M' = 0$.

The relationship between the sign of M' and T is not intuitively obvious. However, knowledge of the signs of both M and M' tells us a lot about the relationship between T and x. Similarly, knowledge of the relationship between T and x (particularly the graph) tells us about the signs of M and M'. Nine possible cases exist to describe any *point* on a smooth continuous graph. Of these nine cases, only seven are possible as describing either an isolated point or an interval. These seven cases are presented here, while the two remaining cases that are applicable *only* at isolated points will be discussed later in this chapter. These cases should be construed as building blocks. Any economic relationship may contain more than one case over its domain. However, in that event it is possible to divide the domain into separate regions, such that each region contains only one case. Below is presented a verbal description of the seven cases as well as the graphs of the total and marginal functions that correspond. In all cases the description posited applies, as x increases.

Case 1: T Increases at a Constant Rate

In this event, a direct relationship between T and x exists, and hence, M > 0. Since the rate of increase is constant, M is a constant, and therefore, M' = 0. In other words, the slope is positive but constant. Recall that the only functions having constant slopes are linear functions. Therefore, T(x) must be a positively sloped linear function of x. The following examples are representative of this case.

A perfectly competitive producer is a price taker, meaning that he or she believes that his or her output decision has no impact on the price that will be received. Therefore, the producer takes the price, as given by the market, and simply decides on the appropriate output level. Total revenue, R, is simply P x Q. For a price taker, P is treated as a constant and the revenue function (in relation to Q) is linear, emanating from the origin, with slope = P. Since the slope of the revenue function = MR, it has been shown that for a price taker, MR = P. Moreover, since this is true for all Q (in the relevant domain), MR is a constant for all levels of output and is always equal to the market price, P. The total revenue function increases at a constant rate as Q increases. Each additional unit produced generates the same extra revenue, P, as the previous unit did.

A simple macroeconomic example would be the linear consumption function (the saving and investment functions could be used as well). Consumption expenditures are posited to be a linear increasing function of disposable income. The linearity tells us that the slope is constant, but the slope is simply the marginal propensity to consume (out of disposable income), MPC. Therefore, we have that the MPC is positive (usually restricted to being between zero and one) but constant at all levels of disposable income.

The graphs depicting this case are presented in Figure 4.3. For this particular case, M(x) must be linear (but horizontal), due to the fact that M is constant over the interval.

Figure 4.3
A Graphical Depiction of the Total (4.3A) and Marginal (4.3B)
Curves Corresponding to Case 1: T Increases at a Constant Rate

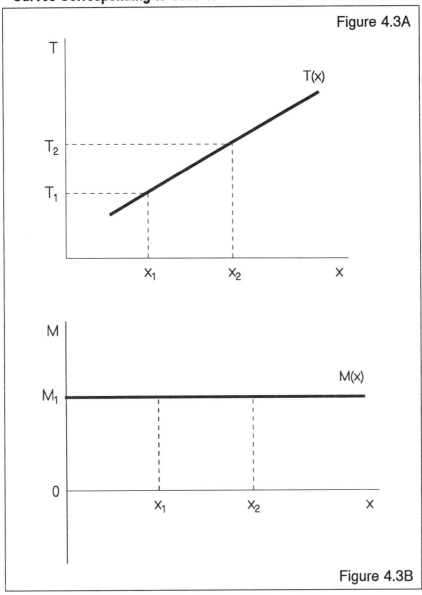

Figure 4.3A

Figure 4.3B

Case 2: T Increases at an Increasing Rate

The fact that T increases as x increases implies that a direct relationship exists between the two, therefore, $M > 0$. In addition, since T is increasing at an increasing rate, the implication is that each additional unit of x is raising T more than the previous unit did (i.e., at a faster rate). Therefore, $M' > 0$, as well. This would very likely be the case over some interval of a cost function, $C = C(Q)$. After some level of output, Q_o, as output expands, total costs may increase at an increasing rate. The above discussion indicates that in that event the marginal cost, MC, would be positive, and increasing as Q increases. In turn, this implies that by producing increments to output, total costs rise and each additional increment to output increases total costs at a faster rate than the previous increment did.

The graphs in Figure 4.4 depict the general properties of the total and marginal functions when Case 2 applies. On the total graph two tangents are drawn at x_1 and x_2. The slopes of these tangents are the values of the marginals at those points. As x increases, these tangents get steeper, indicating that the marginal is increasing. While only two tangents have been drawn, the properties described hold over the whole curve. Notice that the sign of T is unspecified as is the sign of x. This is due to the fact that any curve having the shape of T(x) in Figure 4.4, irrespective of the signs of T and x, will generate an M(x) curve similar to the one depicted. In most economic examples, however, the graphs are drawn in the first quadrant, indicating that T and x are nonnegative, in order to be meaningful economically. Note also that M(x) is drawn as a linear function. This linearity need not always apply. The actual M(x) curve may be linear, or may look like the T(x) curve in Case 2 or Case 3 (below). Without information about the *slope* of M, it is impossible to determine which is true.[4] (This problem is prevalent in the other cases as well.) We have therefore depicted the M(x) curve as linear, since that is an intermediate case. Alternatively, returning to the marginal cost example, if we assume that MC rises at an increasing rate as Q increases, the marginal curve would look like the T(x) curve in Case 2.

Case 3: T Increases at a Decreasing Rate

Again, a direct relationship is posited between T and x, indicating that M > 0. However, the rate of increase is decreasing. This implies that each

Figure 4.4
A Graphical Depiction of the Total (4.4A) and Marginal (4.4B)
Curves Corresponding to Case 2:
T Increases at an Increasing Rate

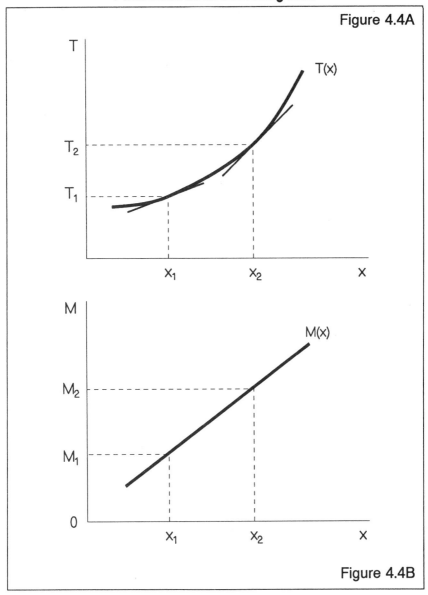

Figure 4.4A

Figure 4.4B

successive increment to x causes T to increase but at a lesser rate than the previous increment. Therefore, although M > 0, M is decreasing as x increases, indicating that M' < 0. An example of this case is the concept of diminishing (but positive) marginal utility. If the amounts of all other goods are held constant, while the amount of one good (say x) increases, then total utility will increase at a decreasing rate. In marginal terms, the same idea can be expressed by saying that the marginal utility of good x, MU_x, is positive but diminishing. Another economic example from the theory of production is the concept of diminishing marginal productivity of an input (i.e., labor). When all other inputs are held constant and only labor is allowed to vary, total output will increase at a decreasing rate (over some interval). In that event, the marginal product of labor, MP_L, will be positive but diminishing. The graphs of T(x) and M(x) representing Case 3 are presented in Figure 4.5.

Notice that the tangents to T(x) are positively sloped but get flatter as x increases. Correspondingly, M is positive but decreasing. As a general principle, the flatter the tangent, the smaller is the **absolute value** of the slope. In the present case, the absolute value of the slope is equal to its actual value, since it is positive. When the slope is negative, however (as in Cases 5 and 6), the distinction between the actual and absolute values is important. Again, the intermediate case of a linear function was used to depict M(x), although other depictions are also possible, when more information is available.

Case 4: T Decreases at a Constant Rate

It should be recognized that the word "decreases" implies an inverse relationship between T and x, indicating that M < 0. However, since the rate of decrease is constant (i.e., M is constant), M' = 0. Combining these two facts, it should be clear that T is a decreasing linear function. The corresponding graphs are depicted in Figure 4.6.

An interesting application of this case is the budget or income constraint. In a two–good (x and y) world, the budget constraint shows the various combinations of the two goods that could be purchased at the prevailing prices, when all income is spent. Denoting the amounts of the two goods as X and Y, their respective prices as P_x and P_y, and income by I, the equation of the budget line is given by:

$$P_x X + P_y Y = I$$

Figure 4.5
A Graphical Depiction of the Total (4.5A) and Marginal (4.5B)
Curves, Corresponding to Case 3:
T Increases at a Decreasing Rate

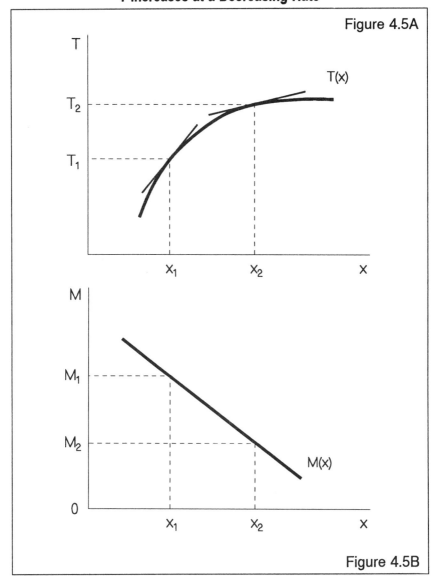

Figure 4.5A

Figure 4.5B

Figure 4.6
A Graphical Depiction of the Total (4.6A) and Marginal (4.6B)
Curves Corresponding to Case 4: T Decreases at a Constant Rate

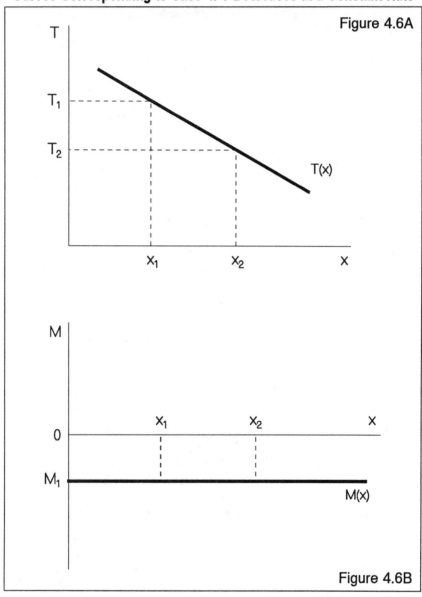

Figure 4.6A

Figure 4.6B

The price of x times its quantity is simply the total expenditure on good x. Similarly, P_yY = total expenditure on good Y. Total expenditure over all is the sum of the two. The equation states that total income equals total expenditure. The two prices P_x and P_y, as well as income, I, are treated as exogenous (predetermined). Given the values of P_x, P_y, and I, the amount of good y that can be purchased (while spending all income), depends on the amount of x that is purchased. The budget constraint can be rewritten to illustrate this point. Solving in terms of Y yields:

$$Y = (I/P_y) - (P_x/P_y)X$$

Notice that since, I, P_y, and P_x are all treated as constants, this is a linear equation with Y intercept = I/P_y and slope = $-P_x/P_y$. Additionally, it is assumed that all variables are positive. The Y intercept informs us of how much y could be consumed, if no x is consumed. In other words, if we only bought good y, how much could we buy? This is given by I/P_y. The slope of the budget constraint is $-P_x/P_y$, which is clearly negative. This implies that if all income is being spent, in order to purchase an additional unit of x, y must change by $-P_x/P_y$. In other words, we must decrease Y by P_x/P_y units of y per additional unit of x. The price ratio, P_x/P_y, is called the relative price of x. This relative price informs us of how much y must be given up to purchase an additional unit of x. It therefore represents the opportunity cost (in terms of units of y) of purchasing an additional unit of x. If the slope of the budget constraint is referred to as M, then the relative price of x is = $-M$. Moreover, since M is constant, so is the relative price of x. It therefore follows that an individual (price taking) consumer faces a constant opportunity cost for each additional unit of x purchased. Similarly, the relative price of y (in terms of units of x) is P_y/P_x. This is the reciprocal of the relative price of x and is equal to $1/(-M)$. It follows that the opportunity cost of y is constant as well. Note also that the relative price of a good is measured not with dollars, but in terms of units of one good/unit of the other good. For example, if P_x = \$4/unit of x and P_y = \$2/unit of y, the relative price of x is 2 units of y/unit of x.

Case 5: T Is Decreasing at an Increasing Rate

As x increases, T is falling, indicating an inverse relationship between them; therefore M < 0. As x increases, the rate of decrease in T is increasing, which implies that T is falling at a faster rate. The rate of decrease is simply the negative of the rate of increase. For example, if a ball is rising at a rate of -10 meters/second, it is falling at a rate of +10 meters/second. If at a later point in time it is rising at a rate of -20 meters/second, at that point it is falling at the faster rate of 20 meters/second. This example illustrates that when something falls at an increasing rate, it is also rising at a negative rate that is getting even more negative (falling). Since M measures the rate of increase (the rate at which the ball is rising), a negative value for M indicates that T is falling as x increases. Moreover, the faster the rate of decrease, the smaller the rate of increase (i.e., -20 < -10). Therefore, the value of M is decreasing as x increases. It is going from some negative value to another negative value whose **absolute** value is greater. (The greater the absolute value of a negative number, the smaller the actual value of that number.) It follows, therefore, that $M' < 0$.

Graphically, this case would be represented by a curve which is negatively sloped throughout, where as x increases, the tangents get steeper. Steeper tangents imply that the absolute value of the slope is greater. However, since the slope is negative, the actual value of the slope is decreasing (becoming even more negative). The curve of the marginal would indicate that it had negative values throughout and decreased as x increased. This is depicted in Figure 4.7.

The revenue function given by $R = 100Q - 10Q^2$ exemplifies this case for values of Q such that $5 < Q \leq 10$. (See Example 4.2 and its corresponding graph.) Over that interval, total revenue decreases at an increasing rate as Q increases. Correspondingly, MR < 0 and is decreasing (becoming even more negative). This implies that over this interval each additional unit of output causes total revenue to fall and that each successive unit causes it to fall by more than the preceding unit. (The table corresponding to Example 4.2 regarding values of MR will corroborate this.)

Case 6: T Decreases at a Decreasing Rate

In this case, an inverse relationship between T and x is indicated and, therefore, M < 0. However, the decreasing rate of decrease means that while increases in x cause T to fall, each successive increment in x causes T to fall by less than the previous unit did. Therefore, although M is negative throughout, as x gets larger, M (while still negative) is getting

Figure 4.7
A Graphical Depiction of the Total (4.7A) and Marginal (4.7B)
Curves Corresponding to Case 5:
T Decreases at an Increasing Rate

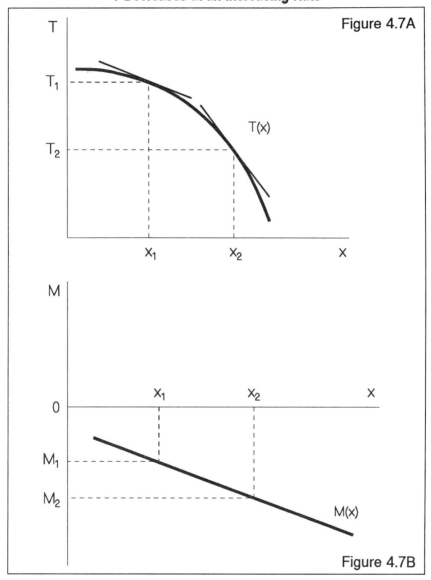

closer to 0. Going from a negative value toward zero is movement in a positive direction (i.e., M is increasing as x increases) and, therefore, M' > 0. The corresponding graphs are depicted in Figure 4.8.

An **indifference curve** shows various combinations of two goods (x and y) that generate the same utility (satisfaction) to a consumer. The consumer is therefore indifferent between any of the combinations on the curve and hence the name, "indifference curve." In most cases, the shape of the indifference curve is similar to that of T(x) in Figure 4.8. However, the vertical axis would be measured in terms of units of good y, while the curve might be labeled U_o, indicating some particular level of utility. The slope of the indifference curve represents the rate at which the consumption of good y can be increased as we increase consumption of x, keeping total utility constant. It is usually assumed that both x and y are goods; therefore, increases in the consumption of either one alone (ceteris paribus) would increase utility. It follows, then, that in order to keep utility constant, if we increase the amount of x, the consumption of y must fall. (Otherwise, utility would have risen.) Therefore, the slope of the indifference curve is negative, showing that we are willing to *give up some y to get more x*, while staying at the same level of utility. The maximum rate at which we are willing to give up y for an additional unit of x (keeping utility constant) is the negative of the slope of the indifference curve. This rate is known as the **marginal rate of substitution**, or MRS. If the slope of the curve is called M (our practice so far), then the MRS = -M. Since M is increasing as x increases (M' > 0), it implies that -M must be falling. Economically, this is referred to as diminishing MRS. The implication being that, as x increases, individuals are increasingly less willing, on the margin, to give up units of y to get successive increments in x.

Case 7: T Is Neither Increasing nor Decreasing and Its Rate of Change Is Constant

When discussion is focused solely on intervals, this case is trivial. It could only occur when T is constant throughout the interval, as x changes. It therefore follows that M = M' = 0. In this case, T(x) would be represented graphically as a horizontal line, where T takes on any value (positive, negative, or zero). The M(x) graph similarly would be a horizontal line; however, it is horizontal at the value M = 0. Therefore, the graph of M(x) is coincident with the x axis. The interpretation of this

Figure 4.8
A Graphical Depiction of the Total (4.8A) and Marginal (4.8B)
Curves Corresponding to Case 6:
T Decreases at a Decreasing Rate

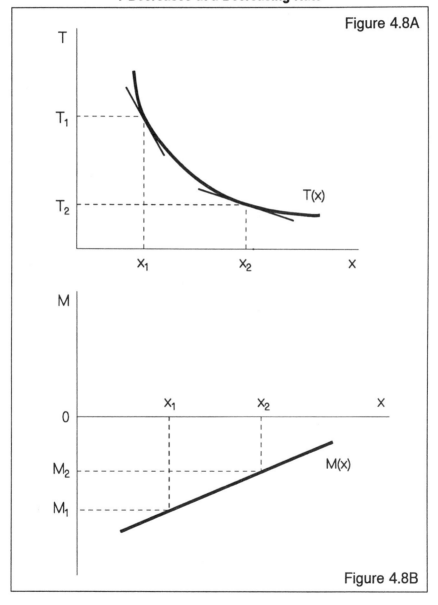

Figure 4.8A

Figure 4.8B

case (over an interval) is that values of x have no impact either on the value of T or its rate of change. In other words, T is independent of x. It is still true that T = T(x) (recall the definition of a function). However, the nature of the function is trivial, as it is a constant function. The graphical depiction of this case is presented in Figure 4.9, followed by economic examples. (When Case 7 prevails at a single point, the situation is more complex. The discussion of that situation is relegated to a later section.)

The level of investment expenditures (I) in the economy may depend on a host of factors including: the interest rate (i), expectations regarding the future (E), and national income (Y). When investment decisions are made·on a long–term basis, the level of I may be considered to be independent of the current level of Y. When investment expenditures are represented by a simple investment function of this type, they are termed autonomous, since they are autonomous of Y, although they may depend upon other independent variables. Graphically, the investment function would be depicted as the T(x) graph in Figure 4.9. Moreover, the slope of the I function with respect to Y is the marginal propensity to invest, MPI. Since the slope = 0, it implies that the MPI = 0. Additionally, the MPI is constant at that level (0) and does not change in response to changes in Y.

Another example relates to cost theory. Total costs of production (C) are assumed to be a function of quantity (Q). However, in the short run, C can be decomposed into two parts, fixed costs (FC) and variable costs (VC). Fixed costs are those that do not vary with output (rent, depreciation, etc.), while as its name implies, variable costs do vary with output, e.g., labor costs. Since FC is independent of Q, its graph would be like the T(x) graph in Figure 4.9. This is important since $\Delta C = \Delta FC + \Delta VC$. Dividing this equation by ΔQ yields $\Delta C/\Delta Q = \Delta FC/\Delta Q + \Delta VC/\Delta Q$. However:

$\Delta C/\Delta Q$ = slope of the total cost function (with respect to Q) = MC
$\Delta FC/\Delta Q$ = slope of the FC function (with respect to Q) = 0 (since FC is independent of Q
$\Delta VC/\Delta Q$ = slope of the VC function (with respect to Q)

It therefore follows that the slopes of the C and VC functions are equal at every Q, and that this slope (of either C or VC) = MC. In addition, MC is independent of FC. This implies that output decisions in the short run that depend upon MC will be unaffected by changes in FC.

Figure 4.9
A Graphical Depiction of the Total (4.9A) and Marginal (4.9B) Curves Corresponding to Case 7: T Is Neither Increasing nor Decreasing and Its Rate of Change Is Constant (Over an Interval)

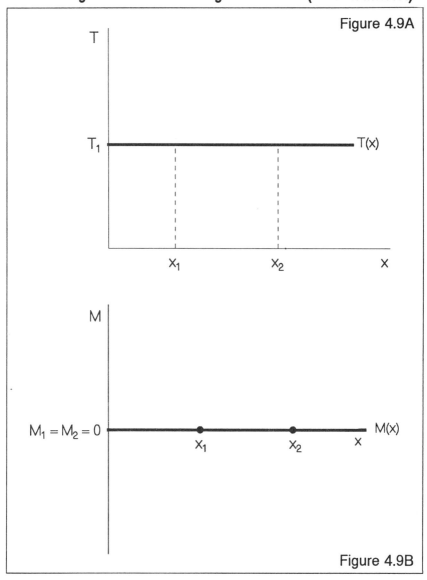

Figure 4.9A

Figure 4.9B

Maxima and Minima; Concavity and Convexity

It is generally assumed that economic agents (e.g., consumers, producers) attempt to maximize or minimize the value of some variable, known as the **objective**. The agent does so by marginally adjusting some other variable(s) under the agent's control that are known to influence the value of the objective. Variables of this type are called **control** or **decision variables**. The relationship between the objective and the decision variable(s) (and possibly other independent variables) is the **objective function**. Consumers may try to maximize utility (given the budget constraint). Producers might maximize profits or possibly revenues. Producers might minimize total costs of a given level of production. Therefore, the determination of points on a function that either maximize or minimize its value is an important concern to economists. When the graph of the objective function is known, casual inspection of it yields the answer immediately. Generally, however, such information is not readily available. But if the conditions under which a maximum or minimum take place are known, then the points satisfying those conditions are the ones being sought.

Some Preliminaries

The general maximization problem, in the univariate case, can be presented as follows. Assume that the objective is to maximize the value of T, where T is a function of x. We are searching for the value of x such that no other value of x, in its domain, yields a higher value for T. When the domain of x contains one or two finite endpoints, two qualitatively different types of maxima are possible. Let the domain of x be all values of x between a and b, inclusive (i.e., $a \leq x \leq b$). In many economic examples, a and b are both finite numbers. For example, the relevant domain (of output) for a profit maximizing producer, in the short run, may lie between 0 and some maximum Q, governed by the capacity of the plant (say, 1,000 units/year). In that event both a and b are finite, with a = 0 and b = 1,000. When the profit maximizing level of output is at either a or b, the solution is termed a **boundary (or corner) solution**, since it occurs on the boundary point of the domain. Alternatively, when the profit maximizing level of output lies on the interior of the domain (i.e., between but excluding a and b), it is termed an **interior solution**. The focus of this section is on interior solutions, since they are more prevalent. The conditions necessary for an interior solution will in general *not* hold at a boundary solution. If one suspects that the true maximum is at the boundary, then the results at the boundary should be compared to the values on the interior.

Another complicating factor is that conditions necessary for a maximum, on the interior, are too general. They may be satisfied at a multiplicity of points rather than at just one. The maximum that is generally sought is a **global maximum**. By global it is meant that this point is the highest over the complete domain. Conversely, the conditions to be specified for a maximum (interior) determine all **local maxima**. The word *local* implies that it is the highest point in that part of the domain that surrounds it (i.e., in a neighborhood around that point). Any global maximum must also be a local maximum, but the reverse isn't true.

The difference between local and global can be readily seen by means of analogy. Imagine that you are trying to find the highest elevation attained on a plot of land. The plot is flat, except for four mountains that lie within it. The peak of each of the mountains would each represent a local maximum. The global maximum would be at the peak of the highest mountain. Once the four local maxima are determined, the global could be ascertained by comparing the values at the four local maxima and choosing the largest amongst them. The same procedure could be applied in economic examples. First, identify all of the local maxima and then compare their results to find the largest. The problems typically encountered by an economics student are usually those where only one local maximum exists. In that event, the local maximum found must also be a global maximum. The typical problem is one with a unique local maximum that lies on the interior, and this will be the case discussed in the remainder of this section. The situation for a minimum is analogous. In other words, the conditions to be discussed here identify all *local* maxima or minima that lie on the interior of the domain.

Maxima and Minima: Necessary Conditions

There are a multitude of problems in economics involving the maximization or minimization of some objective function. In each case, the actual function utilized can take on many forms. It would be useful, under those circumstances, if some general rule could be found that would identify the point on the function at which the maximum or minimum occurred. There are two types of rules or conditions that are associated with this problem of identification, these being **necessary conditions** and **sufficient conditions**.

The distinction between necessary and sufficient conditions can be illustrated by the following general example. Assume that phenomenon z is being investigated. A necessary condition (NC) for phenomenon z is such that, in order for z to occur, NC must be present. This implies that *all* points where z occurs have the NC property and conversely *all* points at which the NC property is absent, z cannot occur. However, the fact that the NC property is present does not imply that z must occur. A condition that is necessary (NC) but not sufficient will hold at all points that z does occur but will also hold at other points at which z does not occur. If z = being a father, then NC might be "being a male." Notice that all fathers are males and no nonmales are therefore fathers. It follows then that "being a male" is a necessary condition for "being a father." Notice also that whereas all fathers have this property, some nonfathers also have this property. Therefore, possessing NC alone does not guarantee that z occurred, since some non–z points also have this property. In this sense, a necessary condition is overly broad.

Alternatively, a sufficient condition (SC) may be viewed as overly restrictive. Continuing the above example, a sufficient condition (SC) for phenomenon z is such that all points possessing SC imply that z also occurs. In other words, the presence guarantees that z is present also. However, z may also occur when SC is absent. When z is "being a father," SC might be "males having 2 children." Notice that anyone satisfying SC must automatically be a father (z) also. However, there exists a group of individuals that do not satisfy SC (males with 1 child or males with more than 2 children), and yet z (being a father) still occurs. Therefore, while the presence of SC guarantees that z also occurs, the absence of SC does not imply that z does not occur. It is of course possible that a condition could be both necessary and sufficient. In that event, all points where z occurs have this property, and no non-z points do. "Males having one or more children" would represent a necessary and sufficient condition for "being a father." The Venn diagram in Figure 4.10 illustrates these relationships.

Notice that SC is a subset of z, which in turn is a subset of NC. If a particular condition is called C, then the following is true.

1) "Every time C occurs, z must also occur," then C = SC.
2) "Every time z occurs, C must be present," then C = NC.
3) If both 1 and 2 hold simultaneously, then C = NC and SC.

Figure 4.10
Venn Diagram Depicting the Relationship Between
Necessary (NC) and Sufficient (SC) Conditions

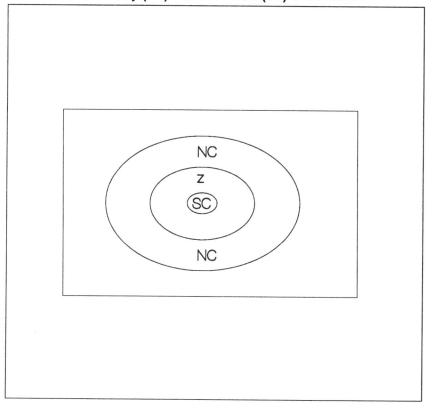

When a condition is both necessary and sufficient, the set of points satisfying that condition is identical with the set of points at which z occurs. Having distinguished between necessary and sufficient conditions, we now ask what conditions are necessary for a local maximum or minimum (on the interior). Of particular concern are properties of the marginal function, M, at such points. The necessary condition (regarding M) can be deduced by a process of elimination. Recall that if M > 0 (at a point or over an interval), it implied that there was a direct relationship between T and x. If x increased from some initial value of x_0, then T would increase as well. Therefore, the value of T at x_0 is smaller than the value of T at a slightly higher value of x. It follows then, that if M > 0 at x_0, x_0 cannot be the value of x that maximizes T, since a higher value of T exists. Similarly, if M > 0 at x_0, then a small decrease in x will cause T to fall as well. Since a smaller value of T exists, x_0 cannot be the value of x that minimizes T. Therefore, any point at which M > 0 cannot represent either a maximum or minimum point. By similar reasoning, it can be shown that if M < 0 at x_0, then x_0 cannot be the value of x that either maximizes or minimizes T. When M < 0, an inverse relationship exists between x and T. Increases in x cause T to fall, indicating that x_0 cannot be a minimum point. Similarly, decreases in x, from x_0, cause T to rise, so that x_0 could not be a maximum point.

Having eliminated the two cases of M > 0 and M < 0, it must be true that all points at which an interior maximum or minimum occur must have M = 0 at those points. Therefore, a necessary condition (NC) for a point to be a maximum or minimum point is that M = 0 at that point.[5] Since the necessary condition for a maximum is identical to the necessary condition for a minimum, it cannot be a sufficient condition (SC) for either. In other words, all maximum points have M = 0, as do all minimum points. So if one is searching for either a maximum or minimum point on a function, the search can be simplified and shortened by looking only at points on that function where M = 0. However, if a point is found at which M = 0, there is no guarantee that that point is a maximum point. Similarly, there is no guarantee that the point found is a minimum point. This indicates that M = 0 is not a sufficient condition for either a maximum or a minimum, although it is a necessary condition for both. In fact, the point may be neither a maximum or a minimum, as a third possibility exists. The third possibility is that the point represents **a point of inflection**. Inflection points will be discussed later in the chapter.

Maxima and Minima Sufficient Conditions

Since M = 0 is a necessary condition for either a maximum or a minimum, how can one distinguish between those cases? In particular, if the necessary condition (M = 0) is satisfied at some point, x*, what are the sufficient conditions that x* is a maximum or minimum point? The seven cases discussed previously (in terms of M and M′) could exist over an interval. In other words, every point on that interval had the property mentioned. The other two cases were omitted since they could not hold over an interval but only at isolated points on that interval. As will be shown, those cases represent maximum or minimum points.

Maxima: Sufficient Conditions

To have a point be a local maximum requires that no point close to it has a higher value of T (although they can have equal values). A typical graph of a maximum as well as its corresponding marginal function is presented in Figure 4.11 and described as Case 8.

Case 8: Maximum Points

A sufficient condition for a point x* to maximize T(x) is that at x*, M(x*) = 0, and M is decreasing (i.e., M′ < 0) as x increases around that point. Notice, for that to happen M must be positive for values of x close to but less than x* (like x_1) and negative for values of x close to but larger than x* (like x_2). In other words, at x*, M = 0, but for points close to x*, M switches from positive to negative. In this event, T(x) increases at a decreasing rate for values of x < x*, while it decreases at an increasing rate for values of x > x*. At x*, T(x) is stationary (neither increasing or decreasing) as x changes infinitesimally. It should be noted that this condition is merely sufficient but not necessary. Technically, if T(x) is a constant function (Case 7), then every point on it is a local maximum even though this condition is absent.

Figure 4.11
A Graphical Depiction of the Total (4.11A) and Marginal (4.11B) Curves Corresponding to Case 8: Maximum Points

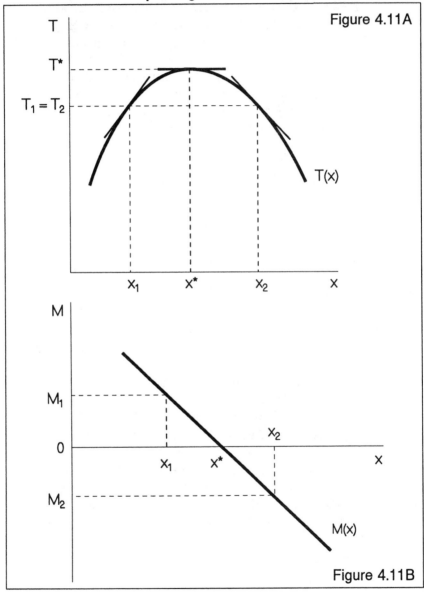

Figure 4.11A

Figure 4.11B

Figure 4.12
A Graphical Depiction of the Total (4.12A) and Marginal (4.12B) Curves Corresponding to Case 9: Minima Points

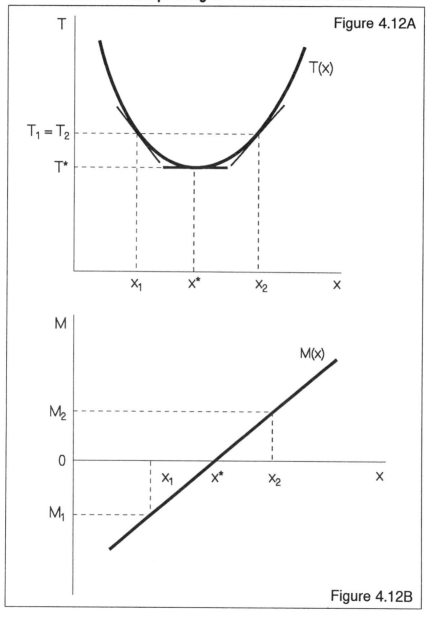

Minima: Sufficient Conditions

In order for a point x* to be a local minimum requires that no point close to it has a lower value of T(x) (although they can have equal values). A typical graph of a minimum and its corresponding marginal function is presented in Figure 4.12 and described as Case 9.

Case 9: Minima Points

A sufficient condition for x* to minimize T(x) is that $M(x^*) = 0$ and that M increases with x around x* (i.e., $M' > 0$). For that to happen, M must be negative for values of x close to but less than x* and positive for values of x close to but greater than x*. Therefore, the sufficiency condition can be stated as "M is equal to 0 at x* and switches from negative to positive as x rises." In this event, T(x) decreases at a decreasing rate before x*, while it increases at an increasing rate after x*. Of course at x* itself, T(x) is stationary. Again, note that this condition is sufficient (but not necessary). Every point on a constant function (Case 7) can be considered a local minimum point.

The exposition so far has been in terms of a univariate function. When $T = T(x)$, necessary conditions for T to be at either its maximum or minimum value include finding the value of x (say x*), so that $M = 0$, at x*. The logic used to derive this rule can be applied to the multivariate case as well. Consider the bivariate case given by $T = T(x_1, x_2)$, and suppose that a maximum or minimum of T is sought. In that event, we are searching for a pair of values (one for x_1, and one for x_2) x_1^*, x_2^* at which T reaches its extreme point. Since there are two decision variables (x_1 and x_2), the partial slopes of T with respect to:

$$x_1 \text{ and } x_2, \quad M_{x_1} \text{ and } M_{x_2}$$

respectively, have to be considered. At any point $(x_{1,0}, x_{2,0})$ that either:

$$M_{x_1} > 0, \, M_{x_2} > 0$$

or both, T can be increased (decreased) by increasing (decreasing) the variable with the positive partial slope. Similarly, if the partial slope with respect to either variable is negative at some point, then an increase (decrease) in that variable will cause T to decrease (increase). Under any of these conditions, changes in x or y can cause T to increase or decrease, indicating that those initial points could not be either maximum or minimum points. The only alternative is that:

$$M_{x_1} = M_{x_2} = 0$$

is a necessary condition for either a maximum or minimum point. This is demonstrated graphically in Figure 4.13. In Figure 4.13 A, the variable T is maximized at the combination x_1^*, x_2^* where:

$$M_{x_1} = M_{x_2} = 0$$

Figure 4.13 B shows that T is minimized at combination x_1^{**}, x_2^{**} where again:

$$M_{x_1} = M_{x_2} = 0$$

In general, if T is a function of n variables (where n might be large), a necessary condition that a point be either a maximum or minimum is that, at that point, all n partial slopes must simultaneously be equal to zero. In order to distinguish between a maximum and a minimum, knowledge of sufficiency conditions is required. Unfortunately, the sufficient conditions unlike the necessary conditions are not a simple generalization of the univariate case. Due to the mathematical complexity of establishing sufficiency conditions for the multivariate case, their development will be omitted.

There are two types of applications to which the above mentioned necessary conditions can be utilized. When the objective function is in **general functional form**, general rules can be developed that describe the conditions necessary for an extremum. These rules will prevail for any specific function, in that general class. However, without knowledge of the specific function, there is insufficient information to determine numerically the actual point at which this extremum occurs. Alternatively, when a specific function is utilized, use of the necessary conditions can aid in the numerical determination of these extreme points.

Figure 4.13
A Graphical Depiction of a Maximum (4.13A) and Minimum (4.13B) for a Multivariate Function

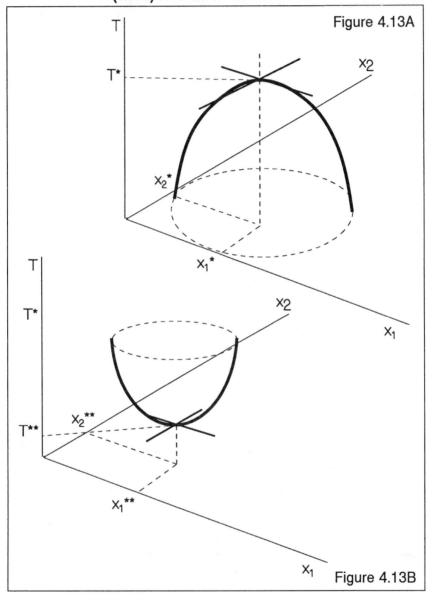

Figure 4.13A

Figure 4.13B

Example 4.8 Maximizing Total Revenue

Total Revenue, R, by definition is equal to P x Q, where P is also a function of Q, i.e., P = P(Q). Therefore, in general functional form, the total revenue function is R = R(Q). If a firm wanted to maximize its total revenue by the appropriate choice of Q, what Q should it choose? The numerically exact answer cannot be determined with the available information. However, using the necessary condition for a maximum, a general rule can be developed that would hold for any specific total revenue function. Since marginal revenue, MR, is the slope of R, the necessary condition would be that MR = 0. In other words, the Q that maximizes R must be a Q at which MR = 0. In addition, the sufficient condition requires that MR is decreasing at that point. This result holds for any total revenue function specified.

Alternatively, when the specific function is known, as in Example 4.2, the numerical value of Q that maximizes R can be determined. In that example using the instantaneous slope method, MR was given by the function, MR = 100 - 20Q. Setting MR = 0 yields 100 - 20Q = 0 or 100 = 20Q. Solving for the value of Q at which MR = 0 yields $Q^* = 5$ (an asterisk implies the solution value). The slope of the MR function is constant (since MR is a linear function of Q) and equal to -20. As such, MR is decreasing from positive values (for Q < 5) to negative values (for Q > 5) around that point. Together with the necessary condition, this is sufficient to guarantee that $Q^* = 5$ is a maximum point.

Example 4.9 Maximizing Total Profits

Total profit, π, is equal to total revenue minus total cost, or $\pi = R - C$. Since R and C are both functions of Q, so is π. Marginal profit, $M\pi$, is the slope of the profit function with respect to Q and is equal to MR - MC. In order to maximize total profit, $M\pi = 0$ is required. Since $M\pi = MR - MC$, this can also be stated as MR - MC = 0. Adding MC to both sides of the equation yields the more familiar necessary condition for profit maximization, MR = MC. Of course, sufficiency conditions must be met to guarantee that a profit maximum (rather than minimum) has been obtained.

Many optimization problems in economics are similar to our profit maximization example in that they involve the maximization of net benefits from a particular action. Net benefits are defined as total benefits

– total costs (where costs and benefits are measured in the same units). The differences between examples include: 1) who is the optimizing agent (and correspondingly whose costs and benefits are being considered), and 2) with which action is the optimization done. Example 4.9 is simply a special case of the above. The optimizing agent in that case is the firm and the action being considered is the quantity to produce. The benefits accruing to the firm from production are its total revenues, while the costs of production (broadly defined) are the total costs accruing to the action. In order to maximize total net benefits, the necessary condition is that marginal net benefits equal zero. In other words, the action (producing more units) should be continued up until the point where the extra net benefits just equal zero. When marginal net benefits are positive, the action should be continued, while if they are negative, less of the action should be undertaken.

Example 4.10 Consumers' Utility Maximization Given an Income Constraint

The goal of a consumer may be to maximize utility. Utility is generated from the consumption of goods. In the case where there are only two goods x and y, the consumer must choose quantities of these goods, X and Y respectively, that maximize utility. The consumer faces a budget constraint, limiting the combinations of X and Y that are affordable. The extra utility per additional unit of x, MU_x, and the extra utility per additional unit of y, MU_y, are the extra benefits respectively from increased consumption of these goods. The extra cost in dollars of consuming an additional unit of either good is its respective price, P_x or P_y. The reciprocal of a good's price is the amount of the good that could be purchased for a dollar. For example, if P_x = $5/unit of x, then one dollar spent on x would enable one to purchase 1/5 unit of good x. Given a fixed budget, an additional dollar spent on x means that one less dollar must be spent on y, when the total budget is utilized. The consumer must decide how much of the limited budget should be spent on each good. The marginal benefit from spending an extra dollar on x is $1/P_x \times MU_x$, which is simply the extra amount of x that could be purchased with that dollar times the extra utility per unit of x. If MU_x = 10 utils/unit of x, and P_x = $5/unit of x, then an extra dollar spent on x enables one to purchase .2 extra units of x, which generates 2 extra utils. The opportunity cost (in utils) of spending an extra dollar on x is the forgone utility of not spending it on y. This would be given by $1/P_y \times MU_y$. The marginal net benefit of spending an additional dollar on x is $(MU_x/P_x) - (MU_y/P_y)$. Net benefits will be maximized when marginal net benefits equal zero. This implies that the consumer should purchase the amounts of x and y such that, at that combination, $(MU_x/P_x) = (MU_y/P_y)$. This condition can also be written as $(MU_x/MU_y) = (P_x/P_y)$. It can be shown that the rate that a consumer would be willing to give up units of y for additional units of x (i.e., the MRS) equals MU_x/MU_y. Therefore, this condition says that the consumer should equate his or her MRS to the price ratio or relative price of x. Recall that the MRS is the negative of the slope of the indifference curve, and the price ratio is the negative of the slope of the budget constraint. Moreover, in combination with the fact that all income is spent, this condition implies that utility maximum will take place at a **tangency** between the indifference curve and the budget constraint.

Concavity and Convexity

The sufficiency conditions for a maximum or a minimum can be described more succinctly using new terminology. Toward this end, the following definitions are presented.

Definition 4.1: Concave curve. A curve is considered concave over an interval if a (chord) line drawn between any two points on that interval lies either on or beneath the curve. When all such lines lie wholly beneath the curve (except at the endpoints) the curve is said to be **strictly concave** over that interval. When a curve is (strictly) concave over an interval, it implies that the curve is (strictly) concave at every point on that interval.

Definition 4.2: Concave at a point. To test whether a curve is concave at some point x_0 (rather than over an interval) the following procedure can be used. Draw a tangent to the curve at x_0. If the tangent lies on or above the curve at all points close to x_0, then the curve is concave at x_0. It is considered **strictly concave** at x_0 if the tangent lies above the curve at all points close to but excluding x_0. These various types of concavity are demonstrated in Figure 4.14.

Figure 4.14
A Graphical Depiction of Concavity (4.14A) and Strict Concavity (4.14B) at a Point and Over an Interval

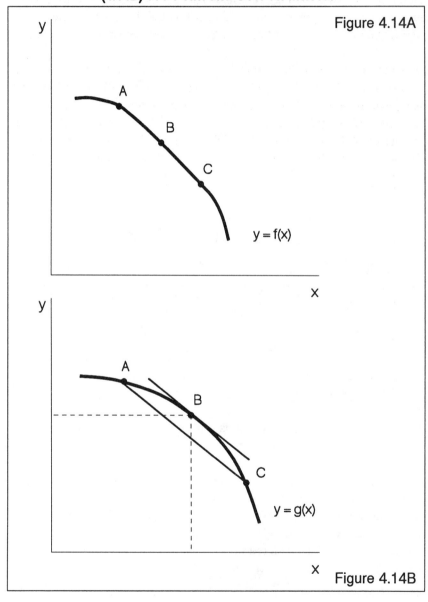

Figure 4.14A

$y = f(x)$

$y = g(x)$

Figure 4.14B

Definition 4.3: Convex curve. A curve is considered convex over an interval if a (chord) line drawn between any two points on that interval lies either on or above the curve. When all such lines lie strictly above the curve (except at the endpoints) the curve is said to be **strictly convex** over that interval. When a curve is (strictly) convex over an interval, it implies that the curve is (strictly) convex at every point on that interval.

Definition 4.4: Convex at a point. To test whether a curve is convex at a point x_0 (rather than over an interval) the following procedures can be utilized. If the tangent to the curve at x_0 lies on or beneath the curve at all points close to x_0, the curve is **convex** at x_0. It is considered **strictly convex** at x_0, if the tangent lies beneath the curve at all points close to but excluding x_0. These various types of convexity are demonstrated in Figure 4.15.

The following points should be noted.

1) What has been termed here as concave is sometimes referred to as **concave down**. Similarly, what has been termed here as convex is sometimes referred to as **concave up**.

2) A linear function satisfies the conditions for both concavity and convexity, since a line drawn between any two points on it lies wholly on the curve. However, while it is both concave and convex, it is neither strictly concave nor strictly convex.

3) The graphs of the nine cases depicted earlier can be classified as follows:

   a) **Concave:** Cases 1, 3, 4, 5, 7, 8

   b) **Convex:** Cases 1, 2, 4, 6, 7, 9

   c) **Strictly Concave:** Cases 3, 5, 8

   d) **Strictly Convex:** Cases 2, 6, 9

In addition, observe that all cases that were classified as strictly concave have the property that $M' < 0$, while those classified as strictly convex have the property that $M' > 0$. A sufficient condition for a curve

Figure 4.15
A Graphical Depiction of a Convexity (4.15A) and Strict Convexity (4.15B) at a Point and Over an Interval

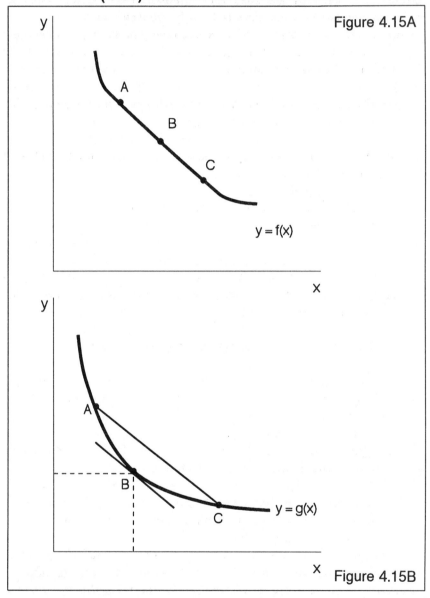

Figure 4.15A

$y = f(x)$

$y = g(x)$

Figure 4.15B

to be strictly concave at a point x_o is that $M' < o$ at x_o. This implies that the value of the slope (M) is decreasing as x increases (for values of x around x_o). Similarly, a sufficient condition for a curve to be strictly convex at x_o is that $M' > 0$ at x_o. That implies that the value of the slope (M) is increasing as x increases (for values of x around x_o).

The sufficiency conditions for a maximum or a minimum can now be restated in these terms. If the necessary condition for an extremum is satisfied (i.e., $M = 0$) at a point x^*, then:

a) A sufficient condition guaranteeing that x^* is a maximum is that the curve is concave at x^*.

b) A sufficient condition guaranteeing that x^* is a minimum is that the curve is convex at x^*.

Notice that Cases 8 and 9 satisfy these conditions.

Inflection Points

An inflection point is a point on the curve where the curve switches from concave to convex or vice versa. An inflection point possesses the following characteristics.

1) The slope of the curve (M) may take on any value (+, -, 0) at an inflection point or it may fail to exist.

2) The sign of the slope is the same at values of x on either side of the inflection point.

3) The rate of change of the slope (value of M') must either be equal to zero or fail to exist at an inflection point.

4) The tangent to the curve at an inflection point will lie above the curve on one side and beneath the curve on the other.

Inflection points provide useful information for the sketching of marginal functions M(x). Recall that M' is simply the slope of M(x). A necessary condition for a function to reach a maximum or minimum at some point x^* is that the slope of the function at that point be equal to zero. Therefore, a necessary condition for M(x) to be at an extremum is that $M' = 0$ at that point. Generally, if x* is an inflection point with $M'(x^*) = 0$, and the curve switches from convex to concave at x*, then M(x) will be maximized at x*. Similarly, if the curve switches from concave to convex at x*, then M(x) will be minimized at x*.

Example 4.11: Production Function

A production function shows the relationship between the level of inputs and the total level of output. While in general there may be many inputs,

Figure 4.16
A Production Function Depicting the Relation Between Output and Labor Input (All Other Inputs Held Constant)

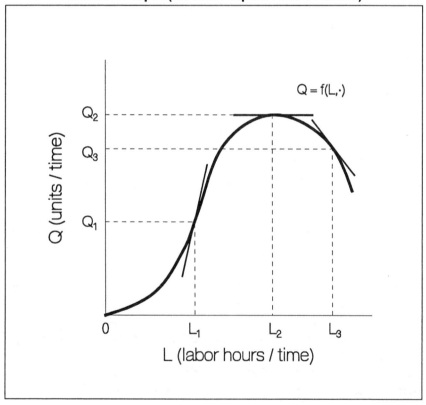

if all but the level of labor (L) is held constant, the production function can be expressed as $Q = f(L, \cdot)$. The level of total output is represented by Q, while the dot symbolizes the fact that all other inputs are held constant. A graph of this function is given in Figure 4.16, with tangents drawn at L_1, L_2, and L_3.

Recall that the slope of this curve represents the marginal product of labor, MP_L. In order to graph the MP_L curve with respect to labor, the following should be recognized. For $0 < L < L_2$, there is a direct relationship between Q and L. Therefore, over this interval $MP_L > 0$. For $L > L_2$, an inverse relationship between Q and L exists, indicating that $MP_L < 0$ over this interval. In addition, at L_2 the slope is zero, so that $MP_L = 0$ at L_2. At L_1 an inflection point exists as the curve switches from convex to concave.

The MP_L graph can be derived from this information and can be described as consisting of three separate ranges separated by two points. The first range is for values of L such that $0 \leq L < L_1$. In this range output is increasing at an increasing rate (Case 2). The curve is convex and upward sloping, indicating that MP_L is positive and increasing. For $L_1 < L < L_2$, Q is increasing at a decreasing rate (Case 3). The curve is upward sloping and concave, implying that MP_L is positive but diminishing. The third range occurs for values of L such that $L > L_2$. In this interval, Q is decreasing at an increasing rate. The curve is concave and downward sloping (Case 5), so that MP_L is negative and decreasing. At L_2 the tangent is horizontal and the curve is concave. This is a sufficient condition for L_2 to represent the level of L at which **total product**, Q, is maximized. Moreover, L_1 represents an inflection point where the slope (MP_L) is positive. Notice that MP_L was increasing for values of $L < L_1$ and decreasing for values of $L > L_1$. This implies that the MP_L is maximized at L_1. The graph of this function is given in Figure 4.17.

Example 4.12: Cost Functions

Total costs, C, may be considered to be a univariate function of the level of output, Q. In general functional notation this can be written as $C = C(Q)$. The graph of a typical cost function is presented in Figure 4.18, with a tangent drawn at Q_1.

The following properties of the graph should be recognized. At an output of zero ($Q = 0$), costs are positive and equal to b_0. This represents the fixed costs component of total cost, while all costs greater than b_0 are

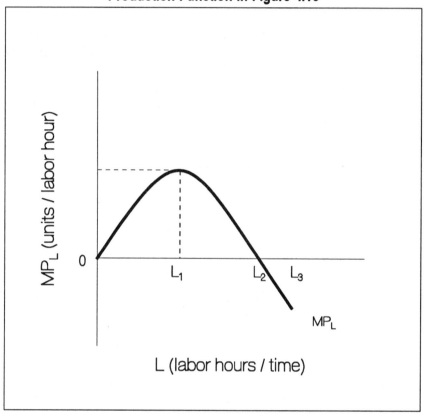

variable costs. Note that the total cost curve is upward sloping through-out, indicating a direct relationship between C and Q. This implies that the marginal cost, MC, (which is simply the slope of this curve) is positive throughout. The curve is positively sloped and concave for $0 \leq Q < Q_1$ and positively sloped and convex for $Q > Q_1$. At Q_1 an inflection point exists. In the concave section costs are increasing at a decreasing rate (Case 3), so that the MC is positive but decreasing. Alternatively in the convex section, costs are increasing at an increasing rate (Case 2), so that MC is positive and increasing. Since MC is decreasing before Q_1 and

Figure 4.18
A Representative Total Cost Curve (as a Function of Output)

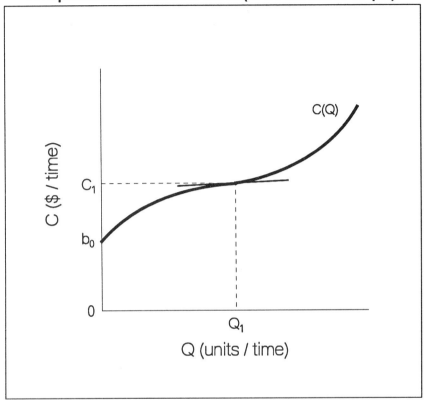

increasing afterward, the inflection point at Q_1 must represent the Q, at which MC is at a minimum. The MC curve is presented in Figure 4.19.

A Final Word on Concavity and Convexity

The previous discussion accurately depicted the case of a univariate function. Unfortunately, the conditions for concavity and convexity in a multivariate setting are more complicated and beyond the scope of this book. It does remain true in a multivariate setting that, if all the

Figure 4.19
The Marginal Cost Curve Corresponding to the
Total Cost Curve of Figure 4.18

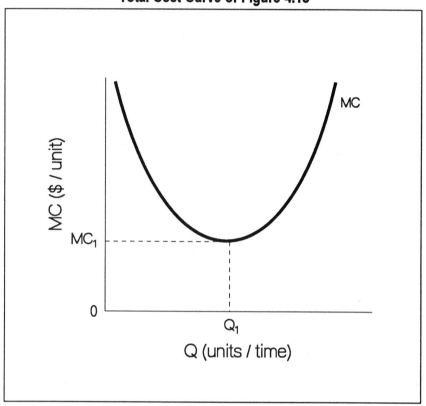

marginals are zero at a point, and the curve is concave at that point, then this is sufficient for a maximum. Sufficient conditions for a minimum are the same as the above except that concave is replaced by convex. A summary of the nine cases is presented in Table 4.2.

Table 4.2
Behavior of T(x) as x Increases:
Nine Cases Based on a Classification of the Signs of M and M′

Values of M′

	Zero	Positive	Negative
Positive (Values of M)	T(x) increases at a constant rate. **Over an interval:** a) T(x) is linear b) concave and convex but strictly neither c) Case 1 **At a point, x*:** a) x* is an inflection point b) M(x) is minimized or maximized at x*	T(x) increases at an increasing rate. **At a point or over an interval:** a) strictly convex b) Case 2	T(x) increases at a decreasing rate. **At a point or over an interval:** a) strictly concave b) Case 3
Negative (Values of M)	T(x) decreases at a constant rate. **Over an interval:** a) T(x) is linear b) concave and convex, but strictly neither c) Case 4 **At a point x*:** a) x* is an inflection point b) M(x) is maximized or minimized at x*	T(x) decreases at a decreasing rate. **At a point or over an interval:** a) strictly convex b) Case 6	T(x) decreases at an increasing rate. **At a point or over an interval:** a) strictly concave b) Case 5
Zero (Values of M)	**Over an interval:** a) T(x) is a constant function (horizontal line) b) concave and convex, but strictly neither c) Case 7 **At a point x*:** the point may be a max, min, or inflection point	Cannot hold over an interval. **At a point, x*:** a) T(x) is stationary b) strictly convex c) x* is a local min d) Case 9	Cannot hold over an interval. **At a point, x*:** a) T(x) is stationary b) strictly concave c) x* is a local max d) Case 8

Important Terms in this Chapter

Boundary solution – A solution of an optimization (maximization or minimization) problem that lies on an endpoint (boundary) of the domain.

Concave (also concave down) – A curve is concave over an interval only if a line drawn between any two points on this interval lies on or beneath the curve. It is concave at a point only if the tangent to the curve at that point lies on or above the curve for points immediately surrounding the initial point.

Convex (also concave up) – A curve is convex over an interval only if a line drawn between any two points on this interval lies on or above the curve. It is convex at a point only if the tangent at that point lies on or below the curve for points immediately surrounding the initial point.

Decision variables (also control variables) – Variables whose values are controlled (chosen) by a decision maker in an optimization problem.

Global maximum – The highest value taken on by a function over its entire domain.

Indifference curve – A curve whose points represent quantities of two goods, such that the consumer receives the same satisfaction (utility) at all points on that curve.

Interior solution – A solution to an optimization problem that lies on the interior (rather than at an endpoint) of the domain.

Local maxima – Points on a function, such that no other point in its immediate vicinity has a higher value, although other points in the domain (not in the immediate vicinity) may have higher values.

Marginal cost (MC) – The rate at which total cost changes in response to changes in output, $\Delta C/\Delta Q$. Also the slope of the total cost function with respect to output.

Marginal product of inputs (MP_K and MP_L) – The rate at which output changes in response to changes in that input (K or L), ceteris paribus. Often denoted as ($\Delta Q/\Delta K$) and ($\Delta Q/\Delta L$) respectively, and represents the slope of the production function with respect to that input.

Marginal profit ($M\pi$) – The rate at which total profit changes in response to output changes, $\Delta\pi/\Delta Q$. Also the slope of the total profit function with respect to output.

Marginal propensity to invest (MPI) – The rate at which investment expenditures change in response to changes in national income, $\Delta I/\Delta Y$. Also the slope of the investment function with respect to national income.

Marginal propensity to save (MPS) – The rate at which saving changes in response to changes in disposable income, $\Delta S/\Delta Y_d$. Also the slope of the saving function with respect to disposable income.

Marginal rate of substitution (MRS) – The rate that a consumer would be willing to give up units of 1 good (y) for additional units of another good (x), while holding total utility (satisfaction) constant. Also the negative of the slope of an indifference curve.

Marginal revenue (MR) – The rate that total revenue changes in response to changes in output, $\Delta R/\Delta Q$. Also the slope of the total revenue function with respect to output.

Marginal utility (MU) – The rate that total utility changes in response to changes in the amount of a good (x), holding the quantities of all other goods constant, $\Delta U/\Delta x$. Also the partial slope of the total utility function with respect to the quantity of a good.

Necessary conditions (NC) – For some phenomenon z, a necessary condition is one such that, every time z occurs, this condition must be present, although it may also be present in cases where z does not occur.

Objective function – In an optimization problem, the function whose value is to be maximized or minimized. The explained (dependent) variable would be the value of the objective, while the decision variables would be some or all of the causal (independent) variables.

Point of inflection (also inflection point) – A point on a curve, where the curve changes from being concave to convex, or vice versa.

Saving function – A function which expresses saving as a function of disposable income.

Strictly concave – A curve is strictly concave over an interval, only if a line drawn between any two points on that interval lies wholly below the curve, except at the two endpoints. It is strictly concave at a point if the tangent at that point lies wholly above the curve for points in the neighborhood of that point.

Strictly convex – A curve is strictly convex over an interval, only if a line drawn between any two points on that interval lies wholly above the curve, except at the two endpoints. It is strictly convex at a point if the tangent at that point lies wholly below the curve for points in the neighborhood of that point.

Sufficient conditions (SC) – For phenomenon z, a condition is sufficient if at all occurrences of this condition, z is also present, although z might also occur even in the absence of this condition.

Exercise Set 4.2

1. A person consumes only two goods, x and y, and has a budget constraint that depends upon their respective prices, P_x and P_y, and the person's income is I. For each case below, express the income constraint as $Y = f(X)$, where Y and X are the quantities of goods Y and X respectively, graph the relationship, and interpret the slope and intercept values.

   a) $P_x = \$10/$unit, $P_y = \$5/$unit, and I = \$100.
   b) $P_x = \$2/$unit, $P_y = \$10/$unit, and I = \$200.
   c) $P_x = \$21/$unit, $P_y = \$3/$unit, and I = \$126.

2. Total revenue, R, is given by:

$$R = 500Q - 5Q^2$$

where:

R = total revenue in dollars per period of time
Q = quantity sold in units per period of time

The corresponding marginal revenue function is:

$$MR = 500 - 10Q$$

where:

MR = marginal revenue in dollars per unit

Graph these two functions. At what value of Q is R maximized? What is the value of R at that point? For both the R and MR functions, identify the regions that are concave or convex and whether they are strictly so. The range of R is assumed to be nonnegative. What is the domain of Q?

3. A production function, $Q = f(L)$, has the following properties (M and M' are defined as in Chapter 4):

    a) for $L = 0$; $Q = 0$, $M = 0$, and $M' > 0$
    b) for $0 < L < 15$; $Q > 0$, $M > 0$, and $M' > 0$
    c) for $L = 15$; $Q > 0$, $M > 0$, and $M' = 0$
    d) for $15 < L < 25$; $Q > 0$, $M > 0$, and $M' < 0$
    e) for $L = 25$; $Q > 0$, $M = 0$, and $M' < 0$
    f) for $L > 25$; $Q > 0$, $M < 0$, and $M' < 0$

    where:
    Q = output in units per day
    L = labor in hours per day

    Sketch the production function. Identify which segments of the function are concave, which are convex, and any inflection points. At what L does Q attain its maximum value? Sketch the MP_L function. At what L does it attain its maximum value? Interpret your results in economic terms.

4. A total cost function is given by:

$$C = C\,(Q)$$

where:
   C = total cost in thousands of dollars per year
   Q = quantity produced in thousands of units per year

This function has the following properties:

a) for Q = 0; C = 50, M > 0, and M′ < 0
b) for 0 < Q < 25; C > 50, M > 0, and M′ < 0
c) for Q = 25; C > 50, M > 0, and M′ = 0
d) for Q > 25; C > 50, M > 0, and M′ > 0

Sketch the total, marginal, and fixed cost functions. For the total cost function identify the regions that are concave, those that are convex, and any inflection points. At what Q is marginal cost at its minimum value? How do you know?

5. Total profits, π, are a function of the quantity produced, Q, and can be expressed as:

$$\pi = (Q)$$

where:
   π = total profits in dollars per period of time
   Q = quantity of output in units per period of time

The function has the following characteristics:

a) for 0 ≤ Q < 5, π < 0, M < 0, and M′ > 0
b) for Q = 5; π < 0, M = 0, and M′ > 0
c) for 5 < Q < 10; π < 0, M > 0, and M′ > 0
d) for Q = 10; π = 0, M > 0, and M′ = 0
e) for 10 < Q < 20; π > 0, M > 0, and M′ < 0
f) for Q = 20; π > 0, M = 0, and M′ < 0
g) for 20 < Q < 40; π > 0, M < 0, and M′ < 0

Graph the π and $M\pi$ functions. Determine the values at which each attains either its maximum or minimum value. How can you distinguish between these points?

6. Graph the following relationships and state whether the graphs are concave or convex. The causal variable (independent) is on the X axis.

   a) The total risk, (R) of a portfolio is the sum of the systematic or market risk (SR), which is independent of the number of holdings (H) in the portfolio and the unsystematic risk (UR) which decreases at a decreasing rate as H increases. Graph R and SR as functions of H. (H is a measure of naive diversification.)

   b) Given the following information: a bond's price, P, depends upon its annual coupon rate (C), yield to maturity, YTM, and years to maturity, M, or P = f(C, YTM, M):

      i) If C = YTM, a bond will sell at par ($1,000) independent of M.
      ii) P is inversely related to YTM (for a given C).
      iii) At maturity (M = 0) a bond will sell at par.
      iv) If C > YTM, P increases at a decreasing rate as M increases.
      v) If C < YTM, P decreases at a decreasing rate as M increases.

   Graph the relationship between P and M for a bond with C = 8%, when the YTM = 6%, 8%, and 10%.

Notes

1. Technically, a marginal change can be big and have a large impact, e.g., the building of a new plant or producing 100,000 more units/year. In most cases, however, it is assumed that variables under the control of the decision maker can be altered by small or perhaps infinitesimal amounts. Under these circumstances it is beneficial to look at small changes as being marginal changes. The smaller the change under consideration, the more accurate is the value of the marginal calculated, when the function is nonlinear.

2. The proof that M = M(x) when T = T(x) is as follows. M is the slope of T with respect to x. The only time that a slope can be defined at a point is when it is unique. Consequently, for all x that M is defined, M must be a function of x. The instantaneous slope of a point on a continuous function is the slope of a line tangent to that point. If the curve has kinks, cusps, or sharp points, it is possible to draw more than one line tangent to those points. Therefore, the slope is not defined at those points. All other points on the curve have one and only one line tangent to it and hence each point for which the slope is defined has one and only one value for M. A smooth continuous curve is one that has no kinks, etc., and consequently has a unique M at every point in the domain. Generally, the functions encountered in economics generate smooth continuous curves. When an average slope is used, the curve is approximated by line segments between pairs of points. Only one line can be drawn between any two points and hence the average slope between those points is unique for all points between those two. When considering two or more adjacent intervals, the terminal point of one interval is the beginning point of the next. When the average slope is different for the adjacent intervals, a kink is formed at the point joining line segments over those intervals. Therefore, no slope is defined at those points. It is for this reason that we define the average slope as holding between these points but not at those points.

3. An interesting case where P and Q are not inversely related occurs when the firm is perfectly competitive. In that event Q ≠ f(P), since multiple quantities will be demanded at the given market price. However, even then P is a function of Q, where the function is a constant one. When P and Q are inversely related, it is possible to express R as a function of P, although conventionally that is not done. When P is a constant function, that possibility doesn't even exist. Therefore, the use of R(Q) is more general, as it allows for both cases.

4. The information required regards the sign of M'', which is the slope of M'. Alternatively, knowledge of the M' curve (i.e., the values of M' over the domain) would suffice as well, since the sign of M'' could then be calculated. Figure 4.4B is drawn on the assumption that $M'' = 0$.

5. Technically, the necessary condition for either a maximum or a minimum is that either the slope is zero ($M = 0$) at that point *or* the slope fails to exist. There are two ways in which the slope fails to exist. The first is when the tangent is vertical, in which case M is said to be infinite. Alternatively, one can say that the slope fails to exist when more than one line is tangent at that point. If attention is restricted to smooth continuous curves (see Endnote 2), then $M = 0$ is the necessary condition for a local interior extremum. It is only when the curve is not smooth (i.e., it has corners, cusps, kinks, or sharp points) that the slope may fail to exist at an extremum, on the interior. Unless otherwise specified, all cases considered will be under the assumption that the curve is smooth.

Average Functions and Elasticities

Introduction

The slope is unquestionably one of the more important mathematical concepts used in economics. In the previous chapter we saw one application of the slope, marginal functions. In addition to total and marginal functions, another type of function frequently encountered is the average function. Examples from microeconomics might include: the average product of labor, average total cost, and average revenue. Macroeconomic examples could include the average propensities to consume and save.

The bulk of this chapter is devoted to average functions. The relationship between average functions and total functions is initially investigated. Then the relationship between average and marginal functions is discussed. The last section of this chapter is devoted to elasticities and their relation to average and marginal functions. The importance of the slope is reemphasized in this chapter, as average functions and elasticities are shown to be related to slopes.

Average Functions and Their Relationship to Total Functions

When the total function is the univariate function given by $T = T(x)$, the average function can be given as $A = A(x) = T(x)/x$. When T is a multivariate function, such as $T = T(x_1, x_2)$, the average with respect to x_1:

$$A_{x_1} = A_{x_1}(x_1, x_2) = T(x_1, x_2)/x_1$$

Similarly the average with respect to x_2:

$$A_{x_2} = A_{x_2}(x_1, x_2) = T(x_1, x_2)/x_2$$

Typically, the behavior of A_{x_1} with respect to x_1, or the behavior of A_{x_1} with respect to x_2, is of interest. Since A_{x_1} is a multivariate function, the relationship between A_{x_1} and x_1 can be given only when x_2 is held constant (i.e., $x_2 = x_{2,0}$). The situation is analogous for the relation between A_{x_2} and x_2. In this event x_1 must be held constant (i.e., $x_1 = x_{1,0}$).

The Average–Total Relationship: A Geometric Approach

There are many instances where the graph of the total function, $T(x)$, is known and the problem is to construct the graph of the average function, $A(x)$, from that information. An interesting result is that the average, at a point, can be represented as a slope. Recall that the average at any point is just the total at that point divided by the level of x at that point, or $A = T/x$. Any line drawn from the origin $(0,0)$ to a point on the total graph (x_o, T_o) has a slope equal to $\Delta T/\Delta x$. However, $\Delta T = T_o - 0$, and $\Delta x = x_o - 0$, so that the slope of that line from the origin $= T_o/x_o$. This, however, is simply the value of the average function $A(x)$ at x_o. Therefore, the value of $A(x)$ at *any* point on $T(x)$ is the slope of a line from the origin to that point. This should not be confused with the marginal, which is given by the slope of a *tangent line* to the curve at that point.

Totals from Averages

In some applications the average function may be known and the problem is to solve for the total from that information. Recalling that, by definition, $A(x) = T(x)/x$, $T(x)$ must in turn be equal to $A(x) \times x$. When the vertical axis measures $A(x)$ and the horizontal axis measures x, the product of the two at any point on the curve can be represented as an area of a rectangle. This area in turn is the value of the total at that point. The relationship between totals and averages can be illustrated by some economic examples.

Example 5.1 Average Products

Consider the production function given by $Q = f(K, L)$, relating the level of total output, Q, to combinations of the two inputs, capital, K, and labor, L. Holding capital fixed at some level, K_o, the **average product of labor**, AP_L, is equal to Q/L. This represents the average contribution to total output of each unit of labor. Similarly, if labor is held constant at some level, L_o, **the average product of capital**, AP_K, is equal to Q/K. The following numerical example will illustrate the difference between the AP_L and the MP_L, which was discussed in the previous chapter. Assume K is fixed and equal to 5 units of capital. The data in Table 5.1 represent distinct points on the production function.

Given this data, the AP_L can be calculated at each of the 3 points. When $L = 9$, the $AP_L = 90/9 = 10$. When $L = 10$, the $AP_L = 99/10 = 9.9$.

Table 5.1
Average and Marginal Products

Q	L	AP_L	MP_L
90	9	10.00	
			9.00
99	10	9.90	
			8.00
107	11	9.72	

When L = 11, the AP_L = 107/11 = 9.72. However, since we have only discrete data we can calculate the MP_L for only two intervals. As labor increases from 9-10, on average, over this interval, the MP_L = $\Delta Q/\Delta L$ = (99 - 90)/(10 - 9) = 9/1 = 9. On average, over the interval from L = 10 to L = 11, the MP_L = (107 - 99)/(11 - 10) = 8/1 = 8.

A typical short run production function given by Q = f(K, L) is depicted in Figure 5.1A for K fixed at K_0 = 5. The corresponding AP_L function is depicted in Figure 5.1B. Three lines from the origin R_1, R_2, R_3 have been included. Notice that the slope of R_3 represents the AP_L at points A and E. Similarly, the slope of R_2 is the AP_L at points B and D, while the slope of R_1 is the AP_L at point C. Observe that, as L increases from 0 to L_2, the AP_L is increasing (the lines from the origin to the curve get steeper, indicating increasing slope values) while after L_2, the AP_L decreases (the lines from the origin to the curve get flatter, indicating decreasing slope values). Therefore, at L_2, AP_L is at its maximum value, when the line from the origin is just tangent to the curve at C. In addition, although point D represents the maximum total product, it has a lower AP_L than point C. Further, since total output, Q, cannot take on negative values, neither can the AP_L.

In Figure 5.1B the values taken on by $AP_{L,1}$, $AP_{L,2}$, and $AP_{L,3}$ are the slopes of R_3, R_2, and R_1 respectively. Therefore, $AP_{L,1}$ = Q_0/L_0 = Q_4/L_4, $AP_{L,2}$ = Q_1/L_1 = Q_3/L_3, and $AP_{L,3}$ = Q_2/L_2. Knowledge of the AP_L function alone allows us to recapture the values of total output, Q, at any point. Consider, for example, point C on Figure 5.1B, where the AP_L is at its maximum value of $AP_{L,3}$, when L = L_2. By dropping perpendiculars to both axes from point C, we form the rectangle $0AP_{L,3}CL_2$. The area of this rectangle is simply $AP_{L,3} \times L_2 = Q_2$ (from Figure 5.1A), since AP_3 = Q_2/L_2. If at point C, AP_3 = 20 and L_2 = 900, then Q_2 = 18,000. The total product at other points on the AP_L curves can be recaptured in a similar manner.

Another frequently encountered production function is the **Cobb–Douglas function**. This takes the form of:

$$Q = AK^{b_1}L^{b_2}$$

where $b_1 + b_2$ = 1, and A is a positive constant. One example of a Cobb-Douglas production function is Q = K^5L^5, which occurs when A = 1 and $b_1 = b_2$ = .5. In the short run, K is fixed. When K is fixed and equal to 1, the short run production function becomes Q = L^5 = $L^{1/2}$ = $\sqrt{L}$. This example of a square root function was analyzed in Chapter 2.

Figures 5.1A & 5.1B
Relationship Between Total and Average Product

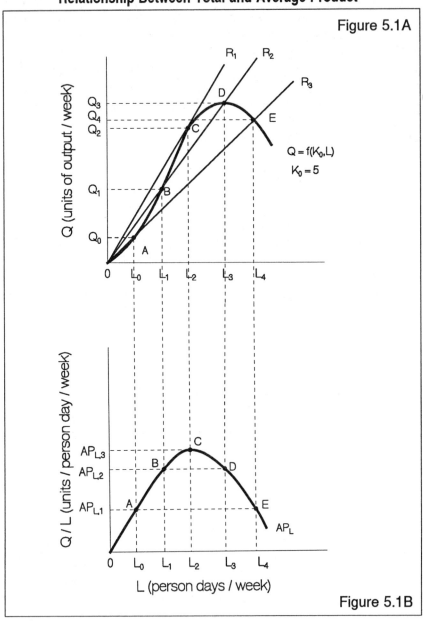

Figure 5.1A

$Q = f(K_0, L)$
$K_0 = 5$

Figure 5.1B

The average product of labor function is given by $AP_L = Q/L$. Substituting for Q we get $AP_L = \sqrt{L}/L = 1/\sqrt{L}$.

This production function and its corresponding AP_L function have properties that differ radically from those of the production function depicted in Figure 5.1. Since $Q = \sqrt{L}$, it follows that, as L increases, Q always increases. In addition, the $AP_L = 1/\sqrt{L} = 1/Q$ is always positive for positive values of Q and L. However as L increases, $\sqrt{L}$, which is equal to Q, increases. Consequently, the AP_L, which is the reciprocal of Q (or $1/\sqrt{L}$) must fall as L increases. At $L = 0$, the AP_L is infinite (or undefined) but decreases steadily as L increases. The values for Q and AP_L are given for selected values of L in Table 5.2.

Example 5.2 Average Cost Relationship

In the short run, total cost (TC) has two components: **fixed cost** (FC) and **variable cost** (VC). This can be expressed as TC = FC + VC. In addition, TC is a function of the quantity produced, Q, or TC = C(Q). Often it is of interest to analyze the costs (on average) per unit of output. Towards this end, the above relationship can be divided by Q, yielding TC/Q = FC/Q + VC/Q. The three terms in this equation represent various average cost concepts. The **average total cost** (per unit), ATC, equals

Table 5.2
AP_L Values for Production Function $Q = L^{1/2}$

L	Q	AP_L
0	0	∞
1	1	1
4	2	.5
9	3	1/3 = .33
16	4	.25
25	5	.20
100	10	.10

TC/Q. This represents on average how much it costs to produce each unit. The **average fixed cost**, AFC, equals FC/Q. Notice that since FC does not vary with Q, AFC must decrease as Q increases. The **average variable cost**, AVC, equals VC/Q. When the only cost that varies with output is labor cost, the AVC is simply the labor cost per unit of output or unit labor cost. Consider the following numerical example. A firm produces 100 units of output at a total cost of $500, of which $100 reflects the fixed cost and $400 represents the variable cost. Following are the data: ATC = $500/100 units = $5/unit, AFC = $100/100 units = $1/unit, and AVC = $400/100 units = $4/unit. Finally, note the average costs are related, since ATC = AFC + AVC.

Another example should provide additional insight. Consider the total cost function given by:

$$C = C(Q) = 25 + 28Q - 9Q^2 + Q^3$$

where:

    C =   total cost in thousands of dollars/year
    Q =   quantity produced in thousands of units/year

The above function is an example of a **cubic function** (of Q) which was discussed in Chapter 2. The FC and VC functions can be deduced from the total cost function. Recall that fixed cost does not vary with output and therefore will be present even when Q = 0. Evaluating the total cost function at Q = 0 yields $C(0) = 25 + 28(0) - 9(0)^2 + (0)^3 = 25$. Therefore, FC = 25, which is the intercept of this function. Since C = FC + VC and FC = 25, we have $VC = 28Q - 9Q^2 + Q^3$. The FC function is a *constant function*, while the VC function is a *cubic function* of Q.

The average functions corresponding to these three cost functions can be obtained by dividing each function by Q. The resultant functions are given by:

$$ATC = C/Q = (25 + 28Q - 9Q^2 + Q^3)/Q = (25/Q) + 28 - 9Q + Q^2$$

$$AFC = FC/Q = 25/Q$$

$$AVC = VC/Q = (28Q - 9Q^2 + Q^3)/Q = 28 - 9Q + Q^2$$

Notice that the sum of AFC and AVC is indeed equal to ATC.

As an aid for plotting purposes, nine values of Q have been chosen. The corresponding values of C, FC, VC, ATC, AFC and AFC have been calculated and are presented in Table 5.3. Note that, since all costs are measured in thousands of dollars/year, and Q is measured in thousands/units per year, all the average measures will be in terms of dollars/unit.

The graph of the total cost function is presented in Figure 5.2A, while those of the AFC and ATC functions are in Figure 5.2B. The graphs of the other cost functions are not provided, but means of constructing them from the available graphs are discussed.

In Figure 5.2A, three rays from the origin, R_1, R_2, and R_3, have been added to the total cost function. The intercept of the total cost function is 25, which represents the fixed cost. Since fixed cost does not change with respect to Q, the fixed cost function is an example of a constant function. As such it would be represented by a horizontal line at a height of 25. The VC function is identical to the total cost function except that, instead of having an intercept of 25, its intercept is 0. In other words, it is the same curve, except that it emanates from the origin. Its value (for all levels of Q) is 25 less than that of C. The VC curve and the C curve

Table 5.3
Components of Total and Average Cost

Q	C	FC	VC	ATC	AFC	AVC
0	25	25	0	infinite	infinite	infinite
1	45	25	20	45.0	25.0	20
2	53	25	28	26.5	12.5	14
3	55	25	30	$18.\overline{33}$	$8.\overline{33}$	10
4	57	25	32	14.25	6.25	8
4.5	59.875	25	34.875	$13.30\overline{5}$	$5.\overline{55}$	7.75
5	65	25	40	13.0	5.0	8
6	85	25	60	$14.1\overline{66}$	$4.1\overline{66}$	10
7	123	25	98	17.5714	3.5714	14

Figure 5.2
Relationships Between Total and Average Cost

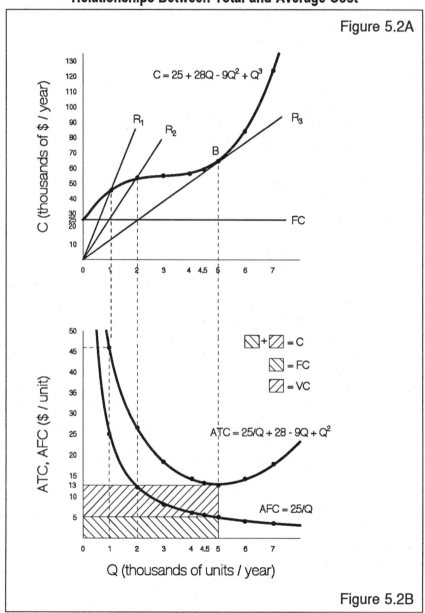

Figure 5.2A

$C = 25 + 28Q - 9Q^2 + Q^3$

R_1 R_2 R_3

B

FC

C (thousands of $ / year)

$\boxtimes + \boxtimes = C$

$\boxtimes = FC$

$\boxtimes = VC$

$ATC = 25/Q + 28 - 9Q + Q^2$

$AFC = 25/Q$

ATC, AFC ($ / unit)

Q (thousands of units / year)

Figure 5.2B

are said to be **vertically parallel**. This means that the *vertical* distance between two curves is a constant (in this case 25). In addition, since their shapes are identical, their instantaneous slopes at any level of Q will be the same for both curves.

The ATC at any point on the total cost function can be obtained by drawing a ray from the origin to that point and finding the slope of the ray. When Q = 1, C is equal to 45, therefore the ray, R_1, passing through that point has a slope of 45/1 = 45. As a consequence, the ATC, when Q = 1, is \$45/unit. In an analogous manner the slopes of R_2 and R_3 represent the ATC for quantities of 2 and 5 respectively. Notice that as Q increases from 0 to 5, rays from the origin to the curve get flatter. This implies that over that range, the ATC is falling. In fact, R_3 is the flattest ray that can be drawn and still touch the curve. Therefore, the ATC for Q = 5 must be the minimum value of ATC. For values of Q > 5, rays drawn from the origin get steeper as Q increases. This implies that the ATC rises with respect to Q over this interval.

The same procedure can be utilized to construct the AFC and AVC curves, from the FC and VC curves, respectively. Since the FC curve is a horizontal line, rays from the origin to the curve will *always* get flatter as Q increases. This implies that the AFC declines steadily as Q increases. The AVC curve can be derived in the same way from the VC curve or directly from the C curve. In the latter event, rays from the intercept, in this case 25, to points on the total cost curve are constructed. For each point chosen, the change in the rise, for each successive ray, is the excess of total cost over fixed cost, which by definition is variable cost, VC. The slope of such a ray is therefore VC/Q = AVC. Notice that rays from a positive intercept to a point are always flatter than rays from the origin to that point. Technically, this is due to the fact that the change in the rise pertaining to rays drawn from a positive intercept is always 25 less than for those drawn from the origin. However, recall that the slope of the former is the AVC, while that of the latter is the ATC, implying that the AVC < ATC. This is intuitively obvious since the AVC reflects only variable cost per unit, while the ATC reflects both variable and fixed cost per unit.

The general shape of the AVC curve will be similar to that of the ATC. Initially, as Q increases, the AVC will fall, hit its minimum value, and then begin to increase. However, the vertical distance between the two curves will get smaller as Q increases. Recall that ATC = AFC + AVC, or AFC = ATC − AVC. The vertical distance between the curves is therefore the AFC, which as previously mentioned declines as Q increases. In addition, the AVC will hit its minimum value at a different level of Q than that of the ATC minimum. In fact, given this type of cost function, the AVC minimum will always occur at a lower Q than the ATC minimum. We have already seen that initially as Q increases, AVC tends to fall, while AFC always falls as Q increases. Over the interval of Q, where both are falling, it must be true that ATC is falling as well. When the AVC hits its minimum, it is stationary, but the AFC is still falling so that ATC must also be falling. When the AVC starts to slowly rise, the AFC is falling at a faster rate than the rise in the AVC, so the ATC still falls. It is only when the AVC rises at a faster rate than the fall of the AFC that the ATC starts to rise. At the point where the AVC is rising at the same rate as the fall in the AFC, the ATC will be stationary and at its minimum value. In our example the AVC is at its minimum value of \$7.75/unit when Q = 4.5. As already noted, the minimum ATC is \$13/unit when Q = 5.

The graphs of the ATC and AFC functions in Figure 5.2B can be utilized to recover the values of AVC, C, FC, and VC. Recall that the vertical distance between the ATC and AFC curves is the AVC. Consider the case when Q = 5. The height of the ATC at that point is 13, while the height of the AFC is 5. The vertical distance between those two points is 8, which represents the AVC for Q = 5. To get the total cost, C, at any Q, simply drop perpendiculars from the ATC curve. The rectangle formed will have height equal to ATC and base equal to Q. The area of this rectangle is the product of its base times height, or Q x ATC. Since ATC = C/Q, this area = Q x (C/Q) = C, which is the total cost at that level of Q. In Figure 5.2B, when Q = 5, ATC = 13, so that the area of the corresponding rectangle = 5 x 13 = 65. Therefore, the total cost of producing 5000 units/year is \$65,000/year. (Recall that both Q and C are in thousands of units or dollars/year, respectively.) The same procedure can be used to recover FC from AFC. When Q = 5, the area of the rectangle formed is 5 x 5 = 25, so FC = 25. Recall, however, that FC is constant for all levels of output. Therefore, perpendiculars dropped from any point on the AFC must form a rectangle with equal area of 25. The only type of curve possessing that property is a **rectangular hyperbola**. The AFC curve must therefore be such a curve. Finally the value of VC can be recovered by subtracting FC from C. When Q = 5, this implies that VC = 40. This can also be interpreted as the area of a rectangle with base = Q, and height = the vertical distance between ATC and AFC,

which is AVC. In Figure 5.2B, the area of the rectangle shaded \\\
represents FC, while that shaded /// represents VC. The area of the
rectangle formed by the addition of those two represents the total cost at
$Q = 5$.

Example 5.3 Average Propensity to Consume (APC)

Given the simple consumption function, $C = b_0 + b_1 Y_d$, where C =
consumption expenditures and Y_d = disposable income, the **average
propensity to consume** is given by APC = C/Y_d. This represents the
proportion of disposable income that is spent for consumption purposes.
In this equation, b_0 = autonomous consumption, and b_1 = the slope of the
consumption function, which is the marginal propensity to consume
(MPC). Substituting $b_0 + b_1 Y_d$ for C, the APC can be written as APC =
$b_0/Y_d + b_1 Y_d/Y_d = b_0/Y_d + b_1$. When autonomous consumption is
positive, the APC must be greater than the MPC. In addition, since b_0 is
a constant, as Y_d increases, b_0/Y_d must decrease. Therefore, as Y_d
increases, the APC (which is greater than the MPC) decreases. When Y_d
is very large, b_0/Y_d approaches zero so that the APC would approach the
MPC. When $b_0 = 0$, the consumption function is an upward sloping linear
function emanating from the origin. In that event the APC = b_1 = MPC.

If the consumption function is given by $C = 100 + .9Y_d$, the APC
will vary inversely with Y_d. When $Y_d = 500$, $C = 100 + .9(500) = 550$.
In that event APC = $550/500 = 1.1$. Notice that although the MPC = .9
(and in general is restricted to be less than 1), the APC is greater than 1.
This implies that the household is spending *more than* its total disposable
income on consumption. In that event it must be *dissaving* (i.e., saving,
S, < 0). When $Y_d = 2000$, $C = 100 + .9(2000) = 1900$, and, therefore, the
APC = $1900/2000 = .95$. A consumption function given by $C = b_0 + b_1 Y_d$
is depicted in Figure 5.3 where it is assumed that $b_0 > 0$ and $0 < b_1 < 1$.

Lines R_0, R_1, and R_2 have been drawn from the origin to three points
on the curve. The slope of $R_0 = C_0/Y_0$, which represents the APC at point
Q. Similarly, the slopes of R_1 and R_2 represent the APC respectively at
R and S. Notice that although the MPC is constant and equal to b_1, the
APC diminishes as disposable income increases. This is evidenced by the
fact that the slope of R_2 < slope R_1 < slope R_0, although each is positive.
Moreover, observe that each of the slopes of all three lines is greater than
the slope of the consumption function itself. This indicates that the APCs
at these points are greater than the MPC.

Figure 5.3
Slopes of Rays from Origin to Consumption Function
Yield APC Values

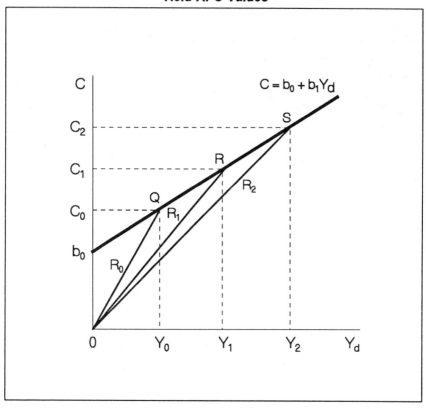

Example 5.4   Average Propensity to Save (APS)

Disposable income, Y_d, can either be spent on consumption, C, or saved, S. This identity can be stated as $Y_d = C + S$ or alternatively as $S = Y_d -$ C. The consumption function from Example 5.3 is $C = b_0 + b_1 Y_d$. Substituting this right-hand term for C into the identity, $S = Y_d - C$, yields:

$$S = Y_d - (b_0 + b_1 Y_d)$$

or
$$S = Y_d - b_0 - b_1 Y_d$$

or
$$S = -b_0 + (1 - b_1)Y_d$$

This equation represents the saving function. The equation is linear with slope, $(1 - b_1)$, and S intercept, $-b_0$. Recall that the slope is the **marginal propensity to save**, MPS, and that b_0 = autonomous consumption. The **average propensity to save**, APS, is simply given by APS = S/Y_d. Substituting for S from the saving function, APS = $[-b_0 + (1 - b_1)Y_d]/Y_d$ = $-b_0/Y_d + (1 - b_1)$. The value taken by the APS represents the proportion of disposable income (in total) that is saved. Notice that it, unlike the MPS, can take on negative values. Using the coefficient values of b_0 = 100 and b_1 = .9, from the previous example, the saving function becomes:

$$S = -100 + (1 - .9)Y_d$$

or
$$S = -100 + .1Y_d$$

Therefore, when Y_d = 500, S = $-100 + .1(500)$ = -50. The associated APS = S/Y_d = $-50/500$ = $-.1$. If Y_d = 2000, S = $-100 + .1(2000)$ = 100, and the APS = $100/2000$ = .05.

Example 5.5 Average and Total Revenue

A firm may decide on its output level, and in the absence of price discrimination it will charge the same price for all units. In that event, the value of the firm's sales, R, equals P X Q, where R = total revenue, P = price per unit, and Q = number of units. In that event, **average revenue**, AR, = R/Q = PQ/Q = P. Also, the price that can be charged depends upon Q and can be represented by an inverse demand function, P = $f^{-1}(Q)$. Thus, the relevant price–quantity combinations are given by the demand curve. The graph of the demand curve, as a result, also represents the average revenue function, as for each quantity it shows the price that will be charged. The total revenue, R, associated with each point on the demand curve, also the AR curve, can be calculated by drawing perpendicular lines to the two axes. This will form a rectangle with height equal to the price and base equal to the quantity. The area of this rectangle is the total revenue at that point. Such a demonstration is depicted in Figure 5.4. At point A, the firm is producing Q_0 and charging

Figure 5.4
Total Revenue from Average Revenue (Demand) Curve

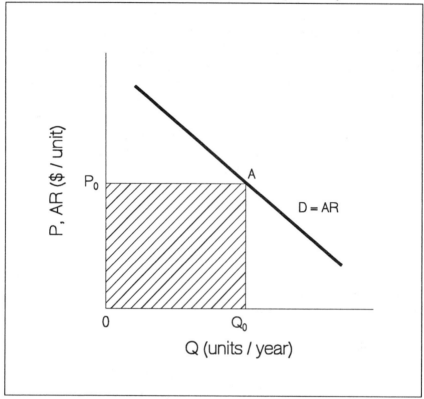

the corresponding price of P_0. Total revenue, R, is then $P_0 \times Q_0$ which is just the area of the shaded rectangle $0P_0AQ_0$.

The Average–Marginal Relationship

It has been demonstrated that for any function $T(x)$, both the average and marginal at some point can be represented as slopes of lines. The former is represented as the slope of a ray from the origin, while the latter is represented by the slope of the tangent line at that point. The question now posed is whether the average and marginal values of a function are related in some way.

The answer to this question is contained in the following scenario to which most students can relate. Assume an economics professor assigns 10 quizzes over the semester and that the grade for the course depends upon the total points achieved on the ten quizzes combined. The quizzes are given sequentially over the semester. For any student, the total number of points achieved to date (T) depends on the number of quizzes taken to date (Q) or $T = T(Q)$. The average quiz grade to date, $A(Q)$, is given by $A(Q) = T(Q)/Q$. For convenience, it is assumed that the marginal grade, $M = \Delta T/\Delta Q$, is the grade received on the last quiz. (Alternatively, the marginal grade might be considered the grade on the next quiz. This problem arises due to the discrete nature of the data.) Assume that you have taken Q_0 quizzes to date and are taking a quiz today. Under what conditions will your quiz average, $A(Q)$, be higher for $Q = Q_0 + 1$, than it was before that quiz, at $Q = Q_0$? The answer is intuitively obvious. If your score on the $Q_0 + 1$ quiz (i.e., your marginal score) is higher than your average score, $A(Q)$, at Q_0, your average will rise. In other words, if your average quiz score after Q_0 quizzes is 8.5 out of a possible 10, and your marginal score on the $Q_0 + 1$ quiz is 9, then your average will rise. Conversely, if your marginal score is lower than the average, say 7, then the average will fall. Lastly, if your marginal is just equal to your average (8.5), then your average will remain the same. These results can be summarized as:

1) If $M > A$, it implies that A is rising.
2) If $M < A$, it implies that A is falling.
3) If $M = A$, it implies that A is stationary.

It should be recalled that in most economic examples, as opposed to this quiz example, stationary points are usually maximum or minimum points. Notice also that it is the level of M that matters, not whether M is falling or rising. In the quiz example, it may have been true that on the Q_0^{th} quiz you received a 10. Even though your marginal score on the $Q_0 + 1$ quiz is lower than it was on the Q_0^{th} quiz, your average will still rise as long as $M > A$. These rules work in reverse as well. If A is rising, then $M > A$ at that point, and so on.[1]

Examples 5.1, 5.2, and 5.5 Revisited

Returning to the production function of Example 5.1, the relationship between average and marginal functions can be demonstrated graphically.

Figure 5.5
Relationship Between Average and Marginal Product Functions

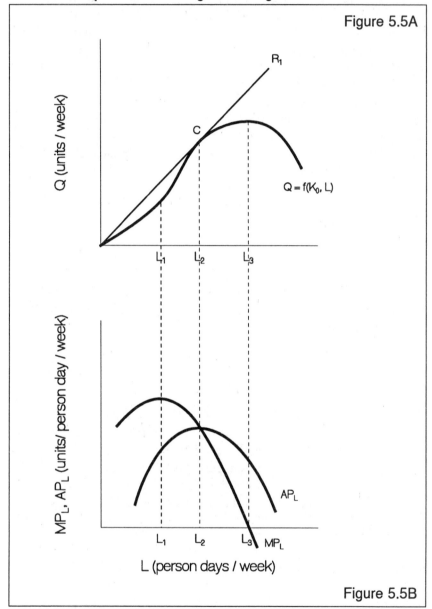

Figure 5.5A

Figure 5.5B

Recall that the average product function is derived by constructing rays from the origin to the production function and plotting the slopes of such rays. The marginal product function is derived by constructing tangents to the production function and plotting the slopes of these tangents. A production function and its related average and marginal product functions are plotted in Figure 5.5, panels A and B, respectively.

The ray, R_1, is the steepest ray that can be drawn from the origin and still touch the production function. Also, notice that it is just tangent to the curve at point C. Therefore, the slope of the ray from the origin to point C is identical to the slope of the tangent line at point C. This implies that at C, $AP_L = MP_L$, and, therefore, the AP_L is stationary at C. In this case it represents the point at which AP_L takes on its maximum value. Geometrically, the AP_L and MP_L intersect at the quantity of labor, L_2, which pertains to point C. For levels of labor less than L_2, $MP_L > AP_L$ and as a result, the AP_L must be rising with increases in L. For levels of labor greater than L_2, $MP_L < AP_L$ and the AP_L must be falling with increases in L.

Analogous reasoning can be applied to the average total cost-marginal cost relationship. Recall the ATC function is derived by constructing rays from the origin to the total cost curve and plotting the slopes of these rays. The MC function is derived by constructing tangents to the total cost curve and plotting the slopes of such tangents. A total cost function and its associated average and marginal cost functions are plotted in Figure 5.6, in panels A and B, respectively. The ray, R_3, is the flattest ray that can be drawn from the origin and still touch the TC curve. Also, it is just tangent to the curve at point B. Therefore, the slope of a ray from the origin to point B on the TC curve is identical to the slope of the tangent line at point B. This implies that at point B, ATC = MC, and as a result, the ATC is stationary at that point. In this example, point B, pertaining to Q_2 units of output, represents the point at which ATC hits its minimum value. Geometrically the ATC and MC curves intersect at this point. For quantities of output less than Q_2, MC < ATC and ATC must be falling with increases in Q. For quantities of output greater than Q_2, MC > ATC and ATC must rise with increases in Q.

A final example of the average-marginal relationship pertains to average and marginal revenue functions. Returning to Figure 5.4, we can see that, for this case, the AR function is downward sloping. Since the average function is falling with increases in Q, it is implied that MR < AR. Since AR = P, it follows that MR < P.

Figure 5.6
Relationship Between Average and Marginal Cost Functions

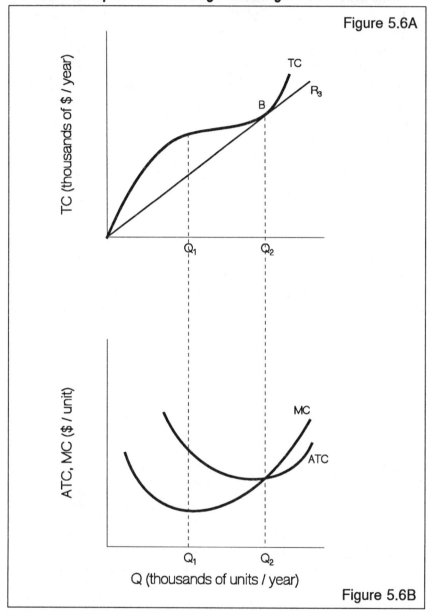

Figure 5.6A

Figure 5.6B

Exercise Set 5.1

1. Total Revenue, R, is a function of output, Q. Three total revenue functions are presented below:

   i) $R = 25$
   ii) $R = 2Q$
   iii) $R = 10Q - Q^2$ for $0 \leq Q \leq 10$

   where R is measured in millions of dollars/year, and Q is in millions of units/year.

   a) Calculate and depict graphically the average revenue (AR) functions (as functions of Q) corresponding to the total revenue functions.
   b) For each of the AR functions, identify the type of function derived (i.e., linear, quadratic, etc.).
   c) Calculate the value of AR for each function, for values of Q between 0 and 10, in increments of one.

2. An Average Total Cost function is given by:

   $$ATC = 5Q + (125/Q)$$

   where:
   ATC = average total cost in $1/unit
   Q = output in thousands of units/year

   a) Draw the ATC curve and geometrically determine the total cost for values of Q between 1 and 10, in unit increments.

   b) Derive the total cost function (as a function of Q). In what units would total costs be measured?

3. The total cost function is given by:

   $$C = 4200 + 145Q - 18Q^2 + 3Q^3$$

where:

  C = total cost in $thousands/year
  Q = output in thousands of units/year

a) Decompose the total cost function into its two component parts, fixed costs (FC) and variable costs (VC). Calculate the values of C, FC, and VC for values of Q (in increments of one) from zero to twenty. Sketch these three curves.

b) Derive the ATC, AFC, and AVC functions. Calculate the values of these functions, for the values of Q specified above.

c) The AVC curve is at its minimum when Q = 3, while ATC is at its minimum when Q = 10. What does this imply about the slopes of rays from the origin to those points on their respective total curves? Use this information to calculate the value of marginal cost, MC, at those two points.

d) For what values of Q will MC exceed AVC, and for which will MC be less than AVC? Answer the same question in terms of MC vs. ATC. [Hint: use the average–marginal relationship.]

4. Given the production function:

$$Q = 100K^{1/2}L^{1/2}$$

where:

  Q = output in thousands of units/year
  K = capital in thousands of machine hours/year and
  L = labor in thousands of labor hours/year

a) Calculate the AP_L function (as a function of L) for K = 4 and K = 9.

b) In both cases above, what happens to the AP_L as L increases? What does this imply about the MP_L?

c) Calculate the AP_K function (as a function of K) for L = 25 and L = 100.

5. In the previous chapter (Example 4.1) it was demonstrated that 1 = MPC + MPS. Prove that 1 = APC + APS, for all positive values of Y_d.

Elasticities

The slope of a function measures the rate of change of the value of that function, as an independent variable changes. As such, it may be considered as a measure of responsiveness of the dependent variable to changes in an independent variable. One drawback to using the slope in this way is that it does not allow for comparisons between two functions, unless the units of measurement (dimensions) are the same in each case. The following example will illustrate this point.

An economist statistically estimates the demand functions for two goods, A and B. He or she is interested in whether consumers are more sensitive to price changes for good A or for good B. He or she estimates that the slope $\Delta Q/\Delta P$ (rather than $\Delta P/\Delta Q$, which is the slope of the plotted curve) for good A = -1000 units of good A (per month) per dollar increase in its price, versus the slope for good B = -.001 units of good B (per month) per dollar increase in its price. To which good are consumers more price sensitive? This question cannot be answered because, although the numerical component of good A's slope is one million times that for good B, the dimensions of the two are different and, therefore, noncomparable. Suppose that good A = slices of pizza, while good B = cars. Would we intuitively accept the view that consumers are more sensitive to changes in pizza prices than to car prices? Observe that a dollar increase in the price of a car would hardly be noticed, but a dollar increase for a slice of pizza would be significant. Another consideration is whether a decrease of 1000 slices is a significant change? It would be, if present consumption is 10,000 slices a month, but it would be a drop in the bucket if consumption is 10 million slices a month. In order to appropriately answer these questions, an alternative measure of responsiveness is needed.

Percentage Changes

Instead of using absolute changes, we can use percentage changes. Let's assume that the price of a good goes up by 50 cents/unit. No matter what the price is initially, the absolute change in price is 50 cents/unit. However, consumers' responses to that price change probably depend upon the value of the initial price. If the price is initially $100/unit, this increase will probably not be significant. On the other hand, if the initial price is $1.00/unit, the increase would be viewed as significant. One way to formalize this phenomenon is to consider percentage rather than absolute changes in price and quantity.

A percentage change in variable x can be given as either $\Delta x/x$ or that value multiplied by 100. In the previous example, where the price increased from $1.00/unit to $1.50 per unit, the change in price, ΔP, equals .50/unit, while the initial value of P is $1.00/unit. Therefore, $\Delta P/P$ = .50/unit/1.00/unit = .5. Since the units cancel out, the term is unitless or without dimension. The calculated value of .5 is relative to a scale of one. In other words, the new price = 1.5 times the old price, and, therefore, the change in price = .5 times the old price. This is clearly a 50 percent increase in price. In other words, in decimal form, the percentage change = .5, while using the % (percentage) notation it gets multiplied by 100 and is equal to 50 percent, i.e., .5 = 50%. In either event, a percentage change in a variable is represented by a number (with no units attached), making it possible to compare across variables with different dimensions.

Elasticity: The Concept

Utilizing the concept of percentage change enables us to create a new measure of responsiveness called the **elasticity.** As the term implies, a greater degree of responsiveness corresponds to something being more elastic. Similarly, a lack of responsiveness would be identified as being **inelastic** (think of a rubber band versus a wire). In the univariate case for which $T = T(x)$, where T is the dependent variable and x is the independent variable, the elasticity of T with respect to x, $E_{T,x}$, is equal to the percentage change in T caused by a percentage change in x. In the cases of E_{T,x_1} and E_{T,x_2}, E_{T,x_1} is defined as the percentage change in T caused by a percentage change in x_1, with the provision that x_2 is held constant. Similarly, E_{T,x_2} is the percentage change in T caused by a percentage change in x_2, when x_1 is held constant.

More formally, these elasticities can be stated as:

$E_{T,x}$ = $\dfrac{\text{percentage change in T}}{\text{percentage change in x}}$ (univariate case)

$E_{T,x}$ = $\dfrac{\text{percentage change in T}}{\text{percentage change in x}}$ / (multivariate case) holding all other causal (independent) variables constant

Given the definition of a percentage change, this relation could be rewritten as:

$$E_{T,x} = \frac{(\Delta T/T)}{(\Delta x/x)}$$

where the condition that all other causal variables are held constant applies in the multivariate case. The right-hand side of the equation is a complex fraction and could be rewritten as:

$$\frac{\Delta T}{\Delta x} \times \frac{x}{T} \quad \text{or as} \quad \frac{\Delta T}{\Delta x} / \frac{T}{x}$$

In this latter formulation, it is clear that although the value of the slope (or partial slope in the multivariate case), $\Delta T/\Delta x$, is important in determining the value of $E_{T,x}$, it is only part of the picture. Notice that (T/x) can be interpreted as the average, A, while the slope, $\Delta T/\Delta x$, represents the marginal, M. This yields interesting insight into the nature of an elasticity. Any elasticity is $E_{T,x} = M(x)/A(x)$, or the marginal divided by the average.

Interpreting Values of the Elasticity

The values calculated as the elasticity of T with respect to x indicate how responsive T is to x. There are three specific values that can be taken on by an elasticity and that have particular importance.

When $E_{T,x} = 0$, it is said that T is **perfectly inelastic** with respect to x. Recalling that the elasticity measures the degree of responsiveness, this implies that T is not responsive at all to changes in x. In order for this to occur, the percentage change in T must be zero, as x changes. By observing the formula:

$$\frac{\Delta T}{\Delta x} \times \frac{x}{T}$$

we can see that this is possible when either $(\Delta T/\Delta x) = M = 0$, or when $x = 0$. In the former case, it could hold over an interval, while in the latter case, it may hold only at an isolated point.

When the elasticity is infinite, $E_{T,x} = \pm\,\infty$, it is said to be **perfectly elastic**. It should be noted that infinity is not a number, but a concept indicating that no limit exists. Perfect elasticity of T with respect to x implies that any small change in x will increase (or decrease) T without bound. This obviously represents a case of ultra–responsiveness. It occurs when either $(\Delta T/\Delta x)$ is infinite or T = 0. Over an interval, this implies that x does not change (i.e., x is constant) but T does.[2] With respect to isolated points, the implication is that, since T equals 0, the average, A, equals 0. Notice that when an initial value of a variable equals zero, any change in that variable represents an infinite percentage change in either the positive or negative direction.

Unitary elasticity is said to apply when $E_{T,x} = +1$ or -1. The positive value applies when a direct relationship exists between T and x, while the negative value holds when they are inversely related. Unitary elasticity represents the intermediate case where T is somewhat responsive to x, but not overly so. This can be better understood if the *absolute value* of the percentage change in x is viewed as the stimulus and the *absolute value* of the percentage change in T is viewed as the response. When unitary elasticity prevails, the size of the stimulus gives rise to an equal sized response, in percentage terms. Notice this occurs when M = A, when T and x are directly related, or M = −A when T and x are inversely related. This assumes A is nonnegative, as is the case in most economic examples. Covering both cases, this can be stated as, $|M| = |A|$, or the absolute value of M equals that of A.

Assuming that T and x are both positive, the average, $T/x = A$, is positive as well. When an inverse relationship exists between T and x, the marginal, M, will be negative, and therefore so will the elasticity. In that event any value taken on by the elasticity such that $-1 < E_{T,x} < 0$ is termed **relatively inelastic**, whereas a finite value less than −1 is called **relatively elastic**. On the other hand, when a direct relationship exists, and $0 < E_{T,x} < 1$, it is termed **relatively inelastic**, while a positive finite value greater than one is called **relatively elastic**. Applying our analogy regarding stimulus and response, a relationship is relatively elastic when the response is finite and larger than the stimulus in absolute value. This prevails when $|E_{T,x}| > 1$, but finite. In that event $|M| > |A|$. In order to be relatively inelastic, the response, while greater than zero, is smaller than the stimulus. This occurs when $0 < |E_{T,x}| < 1$, indicating that $|M| < |A|$.

In investigating the properties of different functional forms, we found that only linear functions have the property, that the slope is constant. For any nonlinear function, the slope varies as x varies. It is natural to ask whether functional forms exist, such that the elasticity is constant, and to identify them if they exist.

Due to the simplicity of linear forms and our familiarity with them, we may ask whether linear functions have this property. Unfortunately, the answer is usually no, although exceptions do exist. Recall that by definition, the elasticity is the ratio of the marginal, M, to the average, A. In order for the elasticity to be constant, this ratio must remain constant as x varies. In other words, $M/A = k$, for all values of x where k is a constant. Multiplying through by A yields $M = kA$, which says that M must be proportional to A for all values of x. The factor of proportionality, k, is the constant elasticity.

Linear forms have the property that although the slope, M, is a constant, generally the average, A, will vary with x. The ratio of the two, being the elasticity, will vary as well. There are three exceptions however, where linear functions have constant elasticities.

The first exception occurs when T is a constant function, $T = T(x) = b_0 + b_1 x$, and $b_1 = 0$. In that event $M = b_1 = 0$, and $M = kA$, provided $k = 0$. Therefore, the elasticity of a constant function is constant as well and is equal to zero. In other words, T is perfectly inelastic with respect to x. As x changes, T does not, and, therefore, T is not responsive at all to changes in x. When T, the dependent variable, is measured on the vertical axis, the graph of this function would be a horizontal line.

The second exception occurs when x is a constant, but T varies. In this case, x is a function of T, but T is not a function of x. Recall that in order for $T = T(x)$, each value of x must have one and only one value of T that corresponds. In this case, for the one value of x, there exists a multiplicity of values of T. We can then say that x is a constant function of T. Since x does not change, but T does, the rate of change of T with respect to x, which is M, must be infinite for all values of T. However, the average, $A = T/x$, is some finite (though changing) number. As such, $M = kA$, where k, the constant elasticity, is infinite. This means that the elasticity is infinite or perfectly elastic. When T is measured on the vertical axis, the graph of this relationship would be a vertical line. However, when the axes are reversed (e.g., the demand curve), the graph would be a horizontal line.

The first two exceptions occur when the slope, M, is constant, while the average, A, varies. However, a linear function exists such that A is constant as x varies. This constitutes the third exception. Recall that the slope of a ray from the origin to the T curve is the value of the average, A, at that point. When the T curve is a ray from the origin, the slope of that ray is constant and, therefore, so is A. Moreover, the instantaneous slope of the curve, M, is constant and equal to A. Since M = A, the elasticity must equal +1 throughout, and the curve is said to have a constant unitary elasticity. Each 1 percent change in x brings about an equal (both in magnitude and sign) percentage change in T. This is the case when $T = b_0 + b_1x$, and $b_0 = 0$. In this case, $M = b_1$ and $A = b_1x/x$ $= b_1$. Therefore, $M/A = b_1/b_1 = +1$, so that $M = kA$, where $k = +1$. As a result, any linear function passing through the origin will be unitary elastic throughout. While the value of b_1 was unspecified, T and x in most economic examples are nonnegative. In that event, b_1 would be positive (but finite). A reversal of the axis does not change this result. The slope in this setting would be the reciprocal of the original slope. Since the original slope, b_1, is positive and finite, so is its reciprocal.

The cases for which linear functions yield constant elasticities are summarized in Figure 5.7. The functions plotted in panels A and B are identical; only the axes have been reversed.

It has been demonstrated that linear forms in general, barring the aforementioned exceptions, do not have the property of possessing a constant elasticity. However, there are forms which do exhibit this property. The general form of a function with a constant elasticity is given by $T = b_1x^k$, where b_1 is an arbitrary constant, and k represents the constant elasticity. The proof of this conjecture relies on mathematical tools developed in Chapter 7 and is deferred to there. Notice, however, that our first and last exceptions, in the linear case, are of this form. In the first exception, the constant elasticity, $k = 0$, so that $T = b_1$, a constant. This results from the fact that $x^0 = 1$, and T is a constant function of x. When $k = 1$, $T = b_1x$, which is simply our third exception. In general, this form has the property that as x varies, the marginal, M, and the average, A, vary proportionately to each other, with the factor of proportionality being the constant elasticity, k, i.e., $M = kA$.

Figure 5.7
Linear Functions Yielding Constant Elasticities

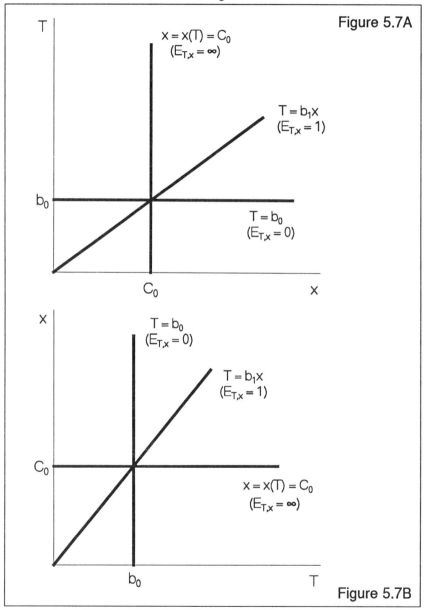

Figure 5.7A

$x = x(T) = C_0$
$(E_{T,x} = \infty)$

$T = b_1 x$
$(E_{T,x} = 1)$

b_0

$T = b_0$
$(E_{T,x} = 0)$

C_0

x

$T = b_0$
$(E_{T,x} = 0)$

$T = b_1 x$
$(E_{T,x} = 1)$

C_0

$x = x(T) = C_0$
$(E_{T,x} = \infty)$

b_0

T

Figure 5.7B

Point Elasticities vs. Arc Elasticities

An elasticity can be calculated for every point on a curve if three facts are known or can be determined from the data. These facts are the slope and the values of T and x at that point. When the data relate only to discrete points on the curve, the *average elasticity* over an interval can be calculated. The term *average* here is similar to that used in referring to the *average slope* over the interval. In fact, if two distinct points on the curve are the only available information, only the average slope, rather than instantaneous, can be calculated. A problem arises, however, in choosing an appropriate point (values of T and x) to represent the interval.

A **point elasticity** represents the elasticity at a specific point on the curve, while an **arc elasticity** corresponds to the average elasticity over some interval. The decision as to which should be used is usually determined by the data. When only two data points are known, it is customary to use the arc elasticity although the point elasticity could be calculated. The choice of an arc elasticity in this case is preferable, because use of the point elasticity results in two different elasticities being calculated. Since the calculated elasticity should be representative of the interval, it is difficult to understand how two figures could be representative of one interval.

Example 5.6 Point Price Elasticity of Demand

Probably the most important elasticity studied in a principles class is the **price elasticity of demand**. Its value reveals how sensitive consumers are, in their demand for a good, to changes in the price of that good. An interesting case to analyze is when the quantity demanded of a good, Q^d, is a linear function of its price, P, ceteris paribus. The general formula would be given by $Q^d = b_0 - b_1 P$, where b_0 is the Q^d intercept, $-b_1$ is the slope, $\Delta Q^d / \Delta P$, and the P intercept is b_0 / b_1. To conform to economic theory, b_0 and b_1 are assumed to be positive. Recall that in graphing a demand curve, the axes are reversed so that the slope of the graph would be $1/(-b_1)$. The specific case where $b_0 = 100$ and $b_1 = 2$ is graphed in Figure 5.8.

The demand function is given by $Q^d = 100 - 2P$. Since it is linear, the slope, $\Delta Q^d / \Delta P$, is constant and equal to -2. In addition, the only other information necessary to calculate the elasticity at any point is either the

Figure 5.8
Linear Demand Curve

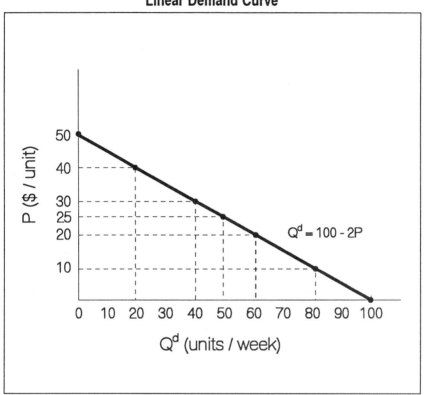

price *or* quantity at that point. Using the demand function, knowledge of either one allows us to calculate the other. Of course, the only relevant combinations of P and Q that satisfy the demand equation lie in the first quadrant where P and Q are both nonnegative.

Seven points on the graph have been calculated in the above manner and are presented in Table 5.4. The formula for the point price elasticity of demand is given by:

$$E_{Q^d,P} = \frac{\Delta Q^d}{\Delta P} \times \frac{P}{Q^d}$$

Since $\Delta Q^d/\Delta P$ is constant and equal to –2, this reduces to $E_{Q^d,P} = -2P/Q^d$.

Table 5.4
Price–Quantity Combinations for Demand Curve: $Q^d = 100 - 2P$

Q^d	0	20	40	50	60	80	100
P	50	40	30	25	20	10	0

At P = 50, $E_{Qd,p}$ = -100/0 = -∞ (perfectly elastic).
At P = 40, $E_{Qd,p}$ = -80/20 = -4 (relatively elastic).
At P = 30, $E_{Qd,p}$ = -60/40 = -1.5 (relatively elastic).
At P = 25, $E_{Qd,p}$ = -50/50 = -1 (unitary elastic).
At P = 20, $E_{Qd,p}$ = -40/60 = -.67 (relatively inelastic).
At P = 10, $E_{Qd,p}$ = -20/80 = -.25 (relatively inelastic).
At P = 0, $E_{Qd,p}$ = 0/100 = 0 (perfectly inelastic).

There are two points that should be observed from the calculations here. Notice that although the demand curve is linear and therefore has constant slope, the elasticity at points along the curve is *not* constant. Instead, it actually runs the gamut of values from being perfectly elastic to being perfectly inelastic. This is not coincidental, but instead stems from the formula for an elasticity. Recall that the elasticity is simply the ratio of the marginal to that of the average, i.e., M/A. In this case M is constant. However, as we move down the demand curve to the right, Q^d is increasing while P is decreasing. Since Q^d/P = A, A must be increasing and nonnegative. M, on the other hand, is negative and constant. The absolute value of M/A, which is the numerical component of the elasticity, ignoring the negative sign, must be decreasing. This can also be understood using percentage changes. Observe that high values of P correspond to low values of Q^d and vice versa. While the absolute rate of change of Q^d with respect to P is constant, the percentage rate of change is not. Every dollar increase in P gives rise to a two unit decrease in Q^d. When Q^d is small, this represents a large percentage change, while the reverse is true when Q^d is large. A similar result holds with respect to P. Equal changes in P represent large percentage changes when P is small and small percentage changes when P is large. Therefore, moving down the demand curve yields, in absolute value terms, smaller percentage changes in Q^d and larger ones for P. When Q^d = 0, any increase in Q^d represents an infinite percentage change while P falls by only some finite percentage. At that point the price elasticity of demand is said to be perfectly elastic. At the other extreme, when P = 0, any change in P similarly represents an infinite percentage change. The percentage change in Q^d at that point is finite. The ratio of something finite to that which is infinite is zero, and the demand curve is perfectly price inelastic at that point.

Linear demand curves possess another interesting property. That is, the midpoint on the curve will have unitary price elasticity. In the preceding numerical example, this occurs where P = 25 and Q = 50. This result holds, however, for any linear demand curve, $Q^d = b_0 - b_1 P$. Recall that the Q^d intercept = b_0, P intercept = b_0/b_1, and the slope $\Delta Q^d/\Delta P = -b_1$. The midpoint of the curve is the (P, Q^d) combination, where each variable's value is half of the value of its intercept. In other words, at the midpoint, $P = b_0/2b_1$ and $Q^d = b_0/2$. The price elasticity at this point is given by:

$$E_{Qd,p} = -b_1 \, P/Q^d = -(b_1 b_0/2b_1)/(b_0/2) = -2b_1 b_0/2b_1 b_0 = -1$$

This proves that, for the general case of a linear demand curve, its midpoint possesses unitary price elasticity.

One point to consider regarding price elasticities of demand is that, barring **Giffen goods** (a good for which the demand function is positively sloped), their value should always be nonpositive. Since positive numbers are generally more easily handled than negative numbers, many authors use the absolute value of the price elasticity. This enables them to refer to the price elasticity as a positive number. With regard to the price elasticity, the sign is understood to always be negative. It is, therefore, the magnitude of the elasticity that is of concern, and the absolute value leaves that unaltered. With regard to other elasticities, for which the sign could be positive or negative, it may be the sign rather than magnitude that is more important. In that event, the absolute value should not be used.

Example 5.7 Point Price Elasticity of Demand When Instantaneous Slope Is Unknown

In the previous example, the demand function and, therefore, the instantaneous slope at each point, was known. Many problems are of the type that the demand function is unknown. Instead, the only information available might be two points on the function. In this case, how should we proceed?

Using the data from the previous example, assume that only two points on the demand curve are known, while the exact shape of the curve is unknown. With only that limited information, it is impossible to calculate the instantaneous slope, at any point. In fact, there exists an infinite number of curves that are negatively sloped, that could go through those two points. The average slope over this interval, on the other hand, can be calculated.

Assume that the two known points are given by ($P = 30$, $Q^d = 40$) and ($P = 20$, $Q^d = 60$). The average slope, $\Delta Q^d/\Delta P$, over this interval is:

$$\frac{\Delta Q^d}{\Delta P} = \frac{60-40}{20-30} = \frac{20}{-10} = -2$$

In this case, we have assumed that the price decreased from 30 to 20 and that Q^d correspondingly increased from 40 to 60. Notice that the value of the slope is identical if we assume that the price increased from 20 to 30. In that event the numerator would be -20, while the denominator would be +10. The ratio, however, would remain equal to -2.

It seems reasonable to choose the initial values of P and Q^d as the bases on which to calculate the percentage changes. However, a problem arises. Whereas the slope is invariant to the choice of the initial point, the percentage changes are not and, therefore, the elasticity is not as well. In the event that P decreases from 30 to 20, our initial point is ($P = 30$, $Q^d = 40$). The price elasticity at this point is given by:

$$E_{Q^d,P} = \frac{\Delta Q^d}{\Delta P} \times \frac{P}{Q^d} = -2P/Q^d = -60/40 = -1.5$$

Alternatively, when P increases from 20 to 30, the initial point is ($P = 20$, $Q^d = 60$). Using these values, the elasticity is given by:

$$E_{Q^d,P} = \frac{\Delta Q^d}{\Delta P} \times \frac{P}{Q^d} = -2P/Q^d = -40/60 = -.67$$

This discrepancy arises since we are considering the same changes in P and Q^d in each case, but the base used to calculate the percentage changes is different. In the first case the percentage change in $Q^d = \Delta Q^d/Q^d = +20/40 = .5 = 50\%$, while the percentage change in $P = \Delta P/P = -10/30 = -.33 = -33\%$. This yields an elasticity of $50\%/-33\% = -1.5$, which is in the relatively elastic range. In the latter case the percentage changes in Q^d and P are -33 percent and $+50$ percent respectively. In that case the elasticity is $-.67$, which is in the relatively inelastic range.

Notice that the elasticities calculated here are identical to the point elasticities, at those points for which the elasticity was calculated in the previous example. In fact, when the demand curve is linear and any two points on it are chosen, this method will *always* yield the point elasticity, at the initial point. This occurs because the average slope is being used. Given only two points, it is implicitly being assumed that the curve is linear over this interval. Therefore, when only two data points are known, this method will always yield two different calculations for the elasticity, one pertaining to each point.

We are left with a quandary. With only two points, our interest is surely with the elasticity over the interval. The use of a point elasticity will generate two different answers. This can be exacerbated, as it was in the numerical example, by the fact that the two answers may not even lie in the same range of elasticity. When price fell from 30 to 20, it was said that demand was relatively price elastic, so that consumers were very responsive to that price change. Alternatively, when price was treated as rising, demand was said to be relatively inelastic, indicating that consumers were fairly insensitive to the price change. Over that interval, how can they be responsive and unresponsive at the same time?

To resolve this paradox, the concept of arc elasticity has been developed. Since the same portion of the demand curve is being analyzed, it would be nice if the elasticity between these two points is invariant to the choice of which is to be the initial point. The average slope over the interval has already been shown to be invariant to the choice of the initial point. The different values calculated for the elasticity are due to choosing one point as a base when P falls and the other when P rises.

A convention can be established, where it is agreed that one of the two points will always be picked. A rule such as, "always use as a base the point with the higher (lower) price" could be employed. This is not done, however. Instead, since responsiveness over the interval is the key concern, an alternative is chosen. Instead of choosing either point, the midpoint is chosen as most representative of the interval. Notice that the midpoint, like the average slope, is invariant to the direction in which the price moves.

When two points on the demand curve are given such as (P_0, Q^d_0) and (P_1, Q^d_1), the midpoint over this interval is the point $[(P_0 + P_1)/2, (Q_0 + Q_1)/2]$. Using this midpoint as the base alleviates the problem caused by the use of point elasticity. Inserting it into the formula for the elasticity yields the *arc elasticity*, or elasticity using the midpoint formula. The revised formula is given below:

$$\text{Arc } E_{Q^d, P} = \frac{\Delta Q^d}{\Delta P} \times \frac{(P_0 + P_1)/2}{(Q_0^d + Q_1^d)/2}$$

In addition, the slope can be written as:

$$\frac{\Delta Q^d}{\Delta P} = \frac{Q_1^d - Q_0^d}{(P_1 - P_0)}$$

Substituting this into the arc elasticity formula yields:

$$\text{Arc } E_{Q^d, P} = \frac{(Q_1^d - Q_0^d)}{(P_1 - P_0)} \times \frac{(P_0 + P_1)/2}{(Q_0^d + Q_1^d)/2}$$

$$= \frac{(Q_1^d - Q_0^d)}{(P_1 - P_0)} \times \frac{(P_0 + P_1)}{(Q_0^d + Q_1^d)}$$

$$= \frac{(Q_1^d - Q_0^d)}{(Q_1^d + Q_0^d)} \times \frac{(P_1 + P_0)}{(P_1 - P_0)}$$

Notice that the use of this formula applied to example 5.8 yields the same result in both cases. The midpoint is $(P = 25, Q^d = 50)$, so that the arc elasticity is -1, or unitary elastic.

Example 5.8 The Price Elasticity of a Linear Supply Curve

A linear supply curve could be given as $Q^S = b_0 + b_1 P$, where $b_1 > 0$, but b_0 can be positive, negative, or zero. When $b_0 = 0$, $Q^S = b_1 P$, which is a positively sloped linear function emanating from the origin. In that event, the point price elasticity of supply is given by:

$$E_{Q^S,P} = \frac{\Delta Q^S}{\Delta P} \times \frac{P}{Q^S}$$

Since the function is linear, $\Delta Q^S/\Delta P = b_1$ at all points on the curve. The elasticity, then, is $b_1 P/Q^S$. Since $Q^S = b_1 P$, this implies that the elasticity is $b_1 P/b_1 P = +1$. This result holds at *all* points on such a supply curve, the implication being that a linear supply curve emanating from the origin has a constant elasticity at every point. In addition to being constant, it is unitary elastic throughout.

When $b_0 < 0$, the Q^S intercept is negative, while the P intercept is positive. The relevant part of that function is for combinations at which Q^S is nonnegative, and, therefore, P is restricted to being greater than or equal to its intercept value. In this case, the price elasticity of supply is:

$$E_{Q^S,P} = \frac{\Delta Q^S}{\Delta P} \times \frac{P}{Q^S} = b_1 P/Q^S = b_1 P/(b_0 + b_1 P)$$

Notice that in this case the elasticity is not constant. Since $b_0 < 0$, $b_1 P > (b_0 + b_1 P)$, so that $E_Q S_P > 1$. Such a supply curve would be relatively elastic over its whole range and perfectly elastic when $Q^S = 0$, i.e., when $b_0 + b_1 P = 0$.

When $b_0 > 0$, the Q^S intercept is positive while the P intercept is negative. Again, to be economically meaningful, both Q^S and P need to be nonnegative. This occurs when $Q^S \geq b_0$ and $P \geq 0$. The relevant portion of this supply curve emanates from the Q^S axis, whereas in the previous case of $b_0 < 0$, it emanated from the P axis. In either event, the formula employed here gives the elasticity as $b_1 P/(b_0 + b_1 P)$. In contrast to the previous case, given that $b_0 > 0$, it follows that $b_1 P < b_0 + b_1 P$. Correspondingly, although the elasticity changes along the curve, it is always in the relatively inelastic range, and perfectly inelastic when $P = 0$.

It is true that most supply curves are nonlinear, rather than linear. This fact would seem to minimize the usefulness of the above results. However, it should be noted that a tangent to a curve shares the tangent point and, at that point, the curve and line share a common slope. Therefore, the elasticity of a point on the curve is the same as it would be if the supply curve is represented as its tangent line. Therefore, if a tangent line is drawn that intersects the P axis at a positive value, it implies that, at that point, supply is relatively elastic. When it intersects the Q^S axis at a positive value, it implies that supply is relatively inelastic. Lastly, if it intersects the origin, it is unitary elastic at that point. This is illustrated in the Figure 5.9.

A supply curve with tangent lines T_1, T_2, T_3 is depicted in Figure 5.9. At point A, the tangent is line T_1. Since T_1 intersects the P axis at a positive value, supply is relatively elastic at point A. Similarly, the tangent to the curve at C is line T_3. Since T_3 intersects the Q^S axis at a positive value, C represents a point that is relatively inelastic. Lastly, the tangent at B is T_2, which intersects the origin. Therefore, at B the curve is unitary elastic.

Figure 5.9
Relatively Elastic, Inelastic, and Unitary Elastic Supply Curves

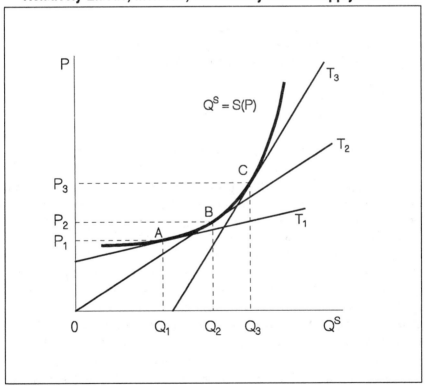

Example 5.9 Income Elasticity of Demand

Another type of elasticity is the **income elasticity of demand**, $E_{Q,I}$. This represents the percentage change in the quantity demanded of a good due to a percentage change in money income. For example, suppose the demand for steak is defined to be a function of income, I, as well as its own price. Also suppose that when income rises by 10 percent, while price remains unchanged, the quantity demanded of steak, Q, increases by 25 percent. The income elasticity of the demand for steak is:

$$E_{Q,I} = \frac{\% \text{ change in } Q}{\% \text{ change in } I} = \frac{25\%}{10\%} = 2.5$$

This means that for every 1 percent change in money income, there will be a 2.5 percent change in the quantity of steak demanded, in the same direction. Since the income elasticity is positive and greater than one, it is in the relatively elastic range. The fact that $E_{Q,I}$ is positive indicates that the good is a **normal good**. The additional result that $E_{Q,I} > 1$ indicates that the good is a **superior good**, or some type of luxury good. Should $E_{Q,I}$ have turned out to be negative, the quantity demanded and income would vary inversely, and the good would be defined as an **inferior good**.

Example 5.10 Cross Price Elasticity

The quantity demanded of a product, Q^d, may be a function of its own price, P, and the price of a related good, P_R, ceteris paribus. Holding all other causal variables constant (including P), our concern might be with the responsiveness of Q^d to P_R. The percentage change in Q^d caused by the percentage change in P_R is called the **cross price elasticity of demand**. If P_R increases by 5 percent, and correspondingly Q^d increases by 4 percent, the cross price elasticity = $4\%/5\%$ = .8. With regard to the cross price elasticity, the sign is of primary importance. In this example it is positive, indicating that increases in the price of good R, the related good, cause consumers to demand more of this good. This indicates that good R is a **gross substitute** for the good in question. On the other hand, if the sign is negative, increases in the price of good R cause consumers to decrease their consumption of the good in question. This indicates that good R is a **gross complement** for this good. Of course, a value of zero, or approximately so, for the cross price elasticity would indicate that the two goods are not related to each other.

Conclusion

In this chapter, average functions and elasticities have been added to our toolbox. Moreover, these new concepts have been related to the slope and to the total and marginal functions presented previously. The material developed in the preceding chapters is useful in analyzing simple models. Such models may be univariate or multivariate but have the common property that only one variable is explained. As such, they are represented as single functions, each of which can be written as a single equation. The process of model building, however, often involves combining two or more of these relationships so that more variables can be explained. Of course, in order to understand the more complex theory, we have to understand the simple theories underlying it. This has been the thrust of the book up to this point. Having mastered the properties of single equation, simple models, we are now ready to tackle simultaneous equation, complex models, as presented in Chapter 6.

Important Terms in this Chapter

Arc elasticity - a type of elasticity calculated over discrete increments of variables.

Average fixed cost (AFC) - a firm's fixed cost per unit of output produced.

Average product of an input (AP_K or AP_L) - the amount of output produced, per unit of an input, holding other inputs constant.

Average propensity to consume (APC) - the fraction of disposable income spent for consumption purposes.

Average propensity to save (APS) - the fraction of disposable income saved.

Average revenue (AR) - a firm's total revenue per unit of output sold.

Average total cost (ATC) - a firm's total cost per unit of output produced.

Average variable cost (AVC) - a firm's variable cost per unit of output produced.

Cobb–Douglas production function - a special type of production function of the form:

$$Q = AK^{b_1}L^{b_2}$$

where A = a constant, and $b_1 + b_2 = 1$.

Cross price elasticity of demand - the percentage change in the quantity demanded of a good due to a percentage change in the price of some other good.

Fixed cost (FC) - a firm's cost that is associated with its fixed inputs and that, therefore, does not vary with the firm's output.

Giffen good - a special type of good for which the demand function is positively sloped.

Gross complements - goods for which the cross price elasticity of demand is negative.

Gross substitutes - goods for which the cross price elasticity of demand is positive.

Income elasticity of demand - the percentage change in the quantity demanded of a good due to a percentage change in money income.

Inferior good - a good for which the income elasticity of demand is negative.

Normal good - a good for which the income elasticity of demand is positive.

Point elasticity - a type of elasticity calculated over infinitesimally small increments of variables.

Price elasticity of demand - the percentage change in the quantity demanded of a good due to a percentage change in its own price.

Superior good - a type of normal good for which the income elasticity of demand is greater than one.

Variable cost (VC) - a firm's cost that is associated with its variable inputs and that, therefore, varies with the firm's output.

Exercise Set 5.2

1. A consumption function is given by:

$$C = b_0 + b_1 Y_d$$

   where:

   C = consumption expenditures in $ billions/year
   Y_d = disposable income in $billions/year

   a) Calculate the average propensity to consume (APC) as a function of Y_d. The marginal propensity to consume (MPC) is given by b_1 and is constant. If $b_0 > 0$, how will the APC vary with Y_d? What if $b_0 = 0$?

   b) The elasticity of consumption expenditures with respect to disposable income, E_{C,Y_d}, can be derived from the knowledge of the APC and MPC. Do so for the case of $b_0 > 0$ as well as for $b_0 = 0$. How does this elasticity vary with Y_d? In what range (elastic, inelastic, unitary elastic) do these elasticities fall? Interpret your results.

2. The demand for money (L), is a function of the level of national income, Y, and the interest rate, i. A researcher finds that the elasticity of money demand with respect to national income, $E_{L,Y}$ = +1, while the elasticity of money demand with respect to the interest rate, $E_{L,i}$ = -.2. Interpret those findings.

3. A demand function is given by:

$$Q^d = 1000 - 4P + 5I + .2P_z$$

   where:

   Q^d = quantity demanded in units/week
   P = price in dollars/unit (of Q)
   I = per capita income in $thousands/year
   P_z = price of good z in dollars/unit of good z

   a) Calculate the demand function for I = 20 and P_z = 100.

b) Calculate the quantity demanded when P = 150. Use that result together with the partial slope (with respect to P) to calculate the point price elasticity of demand. Do the same for P = 130 and P = 140.

c) Calculate the arc price elasticity as P goes from 130 to 140 and 130 to 150. In each case interpret your result.

d) Calculate the point income elasticity of demand and the point cross price elasticity of demand when P = 140. [Hint: use the partial slope.] Interpret your results.

4. A demand function is given as:

$$Q^d = 100P^{-1}$$

where:
Q^d = quantity demanded in units/month
P = price in dollars/unit

a) Does this demand function have a constant price elasticity? If so, what is the constant elasticity "k"?

b) Calculate the values of Q^d that correspond to integer values of P for $1 \le P \le 10$ and plot the demand curve in its inverse form.

c) Using the arc price elasticity formula, calculate the price elasticity of demand for several unit intervals. Compare this result to that from Part a.

d) Calculate the total revenue, R, at each point on the demand curve, and the total revenue function by multiplying the demand equation by P. What functional form does the R function have?

5. Which of the following demand and supply relationships have a constant elasticity? If they do, what is it? Interpret your result.

a) $Q^s = 2P$
b) $Q^s = 100 + 5P$
c) $Q^s = -10 + 3P$
d) a demand curve parallel to the price axis
e) a demand curve parallel to the quantity axis
f) $Q^d = 250P^{-2}$
g) $Q^d = 100 - 4P$

6. The marginal–average relationship was discussed on page 162. Use it to determine the range of $E_{T,x}$ in the following cases. Assume that T and x are positive and directly related.

a) A(x) is directly related to x.
b) A(x) is inversely related to x.
c) A(x) is stationary.

7. The concept of elasticity can be utilized to determine the interest rate risk associated with a bond. Conceptually, this elasticity represents the percentage change in the price of a bond resulting from a percentage change in 1.0 plus the yield to maturity associated with the bond. The yield to maturity is the actual rate of return on the investment. Suppose a bond is issued having two years to maturity and a face value of $5,000. Also, the bond has a coupon rate of 5 percent, so the yield to maturity is 1.05. If this yield increases to 10 percent, what is the associated elasticity? How do you interpret this result in terms of the interest rate risk?

8. At the beginning of the year your portfolio is valued at $X and the year is divided into two periods. All interest and dividends are reinvested and no withdrawals are made. The value of your portfolio at the end of the year is $V = X(1 + R_1)(1 + R_2)$ where R_1 and R_2 are the actual rates of return (not annualized) for periods 1 and 2 respectively, in decimal form. Your rate of return over the year = R $= (1 + R_1)(1 + R_2) - 1$ or $(V/X) - 1$. Prove that when $R_1 = -R_2$ (your rate of return for the first period is equal but opposite of the second period, e.g., +10% and -10%), rather than having a 0 rate of return, R is negative. Explain why this occurs. [Hint: This is related to the problem of using point elasticities over an interval which was solved by using the midpoint formula.]

Notes

1. When T, A, and M are all functions of x, the results described only hold if x is nonnegative. This was the case in the quiz example where negative values of quizzes don't make any sense. In most, if not all economic examples, $x \geq 0$, so these results are quite general. If $x < 0$, the inequality signs would be reversed.

2. If $T = T(x)$, it is possible for the marginal M to be infinite at isolated points, but not over an interval. If M is infinite over an interval, then T cannot be a function of x, although x could be a function of T.

6

Simultaneous Equation Models

Introduction

One purpose of economic theory is to provide a systematic explanation for economic phenomena. It would seem reasonable that in formulating these theories one should proceed from the simple to the complex. A **simple model** is one that can be expressed with a single equation, whereas a more **complex model** requires more than one equation. The most basic of simple models is one that has a single dependent variable and a single independent variable. When a model of this type fails to have sufficient explanatory power, the next step of generalization is to include more than one independent variable, while maintaining a single dependent variable. Notice that with one dependent variable, the model is still expressed as a single equation and is, therefore, in the realm of being a simple model. This type of generalization of simple models was performed in Chapter 3.

Complex models are built in the same way that a child builds a house out of blocks. Sometimes only two or three blocks may be used while when a more elaborate house is envisioned, many blocks may be employed. In model building "our blocks" are simple theories. Some complex theories simply combine two or three simple theories together. Other more elaborate complex theories might entail hundreds of variables and hundreds of equations. The relation between a complex theory and the simple theories upon which it is built is analogous to that between the house and the blocks used to build it. Just as a house maintains some of the properties of the blocks and acquires others due to the relationship between those blocks, a complex theory maintains some of the properties of its simpler components, while acquiring some new ones. This is particularly true in regard to the classification of variables as either independent or dependent. Any variable that is dependent in the context of a simple theory will still be a dependent variable in the context of a complex theory utilizing that simple theory. On the other hand, a variable that is independent in the context of a simple theory might become a dependent variable in the context of the more complex theory. This is the case, for example, in a model of supply and demand, generating the market equilibrium. While price is treated as independent in both the supply and demand relationships, once we go to a model of supply and demand, the equilibrium price becomes one of the variables that we seek to explain, i.e., dependent.

Each simple theory can be represented by a single equation. A complex theory composed of a group of simple theories must, therefore, need a multi-equation system in order to be represented. Typically, one equation is needed for each variable that we seek to explain. A complicating factor in complex theories is that values of one dependent variable may enter into an equation of another dependent variable. The solution to such a system of equations is given by a set of values for each of the dependent variables, such that each equation within the system holds simultaneously. Such systems, which are the focus of this chapter, are therefore referred to as **simultaneous equation systems**.

Equilibrium

The most common use of simultaneous equation systems is to solve for points at which the system is at equilibrium. The word *equilibrium* stems from a latin word meaning "equal balance." This meaning might bring to mind the image of a primitive scale like that of the scales of justice. If a known weight is placed on one side, then the scale would be considered to be in equilibrium when sufficient weight is placed on the other so that the scales balance. An equation can be viewed as being analogous to a scale. On the one side, we place the independent variables and parameters whose values are treated as given or known. On the other side is placed the dependent variable. The value of the dependent variable that balances the equation is referred to as the **equilibrium value** of the dependent variable. This description of an equilibrium is equally valid in the context of either a simple or a complex model.

The point at which an equilibrium takes place can be viewed as a rest point of the system. This interpretation of equilibrium brings to mind Newton's Law of Inertia, that a body at rest tends to stay at rest unless acted upon by an outside force. A rest point implies that there is no tendency to change if the dependent variables are at their equilibrium values. In the context of an economic model, this implies that economic agents have no reason to change their behavior in a way that would change the value of these dependent variables, unless one or more of the independent variables were to change. When independent variables change, there would be a change in behavior and a different equilibrium would result. These changes in independent variables are our equivalent to being acted upon by an outside force.

The theory predicts that, given the values of all of the independent variables, the *actual* values taken on by the dependent variables will be the equilibrium values of those variables. In some instances, a given set of values of the independent variables may correspond to more than one set of values for the dependent variables. In that event, the system is said to possess **multiple equilibria**. Typically, however, only one set of values of the dependent variables corresponds to each set of values of the independent variables. In that event the equilibrium obtained is said to be unique. All equilibria discussed in this chapter will be assumed to be unique.

The conditions necessary for an equilibrium to take place depend upon the context of the problem. Many types of equilibria are discussed in economics. Some examples are consumer equilibrium, equilibrium of the firm in the long run and in the short run, equilibrium for the market in isolation (i.e., partial equilibrium), general equilibrium, and the equilibrium level of national income for the economy. One might be tempted to suppose that since an equilibrium is a rest point, it represents an ideal state. However, such is not *necessarily* the case. Equilibria stemming from an optimization problem may be viewed as desirable from the standpoint of the decision maker, though not necessarily of others. Consumer equilibrium and firm equilibrium are examples of this type. If consumers and firms are maximizing utility and profits respectively, they would have no tendency to change their behaviors. In other cases, however, the equilibrium that is obtained may not be viewed as either desirable or ideal. Those equilibria may result from the interaction of impersonal economic forces. National income equilibrium and market equilibrium are of this type. In some models national income may obtain its equilibrium value at levels below full employment or at levels generating inflation. Similarly, a market may overproduce or underproduce a particular good relative to the social optimum when externalities are present.

Equilibrium Conditions, Behavioral Equations, and Identities

In searching for an equilibrium, we specify the conditions under which that equilibrium will take place. These conditions determine the values of the dependent variables that are predicted to be observed. In order for the theory to be meaningful, there must exist other combinations of values for the dependent variables that our theory predicts will not be observed. These are termed **disequilibrium** points. When the equilibrium is unique, these conditions will hold at only a single point given the values of the independent variables. The theory then predicts that the point observed will be that at which the conditions hold, while the multitude of points at which the conditions do not hold will not be observed.

In addition to equilibrium conditions, a complex theory may contain two other types of equations. These are **behavioral equations** and **identity relationships**. A behavioral equation shows how a dependent variable behaves in response to changes in the independent variables. Each of the simple theories contained in a complex theory is generally a behavioral equation. Examples of behavioral equations are demand functions, supply functions, cost functions, profit functions, production functions, consumption functions, and the like. Identity relationships, on the other hand, are basically **definitional equations**. In an identity relationship, the two sides of the equation must by definition be equal to one another since they are two ways of expressing the same thing. To illustrate that a relationship is an identity, the equal sign utilized may have three lines ($\equiv$) rather than the customary two ($=$). However, it is not uncommon to use the normal two-lined equal sign in representing identities as well. An equation stating that total profits are equal to total revenue minus total cost, or that GNP is equal to consumption expenditures + investment expenditures + government expenditures + net exports, are examples of identity relationships.

Identity relationships are sometimes useful when constructing behavioral equations. The profit equation specified here as an identity can be transformed into a behavioral equation. Recognizing that both total revenue and total cost are functions of quantity (i.e., behavioral equations), we can specify that total profit is equal to a function of quantity. Replacing total revenue and total cost by their respective functions, the total profit function is given by the total revenue function minus the total cost function. Similarly, with regard to the GNP equation, if the components of GNP are specified as functions of some independent variables, we can add all of those functions together and specify that GNP is also a function of those variables. The resultant equation would then be a behavioral one, although it originated from an identity relationship.

The distinction between equilibrium conditions and identity relationships is very important. They often look and sound alike and, therefore, tend to be confused. It is one thing to say "the quantity bought equals the quantity sold" and quite another that "the quantity demanded equals the quantity supplied." The former is an identity relationship, as every unit bought must have been sold. The latter, on the other hand, is an equilibrium condition. In macroeconomics, this problem may be even more acute. In a simple model of national income determination with only firms and households, the equation $S = I$, or saving equals investment, may be interpreted to be either an equilibrium condition or an identity. If the variables are treated as ex ante (planned or before the fact) variables, then the equation describes an equilibrium condition. In other words, it says that the level of national income will be at its equilibrium value when the amount that households plan to save is equal to the amount that firms want to invest, at that income level. On the other hand, if the variables are treated as ex post (after the fact), then the equation is simply an identity. For any realized (after the fact) value of national income, whatever amount was invested must be the amount that was saved.

One can easily distinguish between equilibrium conditions and identities by recalling that identities will hold at all points, while equilibrium will not. For example, when markets set the price at its equilibrium value, the quantity demanded will equal the quantity supplied. However, at prices above the equilibrium, the quantity supplied will exceed the quantity demanded, while the reverse is true at prices below the equilibrium. Whatever price is set, regardless of whether it is an equilibrium price, the quantity bought must equal the quantity sold. In the national income example, if national income is higher than its equilibrium level, consumers will plan to save more than firms choose to invest. At income levels lower than the equilibrium, households will plan to save less than firms plan to invest. Only when the planned levels are equal will national income reach its equilibrium level. At that income, both the plans of the households and of the firms are met. Therefore, there is no reason for them to change their behavior in a way that would alter the national income.

Solving Simultaneous Equation Systems

Two approaches are typically used to solve simultaneous equation systems. The first is graphical while the second is algebraic. The graphical approach is most useful when only the general, rather than the specific, functions are known. When the specific functions are known, then either approach can be used. Both methods rely on the fact that at equilibrium all the equations simultaneously hold. Graphically, this implies that the equilibrium point will lie on the intersection of two or more curves. The same result is obtained algebraically by solving for one variable in one equation in terms of the others and then substituting that result into the other equations. This is done sequentially until we are left with one equation and one unknown, which can be easily solved. That result is then substituted back in to solve for a second variable and so on and so forth. Solving simultaneous equations is somewhat like swimming. The best way to learn how to do it is not by reading about how to do it. Rather, one should enter the water and actually attempt it. So let's take a dip.

Market Equilibrium:
The Graphical Approach

The market demand for a good may depend on the price of that good, P, per capita income, Y, price of a substitute, P_S, price of a complement, P_C, and population, POP, ceteris paribus. The market supply of that good may depend upon its price, P, technology, T, price of an input, P_I, and the price of an alternative good that could be produced, P_A, ceteris paribus. The demand and supply functions are given as:

$$Q^d = D(P, Y, P_S, P_C, POP)$$

$$Q^s = S(P, T, P_I, P_A)$$

where:
  Q^d = quantity demanded per period of time
  Q^s = quantity supplied per period of time

Assuming that the good is normal, the partial slope coefficient of Q^d with respect to Y is positive, as are those with respect to P_S and POP. The partial slope coefficients with respect to P and P_C are negative. The partial slope coefficients of Q^s with respect to P and T are positive, while those with respect to P_I and P_A are negative.

Each of these equations in isolation represents a simple theory. In the demand equation, Q^d is the dependent variable while P, Y, P_S, P_C, and POP are independent variables. Similarly in the supply equation, Q^s is dependent, while P, T, P_I, and P_A are independent. Both of these equations are behavioral. The former explains the behavior of consumers, while the latter explains the behavior of firms offering the good for sale. Notice that in both relationships, price is treated as an independent variable. This is true when both consumers and firms are price takers. In that event we can consider them as responding to changes in P.

Consumers and firms interact in a market, and a theory explaining the consequences of that interaction is sought. It is generally assumed that the market will attain an equilibrium. What conditions are necessary for an equilibrium to take place? In other words, under what conditions will neither consumers nor firms have an incentive to change their behaviors, given the values of the independent variables? The answer is when their plans are not frustrated. That would occur when consumers buy as much as they planned, while firms sell the amount they were willing to offer. Since the amount bought must equal (as an identity) the amount sold, this will only take place if the planned amounts for each are equal. This can be stated as:

$$Q^d = Q^s$$

This equation represents the equilibrium condition for this system. As P increases, ceteris paribus, Q^d falls, while Q^s rises (recall the partial slope coefficients of each). Therefore, there exists at most one price, given the values of the other independent variables, at which this equilibrium condition holds. The price at which this condition is satisfied is termed the **equilibrium price**.

In a model of market equilibrium, it is assumed that the market sets the equilibrium price. At that price, $Q^d = Q^s$, so that the quantity actually transacted at that price, Q, is the equilibrium quantity. Of course, $Q = Q^s = Q^d$. This simply says that the actual amount transacted (bought and sold) is equal to the planned amounts of the consumers and firms. When markets are assumed to operate without interference, the observed values of P and Q are supposedly those determined as the equilibrium in the market.

This is obviously a complex model built upon the foundation of the two simple models of demand and supply. Notice that the equilibrium value of P is now dependent, whereas in the simple models it was independent. In this model P and Q are both dependent, while Y, P_S, P_C, POP, T, P_I, and P_A are independent. In other words, given a set of values for the independent variables, we can determine the values that P and Q will reach in equilibrium. In addition, the values of Q^s and Q^d can also be found, although they are of little interest by themselves. The graphical presentation of this model is depicted in Figure 6.1.

In Figure 6.1, the demand and supply curves are depicted. Recall from Chapter 3 that, in order to depict these curves, all of the other independent variables, except P, have to be held constant at some specified level. The subscript 0 on these variables indicates that the curves are drawn for some particular initial value of those variables. The equilibrium condition is that $Q^d = Q^s$, which is graphically represented by the intersection of the demand and supply curves. The market will set the price at P*, its equilibrium value, which is the only price at which the equilibrium condition is met. At any P > P*, $Q^s > Q^d$, while for P < P*, $Q^d > Q^s$. At P*, $Q^d = Q^s$, so that the quantity that will be transacted in equilibrium is Q*. The graph shows us that when all the values of the independent variables are specified as $(Y_0, P_{S,0}, P_{C,0}, POP_0, T_0, P_{I,0}, P_{A,0})$, the equilibrium will take place when P = P* and Q = Q*. In addition, at P* the values of Q^d and Q^s would also be equal to Q*.

Now assume that the value of $Y = Y_1$, where $Y_1 > Y_0$. Since there is a direct relationship between Q^d and Y, ceteris paribus (the partial

Figure 6.1
Market Equilibrium

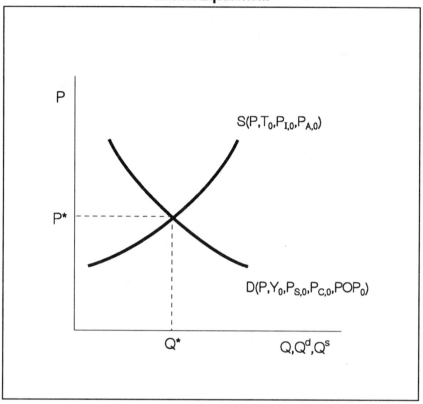

slope coefficient is positive), the demand curve for $Y = Y_1$ will lie to the right of that drawn for $Y = Y_0$. This will have an impact on the equilibrium values of P and Q. The effect of a higher value of Y on the equilibrium is depicted in Figure 6.2

Relative to the original demand curve for $Y = Y_0$, the higher value of Y gives rise to an increase in demand. For a review of the difference between a change in demand and a change in quantity demanded, see Chapter 3. The equilibrium with $Y = Y_1$ will be attained when $P = P^{**}$ and $Q = Q^{**}$. Our theory thus predicts that increases in Y will tend to raise the equilibrium values of P and Q.

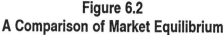

Figure 6.2
A Comparison of Market Equilibrium

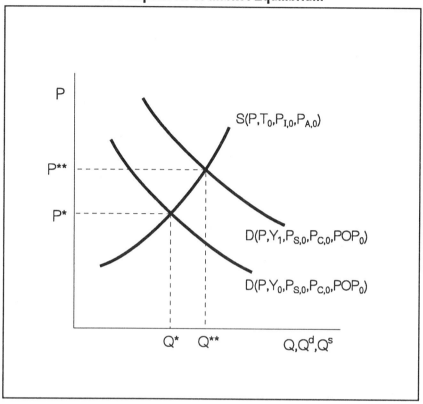

This type of analysis can be performed with respect to each of the independent variables. The theory predicts that a change in any independent variable, ceteris paribus, will have an impact on the equilibrium values of P and Q. By varying each independent variable in isolation, we can observe whether a direct or inverse relationship exists between it and the equilibrium value of P. The relationship between the independent variable and the equilibrium value of Q can be similarly obtained. Due to the fact that general rather than specific functions were used, only qualitative, rather than quantitative, results can be obtained. In the above example, the theory predicts that, as income increases, so will the equilibrium price and quantity. There is insufficient information to indicate by how much each would change.

Since only qualitative results are obtained, the process can be simplified by classifying changes in independent variables into groups. In Figure 6.2 income increased, causing demand to increase. As a result, the equilibrium values of P and Q both increased. Notice however that a change in any independent variable that increases demand would have the same qualitative though not necessarily quantitative impact on P and Q. Therefore, an increase in P_S or POP, or a decrease in P_C, would each give rise to a higher equilibrium value of P and of Q.

The problem can be further simplified, due to its symmetric nature. If an increase in income increases demand, then a decrease in income decreases demand. A decrease in demand has the opposite qualitative impact on the equilibrium values of P and Q of that caused by an increase in demand. Therefore, an increase in P_C, or a decrease in Y, P_S, or POP, will cause demand to decrease. Consequently, the equilibrium values of P and Q will both fall.

The effects of changes of independent variables that affect supply can be analyzed in a similar manner. In Figure 6.3, the effect of a change in technology, T, is considered. An increase in technology will increase supply, i.e., a greater quantity will be supplied at every price. The supply curve for $T = T_1$ will, therefore, lie to the right of the one for $T = T_0$, given that $T_1 > T_0$.

The increase in T from T_0 to T_1 causes the equilibrium price to fall from P* to P**, while the equilibrium quantity rises from Q* to Q**. Similarly, a decrease in either P_I or P_A would have the same qualitative effect, since they would also induce an increase in supply. A decrease in T, or an increase in either P_I or P_A, would decrease supply. The effect of any of those changes would be that P would rise in equilibrium, while Q would fall.

When more than one variable changes, or when one variable affects both relationships, the separate effects of each should be added. However, since the results are qualitative, we may not be able in some cases to get a determinate answer. For instance, if T increases at the same time that Y increases, supply and demand would both increase. The increase in supply would cause Q to rise but P to fall. The increase in demand would cause Q to rise and P to rise as well. Since both cause Q to rise, we can clearly say that the theory predicts that Q will rise. The effect on P, however, is indeterminate because it depends on the magnitude of the two

Figure 6.3
The Effect on Equilibrium of a Change in Supply

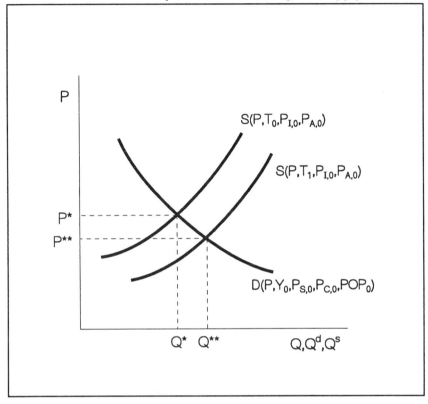

changes. If the increase in Y causes P to rise more than the fall in P induced by an increase in T, then P will rise. On the other hand, P will fall if the reverse is true. Finally, if the two effects are equal and opposite, P will remain unchanged. Without further information, any of these three cases could be true, and we say that P is indeterminate. When a change or changes in the independent variable(s) induces a change in both demand and supply simultaneously, care should be taken in its graphical depiction. Any graph drawn will depict one of the three cases, while in truth, any of the three is possible. To avoid this problem, we must add up the separate effects. Table 6.1 summarizes the effects on the equilibrium price and quantity caused by changes in demand and supply, and combinations thereof.

The effect of a change in any independent variable can be determined in the following manner. First, analyze the supply and demand equations to determine which of the above cases applies. Then refer to Table 6.1 to see the effect. Of the eight cases, the first four are the basic ones, and by adding effects, the remaining four can be derived from them.

It should be recalled that the actual data observed are assumed to be the equilibrium points. As such, each observed price–quantity combination lies at the intersection of some supply curve with some demand curve. When data are collected on different combinations of price and quantity actually transacted, these points may lie on different supply curves, demand curves, or both. When the factors affecting supply change, but those affecting demand do not, the observed points will lie on one demand curve. They will, however, lie on various supply curves. The opposite is true when only demand factors change. When both factors change, the resultant points will lie on various demand and supply curves. It is therefore often difficult to determine the nature of the demand and supply relationships from these equilibrium points. Broadly speaking, this is referred to as the **identification problem**.

Table 6.1
The Effects of Changes in Demand and Supply
on Equilibrium Values of P and Q

	Changes in Demand and Supply	Effects on Equilibrium Values of P and Q
1)	Demand increases, supply unchanged	P rises, Q rises
2)	Demand decreases, supply unchanged	P rises, Q falls
3)	Demand unchanged, supply increases	P falls, Q rises
4)	Demand unchanged, supply decreases	P rises, Q falls
5)	Demand increases, supply increases	P indeterminate, Q rises
6)	Demand increases, supply decreases	P rises, Q indeterminate
7)	Demand decreases, supply increases	P falls, Q indeterminate
8)	Demand decreases, supply decreases	P indeterminate, Q falls

Market Equilibrium: The Algebraic Approach Using a Linear Model

When general functional form is used to represent the demand and supply curves, only qualitative results can be obtained. However, when specific functions are used, quantitative results are obtainable. This will be demonstrated for the case where both the demand and supply functions are assumed to be linear.

Suppose that linear versions of aforementioned demand and supply functions are:

$$Q^d = b_0 + b_1P + b_2Y + b_3P_S + b_4P_C + b_5POP$$

$$Q^s = a_0 + a_1P + a_2T + a_3P_I + a_4P_A$$

The parameters b_0, b_2, b_3, b_5, a_1, and a_2 are positive, while b_1, b_4, a_3, and a_4 are negative. The parameter a_0 may be positive, negative, or zero, as it represents the Q^s intercept. These relationships are meaningful only for combinations of P and Q that lie in the first quadrant, which includes nonnegative values for each. The sign of a_0 depends upon which axis in the first quadrant is intersected by the supply curve. It will be positive when the Q axis is intersected and negative when the P axis is intersected. When the supply curve passes through the origin, a_0 equals zero. The partial slopes of Q^d with respect to its independent variables are the coefficients of those variables. The same is true with regard to the partial slopes in the supply equation.

In order to solve for the equilibrium values of P and Q, the values of the independent variables must be given. Treating these values as constants, we can rewrite the above equations as:

$$Q^d = \hat{b}_0 + b_1P$$

and

$$Q^s = \hat{a}_0 + a_1P$$

where $\hat{b}_0 = (b_0 + b_2Y_0 + b_3P_{S,0} + b_4P_{C,0} + b_5POP_0)$ and $\hat{a}_0 = (a_0 + a_2T_0 + a_3P_{I,0} + a_4P_{A,0})$. Notice that the values of the independent variables affect the intercept of each equation, while leaving the slope, with respect to P, unchanged. It is expected that $\hat{b}_0 > 0$, while $\hat{a}_0$ may still be of any sign.

The equilibrium condition is that $Q^d = Q^s$, which in turn is equal to Q, the quantity transacted. Replacing Q^d and Q^s by Q yields:

$$Q = \hat{b}_0 + b_1 P$$

and

$$Q = \hat{a}_0 + a_1 P$$

This is a system with two equations and two unknowns. Since Q = Q (an identity), this can be written as:

$$\hat{b}_0 + b_1 P = \hat{a}_0 + a_1 P$$

which is a single equation in one unknown, P. Subtracting $a_1 P$ and $\hat{b}_0$ from both sides yields:

$$(b_1 - a_1)P = \hat{a}_0 - \hat{b}_0$$

Now divide both sides by $(b_1 - a_1)$, with the result that:

$$P = (\hat{a}_0 - \hat{b}_0)/(b_1 - a_1)$$

The value of P given by the above equation is its equilibrium value. The denominator is negative since b_1 is negative and a_1 is positive. In order to be economically meaningful, P should be positive. This requires that the numerator $\hat{a}_0 - \hat{b}_0$ is negative or, equivalently, that $\hat{b}_0 > \hat{a}_0$.

Having solved for the equilibrium value of P, we can now use that information to solve for the equilibrium value of Q and, therefore, Q^d and Q^s. This can be done by replacing P in either the demand or supply equation by its solution value. Using the demand equation yields:

$$Q = \hat{b}_0 + b_1(\hat{a}_0 - \hat{b}_0)/(b_1 - a_1) = [(b_1 - a_1)\hat{b}_0 + b_1(\hat{a}_0 - \hat{b}_0)]/(b_1 - a_1)$$

$$= [b_1\hat{b}_0 - a_1\hat{b}_0 + b_1\hat{a}_0 - b_1\hat{b}_0]/(b_1 - a_1)$$

$$= (b_1\hat{a}_0 - a_1\hat{b}_0)/(b_1 - a_1)$$

To be economically meaningful Q should be positive, which requires that

$$(b_1\hat{a}_0 - a_1\hat{b}_0) < 0, \text{ or } a_1\hat{b}_0 > b_1\hat{a}_0$$

Notice that the solutions are in terms of the parameters and implicitly, through the $\hat{b}_0$ and $\hat{a}_0$ terms, the values taken on by the independent variables. Equations of this type are called **reduced form equations**. One can substitute for $\hat{b}_0$ and $\hat{a}_0$ the expressions that represent them in terms of the independent variables. The reduced form equations that result will then be multivariate functions of the independent variables, given by:

$$P = \frac{a_0 - b_0}{b_1 - a_1} + \frac{a_2}{b_1 - a_1}T + \frac{a_3}{b_1 - a_1}P_I + \frac{a_4}{b_1 - a_1}P_A - \frac{b_2}{b_1 - a_1}Y$$

$$- \frac{b_3}{b_1 - a_1}P_S - \frac{b_4}{b_1 - a_1}P_C - \frac{b_5}{b_1 - a_1}POP$$

and

$$Q = \frac{b_1 a_0 - a_1 b_0}{b_1 - a_1} + b_1\frac{a_2}{b_1 - a_1}T + b_1\frac{a_3}{b_1 - a_1}P_I + b_1\frac{a_4}{b_1 - a_1}P_A$$

$$- a_1\frac{b_2}{b_1 - a_1}Y - a_1\frac{b_3}{b_1 - a_1}P_S - a_1\frac{b_4}{b_1 - a_1}P_C - a_1\frac{b_5}{b_1 - a_1}POP$$

The effect of a unit change of any independent variable on the equilibrium values of P and Q will be the partial slope coefficient of that variable in the reduced form equation. For example, a one unit increase in income, Y, will cause the equilibrium price to change by $-b_2/(b_1 - a_1)$ units, and the equilibrium quantity to change by $-a_1 b_2/(b_1 - a_1)$ units, ceteris paribus. Given the sign configurations stipulated earlier, both these magnitudes are positive. The effects of the other independent variables on the equilibrium price and quantity can be found in a similar manner. The reader might find it a useful exercise at this point to calculate the partial slope coefficients of the other independent variables, evaluate their signs, and interpret their meanings.

Example 6.1 Equilibrium in a Linear Model: A Numerical Example

The demand and supply functions are given as:

$$Q^d = 100 - 5P + 2Y$$

and

$$Q^s = -10 + 3P - 3P_A$$

where all variables are as previously defined. Let's assume that Y = 17.5 (measured in thousands of dollars per year) and P_A = 5 (in dollars per unit). Substituting in the above equations yields:

$$Q^d = 100 - 5P + 2(17.5) = 135 - 5P$$

$$Q^s = -10 + 3P - 3(5) = -25 + 3P$$

At equilibrium, $Q = Q^d = Q^s$ so that 135 - 5P = -25 + 3P. Solving for P gives us 8P = 160, so that P = 20. Setting P = 20 in either the demand or supply function enables us to solve for Q. From the demand relationship we have that Q = 135 - 5P = 135 - 5(20) = 35. Substituting in the supply function yields the same result. In this case, Q = -25 + 3P = -25 + 3(20) = -25 + 60 = 35. The equilibrium thus will be attained at P = 20 and Q = 35.

Example 6.2 Numerical Solution of Equilibrium: A Nonlinear Case

The same methods of solution that apply to the linear case apply to the nonlinear model. Consider the following example where the demand function is nonlinear. The model is given by:

$$Q^d = 100 - P^2$$

and

$$Q^s = 21P$$

In equilibrium, $Q = Q^d = Q^s$, so that $100 - P^2 = 21P$. This can be written as $100 - P^2 - 21P = 0$, or after multiplying both sides by -1, as $P^2 + 21P - 100 = 0$. This is a quadratic equation in P, which can be solved either by factoring or by use of the quadratic formula. By factoring, we have (P + 25)(P - 4) = 0, with solution values P = -25, P = 4. Since prices are restricted to be positive, the relevant solution is P = 4.

In cases where factoring is difficult, the roots of a quadratic equation can be obtained by use of the quadratic formula. It is given by:

$$P = (-b \pm \sqrt{b^2 - 4ac} / 2a$$

where a is the coefficient for the squared term, b is the coefficient of P, and c is the value of the intercept. In our example, a = 1, b = 21, and c = -100. Substituting these values in the quadratic formula yields:

$$P = [-21 \pm \sqrt{441 - 4(1)(-100)}]/2(1)$$

$$= (-21 \pm \sqrt{841})/2$$

$$= (-21 \pm 29)/2$$

Therefore P = -50/2 = -25, and P = 8/2 = 4. We are again left with P = 4 in order to be meaningful. Replacing P by 4 in either the demand or supply equation yields Q = 84. The equilibrium thus takes place when P = 4 and Q = 84.

A Simple Model of National Income

The methods used to solve for the market equilibrium are identical to those used to solve for national income in a macroeconomic model. Consider the following linear model for a closed economy.

The behavioral equations are:

$$C = b_0 + b_1 Y_d$$

$$I = I_0$$

$$G = G_0$$

$$T = T_0$$

The following are identities:

$$Y_d = Y - T$$

$$AE = C + I + G$$

The equilibrium condition is:

$$AE = Y$$

The variables are defined as C = consumption expenditures, Y_d = disposable income, I = investment expenditures, G = government expenditures, T = net taxes, Y = national income, and AE = aggregate expenditures. All of the above variables are measured in billions of dollars per year. In addition, b_0 = autonomous consumption expenditures and b_1 = the MPC.

This model contains seven equations in seven variables. The most important variable, however, is the equilibrium value of Y, since the goal is the determination of national income. To solve for Y, the following procedure can be used.

1) Replace Y_d in the consumption function by Y - T. This yields C = $b_0 - b_1 T_0 + b_1 Y$, since T = T_0.
2) Add the new consumption function to I + G, to generate an AE function of Y, given by AE = $(b_0 - b_1 T_0 + I_0 + G_0) + b_1 Y$.
3) Replace AE by Y utilizing the equilibrium condition. This yields Y = $(b_0 - b_1 T_0 + I_0 + G_0) + b_1 Y$.
4) Solve for the equilibrium level of Y by subtracting $b_1 Y$ from both sides and then dividing by $(1 - b_1)$:

$$Y - b_1 Y = (b_0 - b_1 T_0 + I_0 + G_0)$$

$$Y(1 - b_1) = (b_0 - b_1 T_0 + I_0 + G_0)$$

$$Y = (b_0 - b_1 T_0 + I_0 + G_0)/(1 - b_1)$$

5) The above equation is the reduced form equation for Y. Notice that it is equal to the sum of all autonomous expenditures (those not dependent on Y) divided by 1 - slope of the AE function. The partial slopes of this equation with regard to G, I, and T are their respective multipliers. The graphical presentation of this model is presented in Figure 6.4.

Equilibrium for a Monopolist: A Numerical Example

A monopolist faces a demand curve given by Q^d = 100 - 2P and a cost function given by C = 10Q. The monopolist's problem is to choose one point on the demand curve, a price–quantity combination, such that

Figure 6.4
National Income Equilibrium

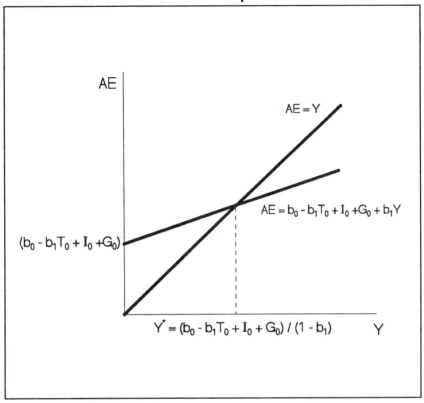

profits are maximized. It is useful to express the demand relation so that price is a function of quantity. This yields $P = 50 - Q/2$, since in equilibrium $Q = Q^d$. The marginal revenue function corresponding to this demand function is given by $MR = 50 - Q$. The marginal cost function is the slope of the total cost function, C. Since C is linear in Q, its slope is the coefficient on Q, which is 10. Therefore, the marginal cost function is given by $MC = 10$. A necessary, and in this case sufficient, condition for maximizing profits is that the quantity, Q, is chosen such that $MR = MC$.

Using the equilibrium condition, $MR = MC$, we can solve for the equilibrium quantity. Since $MR = 50 - Q = MC = 10$, the equilibrium Q

is the solution to 50 – Q = 10, or 40 – Q = 0. Therefore, the monopolist at equilibrium should produce Q = 40. The equilibrium price can now be solved by replacing Q with 40 in the inverse demand function. Since P = 50 – Q/2, and Q = 40, the solution is P = 50 – 40/2 = 50 – 20 = 30. The equilibrium for the monopolist will therefore occur when Q = 40 and P = 30. Graphically, this is presented in Figure 6.5.

Using the graphical approach, the optimal quantity is determined by the intersection of the MR and MC curves, which simply reflects the equilibrium condition. This yields Q = 40. At this Q, the price that will clear the market (Q^d = Q) is obtained by going vertically up to the demand curve. This occurs when P = 30.

Figure 6.5
Equilibrium for a Monopolist

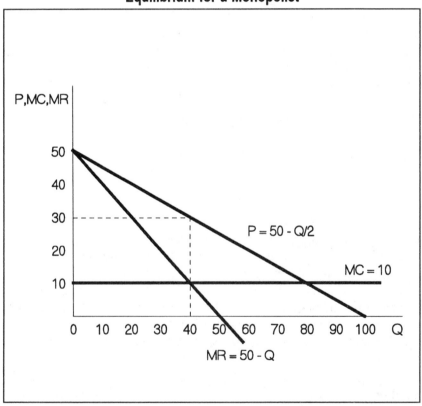

In addition to solving for the equilibrium values of MR, MC, Q and P, given by 10, 10, 40, and 30 respectively, solution values of C, R (total revenue), and π (total profits) can also be obtained. Total costs at the equilibrium are given by C = 10Q = 10(40) = 400. Total revenue is given by the identity, R = P X Q, which at equilibrium = (30)(40) = 1200. The total profit identity is π = R - C. Therefore, the equilibrium value of π = 1200 - 400 = 800.

Conclusion

The preceding chapters have developed tools useful in the analysis of simple models. In this chapter the relation between simple, or one equation, models and complex, or simultaneous equation, models was developed. The tools of analysis so far have been relatively simple, relying primarily on graphical and algebraic techniques. More powerful tools enable us to solve problems that could not be solved with simpler tools. Even in cases when simple tools suffice, more powerful ones may enable us to solve a problem more easily. Finding the slope of a nonlinear function is a case in point. The following two chapters develop tools that simplify such calculations for univariate and multivariate functions, respectively.

Important Terms in this Chapter

Behavioral equations - equations that show how a dependent variable behaves in response to changes in the independent variables.

Complex model - a model having more than one dependent variable and having more than one equation.

Definitional equations - an identity relationship where the two sides of the equation must by definition be equal to one another, since they are two ways of expressing the same thing.

Disequilibrium (points) - values of the dependent variables that do not satisfy the equilibrium condition. Since a theory generally predicts that only equilibrium points will be observed, these points are those that the theory predicts will not occur.

Identification problem (in relation to demand and supply) - the problem of ascertaining the demand and supply curves from knowledge of observed price-quantity combinations. The observed combinations are equilibrium values occurring at the intersection of a specific demand and supply curve. The observed points, therefore, may lie on different demand and supply curves.

Identity relationship - relationship where the two sides of the equation must by definition be equal to one another since they are two ways of expressing the same thing (see definitional equation).

Multiple equilibria - exists when a given set of values of the independent variables may correspond to more than one set of values for the dependent variables. Each set of values for the dependent variables satisfies the equilibrium condition.

Reduced form equations - equations where the solutions are in terms of the parameters and implicitly (or explicitly) the values taken on by the independent variables.

Simple model - a model that can be expressed with a single equation.

Simultaneous equation system - a model containing more than one equation, for which the solution requires that each single equation is satisfied at the predetermined level of the independent variables and the solution values of the dependent variables.

Exercises

1. Given the following demand and supply functions:

    $$Q^d = 1000 - 5P + 50I$$

    $$Q^s = -100 + 10P - 5P_A$$

    where:
      Q^d = quantity demanded in units per period of time
      P = price in dollars per unit
      I = per capita income in thousands of dollars per year
      Q^s = quantity supplied in units per period of time
      P_A = price of an alternative good in dollars per unit of that good

a) What is the equilibrium condition for this model? Explain conceptually why fulfillment of that condition will generate equilibrium.

b) Assuming that the model is explaining the equilibrium that will take place, which variables are independent and which are dependent?

c) Calculate the reduced form equation for P_e, where P_e is the equilibrium price, in terms of the parameters and values of the independent variables. Do the same for Q_e, where Q_e is the equilibrium quantity.

d) What are the values of P_e and Q_e when $I = 30$ and $P_A = 9$? When $I = 24$ and $P_A = 12$?

e) Interpret the partial slope coefficients of I and P_A in the reduced form equations.

2. A monopolist faces a demand curve given by:

$$Q^d = 500 - 10P$$

and a total cost function given as:

$$C = 25 + 2Q$$

where:
  Q^d = quantity demanded in units per period of time
  P = price in dollars per unit
  C = total cost in dollars per period of time
  Q = quantity produced in units per period of time

Assuming that $Q = Q^d$, the total revenue function is given as:

$$R = 50Q - .1Q^2$$

where $R = P \times Q$ = total revenue in dollars per period of time. Marginal revenue, MR, is then:

$$MR = 50 - .2Q$$

where MR is marginal revenue in dollars per unit, while marginal cost, MC, is the slope of the total cost function (i.e., MC = 2). Total profit, π, is given by the identity, $\pi = R - C$, while the necessary condition to maximize total profit is MR = MC.

a) Using all of the above information, solve for the equilibrium values of Q, Q^d, MR, C, P, R, and π.
b) Graphically depict the MR, MC, and demand functions to show how the equilibrium price and quantity are obtained.

3. Given the model of income determination for a closed economy:

$$C = b_0 + b_1 Y_d$$

$$I = I_0 + a_1 Y$$

$$G = G_0$$

$$T = T_0$$

$$Y_d = Y - T$$

$$AE = C + I + G$$

$$AE = Y$$

where all variables are defined as in the chapter and $a_1 = \Delta I/\Delta Y$ = the marginal propensity to invest, MPI:

a) Which equations are behavioral? Identities? Equilibrium conditions?
b) Solve for the reduced form equation of the equilibrium level of Y under the assumption that $a_1 = 0$.
c) Do the same under the assumption that $a_1 > 0$. In general what effect does a nonzero MPI have on the equilibrium level of income?
d) What are the government expenditures, autonomous investment, and autonomous tax multipliers? Compare the results when $a_1 = 0$ as opposed to $a_1 > 0$.

e) What are the solution values of all of the dependent variables when $b_0 = 600$, $b_1 = .8$, $I_0 = 50$, $G_0 = 150$, $T_0 = 100$, and $a_1 = 0$.

f) Given that all parameters are at the same values as in Part e, except that $a_1 = .1$, how do your answers to Part e change?

4. The expected return on a security is:

$$E(R_i) = [E(P_{i1}) - P_{i0} + E(P_i)]/P_{i0}$$

where:

$E(P_{i1})$ = expected price of security i at the end of period 1

P_{i0} = actual price of security i at beginning of period 1

$E(D_{i1})$ = expected dividends received during the period 1

According to the security market line (SML), the expected rate of return required on this security $E(RR_i) = RF + \beta_i RP_M$ where:

RF = risk free return

β_i = beta of security i

RP_M = the market portfolio risk premium

In equilibrium, the price of the security must be set such that $E(R_i) = E(RR_i)$.

a) Solve for the equilibrium price $P_{i0}*$ as a function of $E(P_{i1})$, $E(D_{i1})$, RF, β_i, and RP_M.

b) Given that $RP_M = 6\%$, $RF = 4\%$, $\beta_i = 1$, $E(P_{i1}) = \$50$, and $E(D_{i1}) = \$2.80$. Currently, the security is selling $P_{i0} = \$45$. Is this an equilibrium price? What is the required rate of return, the actual expected rate, and the equilibrium price of the security?

Derivatives: Univariate Functions

Introduction

In Chapter 2, it was demonstrated that linear functions have a constant slope, while nonlinear functions do not. Two methods of calculating the slope were presented. Using discrete changes in the independent variable X, it was shown how the average slope over the interval could be calculated. Further, it was shown that the average slope represents the slope of a secant drawn between two points on a curve. Alternatively, the instantaneous slope at a point was discussed and shown to represent the slope of a tangent to the curve at that point. With regard to linear functions, both methods yield the same solution, due to the constancy of the slope. However, with regard to nonlinear functions, for which the slope varies along the curve, the two methods yield different values. This problem is compounded by the fact that in general it is the instantaneous slope that is more relevant and precise but whose determination is impossible without resorting to complicated graphs or the tools to be developed in this chapter. The average slope, on the other hand, is easy to calculate, but at best, represents an approximation to the instantaneous slope. Moreover, a knowledge of the instantaneous slope is required in order to solve optimization problems.

The goal of this chapter is to provide a relatively easy method of calculating the instantaneous slope of a function. This method involves calculus, and it works for both linear and nonlinear functions. It will be shown that the instantaneous slope is the **derivative** of a function, and in the context of discussing the meaning of the derivative and methods of its calculation, the relationship between the average slope and the instantaneous slope will be examined.

After developing rules for differentiation, economic applications of the derivatives are presented. However, the applications are not new, as they have already been discussed in detail in Chapters 4 and 5. Derivatives will be used to derive marginal functions from total functions, to aid in calculating elasticities, and to solve optimization problems. In the appendix to this chapter, higher order derivatives and their relation to concavity and convexity are explored.

Limits and Derivatives

In comparing the average slope to the instantaneous slope it was noted that the average slope applied to discrete changes in the independent variable, while the instantaneous slope applied to infinitesimal changes. Calculus is the branch of mathematics that deals with infinitesimal changes of a variable and the impact of that change on another variable. The nature of an infinitesimal change can only be understood with the aid of a concept called the **limit**. The limit is probably the most important concept in calculus and is intimately tied to that of the derivative. Therefore, the concept of the limit will be explained before proceeding to the derivative.

The Limit of a Function

Assume that a functional relationship exists between Y and X such that Y = f(X), and that this function is defined over some interval containing X = a, except perhaps at X = a. By choosing values of X closer and closer to a, but not equal to a, we can observe what happens to the value of f(X) = Y. In the event that the value of f(X) gets closer to some number L, as X gets closer to a, then the number L is said to be the **limit of the function,** f(X), as X approaches a. In other words as X → a, f(X) → L, where the symbol, "→" is read "approaches." The implication of this statement is that we can make the value of f(X) as close to L as we choose by picking values of X sufficiently close to a. When point a lies on the interior (not at an endpoint) of the interval, X may approach a from the left (X < a) or from the right (X > a). Similarly, f(X) may approach L from above (f(X) > L) or below (f(X) < L). The words right and left for X and above and below for f(X) are in the context of Cartesian coordinates developed in Chapter 2. Recall that the X axis is horizontal, while the Y axis is vertical. In order for L to be the limit, f(X) must approach the same L whether X → a from the left or the right. In the event that f(X) increases or decreases without bound as X → a, we say that f(X) has no limit as X → a. Another way of saying the same thing is that the limit of f(X) is infinite (+ ∞ and - ∞ respectively) as X → a. Of course infinity is not a number but merely signifies that no bound exists. In a similar fashion one can take the limit of f(X) as X grows without bound or decreases without bound. That would be signified as X → + ∞ and X → - ∞ respectively. In those events X can only approach from one side, and the limit would be termed a one-sided limit.

A concise way of writing that the limit of f(X), as X → a, is L is:

$$\lim_{X \to a} f(X) = L$$

This notation will be employed whenever a limit is discussed. To better understand the concept of a limit, it is advisable to actually work out a few examples. Consider the function given by Y = f(X) = 2X + 1, where f(X) is defined over the interval $0 \le X \ge 10$, except possibly at X = 5. Does this function have a limit as X → 5, and if so what is it? To answer this question we can take values of X close to 5 (from both sides) and observe what happens to f(X). This is done in Table 7.1.

We can see from Table 7.1 that as X increases from 4 toward 5, the value of f(X) increases and gets closer and closer to 11. Similarly as X decreases from 6 toward 5, f(X) decreases and gets closer and closer to 11. Therefore it would seem that:

$$\lim_{X \to 5} (2X + 1) = 11$$

We can make f(X) as close to 11 as we choose by picking values of X close enough to 5. For example, if we want f(X) to differ from 11 by no more than .02, we would choose values of X that differ from 5 by no

Table 7.1
Values of f(X) = 2X + 1, as X Approaches 5

X	f(X)	X	f(X)
4	9	6	13
4.5	10	5.5	12
4.8	10.6	5.2	11.4
4.9	10.8	5.1	11.2
4.99	10.98	5.01	11.02
4.999	10.998	5.001	11.002

more than .01. In other words, $|f(X) - 11| < .02$ whenever $|X - 5| < .01$. In fact, we can get the value of f(X) as close to 11 as we please by restricting $|X - 5|$ to one half of that amount. Notice in this case that if f(X) is defined for X = 5, then f(5) = 11. That result will not always hold, and the limit calculated does not depend upon it. Recall that in defining a limit as X → a, we let X approach a, but specifically excluded the case of X = a.

Another example could be the hyperbolic function given by Y = f(X) = 1/X. Assume that the domain of this function is restricted to X > 0, and we seek the limit of this function as X grows without bound. In this case we seek the one-sided limit as X → ∞. Some values of f(X) are calculated and presented in Table 7.2 for large values of X. In this case, as X gets larger, f(X) approaches zero and consequently:

$$\lim_{X \to +\infty} (1/X) = 0$$

Notice that no matter how large a value we choose for X, f(X) will never equal 0. However, we can make f(X) as close to zero as we please by picking sufficiently large values for X. When:

$$\lim_{X \to +\infty} f(X) = L$$

Table 7.2
Values of the Hyperbolic Function, Y = 1/X,
for Large Values of X (i.e., X Approaches Infinity)

X	f(X)
100	.01
1000	.001
10,000	.0001
100,000	.00001
1,000,000	.000001
1,000,000,000	.000000001

the line given by Y = L is a horizontal asymptote of the function. Recall from Chapter 2 that Y = 0 was, in fact, the horizontal asymptote of 1/X. Alternatively, if as X → a from either the left or the right, the limit fails to exist (i.e., it equals + ∞ or - ∞), then the line X = a is a vertical asymptote. In this example, the vertical asymptote is given by X = 0, as was demonstrated in Chapter 2, and should be verified by the reader.

The Derivative

The concept of a limit is important in its own right. It has already been demonstrated that the use of a limit can be instrumental in finding asymptotes. This alone would make it a valuable tool for use in curve sketching. However, our major purpose in developing this tool is to develop the derivative. This is necessitated by the fact that the derivative is merely the limit of a special function.

Recall from Chapter 2 that the slope of a secant between two points on a curve is the average slope, while the slope of the tangent line at a point on the curve is the instantaneous slope. In addition, the relationship between the two slope concepts was discussed as well. It was explained that the slope of the secant over an interval could be made as close as we wanted to the slope of the tangent, if we consider smaller and smaller intervals. This statement should now be recognized as being equivalent to the statement, "the limit of the slope of the secant, as the length of the interval approaches zero, is equal to the slope of the tangent." The derivative of a function, Y = f(X), is denoted as dY/dX or df(X)/dX and is defined as the limit of the slope of the secant as the interval approaches zero. When that limit exists, it is equal to the slope of the tangent at that point. As such, the derivative is simply another name for the instantaneous slope. Moreover, since the slope has been identified as the marginal, M, the derivative of a function also represents the marginal function. The derivative of a function f(X) is another function of X that is sometimes denoted as f'(X) or simply f'. This is simply a restatement of the fact that the marginal of some function of X is itself a function of X, i.e., M = M(X).

Recall that for a limit to exist at a point, the same value L must be approached by the function whether X approaches that point from the left or the right. This implies that, for values of X for which the derivative is defined, there exists only one tangent line for each value of X. Since the slope of any tangent line is unique, or has only one value, and is equal to the derivative at that point, there is one value of the derivative for each value of X. Therefore, the derivative itself is a function of X.

How can the derivative of a function be calculated? The general method upon which all the rules in the next section are based is called the "delta method." While this method is seldom used in practice due to its cumbersome and time-consuming nature, it provides insight into the concept of the derivative. In addition, the last step in this method provides a more formal definition of the derivative.

The Delta (Δ) Method

There are five steps in calculating the derivative of the function f(X) using the delta method. For each step, the mathematical statement will be on the left, and its verbal interpretation will appear on the right.

Step 1:
Y = f(X)

Write down the actual functional relationship between Y and X.

Step 2:
Y + ΔY = f(X + ΔX)

Let the value of X change by some increment ΔX. Whatever was done to X in the initial function is now done to X + ΔX. The value of the function at this new point will equal f(X + ΔX), which in general will differ from its initial value f(X). As a consequence, the value of the function will change and will equal Y [the original value of f(X)] plus some increment, ΔY. (Of course, if the value does not change, the mathematical formulation is still correct as ΔY would equal 0.)

Step 3:
ΔY = f(X + ΔX) - f(X)

Subtract the initial value Y from both sides of the equation in Step 2. On the left, that leaves us with ΔY. On the right, after substituting f(X) for Y, we have f(X + ΔX) - f(X). Both sides of this equation are alternative ways of expressing the increment in the value of the function (ΔY), caused by some increment in X (i.e., ΔX).

Step 4:

$$\frac{\Delta Y}{\Delta X} = \frac{f(X + \Delta X) - f(X)}{\Delta X}$$

Divide both sides of the equation in Step 3 by ΔX. For any specific ΔX ≠ 0, this yields the slope of the secant line from [X, f(X)] to [X + ΔX, f(X + ΔX)]. Therefore it also represents the average slope of this function, over that interval.

Step 5:

$$\frac{dY}{dX} = \lim_{\Delta X \to 0} \frac{\Delta Y}{\Delta X}$$

$$= \lim_{\Delta X \to 0} \frac{f(X + \Delta X) - f(X)}{\Delta X}$$

assuming this limit exists.

Take the limit of the average slope (slope of the secant) as the change in X (ΔX) approaches zero. The derivative, dY/dX is defined as this limit, assuming it exists. If this limit exists, it is equal to the slope of the tangent or the instantaneous slope. Recall that in taking a limit as ΔX → 0, we specifically exclude the case of ΔX = 0.

When the derivative is calculated in this manner, the result is another function of X. If we are interested in the value of the derivative at some specific point, X = a, we can evaluate the derivative function at that point. Alternatively, the derivative of the function at X = a can be found directly with the delta method, if X is replaced by the term, a, in the above five steps. In that event Step 5 is:

$$\frac{dY}{dX}\bigg|X = a = \lim_{\Delta X \to 0} \frac{\Delta Y}{\Delta X}\bigg|X = a = \lim_{\Delta X \to 0} \frac{f(a + \Delta X) - f(a)}{\Delta X}$$

The vertical lines next to the first two terms are read, "evaluated at." A simpler notation for the above would be f'(a), where f' is the derivative function and "a" means evaluated at X = a. If concern is with a point X = a, it should be noted that as $\Delta X \to 0$, that $X \to a$, since $\Delta X = X - a$. Therefore, an equivalent formulation of the derivative of f(X) at X = a is:

$$f'(a) = \lim_{X \to a} \frac{f(X) - f(a)}{X - a}$$

where X ≠ a, and the limit exists.

To illustrate the delta method, let's consider the function given by Y = f(X) = X^2, whose domain is given by X ≥ 0. To find the derivative (as a function of X) over its whole domain, we can follow the five–step procedure previously discussed. The calculation would proceed as follows:

Step 1: Y = f(X) = X^2

Step 2: Y + ΔY = f(X + ΔX) = $(X + \Delta X)^2$ = $X^2 + 2X(\Delta X) + (\Delta X)^2$

Step 3: ΔY = f(X + ΔX) – f(X) = $[X^2 + 2X(\Delta X) + (\Delta X)^2]$ – X^2
$= 2X(\Delta X) + (\Delta X)^2$

Step 4: $\dfrac{\Delta Y}{\Delta X} = \dfrac{f(X + \Delta X) - f(X)}{\Delta X} = \dfrac{2X(\Delta X) + (\Delta X)^2}{\Delta X} = 2X + \Delta X$

Step 5:
$$\frac{dY}{dX} = \lim_{\Delta X \to 0} \frac{\Delta Y}{\Delta X} = \lim_{\Delta X \to 0} \frac{f(X + \Delta X) - f(X)}{\Delta X}$$

$$= \lim_{\Delta X \to 0} (2X + \Delta X) = \lim_{\Delta X \to 0} 2X + \lim_{\Delta X \to 0} \Delta X$$

$$= 2X + 0 = 2X$$

In Step 5, we utilized the rule that the limit of a sum $(2X + \Delta X)$ is equal to the sum of the limits:

$$\left(\lim_{\Delta X \to 0} 2X + \lim_{\Delta X \to 0} \Delta X \right)$$

Since the term $2X$ does not depend upon ΔX, its limit is simply $2X$. However, as $\Delta X \to 0$, the limit of $\Delta X = 0$. Therefore, the derivative function is given by $dY/dX = f'(X) = 2X$. For any value of X in the domain, the instantaneous slope is twice that value of X. For example, the slope of X^2 when X =1 is $f'(1) = 2(1) = 2$.

Alternatively, if our concern is only about the value of the derivative function at X = 1, we could replace X by 1 in the above five steps. In that case, we would have:

Step 1: $Y = f(1) = 1^2 = 1$

Step 2: $Y + \Delta Y = f(1 + \Delta X) = (1 + \Delta X)^2$
$$= 1^2 + 2 \times 1 \times \Delta X + (\Delta X)^2 = 1 + 2\Delta X + (\Delta X)^2$$

Step 3: $\Delta Y = f(1 + \Delta X) - f(1)$
$$= [1 + 2\Delta X + (\Delta X)^2] - 1 = 2\Delta X + (\Delta X)^2$$

Step 4:
$$\frac{\Delta Y}{\Delta X} = \frac{f(1 + \Delta X) - f(1)}{\Delta X} = \frac{2\Delta X + (\Delta X)^2}{\Delta X} = 2 + \Delta X$$

Step 5:

$$\frac{dY}{dX}\bigg|X = 1 = \lim_{\Delta X \to 0} \frac{\Delta Y}{\Delta X}\bigg|X = 1$$

$$= \lim_{\Delta X \to 0} \frac{f(1 + \Delta X) - f(1)}{\Delta X} = \lim_{\Delta X \to 0} (2 + \Delta X)$$

$$= \lim_{\Delta X \to 0} 2 + \lim_{\Delta X \to 0} (\Delta X) = 2 + 0 = 2$$

Figure 7.1
$Y = X^2$, with a Tangent at $X = 1$ and Assorted Secants Nearby

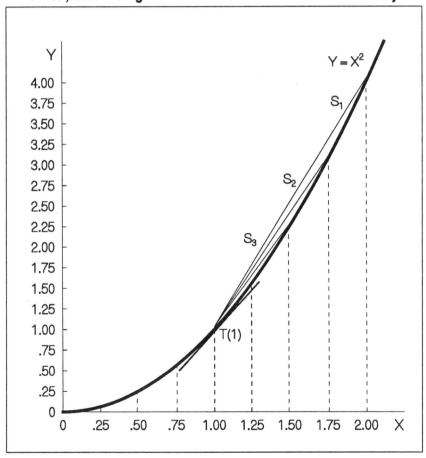

The graph of $Y = f(X) = X^2$ is depicted in Figure 7.1. A tangent line is drawn at $X = 1$, whose slope is the derivative at that point (i.e., 2). In addition, secants are provided for values of ΔX close to zero. Starting from $X = 1$, three secants S_1, S_2, and S_3 are depicted corresponding to ΔX = 1, .75, and .5 respectively. Notice that, as ΔX approaches zero, the slope of the secant lines get closer to that of the tangent line $T(1)$. The values of X, Y, and the slope of the secant, or the average slope, for small values of ΔX (including the aforementioned ones), are presented in Table 7.3. Notice that although graphically we have depicted only positive values of ΔX, negative values of X could be depicted as well. In either event, as indicated by the figures in Table 7.3, as $\Delta X \rightarrow 0$, the slope of a secant starting at $X = 1$ gets closer and closer to 2.

Table 7.3
Assorted Values of the Function, $Y = X^2$, its Average Slope, and ΔX, Close to $X = 1$

ΔX	$X+\Delta X$	$Y+\Delta Y$	ΔY	$\Delta Y/\Delta X$
+1.0000	2.0000	4.0000	3.0000	3.0000
+.7500	1.7500	3.0625	2.0625	2.7500
+.5000	1.5000	2.2500	1.2500	2.5000
+.2500	1.2500	1.5625	.5625	2.2500
+.1000	1.1000	1.2100	.2100	2.1000
+.0500	1.0500	1.1025	.1025	2.0500
-.0500	.9500	.9025	-.0975	1.9500
-.1000	.9000	.8100	-.1900	1.9000
-.2500	.7500	.5625	-.4375	1.7500
-.5000	.5000	.2500	-.7500	1.5000
-.7500	.2500	.0625	-.9375	1.2500
-1.0000	0.0000	0.0000	-1.0000	1.0000

Recall from Step 4 that the slope of the secant, for any ΔX starting from $X = 1$, is equal to $2 + \Delta X$. While actual values of ΔY have been calculated, a simpler method of solving for the slope of the secant is to add ΔX to 2. In any event, as $\Delta X \to 0$, the slope of the secant then approaches 2. Therefore, the derivative at $X = 1$ is $f'(1) = 2$.

While the delta method of calculating derivatives is accurate and insightful, it is also tedious and time-consuming. Once the concept of the derivative is understood, it is more efficient to use short-cut rules that save time. These rules are presented in the following section.

Rules for Differentiation

The following rules facilitate the calculation of derivative functions. The types of functions, and operations on functions for which these rules apply, are those most commonly encountered in economic models. These rules can be used in isolation, or for more complicated functions, they can be combined. Each rule will be stated in general form, followed by a specific application. The application in turn is followed by comments regarding the importance and uses of that rule.

Rule 1: The derivative of a constant, or constant function, is zero. If Y $= f(X) = b_0$, where b_0 is a constant, then $dY/dX = f'(X) = 0$. This result has been demonstrated previously and can be easily verified using the delta method. When Y is a constant (i.e., doesn't vary with X), then the slope must be zero.

Rule 2: The derivative of the **identity function** is equal to 1. The identity function associates for each value of X an identical value for Y. As such, the identity function is given by $Y = f(X) = X$. Its derivative, $dY/dX = f'(X) = 1$. The identity function is a special case of a linear function, which emanates from the origin. Its graph is a 45° line, emanating from the origin and possessing a constant slope $= 1$. Rule 2 can be easily verified using the delta method.

Rule 3—Power Rule: If $Y = f(X) = X^n$, where n is a constant power to which X is raised, then $dY/dX = f'(X) = nX^{n-1}$. The derivative of $Y = f(X) = X^2$, which was solved using the delta method, could be solved more rapidly using Rule 3. In that example, $n = 2$, so $dY/dX = 2X^{2-1} = 2X^1 = 2X$. Notice that Rule 2 is a special case of this rule, when n

= 1. In other words, $Y = f(X) = X$ can also be expressed as $Y = f(X) = X^1$. The derivative, $dY/dX = f'(X) = 1X^{1-1} = 1X^0 = 1$, since $X^0 = 1$. In fact, anything raised to the 0 power is equal to 1.

Rule 4—Generalized Power Rule: If $Y = f(X) = b_2X^n$, where b_2 and n are constants, then $dY/dX = f'(X) = nb_2X^{n-1}$. The function, $Y = f(X) = 10X^{1/2}$, has as the derivative, $dY/dX = f'(X) = 1/2(10)X^{1/2-1} = 5X^{-1/2}$. This can also be expressed as $5/\sqrt{X}$, since anything raised to the 1/2 power is its square root, and a negative exponent is the reciprocal of the variable to that positive exponent. In this case, $X^{-1/2} = 1/X^{1/2} = 1/\sqrt{X}$, which is then multiplied by 5, yielding $5/\sqrt{X}$. The three preceding rules are all special cases of this rule. Rule 3 evolves when $b_2 = 1$, while Rule 2 is a special case where $b_2 = 1$ and $n = 1$ simultaneously. Rule 1 evolves when $n = 0$ and $b_2 = b_0$. In that case $Y = b_0X^0$, and its derivative, $dY/dX = 0(b_0)X^{0-1} = 0X^{-1} = 0$. In addition, we have the following corollary.

Corollary 1 to Rule 4: If $Y = f(X) = b_1X$, where b_1 is a constant, then $dY/dX = f'(X) = b_1$. The type of function specified above is a linear function emanating from the origin. In Chapter 2 it was demonstrated that such a function has a constant slope equal to b_1. This result is a special case of Rule 4 where $n = 1$ and $b_2 = b_1$. In that event $Y = f(X) = b_1X^1$, and correspondingly its derivative is $dY/dX = f'(X) = 1(b_1)X^{1-1} = b_1X^0 = b_1(1) = b_1$, since $X^0 = 1$.

Rule 5—The Sum–Difference Rule: If $u(X)$ and $v(X)$ are two functions of X, and $Y = f(X) = u(X) \pm v(X)$, then $dY/dX = f'(X) = du/dX \pm dv/dX$, or $u'(X) \pm v'(X)$. Consider the general linear function given by, $Y = b_0 + b_1X$. Letting $u(X) = b_0$ and $v(X) = b_1X$ yields $Y = u(X) + v(X)$. By Rule 1, we have $u'(X) = 0$, and by the corollary to Rule 4 we have $v'(X) = b_1$. Therefore, by Rule 5 we have $dY/dX = u'(X) + v'(X) = 0 + b_1 = b_1$. This well-known result has been demonstrated in Chapter 2 and can be verified using the delta method. As another example, consider the quadratic function $Y = 3X^2 - 2X$. In this case $u(X) = 3X^2$, and $v(X) = 2X$ so that $Y = u(X) - v(X)$. From Rule 4 we obtain $u'(X) = 2(3)X^{2-1} = 6X^1 = 6X$, and from the corollary to Rule 4 we have $v'(X) = 2$. Therefore, using the sum difference rule (Rule 5) for $Y = u(X) - v(X)$, the derivative obtained is $dY/dX = 6X - 2$.

The usefulness of this rule cannot be overstated. While the rule was stated for the algebraic sum, or difference, of two functions, it is valid for the sum of any finite number of functions. In its more general form it could be stated as, "the derivative of the sum of any finite number of differentiable functions is equal to the sum of the derivatives of those functions." Recall that subtraction is equivalent to the addition of negative values. Therefore, both additions and subtractions are included by the word **sum**. This generalized rule allows us to easily calculate the derivative of a multi-term function (e.g., polynomial function). Since each term within the function is a function itself, the derivative of a multi-term function is equal to the sum of the derivatives of each of the terms in that function.

Rule 6—Product Rule: If $u = u(X)$ and $v = v(X)$ are two functions of X, and $Y = f(X) = u \times v$, then the derivative, $dY/dX = u(X) \times v'(X) + v(X) \times u'(X) = u \times dv/dX + v \times du/dX$, where u' and v' are the derivatives of u and v respectively. In other words, if Y is the product of two functions $u(X)$ and $v(X)$, then the derivative is equal to the first function, $u(X)$, times the derivative of the second function, $v'(X)$, plus the second function, $v(X)$, times the derivative of the first function, $u'(X)$. Consider the function $Y = (3X^3 + 6X^2 + 5X - 10)(2X^4 - 3X^2 + 7)$. In this case let $u(X) = (3X^3 + 6X^2 + 5X - 10)$ and $v(X) = (2X^4 - 3X^2 + 7)$. By use of Rules 4 and 5 we have $u'(X) = 3(3)X^{3-1} + 2(6)X^{2-1} + 1(5)X^0 - 0 = 9X^2 + 12X + 5$, and $v'(X) = 4(2)X^{4-1} - 2(3)X^{2-1} + 0 = 8X^3 - 6X$. Therefore by Rule 6, $dY/dX = (3X^3 + 6X^2 + 5X - 10)(8X^3 - 6X) + (2X^4 - 3X^2 + 7)(9X^2 + 12X + 5)$. Similar to Rule 5, this rule can be generalized to the product of a finite number of functions by repeated use of this rule. Rules 3 and 4, the power and generalized power rules, can be shown to be special cases of the generalization of this rule.

Rule 7—Quotient Rule: If $u = u(X)$ and $v = v(X)$ are two functions of X, and $Y = u(X)/v(X)$, then $dY/dX = [v(X) \times u'(X) - u(X) \times v'(X)]/[v(X)]^2 = [v \times du/dX - u \times dv/dX]/v^2$. In other words, when Y is the quotient of two functions, the derivative, dY/dX, is equal to the denominator times the derivative of the numerator, minus the numerator times the derivative of the denominator, all divided by the square of the denominator. When $u = 5X^2 + 10X + 3$, $v = 2X - 1$, and $Y = u/v = (5X^2 + 10X + 3)/(2X - 1)$, then (by Rules 4 and 5) $u'(X) = du/dX = 10X + 10$, and $v'(X) = dv/dX = 2$. Therefore $dY/dX = [(2X - 1)(10X + 10) - (5X^2 + 10X + 3)(2)]/(2X - 1)^2$. The primary applications of this rule are for calculating the slope of average functions, which are the quotients of two functions, or of inverse functions, which are the reciprocals of another function.

Rule 8—Chain Rule for Composite Functions: If $Y = f(u)$ and $u = u(X)$, then $Y = f[u(X)]$ is a composite function whose independent variable is X. The expression $f[u(X)]$ is read "f of u of X" where f and u are the names of the functions. Composite functions of this type have as a derivative, $dY/dX = (dY/du)(du/dX)$. Consider the function $Y = f(u) = u^2$ where $u = 3X^2 + 2X - 6$. By Rule 3, we obtain $dY/du = 2u$, while by Rules 4 and 5 we have $du/dX = 6X + 2$. Therefore by the chain rule, $dY/dX = (2u)(6X + 2) = 2(3X^2 + 2X - 6)(6X + 2)$.

The chain rule allows us to simplify the differentiation of a complex function by use of substitution. The function $Y = [3X^3 + 9X - 2]^{10}$ can be represented as $Y = u^{10}$, where $u = 3X^3 + 9X - 2$. Instead of raising that expression to the tenth power and then using Rules 4 and 5 to solve for the derivative, we simply substitute $u = 3X^3 + 9X - 2$, and use the chain rule. The derivative, $dY/dX = (dY/du)(du/dX) = (10u^9)$ $(9X^2 + 9) = 10(3X^3 + 9X - 2)^9(9X^2 + 9)$. The power rule (Rule 3) helps in calculating dY/du, while Rules 4 and 5 simplify the calculation of du/dX.

While eight rules have been presented, only Rules 4–8 are required, since the first three rules are special cases of Rule 4. Rule 4 provides a means for differentiating a particular type of of function, while Rules 5–8 refer to operations on functions of any type. Typically, Rules 4–8 are sufficient to differentiate most functions encountered in economic applications. There exist, however, functions that are not covered by these rules. Logarithmic, exponential, and trigonometric functions would be examples of this type. Rules exist for the differentiation of these types of functions, and they are accessible in any college calculus text.

Implicit Differentiation

Functions of the form $Y = f(X)$, where the variable Y is isolated and is explicitly expressed as a function of X, are termed **explicit functions**. The rules for differentiation discussed earlier have all relied on the fact that only explicit functions have been utilized. There are, however, expressions involving both Y and X, where the variable Y is not isolated. When it is possible to associate a unique value of Y with each value of X over some domain, possibly by restricting the range, the expression is said to define Y as an implicit function of X. Expressions of this type are called **implicit functions**. In some instances, it is easy to solve the implicit function for Y in terms of X, in essence transforming it into an explicit function. In other cases it may be difficult or impossible to do so. In either event, methods of finding dY/dX of an implicit function exist. These methods are termed implicit differentiation, and they allow us to operate on implicit functions directly. Moreover, implicit differentiation can be viewed as an application of the chain rule.

The typical form of an implicit function, which implicitly is a univariate function of X, is given by $F(Y, X) = b_0$, where b_0 is a constant. The addition or subtraction of a constant to a function creates a new function, whose value differs from the original by that constant. Therefore, without a loss of generality, b_0 can be replaced by zero, as is frequently done.

When an explicit function of the form $Y = f(X)$ exists, it is always possible to transform it into an implicit function. This is done by subtracting $f(X)$ from both sides of the equation, yielding $F(Y, X) = 0$, where $F(Y, X) = Y - f(X)$. Consider the explicit function $Y = X^2 + 2$. In implicit form this could be expressed as $F(Y, X) = Y - X^2 - 2 = 0$. Alternatively, the equation $Y - X^2 = 2$ is an equivalent form of this implicit function.

While an explicit function can always be easily transformed into an implicit one, the reverse is not necessarily true. In fact, implicit differentiation is most useful when it is difficult or impossible to transform an implicit function into an explicit one. In addition, there are implicit functions that can be transformed into more than one explicit function. In those cases, the derivative solved by implicit differentiation holds for each of the corresponding explicit functions.

The major advantage of implicit differentiation is that it allows us to calculate dY/dX directly from the implicit function without transforming it into an explicit function. Moreover, the method of implicit differentiation described below involves a straightforward application of the rules discussed in the previous section. A simple method of implicit differentiation involves the following three steps:

Step 1: Treat both sides of the equation that define the implicit function as explicit functions of X. The right-hand side is the constant, b_0, which is a constant function of X. This is true, independent of the value of b_0, i.e., whether $b_0 = 0$ or $b_0 \neq 0$. The left-hand side of the equation can be treated as an explicit function of X by assuming that $Y = f(X)$. In that event, $F(Y, X) = F(f(X), X)$, which is a univariate function of X. This is true by virtue of the fact that, for each value of X, there corresponds a unique value $f(X) = Y$, and for each admissible pair of values (Y, X), there corresponds a unique value for $F(Y, X)$. It follows that the value of the function F is uniquely determined by the value of X.

Step 2: Differentiate both sides of the equation defining the implicit function, with respect to X. This step is permissible since both sides are treated as functions of X. The derivative of the right-hand side, b_0, is equal to 0, by Rule 1. The derivative of the left-hand side is more complicated, as $F(Y, X)$ may contain terms, each of which may be a function of Y, X or both. Whenever a term is a function of Y, or Y and X, the variable Y should be treated as a function of X. The derivative of that term will necessarily require the use of the chain rule. As such, the derivative of that term with respect to X is the product of its derivative with respect to Y, times the derivative of Y with respect to X. However, the derivative of Y with respect to X is dY/dX. Therefore, the derivative of the left-hand side will contain terms involving dY/dX. Terms that are functions of X alone can be treated in the conventional manner using the rules from the previous section. Since they do not contain Y, their derivatives will not contain dY/dX.

Step 3: Algebraically, solve the equation generated in Step 2 for dY/dX. This is done by isolating all terms involving dY/dX on one side of the equation. Due to the chain rule, each term containing dY/dX will be the product of some function of X, Y, or both, times dY/dX. These terms can be consolidated due to their common factor, dY/dX. The result is some function of X, Y, or both, times dY/dX. The derivative, dY/dX, can then be isolated by dividing both sides of the equation by that function. This is permissible as long as the value of that function is not equal to zero.

This method can be better understood by means of a concrete example. Consider the implicit function given by X^2

+ $Y^2 = 9$, or alternatively as $X^2 + Y^2 - 9 = 0$. In this latter formulation, we can differentiate both sides of the equation with respect to X, if Y is treated as f(X). Using the symbol $d(\ )/dX$ to denote the derivative of each term with respect to X, yields $d(X^2)/dX + d(Y^2)/dX + d(-9)/dX = d(0)/dX$. This result is due to the sum-difference rule (Rule 5). Solving for the derivative of each term gives us $d(X^2/dX) = 2X$, by the power rule (Rule 3), and $d(Y^2)/dX = 2Y(dY/dX)$, by the chain rule (Rule 8). The derivative of Y^2 with respect to $Y = 2Y$, by the power rule. The chain rule informs us that the derivative of Y^2 with respect to X is the product of the aforementioned derivative, $2Y$, times the derivative of Y with respect to X, dY/dX. Finally, $d(-9)/dX = 0$, by Rule 1 (i.e., the derivative of a constant is zero) and $d(0)dX = 0$, again by Rule 1. Using these results yields $2X + 2Y(dY/dX) + 0 = 0$, or more simply, $2X + 2Y(dY/dX) = 0$. Isolating terms involving dY/dX, on the right, can be accomplished by subtracting 2X from both sides of the equation. The result is given by $2Y(dY/dX) = -2X$. Finally, dividing both sides by 2Y yields $dY/dX = -2X/2Y = -X/Y$. This last step is allowable only if $Y \neq 0$; therefore, points where $Y = 0$ must be excluded, as the derivative does not exist at those points. Notice that we are able to solve for the derivative, dY/dX, without solving the equation for Y. Any pair of values (X, Y) satisfying the equation $X^2 + Y^2 - 9 = 0$ will have as the instantaneous slope the value given by $-X/Y$.

This result can be verified by solving the equation as an explicit function of X and taking the derivative of the explicit function. Solving the equation for Y in terms of X can be accomplished as follows:

1) Isolate terms involving Y on the left. The equation $X^2 + Y^2 - 9 = 0$ can be written as $Y^2 = 9 - X^2$ by subtracting $(X^2 - 9)$ from both sides of the equation.

2) Solve explicitly for Y. This is done by taking the square root of both sides of the equation. This yields $\sqrt{Y^2} = \sqrt{9 - X^2}$. However, $\sqrt{Y^2} = \pm\, Y$, so two explicit functions are defined by this implicit equation. These functions are $Y = \sqrt{9 - X^2}$ and $Y = -\sqrt{9 - X^2}$.

The derivatives of these functions can be solved in the conventional manner. Recall that the square root of an expression is equivalent to raising that expression to the one half, or .5, power. Let u = u(X) = 9 − X^2. The two functions can now be expressed as Y = $u^{1/2}$ and Y = $-u^{1/2}$, respectively. Using the power rule together with the chain rule on the first function yields dY/dX = (1/2 $u^{-1/2}$)(du/dX). Since u = 9 − X^2, du/dX = d(9)/dX − d(+X^2)/dX by the sum–difference rule. However, d(9)/dX = 0 by Rule 1, and d(X^2)/dX = 2X by Rule 3, the power rule. Therefore, du/dX = 0 − 2X = −2X. Substituting this result back into the dY/dX equation yields dY/dX = (1/2)($u^{-1/2}$)(−2X) = $-Xu^{-1/2}$. However, $u^{-1/2}$ = 1/$u^{1/2}$, so dY/dX = $-X/u^{1/2}$. Replacing u by 9 − X^2 yields dY/dX = $-X/\sqrt{9 - X^2}$. For this function, Y = $\sqrt{9 - X^2}$, so that dY/dX = −X/Y. This result is identical to that found by implicit differentiation.

The same procedure can be utilized in solving for the derivative of the second function, Y = $-\sqrt{9 - X^2}$ = $- u^{1/2}$. The chain rule tells us that dY/dX = (dY/du)(du/dX). The generalized power rule tells us that, dY/du =(−1/2)$u^{-1/2}$, while du/dX has already been solved and equals −2X. Therefore, dY/dX = (−1/2)($u^{-1/2}$)(−2X) = $Xu^{-1/2}$. Utilizing the simplifications used for the first function yields dY/dX = $X/u^{1/2}$ = $X/\sqrt{9 - X^2}$. For this function Y = $-u^{1/2}$ = $-\sqrt{9 - X^2}$; therefore, the denominator of the derivative $\sqrt{9 - X^2}$ = −Y. Substituting this result yields dY/dX = X/(−Y) = −X/Y, which is the result achieved more easily through implicit differentiation. Notice that although two explicit functions correspond to the one implicit function, the derivative found through implicit differentiation satisfies both functions.

The previous example illustrates that even when it is possible to transform an implicit function into an explicit one, there is no need to do so. The use of implicit differentiation permits us to solve for derivatives, without that extra effort. Moreover, there are implicit functions that cannot be solved explicitly. For those functions we have no choice but to use implicit differentiation.

Consider the implicit function given by X^2 + XY + Y^5 = 3. It is impossible to express this function explicitly. However, the derivative dY/dX can be solved through implicit differentiation. Again we treat Y as a function of X. Differentiating both sides of the equation with respect to X yields d(X^2)/dX + d(XY)/dX + d(Y^5)/dX = d(3)/dX, by the sum–difference rule. In addition, by the power rule we have:

$$d(X^2)/dX = 2X$$

by the product rule:

$$d(XY)/dX = X \times d(Y)/dX + Y \times d(X)/dX$$

where:

$$d(Y)/dX = dY/dX \text{ and } d(X)/dX = 1$$

by the chain rule:

$$d(Y^5)/dX = d(Y^5)/dY \times dY/dX$$

and by Rule 1:

$$d(3)/dX = 0$$

However, $d(Y^5)/dY = 5Y^4$, so $d(Y^5)/dX = 5Y^4 (dY/dX)$.

Combining these results yields:

$$2X + X(dY/dX) + Y + 5Y^4(dY/dX) = 0$$

Consolidating terms and isolating those with dY/dX on the left results in:

$$X(dY/dX) + 5Y^4(dY/dX) = -(2X + Y), \text{ or}$$

$$(X + 5Y^4)(dY/dX) = -(2X + Y), \text{ or}$$

$$dY/dX = -(2X + Y)/(X + 5Y^4), \text{ where } (X + 5Y^4) \neq 0.$$

Economic Applications Utilizing Derivatives

The preceding sections have developed methods of calculating derivatives. These methods can now be added to our toolbox. Without these tools we could only use average slopes when dealing with nonlinear functions. With them, we can calculate the instantaneous slope of a nonlinear function almost as quickly and easily as that of a linear function. A tool, however powerful it seems, is useless unless some application exists. Fortunately, the derivative is blessed with numerous applications in economics. The remainder of this section is devoted to some of those applications.

The Derivative as Marginal Function

It has been demonstrated that the derivative of a function, $Y = f(X)$, is itself a function of X, representing the instantaneous slope of the original function. Recall from Chapter 4 that the instantaneous slope of a function is the marginal, M, of that function. Therefore, the derivative function is a marginal function as well. In the examples that follow, certain derivatives will be identified with marginal functions. We will assume throughout that the functions dealt with are univariate. In cases where the function is generally considered to be multivariate, we will assume that all causal variables except the one under consideration are constant. In that event, it is permissible to treat the function as a univariate one. The methods of calculating derivatives of multivariate functions, and their economic applications, are deferred until Chapter 8.

Example 7.1 Marginal Propensity to Consume (MPC)

A consumption function relates the level of consumption expenditures, C, to the level of disposable income, Y_d. In general functional form it could be expressed as $C = C(Y_d)$. The **marginal propensity to consume, MPC,** is the rate that consumption expenditures change in response to changes in disposable income. As such, it represents the slope of the consumption function, with respect to disposable income. Since the derivative of a function is the instantaneous slope of that function, it follows that the derivative, dC/dY_d, is another expression for the marginal propensity to consume. Consider the consumption function given by:

$$C = 300 + .9Y_d$$

where:
   C = consumption expenditures in $billions/year
   Y_d = disposable income in $billions/year

The derivative of C with respect to Y_d, dC/dY_d, is the marginal propensity to consume, MPC. Using the sum-difference rule generates $dC/dY_d = d(300)/dY_d + d(.9Y_d)/dY_d$. Further, $d(300)/dY_d = 0$, by Rule 1, and $d(.9Y_d)/dY_d = .9$, by the generalized power rule. It follows that $dC/dY_d = 0 + .9 = .9$, which implies that the MPC = .9 for all levels of Y_d. In other words, households will spend an additional $.9 or 90 cents on consumption expenditures per year, for each additional dollar received as disposable income per year.

Example 7.2 Marginal Propensity to Save (MPS)

Disposable income received by the households can either be spent on consumption expenditures or saved. The portion of disposable income not spent on consumption is termed saving, S. The level of saving depends upon the level of disposable income, Y_d. The relationship between the two is called the saving function, which could be expressed as $S = S(Y_d)$. The rate that saving changes in response to changes in disposable income is called the **marginal propensity to save**, or **MPS**. The MPS is, therefore, the slope of the saving function, which is also the derivative of that function with respect to Y_d. In general functional form, this derivative is given by dS/dY_d.

The saving function is related to the consumption function by virtue of the fact that saving plus consumption expenditures must equal disposable income. Therefore, $Y_d = C + S$ or $S = Y_d - C$. The marginal propensity to save, MPS = $dS/dY_d = d(Y_d)/dY_d - d(C)/dY_d$, by the sum difference rule. However, $d(Y_d)/dY_d = 1$, (by Rule 2) while $d(C)/dY_d$ was defined as the MPC in Example 7.1. It follows that the MPS = 1 - MPC. This general result holds for both linear and nonlinear functions. In particular, for the consumption function utilized in the previous example, the MPS = 1 - .9 = .1. This implies that for each additional dollar in disposable income per year, households will increase saving by an additional $.1 or 10 cents per year.

Example 7.3 Marginal Propensity to Invest (MPI)

The level of investment expenditures, I, is a function of the level of national income, Y. In general functional form, this can be stated as $I = I(Y)$. The rate at which firms change their investment expenditures in response to changes in national income is termed the **marginal propensi-**

ty to invest, or **MPI**. The MPI is, therefore, the slope of the investment expenditures function with respect to national income. As such the derivative of that function, dI/dY, is another expression representing the MPI.

A specific investment expenditures function might be given by:

$$I = 100 + .05Y$$

where:
  I = investment expenditures in $ billions/year
  Y = national income in $ billions/year

The marginal propensity to invest is the derivative of that function with respect to national income, Y. Utilizing the sum–difference rule generates $dI/dY = d(100)/dY + d(.05Y)/dY$. By Rules 1 and 4 we find that $d(100)/dY = 0$, and $d(.05Y)/dY = .05$. Therefore, $dI/dY = 0 + .05 = .05$. This informs us that the MPI = .05, indicating that firms in total will invest an additional $.05 or 5 cents per year for each additional dollar per year of national income. Since the derivative is a constant, this implies that the MPI is a constant for all levels of national income. Notice that in this case, as well as in Example 7.1, the functions that were specified were linear. It should be recalled from Chapter 2 that all linear functions have a constant slope. Using our present terminology, this can be translated as, "all linear functions have a constant derivative." The reverse is also true. Any function having a constant derivative is a linear function. Alternatively, when the derivative of a function is not constant, then the function is nonlinear.

Example 7.4 Marginal Product (MP)

A production function associates the maximum output attainable, Q, to each admissible combination of input levels. In general, the production function is a multivariate function. When only two inputs, capital and labor, are utilized, the production function would be:

$$Q = f(K,L)$$

where:
K = units of capital/period of time
L = units of labor/period of time

A specific example of the above would be a Cobb–Douglas production function given by:

$$Q = 10K^{.25}L^{.75}$$

where:
Q = output in units/day
K = machine hours/day
L = person hours/day

In the short run, capital may be a fixed input while labor is a variable input. Assume in the short run that K = 16 and is fixed. In that event, the short run production function is $Q = 10(16)^{.25}L^{.75} = 10(2)L^{.75} = 20L^{.75}$, which is a univariate function of L. The marginal product (MP) of any input is the rate of change of output caused by changes in the amount of that input. Specially, in this example the marginal product of labor, MP_L, is the rate of change of output caused by changes in the amount of labor input. This is simply the slope of the production function with respect to labor. It is, therefore, also the derivative, dQ/dL. For the specific function utilized, this derivative can be calculated using the generalized power rule. It is given by $dQ/dL = .75(20)L^{.75-1} = 15L^{-.25}$, which is also the MP_L function. As opposed to the previous examples, where the derivative was constant, in this case its value depends on the value of L. For example, when L = 1, the $MP_L = 15(1)^{-.25} = 15$. Alternatively when L = 16, the MP_L is $15(16)^{-.25} = 15/\sqrt[4]{16} = 15/2 = 7.5$. Notice, however, that the marginal product of labor is always positive for nonnegative values of L. This implies that a direct relationship always exists between Q and L.

Example 7.5 Marginal Cost (MC)

Total cost, C, is a function of the quantity produced, Q, or C = C(Q). Total cost can be decomposed into its two component parts, fixed cost, FC, and variable cost, VC. This relationship can be expressed as C = FC + VC. Fixed cost is the cost that does not vary with quantity and, therefore, FC = FC(Q), where FC is a constant function of Q. Variable cost is the cost that varies with quantity and, therefore, VC = VC(Q), where VC is not a constant function. **Marginal cost, MC,** is the rate that total cost changes due to changes in quantity produced. It follows that marginal cost is also the slope of the total cost function with respect to quantity produced. More formally, marginal cost is the derivative of the total cost function with respect to quantity produced, i.e., dC/dQ.

The derivative dC/dQ = dFC/dQ + dVC/dQ by the sum–difference rule. This implies that the slope of the total cost function is equal to the sum of the slopes of the fixed cost and variable cost functions. However, the fixed cost function is a constant function. Therefore, by Rule 1, its slope and, therefore, its derivative, dFC/dQ, is equal to zero. Adding zero to the slope of the variable cost function yields the slope of the variable cost function. It follows that the slope of the total cost function at every Q is equal to the slope of the variable cost function for that Q. This implies that dC/dQ = dVC/dQ. Recall that dC/dQ is the marginal cost. We can see that another way of viewing marginal cost is as the rate of change of variable cost with respect to quantity produced.

Consider the specific total cost function given by:

$$C = 50 + 2Q + Q^2$$

where:
C = total cost in \$/day
Q = output in units/day

For this function, it should be clear that FC = 50, and VC = $2Q + Q^2$. The marginal cost function is given by MC = dC/dQ = dFC/dQ + dVC/dQ. However, dFC/dQ = 0, by Rule 1, and dVC/dQ = 2 + 2Q, by application of the sum–difference rule together with the generalized power rule. Therefore, MC = 2 + 2Q. Notice that marginal cost in this case is always positive and directly related to Q, for all nonnegative values of Q.

Example 7.6 Marginal Revenue (MR)

Total Revenue, R, is the value of total sales and, therefore, depends on the quantity sold, Q. In other words, R = R(Q). A firm may decide on a specific price, P, to charge per unit of output. The price may itself depend upon the quantity, Q, it plans on selling. In that event, P = P(Q), i.e., P is a function of Q. Moreover, in that event, total revenue is given by the product of price times quantity or R = P x Q, or R = P(Q) x Q. In this latter form it is clear that the total revenue function is the product of two functions of Q. Remember that Q is itself a function of Q (i.e., the identity function).

Marginal Revenue, MR, is the rate of change of total revenue with respect to quantity. It follows that marginal revenue is the slope of the total revenue function with respect to quantity, Q, as well as the derivative, dR/dQ. This derivative can be calculated using Rule 6 — the product rule. This derivative is given by:

$$MR = dR/dQ = P(Q) \times 1 + (dP(Q)/dQ) \times Q = P + (dP/dQ) \times Q$$

In this form, we can see that marginal revenue has two component parts. The first part is the price per unit, P. This represents the direct effect on total revenue of increasing quantity. Each additional unit sold will directly increase total revenue by P. The second part, (dP/dQ) x Q, represents the indirect effect on total revenue of increasing Q. The term dP/dQ represents the slope of the demand curve as it is conventionally drawn. It represents the rate at which price must change in order to sell additional units. When the demand curve is negatively sloped, dP/dQ will be negative. This implies that in order to sell additional units the price must be lowered. Since the same price is charged for all units, the price is lowered not only on the marginal units but also on all previous units. Therefore, the revenue on these previous units is lower by (dP/dQ) x Q than what it was before extra units were offered for sale. It follows that a price-making firm having a negatively sloped demand curve will have MR < P. Alternatively, the same formula gives us the MR for a price-taking firm. For a price taker, the price is treated as given, i.e., a constant and consequently dP/dQ = 0. In other words, for a price taker the price that can be charged is independent of the quantity offered for sale. In that event MR = P + 0 = P. This is the standard result for a perfectly competitive firm. Notice that the formula works both for price makers as well as price takers.

When the inverse demand function P(Q) is specified as:

$$P = 98 - 2Q$$

where:

P = price in dollars/unit
Q = quantity in units/day

two methods can be utilized to solve for marginal revenue. The first is a straightforward application of the product rule. Recall that MR = $P(Q)$ + $(dP(Q)/dQ)$ × Q. Since $P(Q)$ = 98 - 2Q, $dP(Q)/dQ$ = $d(98)/dQ$ - $d(2Q)/dQ$, using the sum-difference rule. However $d(98)/dQ$ = 0, by Rule 1, and $d(2Q)/dQ$ = 2, by the generalized power rule. Therefore, $dP(Q)/dQ$ = -2. Substituting for $P(Q)$ and its derivative in the marginal revenue function yields:

$$MR = (98 - 2Q) + (-2)Q = 98 - 2Q - 2Q = 98 - 4Q$$

Alternatively, one could solve for the total revenue function in terms of Q. Since R = $P(Q)$ × Q and $P(Q)$ = 98 - 2Q, we have R = $(98 - 2Q)$ × Q = $98Q - 2Q^2$. The derivative dR/dQ, which is MR, is given by MR = dR/dQ = $d(98Q)/dQ$ - $d(2Q^2)/dQ$, by the sum-difference rule. Utilizing the generalized power rule for both terms yields:

$$MR = 1 \times 98 \times Q^{1-1} - 2 \times 2 \times Q^{2-1} = 98 - 4Q$$

Example 7.7 Marginal Revenue Product (MRP)

A problem faced by producers is determining the optimal level of an input to employ. In order to solve this problem, several factors must be considered. One important factor is the rate at which total revenue changes as the level of the input employed changes. This rate of change is referred to as the **marginal revenue product** of that input, or simply **MRP**. When the input in question is labor, the marginal revenue product of labor, MRP_L, is the slope of the total revenue function with respect to L, or the derivative of R with respect to L, dR/dL. The impact on R of a change in L is somewhat complex, as it involves two calculations. The most direct impact of changing L is that total output, Q, changes. The rate of change of Q with respect to L, dQ/dL, is the marginal product of labor, MP_L. The MP_L informs us of the marginal contribution of an additional unit of labor in physical (output) terms, rather than in monetary terms. To convert the physical contribution into a monetary one requires knowledge of the rate at which R changes with respect to Q. This rate of change is simply marginal revenue, $MR = dR/dQ$. The MRP_L then is simply the $MR \times MP_L$, and it derives its name from this relationship. In other words, if an additional unit of labor generates 2 extra units of output per day (i.e., $MP_L = 2$) and each additional unit of output per day generates $5/day extra revenue (i.e., $MR = 5$), then the MRP_L of that unit of labor is $5 \times 2 = \$10$/unit of labor.

This result can be derived in a more formal manner. Recall from Example 7.6 that $R = R(Q)$, and from Example 7.4 that Q in the short run was a function of L. Combining these relationships, we can express R as a composite function of L, given by $R = R[Q(L)]$. The derivative of this function is the MRP_L.

This derivative can be solved by use of the chain rule for composite functions. It is given by:

$$dR/dL = (dR/dQ)(dQ/dL)$$

Recall that $dR/dQ = MR$ and $dQ/dL = MP_L$, so that the marginal revenue product of labor is simply the marginal revenue times the marginal product of labor, as was claimed earlier. Utilizing the functions from Examples 7.6 and 7.4 and evaluating them at $L = 1$ yields:

$$MRP_L = (98 - 4Q)(15L^{-.25})$$

However, the production function is given by $Q = 20L^{.75}$. This implies that, for $L = 1$, $Q = 20$. Using these values in the above equation yields:

$$MRP_L = [98 - 4(20)](15 \times 1^{-.25}) = (98 - 80)(15 \times 1) = 18 \times 15$$

$$= \$270/\text{person hour/day}$$

Example 7.8 Marginal Rate of Substitution (MRS)

An individual's total utility depends on the quantities of each good consumed per period of time, ceteris paribus. In the case of only two goods whose quantities are denoted Y and X, the utility function could be expressed as:

$$U = U(Y, X)$$

where:

U = total utility in utils/period of time
Y = units of good Y/period of time
X = units of good X/period of time

Combinations of the two goods that generate the same level of utility are referred to as **indifference curves**. It is generally assumed that increases in either good alone will increase utility. Therefore, indifference curves tend to be negatively sloped. This implies that increases in one good must be offset by decreases in the other good in order to keep total utility constant. The negative of the slope of the indifference curve is the **marginal rate of substitution, or MRS**. The MRS is the rate at which a consumer is willing to give up units of Y for additional units of X, while holding total utility constant.

Consider the specific utility function, $U = YX$, which is defined for nonnegative values of Y and X. An indifference curve can be constructed by setting U equal to some specified value. The indifference curve for $U = 100$ is given as $100 = YX$. The combinations of Y and X that satisfy this equation define Y as an implicit function of X. The slope of the indifference curve is the derivative dY/dX, whose value is the negative of that of the marginal rate of substitution. Treating Y as a function of X, and differentiating both sides of the equation with respect to X, yields $d(100)/dX = d(YX)/dX$. Using the chain rule together with the product rule lets us solve for $d(YX)/dX$ as:

$$d(YX)/dX = Y \times 1 + XdY/dX$$

In addition, $d(100)/dX = 0$, by Rule 1. Substituting these values in the above equation yields:

$$0 = Y + X(dY/dX)$$

Solving for dY/dX, we have $-X(dY/dX) = Y$, or $dY/dX = Y/-(X) = -(Y/X)$, for all $X \neq 0$.

The MRS is therefore given as (Y/X). Notice that while we have chosen the indifference curve for $U = 100$, the derivative found holds for any indifference curve. This results from the fact that, along any indifference curve, U is a constant. The derivative of any constant is always equal to zero. Therefore, the slope of any indifference curve from this utility function is $-(Y/X)$.

An alternative method of calculating the slope of the indifference curve is to define Y as an explicit function of X and solve for the derivative. Since $100 = YX$, we can also state that $Y = 100/X = 100X^{-1}$. Using the generalized power rule on the latter expression yields $dY/dX = (-1)(100)X^{-1-1} = -100X^{-2} = -100/X^2$. However, $Y = 100/X$ so $dY/dX = -(100/X)/X$, or $-(Y/X)$. When $Y = 50$ and $X = 2$, $dY/dX = -25$, and the MRS = 25. This implies that the consumer would be willing to trade at the rate of 25 units of Y for each additional unit of X. This result holds for infinitesimal changes in X.

Example 7.9 Marginal Rate of Product Transformation (MRPT)

A production possibilities frontier or curve shows the maximum amounts of two goods, Y and X, that a society could produce in a period of time, given the level of resources at its disposal and its technology. The slope of a production possibilities curve is negative, indicating that more of one good can be produced only if society produces less of the other good. Ignoring the negative sign, the numerical component of the slope indicates the opportunity cost of an additional unit of X, in terms of foregone units of Y, at the margin. A more sophisticated name for this opportunity cost is the **marginal rate of product transformation**, or **MRPT**. When the slope of the production possibilities curve is given as dY/dX, the MRPT is that value, times negative one.

In Example 2.6, the production possibilities frontier was given as,

$$Y = 9 - X^2$$

where:

    Y = quantity of good Y in billions of units per period of time
    X = quantity of good X in billions of units per period of time

In addition, the average slope was calculated for various intervals. Using techniques developed in this chapter we can calculate the instantaneous slope at each value of X. It is given by $dY/dX = d(9)/dX - d(X^2)/dX$, by the sum–difference rule. However, $d(9)dX = 0$, by Rule 1, and $d(X^2)/dX = 2X$, by the generalized power rule. Therefore, $dY/dX = 0 - 2X = -2X$. Furthermore, the MRPT is given by $-dY/dX = 2X$, for all admissible values of X. This result can be compared to the values of the average slope, computed in Example 2.6.

While in this case the production possibilities curve was specified as an explicit function, it is not uncommon for it to be specified in implicit form. The production possibilities curve in this example could have been stated in implicit form as $Y + X^2 = 9$, or $Y + X^2 - 9 = 0$. In this form, implicit differentiation could be used to find dY/dX and the MRPT.

The Derivative and Elasticities

In Chapter 5, the elasticity of T with respect to X, $E_{T,X}$ was defined as the percentage change in T caused by a percentage change in X, ceteris paribus. One formula given for this elasticity was $E_{T,X} = (\Delta T/\Delta X) \times (X/T) = (\Delta T/\Delta X)/(T/X)$. In the latter formulation, $(\Delta T/\Delta X)$ is the slope or marginal, M, of T with respect to X, while the average of T with respect to X, A, is given by (T/X). Therefore, the elasticity of T with respect to X is the ratio of the marginal to the average, or M/A. In this chapter, we discovered that when T can be treated as a univariate function of X, the derivative, dT/dX, represents the instantaneous slope of the function. As such, dT/dX also represents the marginal function, M. Substituting this result into the elasticity formula yields:

$$E_{T,X} = (dT/dX)/(T/X)$$

The advantage of expressing elasticities in this form is for the calculation of point elasticities of nonlinear functions. Notice that in Chapter 5, when point elasticities were introduced, linear functions were utilized. Linear functions have constant slopes which are easy to calculate. In order to calculate a point elasticity, the values of T and X must be known, as well as the slope at that point. In Example 5.6, a linear demand function was utilized. The point price elasticity of demand was calculated at various points on that function. The use of a linear function was necessitated by the fact that the instantaneous slope could be calculated without resorting to derivatives. It is obviously true that dQ/dP could be used in place of $\Delta Q/\Delta P$ in that example. Both have a constant value equal to -2.

For nonlinear functions, the arc elasticity was preferable since the instantaneous slope could not be calculated without resorting to derivatives. The arc elasticity represents the average elasticity over an interval and depends upon the average slope over that interval. When the function is known, one can easily calculate a point elasticity, at any point on that function, by first calculating the derivative and evaluating it at that point. This generates the marginal, M, at that point, which can then be divided by the average, A, to find the elasticity.

Example 7.10 Constant Elasticity Functions

In Chapter 5 it was stated that, in general, linear functions do not have a constant elasticity. It was stated without proof that functions of the form, $T = b_1X^k$ had a constant elasticity equal to k. This proposition will now be proved.

In order to have a constant elasticity equal to k, the ratio of the marginal to the average must be equal to k for all admissible values of X. This implies that $M/A = k$, or $M = kA$. Recall that the marginal, M, is equal to dT/dX, while the average, A, is equal to T/X. For the function $T = b_1X^k$, the derivative dT/dX can be calculated using the generalized power rule. It is given by $dT/dX = kb_1X^{k-1} = M(X)$. The average, A, can be calculated by dividing T by X. For this function it is given by $T/X = (b_1X^k)/X = b_1X^{k-1} = A(X)$. The elasticity of T with respect to X is the ratio of the two, given by $E_{T,X} = M(X)/A(X) = (kb_1X^{k-1})/(b_1X^{k-1}) = k$. Since k is a constant, the elasticity is a constant equal to k. Notice that this is true independent of the value of X, as long as $b_1X^{k-1} \neq 0$.

Consider the demand function given by:

$$Q = 100/P = 100P^{-1}$$

where:
    Q = quantity demanded in units/week
    P = price in dollars/unit

The price elasticity of demand is given by:

$$E_{Q,P} = (dQ/dP)/(Q/P)$$

By the generalized power rule we have:

$$dQ/dP = (-1)(100)(P^{-1-1}) = -100P^{-2} = -100/P^2$$

The average, $Q/P = 100P^{-1}/P = 100P^{-2} = 100/P^2$. The price elasticity of demand, therefore, is:

$$E_{Q,P} = (-100/P^2)/(100/P^2) = (-100P^2)/(100P^2) = -1$$

The demand curve specified above has a constant price elasticity of demand equal to -1. It is therefore unitary elastic throughout, indicating that each 1 percent change in price gives rise to a 1 percent change in quantity in the opposite direction.

Example 7.11 The Relationship Between $E_{Q,P}$ and Marginal Revenue

In Example 7.6, marginal revenue was defined as:

$$MR = P + (dP/dQ) \times Q$$

Utilizing the derivative concept, the price elasticity of demand was defined in Example 7.10 as:

$$E_{Q,P} = (dQ/dP)/(Q/P) = (dQ/dP) \times (P/Q)$$

These two equations, while different, are similar. Given the similarity we might suspect that the two concepts, price elasticity of demand and marginal revenue, are related. This is in fact the case, as shall be demonstrated.

The reciprocal of the price elasticity of demand is:

$$1/E_{Q,P} = (dP/dQ) \times (Q/P)$$

Multiplying both sides of this equation by P yields:

$$P/E_{Q,P} = (dP/dQ) \times Q$$

Substituting this result into the marginal revenue equation yields:

$$MR = P + (P/E_{Q,P})$$

$$MR = P(1 + 1/E_{Q,P})$$

This last equation shows that P, MR, and $E_{Q,P}$ are related. Therefore, knowledge of any two of the above is sufficient to determine the third. In general the price, P, is positive, while the price elasticity of demand, $E_{Q,P}$, is negative. Using this equation we can analyze the relationship between MR and $E_{Q,P}$.

When the demand function is perfectly elastic, $E_{Q,P} = -\infty$. In that event the limit of $1/E_{Q,P} = 0$. Therefore, MR = P(1 + 0) = P. In other words at any point, or over any interval of the demand curve, where it is perfectly price elastic, marginal revenue is equal to the price. When the demand curve is linear and negatively sloped this occurs only at the price intercept. However, the demand curve for a price taker is perfectly elastic throughout, and in that case it has already been demonstrated that MR = P for all values of Q.

When the price elasticity of demand is unitary, $E_{Q,P} = -1$. Therefore, MR = [P1 + 1/(-1)] = P[1 + (-1)] = P × (0) = 0. At a point, this implies that at that point, changes in quantity have no effect on total revenue. In other words, total revenue is stationary with respect to quantity. When this occurs over an interval it implies that all points over that interval generate the same total revenue. Consider the constant elasticity of demand function from Example 7.10, given by Q = 100/P = $100P^{-1}$. That demand function was shown to be unitary elastic throughout. Total revenue for that demand function is given by R = P × Q = P(100/P) = (100P/P) = 100, which is a constant, independent of Q. In that event, MR = 0 throughout the curve.

When the price elasticity of demand is in the relatively elastic range, $E_{Q,P} < -1$, but finite. In that event the reciprocal of the price elasticity, $1/E_{Q,P}$, is a fraction between zero and negative one, i.e., $0 > (1/E_{Q,P}) > -1$. Adding one to this amount yields a positive fraction between one and zero or, $0 < (1 + 1/E_{Q,P}) < 1$. Therefore in that case, MR is equal to a positive fraction times the price. It follows that MR is positive but less than P when demand is relatively elastic.

When demand is relatively price inelastic, $0 > E_{Q,P} > -1$. The reciprocal of the price elasticity in that case is less than -1, i.e., $(1/E_{Q,P}) < -1$. Adding the value "one" to this results in a negative number. Therefore, MR is equal to the product of P and a negative number. Given that P is positive, MR must be negative in this case. This implies that in the inelastic range total revenue and quantity are inversely related. Increases in quantity reduce total revenue, while decreases in quantity increase total revenue.

Exercise Set 7.1

1. Using the consumption function from Example 7.1, derive the saving
    function and solve for the marginal propensity to save, MPS.

2. A total revenue function is given by:

    $$R = 1000Q - 10Q^2, \text{ for } 0 \leq Q \leq 100$$

    where:
    R = total revenue in thousands of dollars per year
    Q = output in thousands of units per year

    a) Derive the marginal revenue function.
    b) For what values of Q will marginal revenue be positive? Nega-
       tive? Zero?
    c) Derive the average revenue function. When average revenue
       equals price, the graph of this function is also the demand curve.
       Draw the demand curve and its corresponding marginal revenue
       function.
    d) On the demand curve, identify the points where the price
       elasticity of demand is perfectly elastic, unitary elastic, perfectly
       inelastic and the regions where it is relatively elastic and
       relatively inelastic. This can be done directly from the inverse
       demand function derived in Part c or indirectly from information
       in Part b.

3. A total cost function is given by:

    $$C = 15Q^2 + 60, \text{ for } Q \geq 0$$

    where:
    C = total cost in thousands of dollars per year
    Q = output in thousands of units per year

    a) Derive the marginal cost function.
    b) Derive the average total cost function.
    c) Solve for the slope of the average total cost function. For what
       values of Q is it positively sloped? Negatively sloped?

4. Given the total utility function:

$$U = 100X^{.5}Y^{.5}$$

which is defined for nonnegative values of X and Y, where:

U = total utility in utils/week
X = units of good X per week
Y = units of good Y per week

a) Construct an indifference curve for U = 800, with Y as an explicit function of X.
b) Determine the marginal rate of substitution using implicit differentiation. What is the MRS when (X = 4, Y = 16)?
c) Verify the above result by forming an explicit function.
[Hint: Recall that the MRS is the negative of the slope of the indifference curve.]

5. Total cost, C, is a function of output, Q. However, in the short run, through the production function, output is a function of the level of labor input, L. In general functional form, we have:

$$C = C(Q) \text{ and } Q = f(L)$$

It is therefore possible to express total cost as a composite function of L. The slope of this function indicates the rate of change of total costs with respect to the level of labor input. It is termed the **marginal factor cost of labor, MFC_L**.

a) Use the chain rule to determine the marginal factor cost function. Give an economic interpretation to the derivatives in the above formulation.
b) Assume that the marginal factor cost of labor is constant and equal to the wage rate, W. Express marginal cost in terms of W.

6. A demand function is given as:

$$Q = 50P^{-1.5}$$

where:
Q = quantity demanded in units per day
P = price in dollars per unit

a) What is the price elasticity of demand? Does it vary as Q varies?
b) Interpret your results from Part a.
c) What are the implications for the marginal revenue function?

Maxima and Minima

The necessary condition for a point to be a maximum or minimum point is that the slope at that point is equal to zero. This condition holds for any local maximum or minimum point that lies on the interior of the domain, when the function is smooth and continuous. In Chapter 4, this condition was stated as M = 0, where M is the marginal function, evaluated at that point. In this chapter it has been demonstrated that the derivative of a function is another name for the marginal. When T, the total function, is a univariate function of the x, the derivative dT/dx represents the marginal function. Therefore, throughout Chapter 4, whenever M appears in reference to a univariate function, it can be replaced by the derivative, dT/dx. In particular, for the function T = T(x), the necessary condition for either a maximum or minimum is that dT/dx = 0, at that point.

Example 7.12 Maximum Revenue and Maximum Profit

Total revenue, R, as well as total cost, C, are both functions of the quantity produced, Q. Total profit, π, is equal to total revenue minus total cost. As such, total profit is also a function of Q. In general functional form, the relationships are:

$$R = R(Q)$$
$$C = C(Q)$$
$$\pi = \pi(Q) = R(Q) - C(Q)$$

where:
R = total revenue in dollars per period of time
C = total cost in dollars per period of time
π = total profits in dollars per period of time

In order to maximize total revenue, the necessary condition is that $dR/dQ = 0$. However, dR/dQ is just another name for marginal revenue, MR. Therefore, the necessary condition for the maximization of total revenue is that MR = 0, at that point. However, in Example 7.11 it was demonstrated that marginal revenue equals zero only if demand is unitary price elastic. Therefore, an alternative method of finding the revenue maximization point is to identify points on the demand curve that have unitary price elasticity of demand.

The necessary condition for total profits to be maximized is $d\pi/dQ = 0$. However, using the sum–difference rule we find that $d\pi/dQ = dR/dQ - dC/dQ$. The derivative $d\pi/dQ$ is simply marginal profit, Mπ. The derivative dC/dQ is marginal cost, MC, while dR/dQ is marginal revenue, MR. Therefore, marginal profit equals marginal revenue minus marginal cost, or Mπ = MR - MC. The necessary condition for a profit maximum is that marginal profit equals zero. In that event, 0 = MR - MC, or as it is customarily presented, MR = MC. Marginal cost is the rate that total cost changes in response to changes in quantity. In general, total cost will increase as more is produced and, consequently, MC > 0. In exceptional cases where all costs are fixed costs, marginal cost would equal zero. It is implausible, however, that marginal cost could be negative. That would imply that total cost actually decreased as quantity increased. Therefore, MC ≥ 0. In order to maximize profit, MR = MC. Since MC is nonnegative, at a profit maximum, so must MR be nonnegative. In the rare case where MC = 0, profit maximization requires that MR = 0 also. In that event profit maximization is identical to revenue maximization. The profit or revenue maximizing point is where MR = 0 or demand is unitary price elastic. Generally, however, MC > 0 and, therefore, at a profit maximizing point, MR is positive as well. In Example 7.11 we saw that marginal revenue will be positive only if the price elasticity of demand is in the relatively elastic range. Therefore, covering both cases, a profit maximizer will never produce on the inelastic portion of the demand curve. In addition, when marginal cost is positive, the profit maximizing point differs from that which maximizes revenue.

These results are illustrated in Figure 7.2. Panel A of that figure portrays total revenue and total cost functions. The graphs are drawn under the assumption that total revenue is a quadratic function of quantity while total cost is a cubic function of quantity. Panel B depicts the total profit function. Subtracting total cost from total revenue in panel A enables us to derive the total profit function. Finally, panel C shows the marginal cost, marginal revenue, and marginal profit functions. These graphs respectively represent the slopes or derivatives of the total cost, total revenue, and total profit functions with respect to quantity.

In panel A, the vertical intercept of the total cost function represents fixed cost. For $Q < Q_2$, total cost exceeds total revenue, implying that profits are negative or that the firm is incurring losses. At Q_2 and Q_4, total revenue equals total cost, so profits equal zero at those points. Those points are sometimes referred to as **break–even points**. For $Q_2 < Q < Q_4$, total revenue exceeds total costs, so total profit is positive over this interval. For $Q > Q_4$, total cost again exceeds total revenue, implying that negative profits or losses are being made. At Q_1 the tangent lines drawn to the total revenue and total cost curves are parallel, indicating that the slopes of these functions are equal at Q_1. The same is true at Q_3. Since the slopes, or derivatives, of those curves are the marginal revenue and marginal cost, respectively, at Q_1 and Q_3, MR = MC. This result is depicted in panel C. However, marginal profit equals MR - MC, so at those points marginal profit equals zero. Marginal profit is also the slope or derivative of the total profit function. In panel B, the tangents drawn to the total profit function at Q_1 and Q_3 are horizontal. It follows that the slope of the total profit function equals zero at those points. Notice, however, that Q_1 represents a profit minimum or maximum loss, while Q_3 is the profit maximum. Recall from Chapter 4 that a sufficient condition for a maximum is that the slope is zero and the curve is concave, at that point. A minimum occurs when the slope is zero and the curve is convex, at that point. Therefore, Q_3 satisfies the sufficient condition for a maximum, while Q_1 satisfies the condition for a minimum. Another method of distinguishing between the two is presented in the Appendix to this chapter.

In panel A we see that the total revenue function reaches a maximum at Q_5. At that point the tangent to the curve is horizontal, indicating that the derivative equals zero at Q_5. For $Q < Q_5$, total revenue rises with Q, while for $Q > Q_5$, total revenue falls as Q increases. This implies that marginal revenue, MR, is positive for $Q < Q_5$, negative for $Q > Q_5$, and equal to zero at Q_5. This result is depicted in panel C.

The following specific functions correspond to the graphical analysis in Figure 7.2. Assume that the quadratic total revenue function is given by $R = R(Q) = 23Q - Q^2$, and the cubic total cost function is:

$$C = C(Q) = 25 + 28Q - 9Q^2 + Q^3$$

Figure 7.2
(A) Quadratic Total Revenue and Cubic Total Cost Function
(B) Corresponding Total Profit Function
(C) Corresponding Marginal Revenue, Marginal Cost, and Marginal Profit Functions

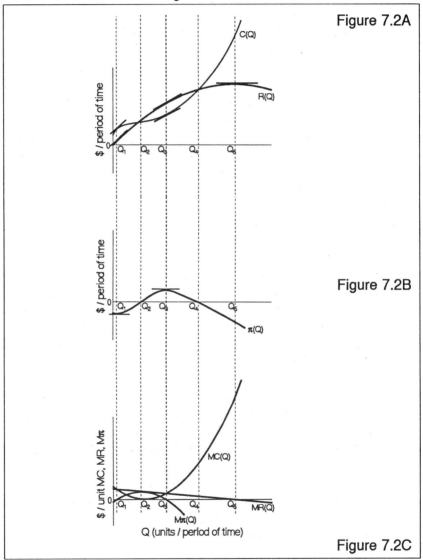

Figure 7.2A

Figure 7.2B

Figure 7.2C

where:
  Q = quantity in thousands of units/year
  R = total revenue in thousands of dollars/year
  C = total cost in thousands of dollars/year

The total profit function is given by:

$$\pi = \pi(Q) = R(Q) - C(Q) = (23Q - Q^2) - (25 + 28Q - 9Q^2 + Q^3)$$

$$= 23Q - Q^2 - 25 - 28Q + 9Q^2 - Q^3 = -Q^3 + 8Q^2 - 5Q - 25$$

where:
  π = total profit in thousands of dollars/year

Solving for marginal revenue from the total revenue function yields:

$$MR = dR/dQ = d(23Q)/dQ - d(Q^2)/dQ$$

by the sum–difference rule. However, $d(23Q)/dQ = 23$ and $d(Q^2)/dQ = 2Q$, both by the generalized power rule. Therefore, marginal revenue is given as $MR = 23 - 2Q$. This equation corresponds to the marginal revenue function in panel C. The necessary condition to maximize total revenue is that marginal revenue, $dR/dQ = 0$. We can solve for the Q at which marginal revenue is zero by setting $MR = 0$. That is, $0 = 23 - 2Q$ and, therefore, $2Q = 23$, so that $Q = 23/2 = 11.5$ is the quantity at which $MR = 0$. Therefore, total revenue is maximized when $Q = 11.5$. In terms of Figure 7.2, this corresponds to Q_5.

There are two approaches that can be utilized to solve for the profit maximum point. The first approach is to find the marginal profit function, $M\pi$, which is simply the derivative of the total profit function with respect to Q, $d\pi/dQ$. This derivative can then be set equal to zero to solve for the Q at which marginal profit is zero. Alternatively, one could solve for the marginal cost function by differentiating the total cost function with respect to quantity. Then by setting $MR = MC$, the profit maximizing Q can be found. Both methods yield identical results since $M\pi = MR - MC$. When $MR = MC$ it must be true that $M\pi = 0$.

From the first approach we have:

$$M\pi = d\pi/dQ = d(-Q^3)/dQ + d(8Q^2)/dQ - d(5Q)/dQ - d(25)/dQ$$

by the sum-difference rule. This is solved as:

$$M\pi = d\pi/dQ = -3Q^2 + 16Q - 5 - 0 = -3Q^2 + 16Q - 5$$

Setting $M\pi$ equal to zero, we can solve for the profit maximizing Q. Therefore, we seek the solution of $0 = -3Q^2 + 16Q - 5$. Using the quadratic formula, we find that the equation has two roots being $Q = 1/3$ and $Q = 5$. Therefore, at both of those quantities, marginal profit equals zero. However, $M\pi = 0$ is a necessary condition for either a profit maximum or a minimum. Substituting these values of Q into the total profit function, we find:

$$\pi(1/3) = -(1/3)^3 + 8(1/3)^2 - 5(1/3) - 25 = -697/27 = -25.8\overline{14}$$

$$\pi(5) = -(5)^3 + 8(5)^2 - 5(5) - 25 = +25$$

Therefore, the profit maximum occurs when $Q = 5$, while a profit minimum occurs at $Q = 1/3$. In terms of the graphical analysis, $Q_1 = 1/3$ and $Q_3 = 5$.

Utilizing the second method we would solve for marginal cost which is given as:

$$MC = dC/dQ = d(25)/dQ + d(28Q)/dQ - d(9Q^2)/dQ + d(Q^3)/dQ$$

This reduces to $MC = dC/dQ = 0 + 28 - 18Q + 3Q^2 = 3Q^2 - 18Q + 28$.

Marginal revenue has already been solved as:

$$MR = 23 - 2Q$$

Setting $MR = MC$ yields:

$$(23 - 2Q) = (3Q^2 - 18Q + 28)$$

Subtracting the right-hand side from both sides of the equation yields $(23 - 2Q) - (3Q^2 - 18Q + 28) = 0 = 23 - 2Q - 3Q^2 + 18Q - 28 = -3Q^2 + 16Q - 5$. Therefore, we seek the solution value of Q such that $-3Q^2 + 16Q - 5 = 0$. The left-hand side is simply the marginal profit derived before and the right-hand side simply sets it equal to zero. The remainder of the solution follows that in method one.

Derivatives of Average Functions: The Marginal–Average Relationships

When the total function, T, is a univariate function of X, $T = T(X)$, the average function, A, is $A = T(X)/X$. Since X is a function of X, being the identity function, the average function is the quotient of two functions of X. As such, its slope or derivative can be found by use of the quotient rule, given as:

$$dA/dX = [X \times dT/dX - T(X) \times d(X)/dX]/X^2$$

Recall that the derivative of the identity function equals 1, so $d(X)/dX = 1$. This derivative can be expressed in a more meaningful manner by dividing both the numerator and denominator by X, yielding:

$$\frac{dA}{dX} = \left(\frac{(X \times dT/dX)}{X} - \frac{T(X) \times 1}{X} \right) / \frac{X^2}{X}$$

which equals:

$$\frac{dA}{dX} = [(dT/dX) - T(X)/X]/X$$

However, dT/dX is the marginal, M, with respect to X, while $T(X)/X$ is simply the average, A. Therefore, the slope of an average function, $dA/dX = (M - A)/X$. In most applications X is restricted to be positive. In that event, the sign of the slope, dA/dX is the same as the sign of $(M - A)$. Technically, this is the basis for the marginal–average relationship exposited in Chapter 5. Notice that when the marginal exceeds the average, $(M - A) > 0$, so $dA/dX > 0$, as well. This implies that whenever $M > A$, the average must be rising, as X rises. Similarly, when the average is rising with respect to X, it must be true that the marginal exceeds the average. When the average exceeds the marginal, $(M - A) < 0$, it follows that $dA/dX < 0$ as well. Therefore, the average is falling as X increases. Similarly, the only way the average could be falling is if the marginal is less than the average. Finally, when the marginal equals the average, $(M - A) = 0$, it follows that $dA/dX = 0$. Therefore, the average is stationary in that case. It also follows that the only way the average could be stationary is if the marginal equals the average.

When $dA/dX = 0$, A is stationary. In addition, the condition that $dA/dX = 0$ is necessary for the average to be at either its maximum or minimum value. Therefore, when searching for either a maximum or minimum value of an average function, two alternatives exist. When the average function is known, we can differentiate it with respect to X, set that derivative to zero, and solve for the value of X. Alternatively, when the total function is known, the marginal function can be found by differentiating the total function with respect to X, while the average function can be derived by dividing the total function by X. The marginal function is then set equal to the average function, and this equation is then solved for X.

Example 7.13 Minimum Average Total Cost

Given the total cost function from Example 7.12, $C = 25 + 28Q - 9Q^2 + Q^3$, where all variables are as previously defined, the average total cost function is:

$$ATC = C/Q = (25/Q) + (28Q/Q) - (9Q^2/Q) + (Q^3/Q)$$

$$= 25Q^{-1} + 28 - 9Q + Q^2$$

The average total cost, ATC, is measured in dollars per unit. The marginal cost, MC, is the derivative of the total cost function with respect to Q and is given as $MC = dC/dQ = 28 - 18Q + 3Q^2$, as was demonstrated in Example 7.12. To solve for the Q at which ATC is at a minimum using the first method, we would first find the derivative, $dATC/dQ$, and set it equal to zero. That is:

$$dATC/dQ = d(25Q^{-1})/dQ + d(28)/dQ - d(9Q)/dQ + d(Q^2)/dQ = 0$$

Solving for the derivatives of each term yields:

$$dATC/dQ = -25Q^{-2} + 0 - 9 + 2Q = 2Q - 9 - 25Q^{-2} = 0$$

Multiplying both sides of the equation by Q^2 yields:

$$(2Q - 9 - 25Q^{-2})(Q^2) = 0(Q^2), \text{ or}$$

$$2Q^3 - 9Q^2 - 25 = 0$$

which is a cubic equation of Q, and therefore has three roots. However:

$$2Q^3 - 9Q^2 - 25 = (Q - 5)(2Q^2 + Q + 5)$$

by factorization. Therefore, one of the roots is Q = 5. The two other roots are the solution of $2Q^2 + Q + 5 = 0$. The two roots of this equation can be found using the quadratic formula, however both are imaginary. These roots are given as $Q = (-1 \pm \sqrt{39}\ i)/4$. Recall from the Appendix to Chapter 2 that i is the purely imaginary number representing the square root of negative one. Therefore, the only real root of this equation is Q = 5. This result was obtained using graphical methods in Example 5.2. The identical result is obtained by setting MC = ATC, yielding:

$$MC = (28 - 18Q + 3Q^2) = ATC = 25Q^{-1} + 28 - 9Q + Q^2$$

Subtracting ATC from both sides yields:

$$MC - ATC = (28 - 18Q + 3Q^2) - (25Q^{-1} + 28 - 9Q + Q^2) = 0, \text{ or}$$

$$MC - ATC = 28 - 18Q + 3Q^2 - 25Q^{-1} - 28 + 9Q - Q^2 = 0, \text{ or}$$

$$MC - ATC = 2Q^2 - 9Q - 25Q^{-1} = 0$$

Multiplying the equation by Q yields:

$$(MC - ATC)Q = (2Q^2 - 9Q - 25Q^{-1})Q = 0(Q)$$

and therefore:

$$2Q^3 - 9Q^2 - 25 = 0$$

This equation was solved using the first method. The graphical implication of the first method is that the tangent to the average total cost curve, at Q = 5, is horizontal. In addition, the second method informs us that the marginal cost curve intersects the average total cost curve at that point. This result was depicted in Figure 5.6B, where for the specific function utilized in this example, Q_2 on the graph is equal to 5. In that figure, one could construct a tangent to the ATC curve at Q_2. The tangent at that point would be horizontal.

Conclusion

The concept of the derivative has been shown to be extremely useful in many economic applications, particularly when the functions utilized are nonlinear. While this tool is powerful, two limitations of its usefulness should be observed. The first limitation regards optimization problems. Notice that in solving for either a maximum or a minimum in this chapter, only the necessary conditions were utilized. Thus we were required to use other methods to determine whether a maximum or minimum point existed when the necessary condition, dT/dX = 0, was met. The second and perhaps greater limitation was that, in order to use derivatives, the functions under consideration had to be univariate or be treated as univariate functions. In the Appendix to this chapter, the concept of the derivative is extended in a manner that removes the first limitation. In Chapter 8, the second limitation is removed as the concept is extended to multivariate functions.

Appendix

Higher Order Derivatives and Their Applications

When Y = f(X), the derivative dY/dX = f'(X) is a function of X as well. Therefore, it may be possible to find the derivative of that function. That is, the derivative of the derivative. That derivative is termed the **second derivative** and is denoted as d^2Y/dX^2, or f''(X). Moreover, since the second derivative is a derivative of a function of X, it too is a function of X. It may therefore be possible to differentiate that function with respect to X. The derivative of the second derivative is termed the **third derivative** and is denoted as d^3Y/dX^3, or f'''(X). This process of taking derivatives of derivatives could go on indefinitely, yielding the fourth, fifth, sixth, etc., derivatives. What has been termed "the derivative" in the body of this chapter is more formally known as the **first derivative**. All derivatives beyond the first are called **higher order derivatives**. The methods of differentiation previously discussed can be used to find the higher order derivatives.

Consider the function $Y = X^3$. The first derivative is $dY/dX = 3X^2$. The second derivative of X^3 is the first derivative of $3X^2$. That is, $d^2Y/dX^2 = 6X$. The third derivative of X^3 is the derivative of the second derivative, $6X$. This is given as $d^3Y/dX^3 = 6$. Similarly, the fourth derivative of X^3 is the derivative of the third derivative. Since the third derivative is a constant, its derivative equals zero, or $d^4Y/dX^4 = 0$. In addition, zero is a constant and, therefore, $d(0)/dX = 0$. It follows that all higher order derivatives beyond the fourth are identically equal to zero for this function.

In most economic applications only the first and second derivatives are of importance. The first derivative has been explained as the instantaneous slope or marginal, M, of a function. Equivalently, it is the rate of change of a function with respect to X. The second derivative is therefore the rate of change of that rate of change. It can also be viewed as the rate of change of the marginal with respect to X. In other words, it is the slope of the marginal function. When the second derivative is positive it implies that the marginal is directly related to X. Therefore, the marginal rises as X rises and falls as X falls. When the second derivative is negative, an inverse relationship exists between the marginal and X. When the second derivative equals zero, the marginal must be stationary.

In Chapter 4, the slope of a function was denoted as M, and the slope of M was denoted as M'. Since M has been identified as the first derivative, it is clear that M' must be another name for the second derivative. All of the results in Chapter 4 relating to values of M and M' also hold if M and M' are replaced by the first and second derivatives respectively. This is particularly true for Table 4.2, which examines nine possible combinations of values for M and M'. There are two important applications of the second derivative, which are related. The first application is a method of determining whether a function is concave or convex. The second application relates to the sufficiency conditions for a maximum or a minimum.

Concavity, Convexity and Inflection Points

In Chapter 4 it was demonstrated graphically that a sufficient condition for a curve to be strictly concave is that M' be negative. Similarly, a sufficient condition for the curve to be strictly convex is that M' be positive. These conditions are equally valid, at isolated points, as well as over some interval. We can now replace M' with the second derivative in stating these sufficiency conditions.

Example 7A.1 The Production Function and Diminishing Marginal Productivity

The short run production function in Example 7.4 was given as, $Q = 20L^{.75}$, for $K = 16$, and the function was defined for $L > 0$. All variables are as previously defined. Determine whether the production function is strictly concave or strictly convex, and interpret that result. **Solution:** The first derivative, being the marginal product of labor is given as:

$$MP_L = dQ/dL = .75(20)L^{.75-1} = 15L^{-.25}$$

The second derivative is the rate of change of the marginal product of labor with respect to labor. It is:

$$dMP_L/dL = d^2Q/dL^2 = -.25(15)L^{-.25-1} = -3.75L^{-1.25}$$

Since $L > 0$, $L^{-1.25}$ is positive as well. Therefore, the second derivative is negative for all positive values of L. As such the production function is strictly concave throughout. However, the second derivative also informs us of the relation between the MP_L and L. Since it is negative throughout, the MP_L and L are inversely related. In other words, the marginal product of labor, although positive throughout, diminishes as L increases. Therefore, a strictly concave production function has diminishing marginal product throughout. Similarly, whenever diminishing marginal product is found, the production function will be strictly concave.

Example 7A.2 Average Total Cost (ATC)

The average total cost function used in Example 7.13 is:

$$ATC = 25Q^{-1} + 28 - 9Q + Q^2$$

where:

ATC = average total cost in dollars per unit

Q = quantity of output in thousands of units/year

The following procedure can be used to determine the concavity or convexity of that function. Start by taking the first derivative of that function. It is:

$$dATC/dQ = d(25Q^{-1})/dQ + d(28)/dQ - d(9Q)/dQ + d(Q^2)/dQ$$

$$= -25Q^{-2} + 0 - 9 + 2Q$$

$$= -25Q^{-2} - 9 + 2Q$$

Then take the second derivative of the ATC function, which is simply the derivative of the first derivative. It is:

$$d^2ATC/dQ^2 = d(-25Q^{-2})/dQ - d(9)/dQ + d(2Q)/dQ$$

$$= +50Q^{-3} - 0 + 2 = 50Q^{-3} + 2$$

Since the average total cost function is defined for only positive values of Q, and a positive number raised to any power is some positive number, it follows that $50Q^{-3} > 0$ and, therefore, $d^2ATC/dQ^2 > 0$. The implication is that this specific ATC function is strictly convex throughout, i.e., for all values of Q in its domain. It follows that it must be strictly convex at Q = 5. However, at Q = 5, the slope $dATC/dQ = 0$. Recall from Chapter 4 that the sufficient condition for a point to be a minimum is that the slope is zero and the curve is convex at that point. Therefore, as asserted in Example 7.13, when Q = 5, average total cost is at its minimum value.

The test for concavity or convexity is conclusive as long as the second derivative is nonzero. Recall, however, that it is a sufficient, rather than necessary condition. When the second derivative equals zero at a point, the curve could be either concave or convex at that point, or it could be a point of inflection. When the first derivative is nonzero at that point, it is an inflection point. When the first derivative is nonzero and the second derivative is zero, over an interval, the function is linear over that interval. In the event that the first and second derivatives are zero over an interval, the function is a constant function, while if this occurs at an isolated point, the point may be a minimum, a maximum, or an inflection point.

Distinguishing Between Critical Values: Sufficiency Conditions Revisited

A **critical point** or **critical value** of a function, $Y = f(X)$, is said to exist at any point X^* if the first derivative, dY/dX, evaluated at X^* equals zero, i.e., $f'(X^*) = 0$. It has been demonstrated that a necessary condition for either a maximum or minimum is that the first derivative of the function equals zero at that point. Therefore, maxima and minima points satisfying this condition are critical points. In addition, an inflection point may also satisfy this condition, in which case it too would be a critical point. Given the three types of critical points, we seek a method of easily distinguishing among them.

The second derivative can be used to test whether a critical point is a maximum or a minimum. Recall that when the second derivative is negative at a point, the curve is strictly concave at that point. In addition, given that the first derivative is zero, by the definition of a critical point, a sufficient condition for a point to be a maximum is that the curve is concave at that point. It follows that when the second derivative evaluated at a critical point is negative, the critical point is a maximum. By similar reasoning, when the second derivative evaluated at a critical point is positive, the point in question is a minimum. This result follows from the fact that a positive second derivative indicates that the curve is strictly convex at that point. A sufficient condition for a critical point to be a minimum is that the curve is convex at that point. Therefore, the sufficient condition for a maximum and a minimum can be expressed in terms of the sign of the second derivative. These conditions are sometimes termed the **second order conditions**. The necessary condition based upon the first derivative is sometimes referred to as the **first order condition**. Combining these conditions, the sufficiency conditions for a maximum or minimum can be stated as:

Maximum–Sufficiency Condition: A point X^* on the function, $Y = f(X)$, satisfies the sufficient condition for a maximum if:
   a) the first derivative evaluated at X^* is zero, i.e., $f'(X^*) = 0$, and
   b) the second derivative evaluated at X^* is negative, i.e., $f''(X^*) < 0$.

Minimum–Sufficiency Condition: A point X^* on the function, $Y = f(X)$, satisfies the sufficient condition for a minimum if:

a) the first derivative evaluated at X^* is zero, i.e., $f'(X^*) = 0$, and
b) the second derivative evaluated at X^* is positive, i.e., $f''(X^*) > 0$.

Example 7A.3 Profit Maximization and Minimization

In Example 7.12 the profit function utilized was:

$$\pi = -Q^3 + 8Q^2 - 5Q - 25$$

where:

π = total profit in thousands of dollars per year
Q = output in thousands of units per year

Marginal profit was given as:

$$M\pi = d\pi/dQ = -3Q^2 + 16Q - 5$$

This profit function had two critical points where $M = 0$. They were given as $Q = 1/3$ and $Q = 5$. The profit function was evaluated at those points and it was asserted that $Q = 1/3$ represented a profit minimum, while $Q = 5$ was a profit maximum. This assertion can now be rigorously proven.

The second derivative of the profit function is:

$$d^2\pi/dQ^2 = dM\pi/dQ = d(-3Q^2)/dQ + d(16Q)/dQ - d(5)/dQ$$

$$= -6Q + 16 - 0 = -6Q + 16$$

Evaluating the second derivative at $Q = 1/3$ yields:

$$(d^2\pi/dQ^2)|(Q = 1/3) = -6(1/3) + 16 = -2 + 16 = +14$$

Therefore, the second derivative at $Q = 1/3$ is positive, indicating the curve is convex at that point. Since $Q = 1/3$ is a critical point, this is sufficient to guarantee that $Q = 1/3$ is a minimum.

Alternatively, evaluating the second derivative at $Q = 5$ yields:

$$(d^2/dQ^2)|(Q = 5) = -6(5) + 16 = -30 + 16 = -14$$

This is clearly negative, indicating that the curve is concave at $Q = 5$ and, therefore, this point represents a maximum.

It should be noted that the conditions specified for a maximum or a minimum are sufficient but not necessary. The implication is that when the conditions are satisfied, we are guaranteed that the critical point in question is a maximum when the second derivative is negative, and a minimum when the second derivative is positive. However, the test is inconclusive when the second derivative evaluated at the critical point equals zero. In that event the point may be a maximum, minimum, or inflection point. The following test relying on higher order derivatives enables us to discuss which is the case. It should be noted that this test incorporates our sufficiency conditions as a special case.

Higher Order Test of Critical Points

Assume that a critical point, X^*, is found such that $dY/dX = 0$, at X^*. Higher order derivatives are taken and evaluated at X^*. The first nonzero value occurs for the nth derivative. In other words, the first, second, third, . . . ,$n-1$, derivatives are all equal to zero at X^*, and the nth derivative is not. Then three possibilities exist.

Case 1: When n is even and $d^nY/dX^n < 0$, X^* is a maximum.
Case 2: When n is even and $d^nY/dX^n > 0$, X^* is a minimum.
Case 3: If n is odd, X^* is an inflection point.

Notice that the second order condition posited for a maximum is covered by Case 1, when n $= 2$. Similarly, the second order condition for a minimum is covered by Case 2, when n $= 2$. However, the importance of this rule increases when the second order condition is inconclusive, i.e., when $d^2Y/dX^2 = 0$.

Example 7A.4   An Inconclusive Second Order Condition

The function $Y = X^4$ has a critical point when $dY/dX = 0$. However $dY/dX = 4X^3$, so this occurs when $X = 0$ and, therefore, $Y = 0$. Is this a maximum, minimum, or inflection point? The second derivative is:

$$d^2Y/dX^2 = 12X^2$$

which equals zero at the critical point, $X = 0$. The second order condition is therefore not conclusive. The third derivative is $d^3Y/dX^3 = 24X$, which also equals zero at $X = 0$. The fourth derivative is $d^4Y/dX^4 = 24$. This is the first of the higher order derivatives which is nonzero at the critical point $X = 0$. Notice that it is a positive constant, independent of the value of X. Therefore, in this case $n = 4$ and $d^nY/dX^n > 0$, so the point $X = 0$ is a minimum. This result can be verified by sketching the graph.

Example 7A.5   Another Inconclusive Second Order Condition

The function $Y = X^3$ has a first derivative given by $dY/dX = 3X^2$. This equals zero at $X = 0$, $Y = 0$ which is a critical point for this function. The second derivative is $d^2Y/dX^2 = 6X$, which evaluated at $X = 0$ also equals zero. The second order condition is, therefore, inconclusive. The third derivative is $d^3Y/dX^3 = 6$, which is a positive constant independent of the value of X. Therefore, in this example, $n = 3$, and the point $(0, 0)$ is an inflection point. This result can be verified graphically.

In this appendix, we have explored the meaning and applications of higher order derivatives. A definitive test of distinguishing among critical values has been presented, thus alleviating one of the shortcomings of the chapter. In the following chapter the other shortcoming is removed, as the concept of the derivative is extended to multivariate functions.

Important Terms in this Chapter

Critical point (Critical value) - a point where the first derivative of the function equals zero. It could be a maximum, minimum, or inflection point.

Derivative – the instantaneous slope of a function. Also the limit of the slope of a secant line as the change in the independent variable approaches zero.

Explicit function – a function for which the dependent variable is isolated and explicitly expressed as a function of the independent variable.

First derivative – see **derivative**.

First order condition for a maximum or minimum – the necessary condition being that the first derivative equals zero.

Higher order derivatives – all derivatives beyond the first (see second and third derivatives as examples).

Identity function – a function that associates for each value of an independent variable an identical value for the dependent variable.

Implicit functions – a relationship between two or more variables, where none of the variables is isolated and expressed as an explicit function of the others, but at least one such function is implied.

Limit of a function (as X approaches "a") – the number L, such that the value of the function can be made as close to L as we please by choosing values of X sufficiently close to "a."

Marginal rate of product transformation – the negative of the slope of the production possibilities curve and, therefore, the rate at which society must give up the production of one good in order to increase production of another, at the margin.

Marginal revenue product – the rate of change of total revenue with respect to an input.

Second derivative – the derivative of the first derivative.

Second order condition (for a maximum or minimum) – the sufficient condition for a critical point to be a maximum or a minimum expressed in terms of the sign of the second derivative.

Sufficiency condition for a maximum – a point on the function where the first derivative of the function is zero and the second derivative of the function is negative.

Sufficiency condition for a minimum - a point on the function where the first derivative of the function is zero and the second derivative of the function is positive.

Third derivative - the derivative of the second derivative.

Exercise Set 7.2

All problems or parts thereof that are marked * rely on material covered in the appendix.

1. A firm has a total revenue function, $R = 1000Q - 10Q^2$, which is defined for $0 \leq Q \leq 100$; and a total cost function, $C = 15Q^2 + 60$, which is defined for $Q \geq 0$:

    where:

    > R = total revenue in thousands of dollars/year
    > Q = output in thousands of units/year
    > C = total cost in thousands of dollars/year

    a) Form the total profit function and derive the marginal profit function from it.
    b) Solve for the value of Q, at which the necessary conditions for a profit maximum are satisfied.
    c) Derive the marginal revenue and marginal cost functions and demonstrate that the solution found in Part b is attained when marginal revenue = marginal cost.
    *d) Using second order conditions, determine whether the point obtained is a maximum. In addition, determine whether the total profit, total revenue, and total cost functions are concave or convex.

2. Total revenue and total cost are each functions of output, i.e., $R = R(Q)$ and $C = C(Q)$ respectively. In addition, the level of output is related to the level of labor input by the production function $Q = f(L)$. Using the chain rule, derive the necessary condition for profit to be maximized with respect to L. Interpret the derivatives utilized.

Lastly, show that the condition found is equivalent to the MR = MC rule.

3. The average product of labor, AP_L, is total output, Q, divided by total labor input, L. Total output is a function of total labor input.
   a) By means of the quotient rule, determine the necessary condition for AP_L to be at its maximum value.
   *b) State the sufficient condition for this to be a maximum.

4. An average total cost function is given by:

$$ATC = (Q - 2)^4 + 10$$

   a) Use the chain rule to solve for the slope of the ATC function, and determine the value of Q that satisfies the necessary condition for a minimum.
   b) Form the total cost function and solve for the marginal cost function.
   c) What is the value of Q such that MC = ATC?
   *d) Using the higher order test for critical points, determine whether the ATC function is concave or convex. What implication does this have for the critical point found in Part a?

*5. For the specific functions utilized in Examples 7.4—7.6, determine whether they are concave or convex.

6. The equilibrium price of a security equates the required rate of return to its expected rate of return. In a simple model (see Exercise Set 6.1, Problem 4) the equilibrium price is determined by:

$$P_0^* = \frac{[E(P_1) + E(D_1)]}{1 + RF + \beta_i(RP_M)}$$

where all variables are defined in Exercise Set 6.1, Problem 4.
   a) Assume $E(P_1)$, $E(D_1)$, RF, and RP_M are given positive constants. What is the slope of P_0^* with respect to β_i? How does that slope change as β changes?

b) Assume that the values of all variables except $E(P_1)$ are given positive constants such that $P_0^* = [E(P_1) + 2.80]/1.1$. What are the first and second derivatives of P_0^* with respect to $E(P_1)$? Interpret your result.

References

Anton, H., *Calculus with Analytic Geometry*, New York: John Wiley and Sons, 1988.

Barnett, R. and M. Ziegler, *Applied Calculus*, San Francisco: Dellen Publishing Company, 1987.

Grossman, S., *Applied Mathematical Analysis*, Belmont, CA: Wadsworth Publishing Company, 1986.

Salas, S. L., E. Hille, and J. T. Anderson, *Calculus*, New York: John Wiley and Sons, 1986.

Thomas, G. B., Jr., and R. L. Finney, *Calculus and Analytical Geometry*, Reading, MA: Addison-Wesley Publishing Company, 1988.

Derivatives: Multivariate Functions

Introduction

The previous chapter introduced the concept of a derivative. It was shown to be the change in a dependent variable due to an infinitesimally small change in some independent variable. For a function, $Y = f(X)$, the derivative of Y with respect to X, dY/dX, is:

$$\lim_{\Delta X \to 0} \frac{\Delta Y}{\Delta X}$$

The derivative has many interpretations and applications. In general, it can be interpreted as the instantaneous slope of a function, or in terms of economic jargon, it represents a method of determining a precise measure of the associated marginal function. In Chapter 7, the derivative was developed and applied within the context of univariate functions. Many functions used in economics, however, are multivariate in nature, i.e., they contain more than one independent variable. Thus, it becomes necessary to extend the concept of a derivative in order to make it applicable to these types of functions. The purpose of this chapter is to accomplish such an extension by developing two categories of derivatives: partial derivatives and total derivatives. While the basic concept of a derivative remains intact, this distinction between partials and totals is now made necessary by the fact that more than one independent variable is included in the function to be examined. Once this distinction has been established, the remainder of this chapter is used to show how they can be applied to economic models.

Partial Derivatives

In general, a multivariate function is of the form $Y = f(X_1, X_2 \ldots, X_n)$, where Y is the independent variable, and $X_1, X_2, \ldots, X_n$ represent n independent variables. Also, we assume here that the independent variables are independent of each other. Recall from Chapter 3 that, for a functional relationship to exist between Y and any *one* of the independent variables, say, X_1, the remaining independent variables must be held constant. This is necessary so that for each value of X_1 there exists a unique value for Y. We can also define the change in Y due to a change in X_1, as a **partial slope,** because all other independent variables are being held constant. Thus, the partial slope of the function Y with respect to X can be designated as:

$$\frac{\Delta Y}{\Delta X_1} \mid X_{2,0}, \ldots, X_{n,0}$$

where the second subscript on the remaining Xs indicate they have been held constant at some level, 0. The level, 0, at which the variables are held constant could represent any fixed value. Similarly, a partial slope can be calculated which describes the relationship between Y and each of the remaining Xs, taken separately. For example, the partial slope reflecting the change in Y due to a change in X_2 can be expressed as:

$$\frac{\Delta Y}{\Delta X_2} \mid X_{1,0}, X_{3,0}, \ldots, X_{n,0}$$

In this case all of the Xs other than X_2 are held constant.

Just as the derivative was shown in Chapter 7 to represent the instantaneous slope of a univariate function, it can be extended here to represent the instantaneous partial slopes associated with a multivariate function. In this case there will be as many derivatives, formally defined as **partial derivatives,** as there are independent variables in the function. What distinguishes a partial derivative from the broader derivative concept, defined as a **total derivative,** is that all independent variables but the one in question are held constant. Thus, for the multivariate function, $Y = f(X_1, X_2, \ldots, X_n)$, we can define the partial derivatives as:

$$\frac{\partial Y}{\partial X_1} = \lim_{\Delta X_1 \to 0} \frac{\Delta Y}{\Delta X_1} \mid X_{2,0}, \ldots, X_{n,0}$$

$$\frac{\partial Y}{\partial X_2} = \lim_{\Delta X_2 \to 0} \frac{\Delta Y}{\Delta X_2} \mid X_{1,0}, X_{3,0}, \ldots, X_{n,0}$$

$$.\qquad.$$
$$.\qquad.$$
$$.\qquad.$$

$$\frac{\partial Y}{\partial X_n} = \lim_{\Delta X_n \to 0} \frac{\Delta Y}{\Delta X_n} \mid X_{1,0}, X_{2,0}, \ldots, X_{n-1,0}$$

where the "∂" symbol indicates that a partial derivative is being taken. We can observe that these partial derivatives are nothing more than the partial slope coefficients calculated for infinitesimally small increments in each relevant independent variable. Also, we can note that each partial will be a function of each of the independent variables listed in the original function; although all but one independent variable held constant when finding a partial, they all still play a role in determining its value. It can be observed, when taking the derivative of a univariate function, that there are no independent variables other than the one in question and, as such, there are none to hold constant. Thus, in the univariate case, there is no difference between a partial derivative and the broader derivative, defined as a **total derivative,** for which none of the independent variables are held constant. The total derivative will be discussed in the next section.

The partial derivative can be illustrated graphically. The multivariate function, $Y = f(X_1, X_2)$, contains two independent variables, or three variables in total, and can be represented by a three dimensional diagram. This function and its related partials are shown in Figure 8.1, panels A and B. When finding the partial with respect to X_1, the variable X_2 must be held constant at some level, thus:

$$\frac{\partial Y}{\partial X_1} = \frac{\partial f(X_1, X_{2,0})}{\partial X_1}$$

Thus, if X_2 is held constant at some level, 0, the partial represents the instantaneous slope of the curve AA′, shown in panel A (i.e., the partial represents the slope of the two dimensional cross section cut out at $X_{2,0}$). As can be seen by observing the tangents drawn to this cross sectional curve, the value of:

$$\frac{\partial Y}{\partial X_1}$$

is positive, but decreasing for increasing values of X_1 up to $X_{1,1}$, at which it is equal to zero. For increases in X_1 beyond this point:

$$\frac{\partial Y}{\partial X_1}$$

becomes negative. If X_2 is fixed at some other value, say $X_{2,1}$, where $X_{2,1} > X_{2,0}$, then the partial derivative:

$$\frac{\partial Y}{\partial X_1} = \frac{\partial f(X_1, X_{2,1})}{\partial X_1}$$

represents the slope of the cross section BB′. Thus, the *value* of the calculated partial:

Figure 8.1
Graph of Multivariate Function with Different Cross Sections

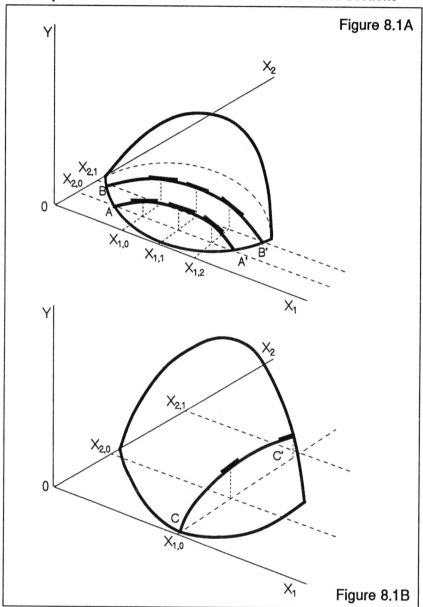

Figure 8.1A

Figure 8.1B

$$\frac{\partial Y}{\partial X_1}$$

depends not only on the value of X_1, but also on the constant value of X_2. For this function, $Y = f(X_1, X_2)$, we can also find:

$$\frac{\partial Y}{\partial X_2} = \frac{\partial f(X_{1,0}, X_2)}{\partial X_2}$$

In this case X_1 is held constant at some level, say 0, and:

$$\frac{\partial Y}{\partial X_2}$$

represents the instantaneous slope of the cross section CC′ in panel B. Of course, for different fixed levels of X_1, different cross sections will be taken, so again, the value of the partial depends on the values of X_1 and X_2.

Some specific functions should further clarify how to calculate partial derivatives. For the function, $Y = X_1^2 X_2^3$, the partial:

$$\frac{\partial Y}{\partial X_1} = 2X_1 X_2^3$$

In performing this computation, X_2 is treated as a constant and, therefore, so is X_2^3. Now, suppose we know X_2 is held constant at the value 4. The partial:

$$\frac{\partial Y}{\partial X_1}$$

now becomes $2X_1(4)^3 = 128X_1$. Finally, if we want to evaluate this partial at some value of X_1, say 3, then $\frac{\partial Y}{\partial X_1} = 128(3) = 384$. The partial:

$$\frac{\partial Y}{\partial X_2}$$

can also be found and evaluated for $X_1 = 3$ and $X_2 = 4$. Thus:

$$\frac{\partial Y}{\partial X_2} = 3X_1^2 X_2^2 = 3(3)^2 X_2^2 = 27X_2^2 = 27(4)^2 = 432$$

As another example, suppose we have the function $Y = X_1^2 + X_1 X_2 + X_2^2$ and want to find and evaluate:

$$\frac{\partial Y}{\partial X_1} \text{ and } \frac{\partial Y}{\partial X_2}, \text{ at } X_1 = 1 \text{ and } X_2 = 2.$$

$$\text{Thus, } \frac{\partial Y}{\partial X_1} = 2X_1 + X_2 = 2(1) + 2 = 4$$

$$\text{and } \frac{\partial Y}{\partial X_2} = X_1 + 2X_2 = 1 + 2(2) = 5$$

Total Derivatives

A total derivative is distinguished from a partial in that it does not necessitate holding any independent variables constant. This derivative becomes particularly useful when interdependencies exist between or among the independent variables in a function, or between the independent variables and some other variable with respect to which the derivative is being taken. As a consequence, a total derivative picks up indirect or interaction effects, as well as direct effects. As an example, suppose that for the multivariate function, $Y = f(X_1, X_2)$, there exists some relationship between the independent variables such that $X_2 = g(X_1)$. Thus, when taking the derivative of Y with respect to X_1, we will want it to be a total derivative so that we can allow not only for the direct effect that a change in X_1 has on Y, but also for the indirect effect that a change in X_1 has on Y, due to the impact on X_2. In other words, a change in X_1 affects X_2, which in turn affects Y. Therefore, the total derivative of Y with respect to X_1, denoted:

$$\frac{dY}{dX_1} \text{ is,}$$

$$\frac{dY}{dX_1} = \frac{\partial f(X_1, X_2)}{\partial X_1} \frac{dX_1}{dX_1} + \frac{\partial f(X_1, X_2)}{\partial X_2} \frac{dX_2}{dX_1}$$

Since:

$$\frac{dX_1}{dX_1} = 1$$

the expression becomes:

$$\frac{dY}{dX_1} = \frac{\partial f(X_1, X_2)}{\partial X_1} + \frac{\partial f(X_1, X_2)}{\partial X_2} \frac{dX_2}{dX_1}$$

This expression is similar to results generated by the chain rule discussed in Chapter 7. Since we are dealing with a multivariate function:

$$\frac{\partial f(X_1, X_2)}{\partial X_1} \text{ and } \frac{\partial f(X_1, X_2)}{\partial X_2}$$

are used rather than:

$$\frac{dY}{dX_1} \text{ and } \frac{dY}{dX_2}$$

The first term:

$$\frac{\partial f(X_1, X_2)}{\partial X_1}$$

records the direct effect of X_1 on Y, and can be recognized as the partial:

$$\frac{\partial Y}{\partial X_1}$$

Accordingly, X_2 is held constant in this term at some level. The second term:

$$\frac{\partial f(X_1, X_2)}{\partial X_2} \frac{dX_2}{dX_1}$$

indicates the indirect effect on Y. The first part of this term:

$$\frac{\partial f(X_1, X_2)}{\partial X_2} \text{ is simply } \frac{\partial Y}{\partial X_2}$$

or the change in Y due strictly to a change in X_2. However, any change in X_2 is a result of the initial change in X_1 and is measured by the term:

$$\frac{dX_2}{dX_1}$$

The total derivative can be written more simply as:

$$\frac{dY}{dX_1} = \frac{\partial Y}{\partial X_1} + \frac{\partial Y}{\partial X_2} \frac{dX_2}{dX_1}$$

Another example for which the total derivative is appropriate is for the multivariate function, $Y = f(X_1, X_2)$, where $X_1 = g(t)$ and $X_2 = h(t)$. In this case, the two independent variables are each functions of some variable, t, which have not been explicitly included in the original function. It is possible, however, given that X_1 and X_2 are functions of t, to find the total derivative of Y with respect to t:

$$\frac{dY}{dt} = \frac{\partial f(X_1, X_2)}{\partial X_1} \frac{dX_1}{dt} + \frac{\partial f(X_1, X_2)}{\partial X_2} \frac{dX_2}{dt}$$

or

$$= \frac{\partial Y}{\partial X_1} \frac{dX_1}{dt} + \frac{\partial Y}{\partial X_2} \frac{dX_2}{dt}$$

The first term:

$$\frac{\partial Y}{\partial X_1} \frac{dX_1}{dt}$$

is the change in Y due to a change in X_1, times the change in X_1 resulting from a change in t. The second term:

$$\frac{\partial Y}{\partial X_2} \frac{dX_2}{dt}$$

represents the change in Y due to a change in X_2, times the change in X_2 resulting from a change in t. It should be noted that the precipitating variable, or the initially changing variable, is t. Thus, in this case both effects on Y are indirect effects which operate through X_1 and X_2, respectively.

Some examples should provide further clarification. For the function $Y = X_1^2 X_2^3$, suppose we also know that $X_2 = 2X_1$. The total derivative of Y with respect to X_1 is:

$$\frac{dY}{dX_1} = \frac{\partial Y}{\partial X_1} + \frac{\partial Y}{\partial X_2} \frac{dX_2}{dX_1}$$
$$= 2X_1 X_2^3 + 3X_1^2 X_2^2 \frac{dX_2}{dX_1}$$

From the equation, $X_2 = 2X_1$, we know that:

$$\frac{dX_2}{dX_1} = 2$$

Therefore, substituting this value for:

$$\frac{dX_2}{dX_1}$$

in the equation for $\frac{dY}{dX_1}$ yields:

$$\frac{dY}{dX_1} = 2X_1 X_2^3 + 6X_1^2 X_2^2$$

As another example, suppose we have the function $Y = X_1^2 - 2X_1 X_2 + 3X_2^2$, and we know that $X_1 = 4t$ and $X_2 = t^2$. We can find the total derivative of Y with respect to t in the following manner:

$$\frac{dY}{dt_1} = (2X_1 - 2X_2)\frac{dX_1}{dt} + (-2X_1 + 6X_2)\frac{dX_2}{dt}$$

We can find:

$$\frac{dX_1}{dt} = 4, \text{ and } \frac{dX_2}{dt} = 2t$$

and substitute these values into the above equation. Therefore:

$$\frac{dY}{dt} = (2X_1 - 2X_2)(4) + (-2X_1 + 6X_2)(2t)$$

$$= 8X_1 - 8X_2 - 4X_1t + 12X_2t$$

Applications of Partial Derivatives to Economic Models

Many of the functions used in economic analyses are multivariate in nature. As a consequence, the application of partial and total derivatives is quite prevalent, and it is important to be able to identify many economic concepts as constituting one of these terms. Partial derivatives tend to be used more frequently in economics, and we shall discuss these applications first.

Example 8.1 Marginal Utility

An individual's utility function might have the form:

$$U = 5X_1X_2 + X_1$$

where:

U = units of satisfaction, in utils per period of time
X_1 = quantity of good X_1 consumed, in units per period of time
X_2 = quantity of good X_2 consumed, in units per period of time

The marginal utility of a good is the rate of change of an individual's utility with respect to consuming another increment of that good, holding all other goods constant. Thus, for infinitesimally small increments of a good, the marginal utility of a good can be represented by the partial derivative of utility with respect to that good. In this example the marginal utility associated with each good, X_1 and X_2, is:

$$MU_{X_1} = \frac{\partial U}{\partial X_1} = 5X_2 + 1$$

and

$$MU_{X_2} = \frac{\partial U}{\partial X_2} = 5X_1, \text{ respectively.}$$

Example 8.2 Marginal Products

The marginal product of an input can also be represented by a partial derivative. This is the increment to output, due to incrementing an input, holding all other inputs constant. If a firm has the production function:

$$Q = K^{1/3} L^{2/3}$$

where:

- Q = units of output produced per period of time
- K = units of capital used per period of time
- L = labor-hours used per period of time

The marginal products of capital and labor, MP_K and MP_L, respectively are:

$$MP_K = \frac{\partial Q}{\partial K} = 1/3 K^{-2/3} L^{2/3}$$

and

$$MP_L = \frac{\partial Q}{\partial L} = 2/3 K^{1/3} L^{-1/3}$$

Example 8.3 Elasticities

Many demand functions contain more than the two variables, quantity demanded of a good and the price of that good. They often contain other important variables such as money income and the price of related goods. One typical such demand function might have the form:

$$Q_X^d = 50 - 3P_X + .5P_R + .0005I$$

where:

$Q_X{}^d$ = quantity demanded of good X in units per period of time
P_X = price of good X in dollars per unit
P_R = price of related good in dollars per unit
I = money income of consumers, in dollars per period of time

It is possible to use the information from this demand curve to calculate the various elasticities described in Chapter 5: own price elasticity of demand, cross price elasticity of demand, and income elasticity of demand. Note that this demand curve is linear and, as a consequence, calculated elasticities vary along the curve. Therefore, it is necessary to specify some particular values for P_X, P_R, and I, in order to calculate the aforementioned elasticities. If P_X = \$5/unit, P_R = \$10/unit, and I = \$10,000/mo, we can find $Q_X{}^d$ by simply substituting these values into the demand function and solving as follows:

$$Q_X{}^d = 50 - 3(5) + .5(10) + .0005(10,000)$$

$$= 50 - 15 + 5 + 5$$

$$= 45$$

Effectively, we have selected a point on the multivariate demand function at which we calculate the elasticities. Thus, any increments in these variables around this point are infinitesimally small, enabling us to apply the concept of a derivative. More specifically, since this function is multivariate, we need to use partial derivatives which allow us to hold all independent variables constant, except the one in question. Accordingly, the elasticity formulas developed in Chapter 5 can be modified and expressed as follows:

$$\text{Own price elasticity of demand} \quad = E_{Q_x^d, P_x} = \frac{\partial Q_x^d}{\partial P_x} \times \frac{P_x}{Q_x^d}$$

$$\text{Cross price elasticity of demand} \quad = E_{Q_x^d, P_R} = \frac{\partial Q_x^d}{\partial P_R} \times \frac{P_R}{Q_x^d}$$

$$\text{Income elasticity of demand} \quad = E_{Q_x^d, I} = \frac{\partial Q_x^d}{\partial I} \times \frac{I}{Q_x^d}$$

Each elasticity can now be calculated by finding the appropriate partial derivative and substituting it, along with the value of Q_x^d, and the relevant P_x, P_R, or I information, into the desired elasticity formula.

Thus, regarding own price elasticity:

$$\frac{\partial Q_x^d}{\partial P_x} = -3 \quad \text{and}$$

$$E_{Q_x^d, P_x} = (-3)5/45 = -.33$$

This result indicates that, for a 1 percent change in its own price, the quantity demanded will change by .33 percent in the opposite direction. Therefore, the own price elasticity of demand can be characterized as inelastic.

Regarding the cross price elasticity:

$$\frac{\partial Q_x^d}{\partial P_R} = .5 \quad \text{and}$$

$$E_{Q_x^d, P_R} = (.5)(\frac{10}{45}) = .11$$

Since this term is positive, it indicates that for a 1 percent change in the price of a related good, there will be a .11 percent change in the quantity demanded of good X in the same direction. Consequently, the positive sign on this cross price elasticity reflects that the two goods are substitutes.

Finally, with regard to the income elasticity:

$$\frac{\partial Q_x^d}{\partial I} = .0005, \quad \text{and}$$

$$E_{Q_x^d, I} = (.0005)(\frac{10,000}{45}) = .11$$

This result indicates that for a 1 percent change in money income, quantity demanded will change by .11 percent in the same direction. The positive sign on this income elasticity reflects that the good is normal.

Example 8.4 Marginal Propensity to Consume

Sometimes consumption functions are expressed as multivariate functions. An example of such a function is:

$$C = 1000 + .6Y_d - 1.0R$$

where:

  C = consumption expenditures in billions of dollars per year
  Y_d = disposable income in billions of dollars per year
  R = interest rate in percentage points

Since this is a multivariate consumption function, the marginal propensity to consume (MPC) is expressed as a partial derivative. By so doing, the other independent variable in the function, R, is held constant, making the MPC a partial slope coefficient. In this example:

$$MPC = \frac{\partial C}{\partial Y_d} = .6$$

indicating that for an extra one billion dollars of disposable income, with interest rates held constant, 600 million more dollars will be spent for consumption purposes. In this example, it is also possible to find the extra consumption expenditures due to an increment in the interest rate, holding disposable income constant. This is:

$$\frac{\partial C}{\partial R} = -1.0$$

which indicates that for a 1 percent change in interest rates, there will be a one billion dollar change in consumption expenditures in the opposite direction. Incredibly, there is no particular name for this partial, though some economist might eventually coin such a term.

Example 8.5 Marginal Propensity to Save

A saving function can also be expressed in multivariate form. Disposable income must be either spent for consumption or saved, i.e., $Y_d = C + S$, where S = saving in billions of dollars per year, and Y_d and C are defined as before. Solving for S, the equation becomes $S = Y_d - C$. Substituting for C from the consumption function given in Example 8.4, the expression becomes:

$$S = Y_d - (1000 + .6Y_d - 1.0R)$$
$$= Y_d - 1000 - .6Y_d + 1.0R$$
$$= -1000 + .4Y_d + 1.0R$$

Since this is a multivariate function, the marginal propensity to save (MPS) can be represented by the partial derivative of saving with respect to disposable income. Therefore, for this example:

$$MPS = \frac{\partial S}{\partial Y_d} = .4$$

reflecting that .4 of each increment in Y_d will be saved.

Applications of Total Derivatives to Economic Models

Total derivatives are also of considerable importance in economic analyses. They are applicable with regard to multivariate functions for which no variables, at least in concept, are held constant when the derivative is taken.

Example 8.6 Marginal Rate of Technical Substitution

An **isoquant** is defined as a function representing the locus of input combinations which can be used to produce some given level of output. The slope of an isoquant is accordingly the rate at which one input can be substituted for the other in a production process, while still producing the same level of output. In economic jargon, the slope of an isoquant is defined as the **marginal rate of technical substitution (MRTS)**, which can be derived directly from a production function. As an example, assume a firm has the production function:

$$Q = K^{1/4}L^{3/4}$$

where:

Q = units of output produced per period of time
K = units of capital used per period of time
L = units of labor used per period of time

The MRTS is represented by:

$$\left| \frac{dK}{dL} \right|$$

for some given level of Q. This can be found by taking the total derivative of the function with respect to L. Thus:

$$\frac{dQ}{dL} = (3/4)K^{1/4}L^{-1/4} + (1/4)K^{-3/4}L^{3/4}\frac{dK}{dL}$$

Since by definition Q must remain constant along an isoquant, we know that:

$$\frac{dQ}{dL} = 0$$

Substituting this information into the equation yields:

$$0 = (3/4)K^{1/4}L^{-1/4} + (1/4)K^{-3/4}L^{3/4}\frac{dK}{dL}$$

Solving for $\frac{dK}{dL}$, which represents the MRTS, yields:

$$\text{MRTS} = \left|\frac{dK}{dL}\right| = \left|\frac{(3/4)K^{1/4}L^{-1/4}}{(1/4)K^{-3/4}L^{3/4}}\right| = \frac{3K}{L}$$

This result indicates that the MRTS varies directly with K and inversely with L.

Example 8.7 Time Derivatives and Growth Rates

Sometimes an economist may want to examine how a variable changes over time. This can be facilitated by taking the derivative of such a variable with respect to time, t, where t = time in units such as days, months, years, etc. Furthermore, the time derivative of a variable divided by the variable's initial level represents the percentage change in that variable over time. This is defined as the **instantaneous growth rate of a variable.**

Suppose we want to determine how the quantity of output produced, Q, in the preceding example changes over time. Since Q is dependent on the inputs (K and L) used it is logical to expect that the growth of Q over time will be dependent on how K and L grow over time. Thus, since Q,

K and L are treated as variable with respect to time, a total derivative must be taken in order to ultimately determine the growth rates of the variables. The production function from Example 8.6 is $Q = K^{1/4}L^{3/4}$, and the total derivative with respect to time is:

$$\frac{dQ}{dt} = K^{1/4}\frac{dL^{3/4}}{dt} + L^{3/4}\frac{dK^{1/4}}{dt}$$

$$= (3/4)K^{1/4}L^{-1/4}\frac{dL}{dt} + (1/4)L^{3/4}K^{-3/4}\frac{dK}{dt}$$

In order to express this in terms of growth rates, we can divide both sides of the equation by Q, generating the term:

$$\frac{\frac{dQ}{dt}}{Q} = \frac{(3/4)K^{1/4}L^{-1/4}\frac{dL}{dt}}{Q} + \frac{(1/4)L^{3/4}K^{-3/4}\frac{dK}{dt}}{Q}$$

Substituting $K^{1/4}L^{3/4}$ from the production function for the Q terms on the right–hand side of this equation yields:

$$\frac{\frac{dQ}{dt}}{Q} = \frac{(3/4)K^{1/4}L^{-1/4}\frac{dL}{dt}}{K^{1/4}L^{3/4}} + \frac{(1/4)L^{3/4}K^{-3/4}\frac{dK}{dt}}{K^{1/4}L^{3/4}}$$

$$= \frac{(3/4)\frac{dL}{dt}}{L} + \frac{(1/4)\frac{dK}{dt}}{K}$$

Thus, the growth rate in output, in percent per time:

$$\frac{\frac{dQ}{dt}}{Q}$$

is equal to the summation of 3/4 times the growth rate in labor or:

$$\left(\frac{3}{4}\right) \times \frac{\dfrac{dL}{dt}}{L}$$

plus 1/4 times the the growth rate in capital or:

$$\left(\frac{1}{4}\right) \times \frac{\dfrac{dK}{dt}}{K}$$

Exercise Set 8.1

1. An individual has the following utility function:

$$U = 5X^2Y^3$$

where:

> U = units of satisfaction in utils per period of time
> X = quantity of good X consumed, in units per period of time
> Y = quantity of good Y consumed, in units per period of time

a) Find the marginal utility function for good X and evaluate it at X = 2 and Y = 3.

b) Find the marginal utility function for good Y and evaluate it at X = 2 and Y = 3.

c) What is unusual about these marginal utility functions (i.e., what economic law is being violated)?

2. A firm has the production function:

$$Q = 8K^2L^2 - 2K^3L^3$$

where:
> Q = output produced in units per period of time
> K = capital input, in units per period of time

$$L = \text{labor input, in units per period of time}$$

a) Find the marginal product functions for capital and labor, respectively.
b) Plot the MP_K function for $L = 1$ unit/time. Does this function exhibit the law of diminishing marginal productivity?
c) Evaluate both marginal product functions at $K = 2$ and $L = 1$.
d) Using a total derivative, find the slope of the isoquant pertaining to $Q = 10$ units. What is the name for the negative of this term? How can it be interpreted?

3. A firm faces the following multivariate demand function:

$$Q_X^d = 400 - 40P_X + 50P_Y + .005I$$

where:

Q_X^d = quantity demanded of good X, in units per period of time
P_X = price of good X, in dollars per unit
P_Y = price of good Y, in dollars per unit
I = per capita money income of consumers, in dollars per period of time

a) If $P_X = \$10$/unit, $P_Y = \$6$/unit, and $I = \$20,000$/year, what is Q_X^d?
b) Calculate the own price, cross price, and income, elasticities of demand.
c) Interpret the own price elasticity you have just calculated.
d) Are goods X and Y substitutes or complements?
e) What type of good is good X, i.e., is it superior, normal, or inferior?

4. A firm has the production function:

$$Q = K^{1/3}L^{2/3}$$

where:

Q = output produced, in units per period of time
K = capital input used, in units per period of time
L = labor input used, in units per period of time

Also, K = 2t and L = 4t, where t = units of time.

What will be the growth rate of Q over time? [Hint: use the total derivative:

$$\frac{dQ}{dt}$$

and apply the chain rule.] Evaluate your solution for K = 1 and L = 8.

Unconstrained Optimization of Multivariate Functions

In Chapter 4 we discussed the concept of finding the values of independent variables which optimize (maximize or minimize) the value of some objective variable. We demonstrated in Chapter 7 how the derivative can be used to facilitate this procedure, within the context of univariate functions, when infinitesimally small increments of the independent variables are taken. Analogously, we can use the derivative to optimize multivariate functions. Depending on the circumstances, this procedure can be accomplished by employing either partial or total derivatives.

Optimization by Using Total Derivatives

A multivariate function containing n independent variables, $Y = f(X_1, X_2, \ldots, X_n)$, can be optimized (maximized or minimized) by using a total derivative. Of course, some information must be known about any relationship, at the solution values, between the independent variables and the variable with respect to which the function is differentiated. This variable could be one of the independent variables in the function or some other variable which has not been included. A point of clarification should be stated here. Although the independent variables in an original function may be independent of each other, they can be related to each other at the **solution values**, which are the values of the independent variables that correspond to an optimal value for the dependent variable. This is due to the fact that, in order to find an optimum, we must impose a condition on the slopes of the independent variables. This condition, termed the necessary condition for an optimum, says that each partial slope must be equal to zero. Once this constraint is imposed, a relationship is established between the independent variables at the solution values. If this relationship between an independent variable in question and the other independent variables is known, part of the problem has already been solved. The necessary condition for an optimum has been reduced to the fact that the total derivative, with respect to the independent variable in question, must be equal to zero. In other words, if we know that $X_2, \ldots, X_n$ are themselves functions of X_1, then the necessary condition for a maximum or a minimum is:

$$\frac{dY}{dX_1} = \frac{\partial Y}{\partial X_1} + \frac{\partial Y}{\partial X_2}\frac{\partial X_2}{\partial X_1} + \ldots + \frac{\partial Y}{\partial X_n}\frac{dX_n}{dX_1} = 0$$

The solution to this equation yields the values of $X_1, X_2, \ldots, X_n$ which correspond to either a maximum or minimum value of Y. The necessary condition for a maximum or a minimum is one and the same. Thus, in order to distinguish between the two, or more generally to determine whether we have calculated an extremum (maximum or minimum) at all, we need to establish a sufficiency condition. Unfortunately, the computation of sufficiency conditions for optimizing multivariate functions can become rather complex and are beyond the scope of this book. As a result, in order to demonstrate optimization of multivariate functions, we will focus on maximization problems, where the corresponding sufficiency conditions are assumed to hold.

As an example, suppose we wish to find the values of X_1 and X_2 which maximize the function:

$$Y = 28X_1 + 2X_1X_2 - 2X_1^2 - 4X_2^2$$

Also assume we know that the independent variables are related in the manner $X_1 = 4X_2$. The total derivative of Y with respect to either X_1 or X_2 can be taken and set equal to zero. In this case:

$$\frac{dY}{dX_2} = 28\frac{dX_1}{dX_2} + 2X_1 + 2X_2\frac{dX_1}{dX_2} - 4X_1\frac{dX_1}{dX_2} - 8X_2 = 0$$

Since we know $X_1 = 4X_2$, we can determine that:

$$\frac{dX_1}{dX_2} = 4$$

Substituting this value for $\frac{dX_1}{dX_2}$ in the equation for $\frac{dY}{dX_2}$ yields:

$$\frac{dY}{dX_2} = 28(4) + 2X_1 + 2X_2(4) - 4X_1(4) - 8X_2 = 0$$

$$= 112 + 2X_1 + 8X_2 - 16X_1 - 8X_2 = 0$$

$$= 112 - 14X_1 = 0$$

or

$$X_1 = 8$$

Substituting this value for X_1 into the equation $X_1 = 4X_2$ yields $8 = 4X_2$, or $X_2 = 2$. Finally, the maximum value for Y is found by substituting the values for X_1 and X_2 back into the original function. Therefore:

$$Y = 28(8) + 2(8)(2) - 2(8)^2 - 4(2)^2$$

$$= 224 + 32 - 128 - 16$$

$$= 112$$

It should be noted that these same results can be obtained by simply substituting $X_1 = 4X_2$ into the original equation and solving for:

$$\frac{dY}{dX_2} = 0$$

This substitution reduces the multivariate function to a univariate one, containing only X_2 as the independent variable. Thus, solving for:

$$\frac{dY}{dX_2} = 0$$

yields the value of X_2 which maximizes the function. The value of X_1 corresponding to a maximum is then found by simply substituting for X_2 into $X_1 = 4X_2$ and solving.

Optimization by Using Partial Derivatives

Most of the time, any extra information regarding a relationship (at the solution values for an optimum, between or among the independent variables) is unknown. In these cases, it is impossible to optimize a multivariate function using a total derivative. It is possible, however, to solve these types of problems using systems of partial derivatives.

For a multivariate function, containing n independent variables, $Y = f(X_1, X_2, \ldots, X_n)$, the necessary condition for optimization is that:

$$\frac{\partial Y}{\partial X_1} = \frac{\partial Y}{\partial X_2} = \ldots = \frac{\partial Y}{\partial X_n} = 0$$

Thus, by taking the partial derivative of the objective variable, Y, with respect to each independent variable, and imposing the condition that each partial must be equal to zero, we create a system of equations which can be solved simultaneously. The solution for this system yields the values for the independent variables $X_1, X_2, \ldots, X_n$, which correspond to an optimum (maximum or minimum) value for the objective variable, Y. Again, assuming that the sufficiency conditions have been established, we will, for expository purposes, dwell on a maximization problem.

The multivariate function, $Y = f(X_1, X_2)$, containing two independent variables, might be of the form shown in Figure 8.1. Recall the partials:

$$\frac{\partial Y}{\partial X_1} \text{ and } \frac{\partial Y}{\partial X_2}$$

will each be functions of both X_1 and X_2. The term:

$$\frac{\partial Y}{\partial X_1}$$

represents the slope of Y with respect to X_1, holding X_2 constant. In other words, it represents the slope of a two dimensional cross section, with variables Y and X_1 taken at some fixed value of X_2, say $X_{2,0}$. The value of X_1 which maximizes Y for this cross section, taken at $X_{2,0}$, can be calculated by employing the condition:

$$\frac{\partial Y}{\partial X_1} = 0$$

If X_2 is kept constant at $X_{2,0}$, the maximization procedure is no different than maximizing a univariate function, because now it contains only two variables, Y and X_1. However, the variable X_2 can be held constant at values other than $X_{2,0}$ as well, e.g., $X_{2,1}$, $X_{2,2}$, etc. For each value at which X_2 is held constant, a different cross section is established, each having a slope represented by:

$$\frac{\partial Y}{\partial X_1}$$

For each cross section, the variable Y can be maximized by finding the value of X_1 at which:

$$\frac{\partial Y}{\partial X_1} = 0$$

Thus, an entire locus of values of X_1, which maximize Y for different fixed levels of X_2, can be traced. Such a locus, labeled DD', is shown in Figure 8.2, panel A. A similar line of reasoning applies to:

$$\frac{\partial Y}{\partial X_2}$$

This term represents the slope of Y with respect to X_2, holding X_1 constant. It represents the slope of two dimensional cross sections taken for each level of X_1, where Y and X_2 are the variables. Thus the maximum value for Y can be obtained by finding the values for X_2 at which:

Figure 8.2
(A) Locus of Values of X_1 Which Maximize Y for Different Fixed Values of X_2
(B) Locus of Values of X_2 Which Maximize Y for Different Fixed Values of X_1

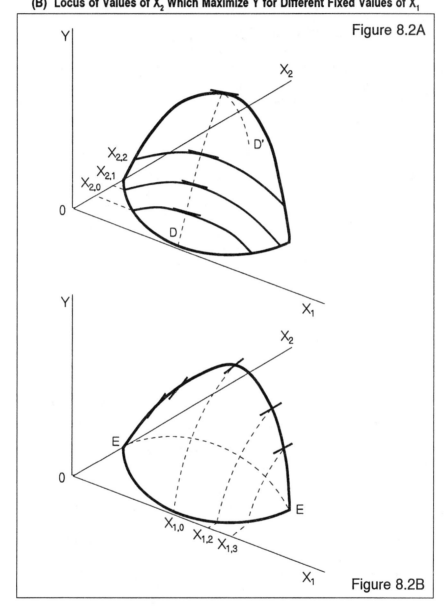

$$\frac{\partial Y}{\partial X_2} = 0$$

for each cross section. The locus of such values is shown as the curve, EE', in panel B of Figure 8.2.

The partials trace out two loci of local extremes:

$$\frac{\partial Y}{\partial X_1} = 0 \text{ and } \frac{\partial Y}{\partial X_2} = 0$$

Our goal, however, is to find the values of X_1 and X_2 which maximize the entire multivariate function. Although the variables X_1 and X_2 are not related to each other in the original function, they will be related to each other in the maximization condition for each partial. This is due to the fact that we have set each partial equal to zero. As a result, we have a system of two equations, in two variables, which can be solved simultaneously. The solution yields the values for X_1 and X_2 which maximize the entire function, i.e., yield the maximum value of the objective variable, Y. The necessary condition for a multivariate maximum is that:

$$\frac{\partial Y}{\partial X_1} = \frac{\partial Y}{\partial X_2} = 0$$

and is shown in Figure 8.3.

This procedure can be illustrated by use of a specific example. Returning to the function, $Y = 28X_1 + 2X_1X_2 - 2X_1^2 - 4X_2^2$, we can find the values of X_1 and X_2 which maximize Y in the following manner:

$$\frac{\partial Y}{\partial X_1} = 28 + 2X_2 - 4X_1 = 0$$

$$\frac{\partial Y}{\partial X_2} = 2X_1 - 8X_2 = 0$$

Figure 8.3
Global Unconstrained Maximization Solution

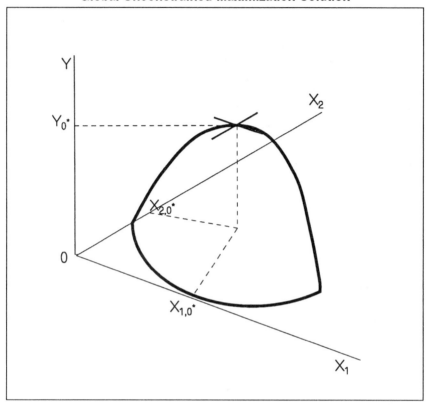

A relationship between X_1 and X_2 now exists at the solution values, so we can choose either one of the equations and solve for one variable in terms of the other. Choosing the second equation and solving for X_1 yields $X_1 = 4X_2$. Substituting $4X_2$ for X_1 in the first equation, we get:

$$28 + 2X_2 - 4(4X_2) = 0$$

$$28 - 14X_2 = 0$$

or

$$X_2 = 2$$

Substituting this value for X_2 into the second equation yields:

$$2X_1 - 8(2) = 0$$

or

$$X_1 = 8$$

These results were obtained previously using the total derivative method. The maximum value for Y is therefore 112, as before. Note that we can solve for the values of X_1 and X_2, which maximize Y, without any beforehand knowledge of the relationship between X_1 and X_2 at the solution values. As a result, this is the method which is, by far, the more useful in solving multivariate optimization problems.

Constrained Optimization

The science of economics, in large part, consists of studying how choices are made. Many choices are often affected by the fact that economic agents are usually limited or constrained in their decision making process by some predetermined factors. For example, an individual consumer may seek to find the combination of goods which maximizes his or her utility. However, in most cases the consumer is limited, or constrained, regarding the maximum amount of utility than can be achieved, by such factors as money income and the prices that must be paid for the goods. Accordingly, the process becomes one of **constrained optimization**. As another example, a firm may seek to find the combination of inputs which correspond to the maximum amount of output it can produce, subject to such constraining factors as the prices it must pay for the inputs and some predetermined expenditure outlay.

In general, these constrained optimization problems are solved by incorporating the relevant limiting factors into some equation defined as a constraint, and then solving it simultaneously with the necessary conditions to obtain optimal values for the variables. These types of problems can be solved using either of two methods. The first involves solving the constraint for one of the variables, substituting the resulting expression into the objective function we want to optimize, and then taking a total derivative and setting it equal to zero. The solution for this equation, together with the constraint, generates the solution values for a constrained optimum. This procedure is defined as the **substitution**

method. The second method for solving constrained optimization problems is defined as the method of **Lagrangean multipliers.** This technique involves incorporating the objective function and the constraint into a single function defined as a Lagrangean function and taking partial derivatives with respect to each variable in the function. These partials are set equal to zero and solved as a system, yielding the solution values.

Constrained Optimization Using the Substitution Method

The substitution method can first be illustrated using general notation. Suppose our goal is to optimize, or more specifically, maximize, some objective function, $Y = f(X_1, X_2)$, subject to some constraint, $X_2 = g(X_1)$. We can take the total derivative of Y with respect to X_1 and set it equal to zero:

$$\frac{dY}{dX_1} = \frac{\partial Y}{\partial X_1} + \frac{\partial Y}{\partial X_2} \frac{dX_2}{dX_1} = 0$$

The term $\dfrac{dX_2}{dX_1}$ can be solved from the constraint, yielding:

$$\frac{dX_2}{dX_1} = \frac{dg(X_1)}{dX_1}$$

This right-hand term can be substituted for $\dfrac{dX_2}{dX_1}$ in the above equation, resulting in the expression:

$$\frac{dY}{dX_1} = \frac{\partial Y}{\partial X_1} + \frac{\partial Y}{\partial X_2} \frac{dg(X_1)}{dX_1} = 0$$

This equation can now be solved together with the original constraint, $X_2 = g(X_1)$, to get the values for X_1 and X_2 which optimize the objective variable, Y. The value of Y can be found by simply substituting these solution values for X_1 and X_2 into the original objective function and solving. A specific example should provide further clarification regarding this procedure.

Example 8.8 Constrained Output Maximization

A firm has the production function:

$$Q = K^{1/2} L^{1/2}$$

where:

$\quad$ Q $\quad$ = $\quad$ output in units per period of time
$\quad$ K $\quad$ = $\quad$ capital input in units per period of time
$\quad$ L $\quad$ = $\quad$ labor input in hours per period of time

The firm is constrained as to the amounts of inputs it can hire, and hence the amount of output it can produce, both by the prices it must pay for the two inputs and by the total expenditure outlay allocated to the production of output. These factors can be formally expressed in an equation defined as an **isocost constraint,** which has the form:

$$P_K K + P_L L = C$$

where, in this example:

$\quad P_K$ $\quad$ = $\quad$ \$100/unit $\quad$ = $\quad$ price of capital in dollars per unit
$\quad P_L$ $\quad$ = $\quad$ \$4/labor hour = price of labor in dollars per hour
$\quad$ C $\quad$ = $\quad$ \$80,000 $\quad\quad$ = $\quad$ total expenditure allocated to producing output in dollars per unit of time.

The total expenditure outlay, C, is equal to sum of the total amount spent on the capital input, $P_K K$, and the total amount spent on the labor input, $P_L L$. If the firm is a price taker in the input market, then P_K and P_L are treated as given, as is C, since the firm has already predetermined its level of expenditures. Thus the only variables in the equation are K and

L. As a result, an isocost constraint represents the locus of combinations of inputs (K and L) a firm is able to purchase, given the levels of P_K, P_L, and C.

Generally, the goal of a rational firm is to maximize profits. However, in the case of perfect competition, price is a constant. As a result, once an expenditure outlay has been allocated, the firm can maximize profits by simply maximizing its level of output. Thus, the goal of this firm is to maximize its production of output, Q, represented by the production function, $K^{1/2} L^{1/2}$, subject to the isocost constraint, $P_K K + P_L L = C$. This can be accomplished by first taking the total derivative of Q with respect to either of the inputs, say:

$$\frac{dQ}{dL}$$

and setting it equal to zero. Thus we get:

$$\frac{dQ}{dL} = (1/2)K^{1/2}L^{-1/2} + (1/2)K^{-1/2}L^{1/2}\frac{dK}{dL} = 0$$

Note that since K and L are both treated as variable, the product rule must be employed. The term:

$$\frac{dK}{dL}$$

can be obtained by solving the isocost constraint for K and taking the derivative of K with respect to L:

$$K = \frac{C}{P_K} - \frac{P_L}{P_K} L \quad \text{and} \quad \frac{dK}{dL} = \frac{-P_L}{P_K}$$

This expression $\dfrac{-P_L}{P_K}$ can be substituted for $\dfrac{dK}{dL}$ in the equation for

$\dfrac{dQ}{dL}$, generating:

$$\frac{dQ}{dL} = 1/2\, K^{1/2} L^{-1/2} + 1/2\, K^{-1/2} L^{1/2} \left(\frac{-P_L}{P_K} \right) = 0$$

$$= \left(\frac{K}{L} \right)^{1/2} - \frac{P_L}{P_K} \left(\frac{L}{K} \right)^{1/2} = 0$$

$$\frac{K}{L} = \left(\frac{P_L}{P_K} \right)^2 \left(\frac{L}{K} \right)$$

$$K^2 = \left(\frac{P_L}{P_K} \right)^2 L^2$$

$$K = \frac{P_L L}{P_K}$$

Substituting this value for K, along with given values, P_L = \$4/man hour and C = \$80,000, into the isocost constraint yields:

$$P_K \left(\frac{P_L}{P_K} \right) L + P_L L = C$$

$$L = \frac{C}{2P_L} = \frac{\$80,000}{\$8/\text{labor hour}} = 10,000 \text{ labor hours}$$

Substituting this value for L along with the given values, P_K = \$100/unit, and P_L = \$4/labor hour into the above equation:

$$K = \frac{P_L L}{P_K}$$

yields:

$$K = \frac{\$4/\text{labor hour}}{\$100/\text{unit}} (10{,}000 \text{ labor hours}) = 400 \text{ units}$$

These are the values of K and L which correspond to a constrained optimum (maximum) for the objective variable Q, which can be found by substituting the solution values for K and L into the objective function (the production function). Accordingly:

$$Q = (400)^{1/2} (10{,}000)^{1/2} = (20)(100) = 2000 \text{ units}$$

This substitution method, while perfectly valid, can become quite cumbersome when complex functions are involved. As a consequence an alternative procedure, the method of Lagrangean multipliers, is often used in its place.

Constrained Optimization Using the Method of Lagrangean Multipliers

The method of Lagrangean multipliers involves incorporating the objective function, which is to be optimized, and the constraint into one function defined as a **Lagrangean function**, $\mathcal{L}$. Generally speaking, more than one constraint could be incorporated, but in our examples, we shall dwell on the use of only one. By taking partials of $\mathcal{L}$ with respect to each variable in the function and setting them equal to zero, we can create a system of equations representing local extremes, which can be solved simultaneously to get solution values for the global optimum. In our examples, this will be a maximum. This technique is less cumbersome than the substitution method, because it allows us to solve the problem using partial, rather than total, derivatives. What makes this a constrained optimization technique is, of course, the incorporation of the constraint into the function, $\mathcal{L}$, which is to be optimized. More specifically, the constraint is included in a manner which, after the partials have been taken and set equal to zero, leaves the constraint itself as one of the equations of local extremes. This equation, the constraint, is then solved with the other equations to get the solution values for a global optimum.

As a general example, suppose we want to optimize the objective function, $Y = f(X_1, X_2)$, subject to some constraint, $g(X_1, X_2) = 0$. We can construct a function, the Lagrangean function, $\mathcal{L}$, which includes both the objective function and the constraint, by solving the constraint so that it is equal to zero, taking it times some created variable, λ, called the Lagrangean multiplier, and adding this term to the objective function. As a result, we get the function:

$$\mathcal{L} = Y + \lambda[g(X_1,X_2)]$$

or

$$\mathcal{L} = f(X_1, X_2) + \lambda[g(X_1,X_2)]$$

This Lagrangean function, $\mathcal{L}$, is a function of X_1, X_2 and λ. The optimization of $\mathcal{L}$ yields an unconstrained optimum, but the solution values for this procedure will be the same as a constrained optimization for the objective function, $f(X_1, X_2)$. This is due to the fact that the constraint, $g(X_1, X_2)$, is equal to zero and, therefore, its inclusion does not change the value of the function, $f(X_1, X_2)$. The new variable, λ, is defined as the **Lagrangean multiplier** and has been included such that, when we take the partial of $\mathcal{L}$ with respect to it, we will get the constraint itself as a result. In a sense, the Lagrangean function is a "stacked deck," designed to generate desired equations for local extremes, when the partials are taken and set equal to zero. Accordingly we get:

$$\frac{\partial \mathcal{L}}{\partial X_1} = \frac{\partial f(X_1,X_2)}{\partial X_1} + \lambda \frac{\partial g(X_1,X_2)}{\partial X_1} = 0$$

$$\frac{\partial \mathcal{L}}{\partial X_2} = \frac{\partial f(X_1,X_2)}{\partial X_2} + \lambda \frac{\partial g(X_1,X_2)}{\partial X_2} = 0$$

$$\frac{\partial \mathcal{L}}{\partial \lambda} = g(X_1,X_2) = 0$$

This system of three equations in three variables, X_1, X_2, and λ can be solved to get the solution values which correspond to an optimal value for Y.

Example 8.9 Constrained Output Maximization Revisited

The method of Lagrangrian multipliers can be illustrated by returning to the constrained output maximization example. A firm has the production function, $Q = K^{1/2} L^{1/2}$, where the variables are defined as before. In addition the firm is faced with the isocost constraint, $P_K K + P_L L = C$, where $P_K = \$100/unit$, $P_L = \$4/labor\ hour$, and $C = \$80,000$, and these terms are defined as in the previous example. The Lagrangean function is:

$$\mathcal{L} = Q + \lambda(C - P_K K - P_L L)$$

or

$$\mathcal{L} = K^{1/2} L^{1/2} + \lambda(C - P_K K - P_L L)$$

The equations of local extremes are:

$$\frac{\partial \mathcal{L}}{\partial K} = 1/2 K^{-1/2} L^{1/2} - \lambda P_K = 0$$

$$\frac{\partial \mathcal{L}}{\partial L} = 1/2 K^{1/2} L^{-1/2} - \lambda P_L = 0$$

$$\frac{\partial \mathcal{L}}{\partial \lambda} = C - P_K K - P_L L = 0$$

Solving the first two equations together, in order to eliminate λ, yields:

$$\frac{1/2 K^{1/2} L^{-1/2}}{1/2 K^{-1/2} L^{1/2}} = \frac{\lambda P_L}{\lambda P_K}$$

$$\frac{K}{L} = \frac{P_L}{P_K}$$

or

$$K = \frac{P_L}{P_K} L$$

We have now reduced the system of three equations in three variables down to just two equations in two variables, K and L. Substituting the term:

$$\frac{P_L L}{P_K}, \text{ for } K$$

into the third equation of local extremes, $P_K K + P_L L = C$ (the constraint), along with the given values for P_L and C yields:

$$P_K \frac{P_L L}{P_K} + P_L L - C = 0$$

$$2P_L L = C$$

or

$$L = \frac{C}{2P_L} = \frac{80,000}{2(4)} = 10,000 \text{ labor hours}$$

The solution value for K is obtained by substituting this value for L, along with the given value of P_K, into:

$$K = \frac{P_L L}{P_K}$$

generating the result:

$$K = \frac{4}{100}(10,000) = 400 \text{ units}$$

Finally, the value of Q which has been maximized is $Q = 400^{1/2}(10,000)^{1/2}$ = 2000 units/time. Note these solution values are the same as those obtained using the substitution method.

A special interpretation can also be associated with the variable, λ. In general, it represents the change in the optimal level of the objective variable due to a one unit change in the constraint. In this case, it represents the extra output which could be produced given a one dollar increase in expenditure outlay. If the constraint is not binding or effective, the variable λ would equal zero, and the problem can be solved by simply finding the unconstrained optimum for the objective function.

Conclusion

This chapter has been an introduction to the application of calculus to multivariate functions. Many functions used in economics are multivariate in nature, in order to provide comprehensive explanations related to variables of interest. As a consequence, it is important that students of economics possess, in their box of tools, the techniques applicable for these types of functions. Furthermore, much of the study of economics culminates in the procedure of optimizing multivariate functions. This is due to the fact that this procedure represents the process of rational decision making, and in large part, this is what the science of economics is all about.

The focus of the book thus far has been the analysis and interpretation of models where the relationship between the independent and dependent variables is known. In most instances theory alone does not inform us of the exact relationship. In those cases, the relationship must be estimated by collecting and analyzing data. The tools used for estimating and testing these relationships are developed in the following chapter.

Important Terms in this Chapter

Constrained optimization – the process of optimizing (maximizing or minimizing) some objective function subject to the limitations imposed by some predetermined factor(s).

Instantaneous growth rate of a variable – a percentage change in a variable over time.

Isocost constraint – an equation representing the locus of input combinations a firm is able to purchase, given the factor prices of the inputs and some predetermined expenditure outlay.

Isoquant: a function representing the locus of input combinations which can be used to produce some given level of output.

Lagrangean function – a function that incorporates the objective function, which is to be optimized, with the constraint function(s).

Marginal rate of technical substitution (MRTS) – the negative of the slope of an isoquant defined as the rate at which one input can be substituted for another in the production process while still producing the same level of output.

Partial derivatives – derivative for which all independent variables but the one in question are held constant.

Solution values – the values of the independent variables that correspond to an optimal value for the dependent variable.

Substitution method – a method of constrained optimization which involves solving a constraint for one of the variables, substituting this expression into the objective function, and utilizing the total derivative to solve the necessary condition for an optimum.

Total derivative – a derivative for which none of the independent variables are held constant.

Exercise Set 8.2

1. An individual has the utility function:

$$U = X^{1/2} + Y^{1/2}$$

where:

   U   =   utility in utils per period of time
   X   =   units of good X consumed per period of time
   Y   =   units of good Y consumed per period of time

The individual faces the budget constraint:

$$P_X X + P_Y Y = I$$

where:

   P_X =   \$1   = price of good X in dollars per unit
   P_Y =   \$2   = price of good Y in dollars per unit
   I   =   \$300 = income in dollars per period of time

What amounts of good X and Y should the individual consume in order to maximize his or her utility?

2. A firm has the production function:

$$Q = 2K^{1/4}L^{3/4}$$

where:

   Q   =   output produced in units per period of time
   K   =   capital input used in units per period of time
   L   =   labor input used in units per period of time

The firm is subject to the following isocost constraint:

$$P_K K + P_L L = C$$

where:

P_K = $100 = price of capital input, in dollars per unit
P_L = $10 = price of labor input, in dollars per unit
C = $100,000 = expenditure outlay for producing Q, in dollars per period of time

Using the substitution method, find the values of K and L which optimize (in this case, maximize) the value of Q.

3. Using the same information given in Problem 2, find the values of K and L which optimize (maximize) Q by using the method of Lagrangean multipliers. Check and make sure your results are the same as those calculated for Problem 2. What is the interpretation associated with the Lagrangean multiplier, λ? Now that you can solve for the value for Q, set up this problem as one of constrained cost minimization (i.e., show that these solution values for K and L result in the least cost expenditure necessary to produce the given value of Q).

4. A firm has the production function:

$$Q = K^{1/2}L^{1/2}$$

where:

Q = 100 = output produced in units per period of time
K = capital input in units per period of time
L = labor input in units per period of time

The firm is subject to the isocost constraint equation:

$$P_K K + P_L L = C$$

where:

P_K = $1 = price of capital input, in dollars per unit
P_L = $4 = price of labor input in units per period of time
C = expenditure outlay (cost) for producing Q in dollars per period of time

What are the values of K and L which minimize the expenditure outlay C, while producing Q = 100 units of output? [Hint: Treat the isocost equation as the objective function, and the production function as the constraint.]

5. Return to the two period consumption problem in Exercise 2.6 at the end of Chapter 2. The constraint facing the individual was:

$$C_2 = Y_2 + (Y_1 - C_1) + R(Y_1 - C_1)$$

where:

C_1 = consumption expenditures for period one, in dollars
C_2 = consumption expenditures for period two, in dollars
Y_1 = income for period one, in dollars
Y_2 = income for period two, in dollars
R = interest rate, in percentage points

Assuming the individual has a utility function of the form U = $C_1^{1/2}C_2^{1/2}$, find the optimal levels for C_1 and C_2 when Y_1 = \$10,000, Y_2 = \$20,000, and R = 10%. Is the individual borrowing or lending in period one?

References

Anton, H., *Calculus with Analytic Geometry*, New York: John Wiley and Sons, 1988.

Barnett, R. and M. Ziegler, *Applied Calculus*, San Francisco: Dellen Publishing Company, 1987.

Grossman, S., *Applied Mathematical Analysis*, Belmont, CA: Wadsworth Publishing Company, 1986.

Salas, S. L., E. Hille, and J. T. Anderson, *Calculus*, New York: John Wiley and Sons, 1986.

Thomas, G. B., Jr., and R. L. Finney, *Calculus and Analytical Geometry*, Reading, MA: Addison–Wesley Publishing Company, 1988.

Estimation of
Simple Models

Introduction

Economic theories are a subset of scientific theories since economics is a science. One property of scientific theories and sciences in general is that they are based on observation. Given that reality is very complex, with multitudes of events occurring simultaneously, it takes an astute observer to discern that some of those events are related in some fashion and that, in particular, a causal link exists between them. The scientist then formulates a hypothesis or theory that generalizes the results observed. This process of reasoning from the specific (observations) to the general is called **induction**. A theory would be useless unless it could be tested in some way. Toward this end, the scientist must deduce the predictions contained within the theory. To be testable, the theory must predict that certain events will occur while others will not. The next step is to make additional observations to see whether the theory has predicted well. In the event that the additional observations do not confirm the predictions of the theory, we would be justified in rejecting that theory. However, if they do correspond to the theory's predictions, can we state that we have proven the theory and can therefore accept it as true? The answer is no. Since the theory is potentially refutable (i.e., predicts that certain events will not occur), there is always the possibility that subsequent observations may lead us ultimately to reject the theory. Therefore, at best we can state that the current evidence is insufficient to reject the theory. In that event, we might tentatively accept the theory as a basis for making predictions rather than accepting the theory as being "the truth." In other words, there is no test of a theory that can prove that a causal relationship exists. Conceptually, however, a test could prove that a causal relationship fails to exist between variables. Therefore, the theory that "A causes B" is usually tested as the hypothesis that "A does not cause B." Rejection of that hypothesis would lead us to the tentative conclusion that A may in fact cause B.

In order for a theory to be testable, it must have the following properties. First, it should assert that a causal relationship exists between certain variables and provide a rationale underlying that relationship. By doing so it will classify the variables under consideration as either independent or dependent. Next, it should make predictions regarding the effect of each of the independent variables on the dependent variable(s). These predictions typically can be expressed in terms of the sign (positive or negative) of the slope or partial slope of the dependent variable with respect to the independent variable(s). At least one of these predictions should be unambiguous, in order for the theory to be testable. A more precise theory could make predictions regarding the magnitude of the slopes and possibly even the form of the functional relationship.

Most economic theories are not that precise and, therefore, only make predictions regarding the sign of the slope coefficient(s). In that event, the researcher must choose the functional form (linear, quadratic, etc.) that he or she believes is most appropriate. Since the theory is tested in the context of a specific functional form, it is possible to reject the specific form without necessarily rejecting the more general theory underlying it.

A theory's usefulness is also tied to its degree of precision. A theory that predicts that quantity demanded will fall by fifty units per month for each dollar increase in its price is more useful than one predicting only that quantity demanded and price are inversely related. A less precise theory can be made more powerful, for prediction purposes, by estimating the values of the unknown coefficients. It is the field of statistics which provides the tools used for such estimation and for ultimately testing theories. This is accomplished by collecting and analyzing actual data pertaining to the included variables.

The preceding chapters have dwelled on the construction and interpretation of theoretical models applicable to economics. Thus far, the coefficients of the models have been treated as "givens." The purpose of this chapter is to provide some basic statistical techniques that can be used to estimate the previously mentioned coefficients, with particular emphasis on the slope coefficient. These statistical tools are developed to enable one to test these theories. The thrust of this chapter is the interpretation of statistical measures rather than the development of statistical theory. Students desiring a more detailed development of statistical theory are advised to consult any of a number of basic probability and statistics texts.

Deterministic vs. Stochastic Relationships

Economic models may be specified as either deterministic relationships or as stochastic relationships. It is common practice in expositing a model to treat it as deterministic. The relationships developed in the preceding chapters, as well as those presented in most basic economic texts, are of this type. However, for purposes of estimation and testing, the relationships here are treated as stochastic.

A **deterministic relationship** is one for which the value of the dependent variable is uniquely determined by the value(s) taken on by the independent variable(s). The relationship $Y = b_0 + b_1X$ is deterministic, because only one value of Y corresponds to each value that is assigned for X.

A **stochastic relationship** is probabilistic in nature. The dependent variable can take on more than one value for each (set of) value(s) of the independent variable(s). The flipping of a coin may be considered a stochastic event. On any given flip, the coin may come up heads or tails. The outcome of the flip cannot be determined uniquely beforehand. All that could be said is that there is a 50 percent chance of either outcome. The relationship $Y = b_0 + b_1X + u$, where u is a random error term, is a stochastic relationship. This relationship has two components. The deterministic component is given by, $b_0 + b_1X$, while the random component is u. The deterministic component tells us on average how the value of Y is determined by the value of X. The random component tells us that the actual value of Y can differ from its average value, predicted by the deterministic component. When using a stochastic model, the characteristics of the random error term, u, should be specified.

When expositing a causal theory, it is natural to use a deterministic relationship. If "A causes B," then every time A occurs, B must follow. In other words, B is uniquely determined by A. If A occurs and B does not follow, even once, how can we say that A caused B? For that one time that B did not follow, A did not cause B. Were we to test a theory in its deterministic form, even one observation of Y that differed from its predicted value would cause us to reject that particular theory. This is so even if all other observations fit the relationship exactly. This condition seems overly restrictive since it leads to the rejection of theories that are essentially correct. On pragmatic grounds it seems reasonable to test the theory as a stochastic relationship.

The inclusion of the error term has been justified on purely pragmatic grounds. When estimating a relationship from actual data there are four reasons for the existence of the error term. First, the dependent variable may be generated in a stochastic rather than deterministic manner. In other words, the true relationship is stochastic, in as much as the dependent variable has a random component in addition to the deterministic one. However, even when the true relationship is deterministic, three reasons exist for including the error term, thus treating the relationship as stochastic.

Theories are abstractions of reality. There may be one thousand independent variables that impact in some way on a dependent variable. The values taken on by the independent variables may uniquely determine the value of the dependent variable. The theorist may be unaware of the influences of some of these variables, or by choice exclude some of them if their impact is assumed to be negligible. In either event we can never be sure that the list of independent variables is complete. This is particularly true of simple models where the number of independent variables is small. If the specification of the relationship between the dependent and independent variables is correct, except for the effects of the omitted variables, it is likely that the actual value of the dependent variable will differ from its predicted value. This would occur due to variation in the omitted variables having some impact on the dependent variable. For example, a consumption function may be specified as solely a function of disposable income. In fact, consumption expenditures may also depend on the interest rate. Since our predicted value of consumption expenditures depends only on the level of disposable income, changes in the interest rate will cause the actual level of consumption expenditures to differ from the predicted level.

Assume that the problem of omitted variables has been overcome, and that luckily our list of independent variables is complete. Even in that unlikely event, the inclusion of an error term is warranted. Recall that, in general, theory does not inform us of the true mathematical form of the relationship. In specifying some functional form, there is always the possibility that we erred. We might specify a linear relationship, when the true relationship may not be exactly linear. Consequently, for selected values of the independent variable(s), the observed values of the dependent variable may differ from those predicted by the theory. In some cases these differences are so large that the postulated model should be rejected and a different model (nonlinear) should be utilized.

Finally, even if the previous problems have been overcome, the inclusion of the error term is still warranted. We can never be sure that we have measured the observed variables accurately. When measurement error exists, it will generally cause our predicted values to differ from the observed values of the dependent variable. It is seldom possible or desirable (due to cost) to collect all of the observations pertaining to a variable (the population). Instead, only a sample drawn from the population is utilized and inferences are made about the population, based upon that sample. To the extent that the sample does not perfectly reflect the true population from which it is drawn, sampling error will exist. The problem of errors in measurement will thereby be compounded. For example, a final exam is designed to measure a student's retention of knowledge obtained in a course. To the extent that questions are not perfectly worded and graded, measurement error exists. Furthermore, questions on an exam correspond to only a sample of the population of knowledge obtained during the course. It is possible for a student to obtain much knowledge and perform poorly on the exam, while another student might know little and perform well. The extent to which this occurs reflects sampling error. The professor may attempt to minimize this error by making the exam (sample) as representative of the body of course knowledge (population) as possible.

The existence of any of these problems in isolation is sufficient to warrant the inclusion of an error term. Furthermore, due to a lack of omniscience, we can never be sure that at least one of these problems exists. In fact, it is highly likely that all three are present simultaneously. Therefore, whether the true model is stochastic or deterministic, we must treat the relationship as stochastic.

Some Statistical Definitions

Before we can use any statistical techniques to estimate and test a model, it is necessary to define and briefly explain some basic statistical terms.

Expected Values and Means

A discrete variable represents quantities that can occur only at certain values. If X represents a discrete random variable which can take on a set of values $X_1, X_2, X_3, \ldots, X_n$, then the expected value of the variable X, more commonly known as the **mean** of X, is equal to the summation of the products of each value of X times its probability of occurrence. In a general sense, an expected value or mean is simply a measure of central tendency. Symbolically, this can be expressed as:

$$E(X) = \sum_{i=1}^{N} P_i X_i$$

where $E(X)$ is read "the expected value of X," Σ simply means "the summation of," P_i represents the probability of each respective X_i occurring, and X_i stands for the different values of the variable X. As an example, suppose we want to find the expected value or mean associated with rolling a pair of dice. In other words, we want to find the expected value of the sum of the two dice. Since each die contains numbers one through six, the possible totals (X_is) are 2, 3, 4, . . . , or 12. A probability of each outcome can be easily established. The probability of rolling a two overall is the product of rolling a one on each die simultaneously. A die is six sided, so the probability of rolling a one is 1/6 for each die, or $(1/6)(1/6) = 1/36$ that both come up one, yielding a total of two. The probability of rolling a total of three is a little better, because there are more combinations that yield a total of three. Specifically, we could roll a one on the first die and a two on the second, or a two on the first die and a one on the second. Therefore, the probability of rolling a three, in total, is $(1/6)(1/6) = 1/36$, for the first combination, plus $(1/6)(1/6) = 1/36$, for the second combination, which equals 2/36. The various possible outcomes, along with their associated probabilities, are given in Table 9.1.

Table 9.1
Outcomes and Unconditional Probabilities
Associated with Rolling a Pair of Dice

X_i	2	3	4	5	6	7	8	9	10	11	12
P_i	1/36	2/36	3/36	4/36	5/36	6/36	5/36	4/36	3/36	2/36	1/36
i	1	2	3	4	5	6	7	8	9	10	11

The expected value (mean) of the Xs is:

$$E(X) = \sum_{i=1}^{11} P_i X_i$$

$$= (1/36)(2) + (2/36)(3) + (3/36)(4) + \ldots + (1/36)(12)$$

$$= 7$$

This value of seven represents the central tendency associated with the set of possible outcomes.

The computational formula for most means can be simplified, if we assume that the probability associated with each outcome is of equal value. Thus, if there are N possible outcomes, the probability of each outcome is 1/N. The formula for an expected value or mean becomes:

$$E(X) = \sum_{i=1}^{N} \frac{1}{N} X_i = \frac{1}{N} \sum_{i=1}^{N} X_i$$

As an example, suppose we roll just one die. Since the die is six sided, the probability of any one of the outcomes, 1, 2, . . . , 6, is 1/6. As a result, the mean value of a roll can be calculated as:

$$E(X) = \frac{1}{6} \sum_{i=1}^{6} X_i = \frac{1+2+3+4+5+6}{6} = 3.5$$

A very important point should be noted here. A mean can be calculated for an entire population, but very seldom is it possible, or even desirable, to obtain observations from an entire population. More generally samples are taken and, consequently, most calculated means are sample means. Due to sampling error it is unlikely that two sample means will be identical. However, it can be shown that with a sufficient number of observations, sample means are good estimators of population means. Those students wishing to see proof of this contention should consult a probability and statistics text.

It should be pointed out that the expected value defined and demonstrated up to this point is technically an **unconditional expectation**. Another type of expectation is a **conditional expectation** also known as a **conditional mean**. Conditional means are relevant when two variables are determined, and the determination of one variable depends on the value of the other. For example, suppose the variables X and D are to be determined, and that the value of X is dependent on the value of D. It is possible to define a conditional mean for X provided prior information is known about the outcome associated with D. More formally:

$$E\ (X\,|\,\text{Information about the outcome of D})= \sum_{i=1}^{N} P_i' X_i$$

The term on the left-hand side of the equation is read "the expected value of X, given some prior information about outcome, D." The probabilities associated with the X_is will be altered by this information and are labeled P_i'. Returning to our example, suppose we roll each die separately in sequence. In this case, D represents the value of the first die and X represents the sum of the two dice. Suppose we know the value of the first die roll is three, i.e., D = 3. Now, we can find the expected value of the total associated with rolling the two dice, except in this case we have some prior information. We know the value of the first die is three. As a consequence, we are dealing with a conditional expectation. The probabilities associated with the possible outcomes have now been altered and are summarized in Table 9.2. Given that the value of the first die is three, there is no way that a total of 2, 3, 10, 11, or 12 can be rolled. Total values of 4, 5, 6, 7, 8, or 9 can be achieved if the value of the second die comes up 1, 2, 3, 4, 5, or 6 respectively. The conditional expectation, or mean, is:

Table 9.2
Outcomes and Conditional Probabilities
Associated with Rolling Two Dies in Sequence

X_i	2	3	4	5	6	7	8	9	10	11	12
P_i'	0	0	1/6	1/6	1/6	1/6	1/6	1/6	0	0	0

$$E(X \mid \text{first die} = 3) = \sum_{i=1}^{11} P_i X_i$$

$$= (0)(2) + (0)(3) + (1/6)(4) + (1/6)(5) + (1/6)(6) + (1/6)(7)$$

$$+ (1/6)(8) + (1/6)(9) + (0)(10) + (0)(11) + (0)(12)$$

$$= 6.5$$

Notice that the value of a conditional mean differs from the unconditional one, due to the existence of the extra information.

Variances and Standard Deviations

Another important statistical measure applied to a random variable is the **variance**. In general, the variance is a measure of the dispersion of a random variable about its mean. It indicates how widely scattered the observations are. The variance is expressed as the expected value of the square of the differences between each observation and its mean. Thus it represents the central tendency of the square of these deviations. The differences are squared for two reasons. First, the differences can be positive or negative, so squaring keeps them from canceling each other out. Second, squaring the differences places more weight on the larger deviations. Mathematically, the variance is:

$$\text{Var}(X) = E[X - E(X)]^2$$

or

$$= \sum_{i=1}^{N} P_i[X_i - E(X)]^2$$

Again, letting each of the N observations have an equal probability of occurrence, 1/N, the formula simplifies to:

$$\text{Var}(X) = \sum_{i=1}^{N} \frac{1}{N}[X_i - E(X)]^2$$

or

$$= \frac{1}{N} \sum_{i=1}^{N} [X_i - E(X)]^2$$

where, recall, E(X) is the population mean. Actually, this is the variance of a population. Seldom, however, do we deal with the entire population, and as a result, population means are seldom known. The purpose of taking samples from a population is to provide estimators for their population counterparts. One such estimator is the sample mean, often designated $\bar{X}$, which is used to estimate the population mean. Another is the sample variance, designated Vâr(X) or $\hat{S}^2$, which is an estimator of the population variance. The formula for this estimator involves only a slight modification of the above equation, yielding:

$$\hat{\text{Var}}(X) = \hat{S}^2 = \frac{1}{N-1} \sum_{i=1}^{N} [X_i - \bar{X}]^2$$

Notice we have divided by N–1 rather than N when calculating a sample variance. The reason for doing so can be explained as follows. A sample variance is intended to represent an estimate of the population variance. Also recall the population mean is seldom known, but the sample mean can be calculated as an estimate of the population mean. With a sample of just one observation, the sample mean would equal the one observation and could be used to approximate the population mean. But in this case there is no way to estimate the variance, because there is no dispersion about the mean. In other words, one **degree of freedom** (d.f.) has been used to calculate the mean, leaving none to calculate the variance. With a sample of two observations, one degree of freedom is used to calculate the mean of the sample, leaving N-1 = 1 degree of freedom to calculate the variance. In general, the number of degrees of freedom equals the number of observations in the sample minus the number of estimated terms. Regarding the calculation of a sample variance, one degree of freedom is always used to calculate the sample mean, thus leaving N-1 d.f. to calculate the sample variance.

Another term frequently encountered in statistics is the **standard deviation**. This term is only a slight alteration of the formula for a variance. Dwelling only on the sample variance, the related sample standard deviation, $\hat{S}$, is:

$$\hat{S} = \sqrt{\hat{S}^2}$$

i.e., it is simply the positive square root of the variance.

Exercise Set 9.1

1. What is the difference between a deterministic and a stochastic relationship? Explain the rationale for including an error term in a function.

2. Suppose you are given a deal where you can flip two coins simultaneously and receive the following payoffs:

Outcome	Coin 1	Coin 2	Payoff
1	Tail	Tail	0
2	Tail	Head	$1
3	Head	Tail	$1
4	Head	Head	$2

    a) What is the probability associated with each of the four outcomes?
    b) What is the unconditional mean payoff?

c) Suppose you can flip the coins in sequence, and you know the first coin comes up a head. Now flip the second coin to determine the payoff as presented on page 329. What is the mean payoff now? What type of mean or expectation have you just calculated? Why does it differ from the unconditional mean calculated in Part b?

3. Two classes, with ten students in each, take a test yielding the following results:

Class 1	Class 2		
90	95	a)	Find the mean test score for each class. (They should be equal.)
60	55		
55	57		
40	38	b)	Find the population variance and standard deviation about the mean for each class.
85	80		
92	91		
72	77	c)	As demonstrated by your calculations, the two means are equal, but the variances differ. What does this tell you about the nature of the students in the two classes?
75	76		
68	58		
78	88		

4. The following table presents the annual rates of return for a security in your portfolio for years 1-10.

Year	Rate of Return	Year	Rate of Return
1	12%	6	-2%
2	5%	7	+8%
3	-20%	8	+10%
4	31%	9	+15%
5	6%	10	-5%

a) What was the average rate of return for this security using the arithmetic mean, as discussed in this chapter? (Note that generally a geometric mean is used to calculate average rates of return.)

b) One measure of the risk of a security is its standard deviation. Compute the standard deviation of the rate of return for this security over the 10 year period.

Simple Regression

Having established some basic statistical terms, let's return to the goal of this chapter, which is to use basic statistical techniques to show how predicted values of a dependent variable can be calculated on the basis of known values of some independent variables. This technique is formally defined as **regression analysis**. Essentially, this procedure involves collecting a sample of observations on the included variables then estimating the coefficients that generate a curve which best "fits" the data. The basic regression equation to be estimated in this chapter is:

$$Y = b_0 + b_1 X + U$$

where Y is the dependent variable to be predicted, X is the independent variable, b_0 and b_1 are the intercept and slope coefficients respectively, and U is a stochastic error term.

Before proceeding, some important clarifications and assumptions need to be noted. First, we are estimating a univariate, linear function. This has been chosen so that we can illustrate regression analysis using the simplest function possible. Second, for reasons established earlier in this chapter, a stochastic error term is included in the function. There are some additional assumptions regarding this error term.

1) The expected value or mean of the error term is equal to zero. This assumption implies that the random effects of omitted variables tend to cancel each other out.

2) The error terms are unrelated to the X's and to each other. This implies that when there is a change in the X variable, we can examine what happens, on average, to the variable Y without worrying about any additional effects on Y caused by changes in the error term.

3) The variance of the error term is constant across different observations. This implies that changes due to omitted variables tend to have the same dispersion.

The goal of regression analysis is to find a way of calculating or predicting values of a dependent variable, Y, on the basis of known values of independent variables, or in this case, known values of a single independent variable, X. This goal should be recognized as one of finding the conditional expectation, or mean, of Y given values of X. Thus the population regression equation is:

$$Y = b_0 + b_1 X + U$$

and the predicted values of Y are:

$$E(Y \mid X) = b_0 + b_1 X$$

Since we will be dealing with observations from a sample rather than a population, the sample regression equation becomes:

$$\hat{Y} = \hat{b}_0 + \hat{b}_1 X + \hat{U}$$

where $\hat{b}_0$, $\hat{b}_1$ and $\hat{U}$ are calculated from a sample and provide estimation for their population counterparts b_0, b_1, and U. Thus an estimate of the conditional mean or predicted value of Y becomes:

$$E(Y \mid X) = \hat{Y} = \hat{b}_0 + \hat{b}_1 X$$

Methods of Collecting Data

In order to estimate a regression equation, it is necessary to collect observations on the included variables. There are essentially two methods of collecting data. The first is defined as a **time series**, which involves collecting data on variables measured at different points in time, i.e., the data varies over time. The second method of collecting data is defined as a **cross sectional analysis**, which involves collecting data on variables measured at one point in time, but variable across sections, e.g., individuals, families, states, etc.

These two methods of data collection can best be described by use of an example. Suppose we want to estimate a consumption function of the theoretical form:

$$C = b_0 + b_1 Y_d$$

where:

C = consumption expenditures in dollars
Y_d = disposable income in dollars

The function can be made stochastic by the inclusion of an error term. Furthermore, since data are to be collected from a sample, the calculated coefficients will be estimators of the population coefficients. As a result, the equation becomes:

$$C = \hat{b}_0 + \hat{b}_1 Y_d + \hat{U}$$

Table 9.3
Cross–Sectional Data Pertaining to Consumption and Disposable Income for Ten Students

Data for the Month of January

Student	N	C($)	Y_d($)
A	1	190	200
B	2	250	220
C	3	140	150
D	4	240	300
E	5	300	350
F	6	210	180
G	7	190	250
H	8	320	400
I	9	240	320
J	10	170	190

The next step is to collect observations on the variables C and Y_d. Suppose our sample consists of 10 students in an Economics 101 class. Also for the sake of example, assume the class (as disheartening as the thought may be) lasts exactly one year, January 1987-December 1987. The data can be collected using either a time series or a cross sectional approach. Let's examine the cross sectional approach first. This involves taking a point in time, say the end of January 1987, and collecting (C, Y_d) observations across the ten people in the class. Each of these (C, Y_d) pairs represents each student's consumption expenditure and disposable income level for the month of January 1987. We will get ten (C, Y_d) pairs of observations, all taken at a point in time. A summary of such hypothetical data is presented in Table 9.3 and plotted in Figure 9.1.

Figure 9.1
Cross Sectional Data Pertaining to Consumption and Disposable Income for Ten Students Plotted Graphically

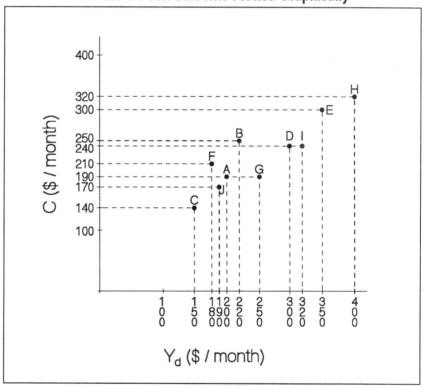

The alternative method of collecting data is via a time series approach. Using the same sample, we could take the class as a whole, collect (C, Y_d) observations, and calculate the mean class values for these variables for each month over the course of one year, thus generating twelve (C, Y_d) pairs of observations. Alternatively, the aggregate levels of C and Y_d for the class could have been chosen. The set of hypothetical observations might resemble those given in Table 9.4 and plotted in Figure 9.2.

Using either approach, we get a scatter of (C, Y_d) points, following somewhat of a linear pattern. Each technique represents an attempt to construct a sample generating the data necessary to estimate a linear consumption function for college students. The results from each type of sample will not be identical, but they should be reasonably close. Since the units of observation have been changed, the interpretation of the equation may be altered somewhat. Both approaches are perfectly valid, so the procedure of choice depends largely on which type of data is available.

Table 9.4
Times Series Data Pertaining to Consumption
and Disposable Income for Twelve Months

Month	C	Y_d
January	225	256
February	140	150
March	210	250
April	200	240
May	300	650
June	350	700
July	400	600
August	370	600
September	200	300
October	130	200
November	220	160
December	280	350

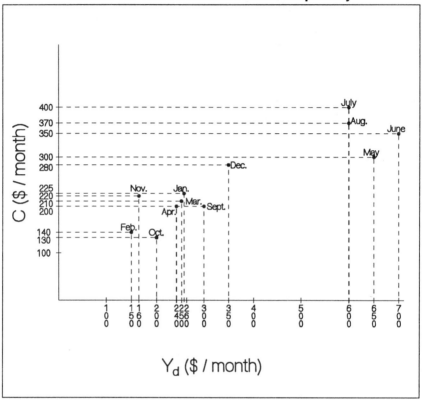

Figure 9.2
Time Series Data Pertaining to Consumption and Disposable
Income for Twelve Months Plotted Graphically

Fitting a Line to a Set of Observations

We have specified a model, along with its associated assumptions, and shown how to collect the data necessary for testing the model. The next step is to demonstrate how to determine the coefficients, $\hat{b}_0$ and $\hat{b}_1$, which are associated with a curve that best fits the collected data. This procedure will generate a specific equation enabling us to calculate the conditional mean and predicted values for an dependent variable on the basis of selected values of an independent variable. The procedure which accomplishes this task is known as **fitting a line** to a set of observations.

In general, to generate a function which most accurately reflects the data, we want to find the best fit possible. There are an infinite number of possible curves passing through a set of data points. Figure 9.3 shows three such curves. The goal is to select the curve which best describes or fits the scatter of observations. By simply observing the figure, we would probably guess that the line AA' best fits the scatter. But how do we really know this? Also, how can we find the coefficients, $\hat{b}_0$ and $\hat{b}_1$, which describe the curve?

There are several techniques designed to perform this task, but the most often used is the procedure of minimizing the sum of squared differ-

Figure 9.3
Three Curves, One of Which Best Fits the
Scatter of Observation Points

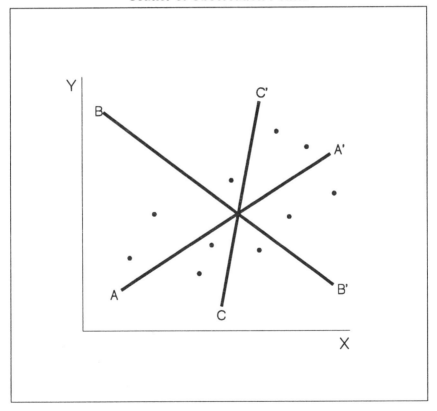

ences between an actual observation and the fitted curve. This procedure is more formally known as minimizing the sum of squared errors or the method of least squares. These error terms are depicted in Figure 9.4. There are several reasons for squaring these error terms. First, because some errors are positive and some are negative, the process of squaring keeps them from canceling each other out when they are summed. Second, squaring tends to place a greater weight on the larger errors. In addition, there are other desirable statistical properties of the least squares estimates that are absent in other methods.

The procedure of fitting a line by minimizing the sum of squared errors is essentially nothing more than an application of the optimization

Figure 9.4
Graphical Depiction of Error Terms

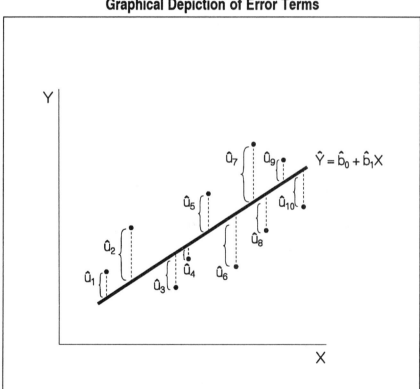

technique described in Chapter 4. The general linear regression equation is:

$$Y_i = \hat{b}_0 + \hat{b}_1 X_i + \hat{U}_i$$

Solving for $\hat{U}_i$, it becomes:

$$\hat{U}_i = Y_i - \hat{b}_0 - \hat{b}_1 X_i$$

Squaring and summing both sides for $i = 1, 2, \ldots, N$ observations, the equation becomes:

$$\sum_{i=1}^{N} \hat{U}_i^2 = \sum_{i=1}^{N} (Y_i - \hat{b}_0 - \hat{b}_1 X_i)^2$$

The goal is to minimize the objective function, the sum of squared errors:

$$\left(\sum_{i=1}^{n} \hat{U}_1^2 \right)$$

with respect to each of the coefficients, $\hat{b}_0$ and $\hat{b}_1$. In other words, we want to find the values of $\hat{b}_0$ and $\hat{b}_1$ which satisfy this objective. The procedure involves basic calculus, and will not be shown here, but the results generate formulas for $\hat{b}_0$ and $\hat{b}_1$. The formula for calculating the estimate of the slope coefficient, $\hat{b}_1$, is:

$$\hat{b}_1 = \frac{\sum_{i=1}^{N} (X_i - \bar{X})(Y_i - \bar{Y})}{\sum_{i=1}^{N} (X_i - \bar{X})^2}$$

where:
$\overline{X}$ = the unconditional expected value, or sample mean, of X
$\overline{Y}$ = the unconditional expected value, or sample mean, of Y

The formula for calculating the estimate of the intercept coefficient, $\hat{b}_0$, is:

$$\hat{b}_0 = \overline{Y} - \hat{b}_1\overline{X}$$

Therefore, the fitted equation or regression line, $Y = \hat{b}_0 + \hat{b}_1 X$, must pass through the means of X and Y. Recognizing that the values $\hat{b}_0$ and $\hat{b}_1$ represent sample estimates of their population counterparts b_0 and b_1, we can interpret them in the usual manner. In other words, $\hat{b}_0$ is the estimate of the intercept coefficient and, therefore, represents the predicted value of the dependent variable, Y, when the independent variable, X, is equal to zero. The term, $\hat{b}_1$, is the estimate of the slope coefficient and, therefore, represents the change in the predicted dependent variable, Y, due to a change in the independent variable, X. It is this term, $\hat{b}_1$, which is of particular importance, because it provides the magnitude of the linkage, if any, between the included variables. Once the coefficients have been estimated, we can use the fitted regression line, $\hat{Y} = \hat{b}_0 + \hat{b}_1 X$, to calculate values for the predictor variable, $\hat{Y}$, after substituting in values for X. This procedure of fitting a curve by estimating the regression coefficients and then using the fitted curve to predict values for the dependent variable can best be illustrated by an example.

Let's return to the cross sectional consumption function data presented earlier. We can fit the curve, $\hat{C} = \hat{b}_0 + \hat{b}_1 Y_d$ to the scatter of observations by using the formulas presented above to calculate $\hat{b}_0$ and $\hat{b}_1$. In this case, again note that $\hat{C}_i$ represents the predicted values for the dependent variable, and Y_{di} represents the values of the independent variable. The calculations for $\hat{b}_0$ and $\hat{b}_1$ are summarized in Table 9.5. Thus:

$$\hat{b}_1 = \frac{\sum\limits_{i=1}^{10} (Y_{d_i} - \overline{Y}_d)(C_i - \overline{C})}{\sum\limits_{i=1}^{10} (Y_{d_i} - \overline{Y}_d)^2} = \frac{37,400}{61,440} = .61$$

Table 9.5
Computations of $\hat{b}_1$ and $\hat{b}_0$ for Consumption Function, $C = b_0 + b_1 Y_d$

Student	N	Ci	$Y_{d,i}$	$Y_{d,i} - \bar{Y}_d$	Ci-$\bar{C}$	$(Y_{d,i} - \bar{Y}_d)^2$	$(Y_{d,i} - \bar{Y}_d)(Ci-\bar{C})$	$\hat{C}i=E(C|Y_{d,i})$	Ci-$\hat{C}i$	$(Ci-\hat{C}i)^2$	$(Ci-\bar{C})^2$
A	1	190	200	-56	-35	3136	1960	190.91	-0.91	0.83	1225
B	2	250	220	-36	25	1296	-900	203.09	46.91	2200.93	625
C	3	140	150	-106	-85	11236	9010	160.48	-20.48	419.24	7225
D	4	240	300	44	15	1936	660	251.78	-11.78	138.86	225
E	5	300	350	94	75	8836	7050	282.22	17.78	316.13	5625
F	6	210	180	-76	-15	5776	1140	178.74	31.26	977.38	225
G	7	190	250	-6	-35	36	210	221.35	-31.35	982.68	1225
H	8	320	400	144	95	20736	13680	312.66	7.34	53.93	9025
I	9	240	320	64	15	4096	960	263.96	-23.96	574.00	225
J	10	170	190	-66	-55	4356	3630	184.82	-14.82	219.76	3025
SUMMA–TION (Σ)	10	2250	2560			61440	37400			5583.74	28650

$$\bar{C} = \Sigma Ci/N = 225$$

$$\hat{b}_1 = \frac{\Sigma(Y_{d,i} - \bar{Y}_d)(Ci - \bar{C})}{\Sigma(Y_{d,i} - \bar{Y}_d)^2} = .61$$

$$\bar{Y}_d = \Sigma Y_{d,i}/N = 256$$

$$\hat{b}_0 = \bar{C} - \hat{b}_1 \cdot \bar{Y}_d = 68.84$$

or:

$$\hat{b}_0 = \bar{C} - b_1 \bar{Y}_d = 225 - .61(256) = 68.84$$

The estimated consumption function becomes $\hat{C} = 68.84 + .61Y_d$. The predicted consumption expenditure levels, $\hat{C}_i$, are presented in column 9 of Table 9.5.

Recall the economic interpretation associated with the coefficients in a consumption function. The intercept coefficient, $\hat{b}_0 = \$68.84$, represents the typical student's level of consumption expenditures, when disposable income is equal to zero and is defined as the level of autonomous consumption. The slope coefficient, $\hat{b}_1 = .61$, represents the change in consumption expenditures due to a change in disposable income and is known as the marginal propensity to consume (MPC). This value of .61 indicates that for every additional dollar of disposable income, a typical student will spend 61 cents of it for consumption. The remaining $1.00 - \$.61 = \$.39$ would, of course, be saved. Thus the coefficients, once estimated, have the same interpretations as those provided by economic theory. We have demonstrated how the statistical tool of regression analysis can be applied to a sample of observations to fit a curve and generate estimates for the coefficients. However, the mere fact that we are able to estimate such an equation does not guarantee that the results are necessarily useful. It is always possible, mechanically speaking, to estimate a univariate regression equation as long as two or more observations can be utilized. However, before we can draw any valid conclusions or make any useful predictions, we need to determine how reliable the estimated coefficients are, and how good the estimated model is at satisfying the objectives set forth by the underlying economic theory. In order to test an estimated model to see how well it satisfies these criteria, we must develop some additional statistical measures.

Statistical Measures and Tests of Significance

Recall that the sample coefficients, $\hat{b}_0$ and $\hat{b}_1$, are intended to represent estimators of their population counterparts, b_0 and b_1. Once these sample coefficients have been estimated, we would like to know with what degree of confidence can we say these are good estimators. A key condition for testing the reliability of a sample coefficient (how well does it represent its population counterpart) is stated here without proof. **The expected value or mean of a sample coefficient is equal to the population coefficient.** Therefore, it follows that by measuring the dispersion of an estimated coefficient from its mean, we can determine its degree of reliability. Recall that, in general, the term which measures the dispersion of the observations associated with some term is referred to as the variance of the term. The square root of a variance is defined as the standard error. Specifically, in this case we need to find the variance and, hence, the standard error of the estimated coefficient. By so doing we can determine its reliability.

We will dwell on a measure of reliability as applied to the slope coefficient, since it is generally of greater importance than the intercept. This measure can be developed by analyzing the factors which determine the standard error of this coefficient, $\hat{b}_1$. First, the standard error depends on the number observations in the sample on which the estimated slope coefficient, $\hat{b}_i$, is based. Logically, the greater the number of observations, the smaller should be the dispersion or standard error of $\hat{b}_1$ around its mean. This is due to the fact that a sample containing a larger number of observations will be more representative, on average, of the population from which it is drawn. Thus the fitted curve should be closer to the actual (population) curve, and the estimated coefficients should be close to their population counterparts. Second, the standard error of $\hat{b}_1$ should depend on the standard error associated with the stochastic, or error, terms ($\hat{U}_i$s) in the regression equation. Recall, the error terms, $\hat{U}_i$'s, represent the differences between the predicted and actual values of the explained variable, or $Y_i - \hat{Y}_i$. The greater the dispersion or standard error of these terms, the further is the fitted line from the true one, and the greater will be the standard error of $\hat{b}_1$. The formula for the standard error of the error terms in a regression, $\hat{S}_{u_i}$, is:

$$\hat{S}_{u_i} = \left(\frac{\sum_{i=1}^{N} (Y_i - \hat{Y}_i)^2}{N - 2} \right)^{1/2} = \left(\frac{\sum_{i=1}^{N} \hat{U}_i^2}{N - 2} \right)^{1/2}$$

Note that $\hat{Y}_i$ is the conditional mean of Y_i. Also note that the number of associated degrees of freedom is $N - 2$. This reflects the fact that two degrees of freedom are lost in estimating the two coefficients, $\hat{b}_0$ and $\hat{b}_1$, in the regression equation. This term is defined as the **standard error of the estimate**. A greater dispersion, $\hat{S}_u$, in the error terms, caused by variation in omitted variables, a large difference between the estimated mathematical form of the equation and the true equation, or sampling error, will lead to a greater level of dispersion in the standard error of $\hat{b}_1$.

A final factor contributing to the dispersion of $\hat{b}_1$ is the dispersion or **standard error of the observations on the independent variable X,** denoted, S_x. The formula for this term is:

$$S_x = \left(\sum_{i-1}^{N} \frac{(X_i - \bar{X})^2}{N} \right)^{1/2}$$

This term will affect the standard error of $\hat{b}_1$ in an inverse manner; it is desirable to have lots of variation in the **independent** variable when fitting a curve. As will be seen below, a larger value of S_x will lead to a smaller standard error of $\hat{b}_1$.

Now that the factors determining the standard error of the coefficient, $\hat{b}_1$, designated as $\hat{S}_{b_1}$, have been presented, the formula for calculating this term can be developed in the following manner. The variance of the estimated coefficient, $\hat{b}_1$, is:

$$\hat{S}_{b_1}^2 = \frac{\displaystyle\sum_{i-1}^{N} \frac{(Y_i - \hat{Y}_i)^2}{n-2}}{\displaystyle\sum_{i-1}^{N} (X_i - \bar{X})^2} = \frac{\hat{S}_{u_i}^2}{\displaystyle\sum_{i-1}^{N} (X_i - \bar{X})^2}$$

The variance of $\hat{b}_1$ is the variance of the error terms per total variation in the independent variable, X. Since:

$$S_x = \left[\sum_{i=1}^{N} \frac{(X_i - \bar{X})^2}{N} \right]^{1/2}$$

$$S_x^2 = \sum_{i=1}^{N} \frac{(X_i - \bar{X})^2}{N}$$

and

$$NS_x^2 = \sum_{i=1}^{N} (X_i - \bar{X})^2$$

Substituting NS_x^2 into the equation for $\sum_{i=1}^{N} (X_i - \bar{X})^2$ yields:

$$\hat{S}_{b_1}^2 = \frac{\hat{S}_{u_1}^2}{NS_x^2}$$

Taking the square root of both sides, we get the formula for the standard error of the estimated slope coefficient:

$$\hat{S}_{b_1} = \frac{\hat{S}_{u_1}}{S_x \sqrt{N}}$$

Observing this result, we can see that $\hat{S}_{b_1}$ varies directly with $\hat{S}_{u_1}$ and inversely with N and S_x.

Testing the Slope Coefficient for Significance

Finding $\hat{S}_{b_1}$ gives us a measure of the dispersion (and hence reliability) associated with the calculated $\hat{b}_1$. In general, the smaller the standard error of $\hat{b}_1$, the more reliable is $\hat{b}_1$ as an estimator of its population counterpart, b_1. Our best estimate of b_1 is $\hat{b}_1$, and $\hat{S}_{b_1}$ is our measure of $\hat{b}_1$'s reliability. The information contained in these measures can be used to determine the likelihood that the true b_1 lies in a certain interval. However, some reference point and framework is needed to make inferences about the value of b_1. Such a framework is provided by the concept of **hypothesis testing**.

Generally the value of a population coefficient, b_1, is not known. As a result, we can only hypothesize as to what is its value. For example, we may hypothesize that $b_1 = b_1^*$, where b_1^* represents some hypothetical value of the population parameter, b_1, based on some additional information (not directly included in our model) which enables us to form some expectation regarding its true value. We now want to compare the estimated value, $\hat{b}_1$, to the hypothetical value, b_1^*, to see if they are significantly different. In order to do so, we must come up with some measure that can be compared to some standard, so that we can make a judgment. Such a measure can be calculated by dividing the difference between the estimated value and the hypothetical one ($\hat{b}_1 - b_1^*$) by the standard error of the estimated coefficient, $\hat{S}_{b_1}$. The result of this calculation is defined as a **"t" statistic**, and is summarized as:

$$t = \frac{\hat{b}_1 - b_1^*}{\hat{S}_{b_1}}$$

The "t" value calculated represents the number of standard deviations between an estimated coefficient and its hypothesized value. This term is called a t statistic because such values follow what is defined as a t distribution. The t distribution is centered around $t = 0$, assuming that $b_1 = b_1^*$. Since it is unlikely that the actual estimated coefficient $\hat{b}_1$ will equal its expected value which is equal to b_1^*, the calculated t will accordingly vary from the value of zero. This calculated t can be viewed, as stated above, as the number of standard deviations of an estimated coefficient, $\hat{b}_1$, from its hypothesized value, b_1^*, which is also the number of standard deviations of an estimated value, $\hat{b}_1$, from its mean, $E(\hat{b}_1)$ = b_1. The shape of this distribution varies with the number of degrees of freedom (d.f.) used in calculating the t statistic. The degrees of freedom are found by subtracting the number of estimated coefficients from the number of observations, N, in the sample. For the univariate case, two coefficients (b_0 and b_1) are estimated, so the general formula for degrees of freedom is equal to N – 2. If the number of observations is large, so will be the number of degrees of freedom, and the t distribution approaches a shape that can be applied to all large samples, formally defined as a normal distribution. A diagram of this distribution is presented in Figure 9.5.

The number of standard deviations of an estimated coefficient, $\hat{b}_1$, from its mean, or hypothesized value, b_1^*, is given on the horizontal axis. The probability that a calculated t value lies within a range of standard deviations from the value of zero is the same thing as the probability that an estimated coefficient lies within a range of standard deviations from its mean which is, by assumption, equal to some hypothesized value. This probability is found by summing, within specified limits, the area under the curve, as shown in Figure 9.5. For example, when dealing with large samples, the probability that a t value lies between –1.0 and +1.0 is the shaded area on the graph, which is equal to 68 percent. The probabilities that a value of t lies within specified ranges, e.g., –1.0 to +1.0., –2.0 to +2.0, etc., are given by t tables included in most statistics textbooks. Rather than presenting an entire table here, we will simply summarize the most often used values, pertaining to large samples:

1. The probability that a calculated t value lies between –1.0 and +1.0 is 68 percent.
2. The probability that a calculated t value lies between –2.0 and +2.0 is 95 percent.
3. The probability that a calculated t value lies between –3.0 and +3.0 is 97 percent.

The choice of which probability to use as a standard is somewhat arbitrary, so we will dwell on the one most frequently used, 95 percent. Specifically, this means there is a 95 percent probability that a value (t) lies between –2.0 and +2.0 standard deviations from its mean value of

Figure 9.5
t Distribution

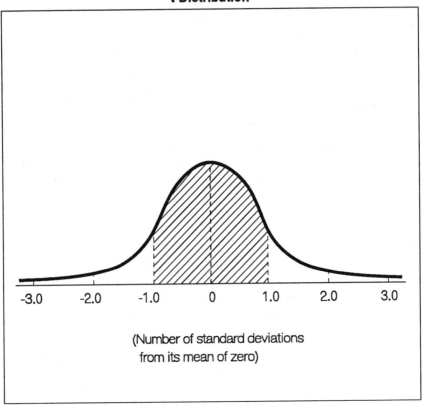

(Number of standard deviations
from its mean of zero)

zero. This implies that there is a 100 percent - 95 percent = 5 percent probability that it lies more than 2.0 standard deviations from its mean, in either the positive or negative direction. Much of the information presented above can be utilized formally through a procedure known as **hypothesis testing**. If, as stated earlier, we expect the true value of b_1 to equal some value b_1^*, we form the hypothesis that $b_1 = b_1^*$ and test it against the alternative that $b_1 \neq b_1^*$. Technically this is defined as a two-tailed test, because we don't care if b_1 is greater or less than b_1^*, only if it is, or is not, equal to it. We can test this hypothesis using the information from our sample estimate, $\hat{b}_1$, and its associated standard error, $\hat{S}_{b_1}$.

The corresponding calculated t statistic is:

$$t^* = \frac{\hat{b}_1 - \hat{b}_1^*}{\hat{S}_{b_1}}$$

We can compare this calculated value of t to the tabulated t-values. More specifically, on the assumption that $b_1 = b_1^*$, any estimated $\hat{b}_1$ should lie within two standard deviations of b_1^* 95 percent of the time. However, it is possible to estimate $\hat{b}_1$ and find that it lies more than two standard deviations from the hypothesized value, b_1^*, while still assuming $b_1 = b_1^*$ is correct. This would occur, however, only 5 percent of the time. Thus, if the calculated $|t^*|$ is greater than 2.0, we will logically reject the hypothesis that $b_1 = b_1^*$, because we would be wrong in so doing only 5 percent of the time (i.e., if b_1 really is equal to b_1^*, $|t^*| > 2.0$ only 5 percent of the time). On the other hand, if $|t^*|$ is less than 2.0, then there is no logical reason to reject the hypothesis that $b_1 = b_1^*$.

The most frequently used type of hypothesis, that $b_1 = 0$, is a subcase of the more general one just presented. This hypothesis is of particular interest because it enables us to statistically test for a relationship (other than a constant one) between the dependent and independent variables in a function. This test is presented in the following manner:

$$H_o: b_1 = 0$$

$$H_a: b_1 \neq 0$$

where H_o represents the **null hypothesis**, and H_a represents the alternative. This is a special case of the more general, where we are simply letting $b_1^* = 0$. The calculated t statistic is:

$$t^* = \frac{\hat{b}_1 - 0}{\hat{S}_{b_1}} = \frac{b_1}{\hat{S}_{b_1}}$$

Using the 95 percent confidence level, we can compare t^* to the tabled value of 2.0. If $|t^*| > 2.0$, we would be wrong in rejecting the null hypothesis only 5 percent of the time (i.e., if the null hypothesis, $b_1 = 0$, is correct, then $|t^*| > 2.0$ only 5 percent of the time). Accordingly, we will reject the null hypothesis and accept the alternative. If, on the other hand, $|t^*| < 2.0$, we would fail to reject the null hypothesis that $b_1 = 0$.

This discussion can be clarified by use of example. Let's return to the estimated consumption function, $\hat{C} = 68.84 + .61Y_d$, where $\hat{b}_0 = 68.84$ and $\hat{b}_1 = .61$. Suppose we want to test if the true slope coefficient, b_1, is equal to zero (i.e., we want to examine if $\hat{C}$ changes as Y_d changes) or formally:

$$H_o: b_1 = 0$$

$$H_a: b_1 \neq 0$$

We can use the estimated slope coefficient $\hat{b}_1 = .61$ and its related information to test this hypothesis. First, we need to calculate the standard error of the estimate:

$$\hat{S}_{u_i} = \left[\frac{\displaystyle\sum_{i=1}^{N} (C_i - \hat{C}_i)^2}{N - 2} \right]^{1/2}$$

There are ten observations, and $\Sigma(C_i - \hat{C}_i)^2$ is determined from column 11 in Table 9.5. Therefore:

$$\hat{S}_{u_i} = \left(\frac{5883.74}{10 - 2} \right)^{1/2} = 27.12$$

The standard error of the independent variable is:

$$S_{Y_d} = \left[\frac{\displaystyle\sum_{i=1}^{N} (Y_{d,i} - \bar{Y}_d)^2}{N} \right]^{1/2}$$

Again using $N = 10$ and obtaining $\Sigma(Y_{d,i} - \bar{Y}_d)^2$ from column 7 in Table 9.5:

$$S_{Y_{d,i}} = \left(\frac{61,440}{10} \right)^{1/2} = 78.38$$

Thus the standard error of the slope coefficient, $\hat{S}_{b_1}$, is found by substituting the calculated values for $\hat{S}_{u_1}$ and $S_{Y_{d_1}}$ into the formula for $\hat{S}_{b_1}$ such that:

$$\hat{S}_{b_1} = \frac{\hat{S}_{u_1}}{S_{Y_{d_1}}\sqrt{N}} = \frac{27.12}{(78.38)\sqrt{10}} = .11$$

We can now calculate the t statistic necessary for testing the hypothesis that the true $b_1 = 0$. The calculated t statistic is:

$$t* = \frac{\hat{b}_1 - b_1}{S_{\hat{b}_1}} = \frac{.61 - 0}{.11} = 5.54$$

Since $5.54 > 2.00$, the calculated $t*$ is more than two standard deviations from the mean value of zero.[1] As a consequence, we can reject the null hypothesis that $b_1 = 0$. Another way to state this result is that the slope coefficient is different from zero at the 100 percent – 95 percent = 5 percent level of significance. Thus, if we reject the null hypothesis that $b_1 = 0$, we can conditionally accept the estimated value $\hat{b}_1$. This implication alone, however, does not necessarily indicate that our model is a good one. In other words, although our model may be valid, there may be better models that can be constructed.

The Coefficient of Determination and the F Test

We should remember that one of the overall goals of building a model is to explain the variation in some "dependent" variable on the basis of the variation in some independent variable. The fact that the estimated coefficient on the independent variable is statistically significant implies that variation in the independent variable contributes to variation in the dependent variable, but it does not tell us the amount of the contribution. A measure of this contribution can easily be developed, however, on the basis of the information we already know.

The general regression equation is $Y_i = b_0 + b_1X_i + U_i$, and the equation for the fitted curve is $\hat{Y}_i = \hat{b}_0 + \hat{b}_1X_i$. Recall that the predicted value for the dependent variable, $\hat{Y}_i$, represents the conditional mean of Y_i, i.e., the mean of Y_i given a value for the independent variable X. Also recall that the error terms, $\hat{U}_i$s, represent the differences between the actual values of the dependent variable, Y_i, and the predicted value for that variable, $\hat{Y}_i$. This error term, $Y_i - \hat{Y}_i$, represents that variation in Y that is due to variation in omitted variables, error in the specified mathematical form, or sampling error. In general, this variation in Y is not explained by the model.

The total variation in the dependent variable, Y, from its unconditional mean can be broken into two components: that which can be explained by its predicted value (the conditional mean) and that which cannot be explained by the model. This decomposition is demonstrated in Figure 9.6.

For any chosen value of the independent variable, say X_1, the difference between the actual observed value of the dependent variable, Y_1, and its mean, $\bar{Y}$, is $Y_1 - \bar{Y}$. Part of this difference, however, is the difference between the predicted value $\hat{Y}_1$ and the mean, $\bar{Y}$, or $\hat{Y}_1 - \bar{Y}$. This is that part of the total difference which is explained by the independent variable, X_1. The remainder of the total difference is $Y_1 - \hat{Y}_1$, or the part that is unexplained or residual, which is due to the error term, U_1. For reasons stated earlier, variation in a variable can be found by squaring the differences and summing over the different $i = 1, 2, \ldots, N$ values. Therefore:

$$\sum_{i=1}^{N} (Y_i - \bar{Y})^2 = \sum_{i=1}^{N} (Y_i - \hat{Y}_i)^2 + \sum_{i=1}^{N} (\hat{Y}_i - \bar{Y})^2$$

total variation in Y (TSS)	= residual variation in Y (ESS)	+ explained variation in Y (RSS)

The total variation in Y is defined as the total sum of squares, TSS, the unexplained or residual variation in Y is defined as the error sum of squares, ESS, and the explained variation in Y is defined as the regression sum of squares, RSS.

As a result of this decomposition, a simple measure indicating the percentage of the variation in the dependent variable, Y, that is explained

Figure 9.6
Decomposition of the Variation in a Dependent Variable
into Explained and Unexplained Components

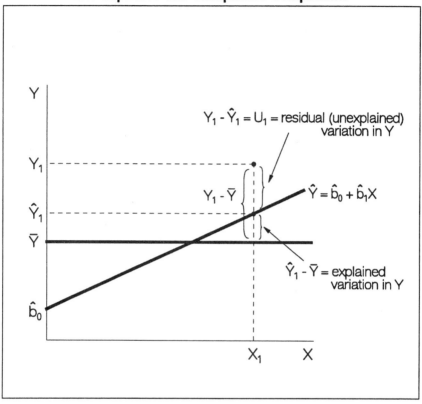

by the independent variable, X can be constructed. This term is defined as the **coefficient of multiple determination** and is labeled "R^2." Thus, the formula for R^2 is:

$$R^2 = \frac{RSS}{TSS} = \frac{\sum_{i=1}^{N} (\hat{Y}_i - \bar{Y})^2}{\sum_{i=1}^{N} (Y_i - \bar{Y})^2}$$

Since TSS = ESS + RSS, another way to express this formula is:

$$R^2 = \frac{TSS - ESS}{TSS} = 1 - \frac{ESS}{TSS} = 1 - \frac{\sum\limits_{i=1}^{N} (Y_i - \hat{Y}_i)^2}{\sum\limits_{i=1}^{N} (Y_i - \bar{Y})^2}$$

A high R^2 indicates that a high percentage of the total variation in the dependent variable is explained by the included independent variable. Therefore, the model is doing a good job of serving its original intent. Another way to state this conclusion is that the model "fits" the data well. A low R^2 on the other hand indicates that a low percentage of the variation is explained by the independent variable. The model may not be inaccurate, but it is relatively uncomprehensive. In other words, there are either additional independent variables, or more important independent variables, that should be included in the model.

A statistical test which is closely related to the R^2 term is the **F–test**. Such a test is designed to test for the equality of two variances. It is defined as:

$$F_{1,N-2} = \frac{\text{explained variance}}{\text{unexplained variance}}$$

where 1 and N - 2 refer to the number of degrees of freedom associated with the numerator and the denominator respectively. The explained variance = $RSS/_1$ and the unexplained variance = $ESS/_{N-2}$. The number of degrees of freedom for the RSS is the number of independent variables in the equation, which in this case is just 1. The number degrees of freedom associated with the ESS is the number of observations less the number of estimated coefficients which happens to be two in this case ($\hat{b}_0$ and $\hat{b}_1$). This statistic follows an F distribution, which will be different for different degrees of freedom.

What is being tested here is whether or not the regression equation significantly explains the variation in the dependent variable, Y. The extreme case is where the explained variance is equal to zero and, therefore, F = 0. In this case we can conclude that the regression equation contributes no explanation for the variation in the dependent variable. Formally, the hypothesis to be tested, again defined as the null hypothesis, is H_o: $b_1 = 0$, where the alternative is H_a: $b_1 \neq 0$. The calculated F statistic can be compared to some critical tabled F value which pertains to the relevant degrees of freedom. As with the t statistic, a level of significance must be chosen. Suppose we choose the .05 level. If the calculated F statistic is greater than the tabled value, we would be wrong to reject the null hypothesis on the assumption that it is true only 5 percent of the time. Thus, in this case it is logical to reject the null hypothesis. The implication of this rejection is that there is a significant difference between the explained and unexplained variation in the model and, therefore, the independent variable, X, does play a role in explaining the variation in Y. If the calculated F statistic is less than the tabled value, then we cannot reject the null hypothesis that $b_1 = 0$, implying that there is no significant difference between the explained and unexplained variation. In other words, the variation in Y explained by the independent variable X is no different than the unexplained variation in Y (caused by other, nonspecified factors).

The related concepts of R^2 and F tests can be illustrated from the consumption function example presented earlier:

$$R^2 = 1 - \frac{ESS}{TSS} = 1 - \frac{\sum\limits_{i=1}^{N} (C_i - \hat{C}_i)^2}{\sum\limits_{i=1}^{N} (C_i - \bar{C})^2}$$

The ESS $= \sum\limits_{i=1}^{N} (C_i - \hat{C}_i)^2$, and the TSS $= \sum\limits_{i=1}^{N} (C_i - \bar{C})^2$ can be obtained from the last two columns in Table 9.5. Accordingly:

$$R^2 = 1 - \frac{5883.74}{28650} = 1 - .21 = .79$$

This can be interpreted as indicating that the 79 percent variation in C about its mean can be explained by the independent variable Y_d. Generally, this is considered to be a pretty good R^2. However, just as one person could say "the glass is 79 percent full," another might say "the glass is 21 percent empty." Thus a more formal indication of explained variation is through the F test. The null hypothesis is H_o: $b_1 = 0$, and the alternative is H_a: $b_1 \neq 0$. The calculated F statistic for this problem is:

$$F_{1,N-2} = \frac{RSS/_1}{ESS/_{N-2}} = \frac{\sum_{i=1}^{N} (\hat{C}_i - \bar{C})^2}{\sum_{i=1}^{N} (C_i - \hat{C}_1)^2}$$

The RSS could be calculated directly from Table 9.5, or more easily from the equation TSS = ESS + RSS, since we already have obtained TSS and ESS. Therefore, RSS = TSS - ESS or RSS = 28650 - 5883.74 = 22766.26 As a result:

$$F_{1,10-2} = \frac{22766.26/1}{5883.74/10-2} = 30.95$$

The tabled value for an F with 1 and 8 degrees of freedom, and a 5 percent level of significance is 5.32. Since 30.22 > 5.32, we can reject the null hypothesis that $b_1 = 0$, and we can conclude that the independent variable, Y_d, does play a role in determining C.

Using both a t statistic and an F statistic to test the hypothesis that $b_1 = 0$ is rather redundant for a univariate model. There is really no point in doubly testing the same coefficient. The F test has been demonstrated here only as an illustration of how it can be used. The major contribution to be made by the F test is with regard to a multivariate regression model, where more than one independent variable is included. In this case, there will exist several **partial** slope coefficients, b_1, b_2, . . . , b_k, or one for each of the k independent variables. The F test makes it possible to jointly test the partial slope coefficients, i.e., $b_1 = b_2 = \ldots = b_k = 0$. Essentially, in this case, we are testing to see if all of the independent variables, as a group, provide a significant explanation for the variation in the dependent variable.

Some Limitations of Regression Analysis

Once a regression model has been estimated and tested for significance, we are ready to draw conclusions and make predictions. Some of the direct conclusions have already been demonstrated within the context of hypothesis testing. However, we must be very careful in stating any broader conclusions or in making any predictions based on our model. In general, we want to be careful not to outrun the assumptions and restrictions on which the model is originally based. This is particularly true with regard to using the model to make predictions beyond the original data set. In our consumption function example, the estimated model, $\hat{C} = \hat{b}_0 + \hat{b}_1 Y_d$, is calculated on the basis of (C, Y_d) pairs of observations collected over ten students in an Economics 101 class. Underlying this estimation procedure is a certain pattern of behavior reflecting how these students determine their consumption levels, C, on the basis of their disposable income, Y_d. This pattern of behavior may reflect factors such as attitudes regarding consumption vs. saving, wealth, and so forth. As we use this estimated function to predict consumption levels on the basis of chosen disposable income levels for individuals outside our sample, we must implicitly make the assumption that these underlying patterns of behavior remain the same as those underlying our sample.

Suppose we apply this function to an art student. Will an art student have the same behavioral attitudes toward consumption and disposable income as an economics student? Can we assume these patterns remain constant across students at different universities? Finally, can this consumption function be applied to nonstudents? The point is, the further we depart from our original sample base and its underlying characteristics, the less accurate will be any predictions associated with our model.

A related concern is that, even for the units (in this case Economics 101 students) on which the original sample is based, there is a danger of extrapolating beyond the original data. Specifically, in this case, it is dangerous to use the estimated function to calculate predicted consumption values for disposable income levels that lie outside the original range of data. This is due to the fact that there is no information regarding the mathematical form of the function, or the effects of omitted variables, outside of the original data set. This is not to say that a model cannot be applied for prediction purposes, but we must be careful not to extrapolate too far.

Another limitation associated with regression models is that they tell us nothing about the direction of causality. We postulate causality when we construct a model, but this is based on theoretical considerations. A regression analysis does not confirm the postulated direction of causality or the fact that causality exists at all. It indicates only that a relationship between the included variables does or does not exist. The existence of a relationship between variables is a necessary condition for causality, but it, alone, is insufficient. For example, a model can be constructed with national income as the dependent variable and the money supply as the independent variable. The theory is that an increase in the money supply stimulates demand leading to an increase in national income. However, a model can be constructed where the money supply is designated as the dependent variable and national income as the independent variable. The theory here is that as national income rises, more money will be supplied to facilitate a greater level of transactions. Regression analysis can be performed for each model, probably generating significant results. But it is virtually impossible, on the basis of the statistical results, to determine which model and hence which direction of causality is correct. In fact, it is possible that neither direction of causality is correct. Both variables might move together, due to the effect of some other independent variable which commonly influences both but has been omitted from the functions.

A final limitation, to be discussed here, is a potential lack of comprehensiveness. This can be particularly acute in the univariate case, where only one independent variable is included. The major purposes of building a model are to explain the variation in some variable and/or to be able to predict values for that variable. Generally, such a variable depends on a number of factors or independent variables. If too many of these factors are left out of a regression equation, too much of the variation is left unexplained, rendering the model rather useless. The coefficient of determination, R^2, is to a large extent a measure of a model's comprehensiveness. However, it is possible to construct a model which generates a high R^2 and is still rather incomplete. This could occur if the included independent variable is some sort of proxy or "representative" for a number of underlying independent variables. In this case, the constructed model may be good for prediction purposes but deficient in providing information about the fundamental linkages between variables.

Multivariate Regression

In some cases a univariate model may serve the intended purposes quite well. But for others, where a more comprehensive model is desired, a multivariate approach is often preferable. A **multivariate regression** analysis is simply a regression model applied to a function containing more than one independent variable. Mathematically it is of the form:

$$Y = b_0 + b_1 X_1 + b_2 X_2 + \ldots + b_k X_k + u$$

where $X_1, X_2, \ldots, X_k$ represent k independent variables, and $b_1, b_2, \ldots,$ b_k represent k partial slope coefficients. Recall from Chapter 3 that for a functional relationship to exist between two variables (e.g., Y and X_1, Y and X_2, etc.) it is necessary to hold all other variables constant. Thus, the partial slope coefficients are:

$$b_1 = \frac{\Delta Y}{\Delta X_1} \quad | \; X_{2,0} \ldots, X_{k,0}$$

$$b_2 = \frac{\Delta Y}{\Delta X_2} \quad | \; X_{1,0}, X_{3,0} \ldots, X_{k,0}$$

$$\vdots \qquad \qquad \vdots$$

Once the regression equation has been estimated, each estimated partial slope coefficient indicates the change in Y due to a change in the respective independent variable, with all other independent variables held constant.

An illustration of multivariate regression can be provided by modifying the consumption function example in this chapter. It is logical to believe that consumption expenditures, while probably dependent on disposable income, are likely dependent on some other factors as well. Since people sometimes borrow for consumption purposes, we might expect the level of interest rates to be one such additional factor. The consumption function can now be expressed in multivariate form as:

$$C = b_0 + b_1 Y_d + b_2 R + U$$

where R = the interest rate in percentage points. The term b_2 is a partial slope coefficient which indicates the change in C due to a change in R, ceteris paribus. On the basis of economic theory, we would expect its sign to be negative, i.e., as interest rates rise, we would expect borrowing, and hence C, to fall. The data collection process would now be extended to include ten observations on R to go with the ten (C, Y_d) combinations for each student in the sample. We would hope that because students are from different towns and borrow from different financial institutions, there will be some variation in the observed interest rate levels.

Suppose the regression equation is estimated and yields the following result:

$$\hat{C} = 145 + .62\,Y_d - 10R$$

The estimated partial slope coefficient for R is -10. This indicates that for a one percentage point rise in R, predicted consumption expenditures, $\hat{C}$, will change by (-10) (1) = -$10, ceteris paribus. This multivariate regression equation contains two independent variables, Y_d and R. Of course, additional independent variables could be included if deemed necessary.

Although this is a hypothetical example, notice that the inclusion of another independent variable alters the intercept and slope coefficients from those estimated for the univariate function. An intercept represents the value of a dependent variable when the independent variables are equal to zero. Thus it represents the level of a dependent variable that is determined by factors not explicitly included in the regression equation. As a result, when an additional independent variable is explicitly included in the function, its impact is now isolated and no longer manifested through the intercept.

In this example, since the interest rate adversely affects consumption, and is always positive, the inclusion of it in the model as an independent variable will lead to a higher intercept value, given no relationship between it and the Y_d variable. As for the partial slope coefficient on Y_d, we would not expect the inclusion of R to affect it significantly. Ideally, there would be no impact because the terms, $\hat{b}_1$ and $\hat{b}_2$, represent partial slope coefficients. Realistically, however, there usually exists some degree of correlation between independent variables and, therefore, the inclusion of additional independent variables will affect these partial slope coefficients somewhat. This interaction effect between or among independent variables is defined as **multicollinearity**. If this effect is large, it can cause a distortion in the partial slope coefficients and render their interpretation virtually meaningless; that is, they reflect interactions between or among independent variables that cannot be separated from the desired isolated impact that an independent variable has on the dependent variable. This material can become rather complex, and is beyond the scope of this book. It should be fairly clear, however, that a model may not always be improved and, in fact, can be made worse by haphazardly including more independent variables. This is something that must be done with extreme caution and should be based on sound theoretical principles.

Conclusion

This chapter has attempted to bring together economic theory and "real world" statistical analysis procedures. Although this chapter has been but a brief introduction to statistical methods, we can see how they can be used hand in hand with economic theory to generate some useful results.

Important Terms in this Chapter

Coefficient of determination (R^2) – a measure indicating the percentage of the variation in the dependent variable that is explained by the independent variable or variables included in the regression equation.

Conditional expectation or conditional mean – the expected value of a variable provided its determination depends on the value of another variable, for which some prior information regarding the outcome is known.

Cross sectional analysis – an analysis involving collection of data at a point in time, but varied across sections, e.g., individuals, families, states, etc.

Degrees of freedom – the number of observations in a sample minus the number of estimated terms.

F–test – a test for the equality of two variances.

Multicollinearity – interdependency between or among independent variables.

Multivariate regression – a regression model applied to a function containing more than one independent variable.

Null hypothesis – a hypothesis stating that the true value of a coefficient is equal to some predetermined value.

Regression analysis – a procedure used to estimate a set of coefficients which generate a curve that best fits a sample of data.

Standard Deviation – the square root of the variance.

Standard error of the independent variable (S_X) – a measure of the dispersion of an independent variable, X, about its mean.

Standard error of the estimate $(\hat{S}_u)$ – a measure of dispersion of the error terms in a regression equation about their mean.

Time series – a method of collecting data on variables measured at different points in time.

t statistic – a value which represents the number of standard deviations between an estimated coefficient and its hypothesized value.

Variance – a measure of the dispersion of a random variable about its mean.

Exercise Set 9.2

1. A retailer varies the price of an item across eight different customers and records the quantity of the item purchased by each customer. By so doing, the retailer hopes to estimate the demand function for the product in question. The demand function is of the form:

$$Q^d = b_0 + b_1 P + u$$

where:
Q^d = quantity demanded of the good in units per period of time
P = price of the good in dollars per unit
u = error term

The observed data are as follows:

P	Q
$5	20
$2	23
$1	26
$7	10
$2	25
$10	2
$5	22
$1	29

a) Plot the scatter of P, Q observations.
b) Calculate the means associated with P and Q.
c) Calculate the estimates for b_0 and b_1.
d) Calculate the standard error of the estimate, the standard error of the independent variable (P), and the standard error of the estimated slope coefficient ($\hat{b_1}$).
e) Calculate a t statistic and determine if $\hat{b_1}$ is significant at the .05 level. Set up this problem within the context of formal hypothesis testing.
f) Find the coefficient of determination (R^2). How do you interpret this term?
g) Conduct an F test, and interpret your results.

2. Suppose a multivariate demand function for some product is estimated, yielding the following:

$$Q^d = 120 - 4P + 2I$$

where:
Q^d = quantity demanded of the good in units per period of time
P = price of the good in dollars per unit
I = income in thousands of dollars per period of time

a) Interpret the intercept and partial slope coefficients.
b) What would happen to the value of the intercept coefficient if income was not explicitly included in the function? Assume that P and I are not related.
c) Suppose you conduct an F test and find significant results at, say, the .05 level. However, you conduct t tests on each of the partial slope coefficients and fail to find significance at this same level. How can this be so? What possible explanations can you put forth describing this situation?

3. An economist wants to construct a model which can be used to explain levels of national income. Suppose he or she comes up with the following:

$$Y = 1000 + 20G$$

where:
   Y = national income in billions of dollars per year
   G = government expenditures in billions of dollars per year

a) What do the terms 1000 and 20 indicate?
b) Suppose the associated t and F tests are significant at the .05 level. Does this mean the model is necessarily a good one?
c) What does the model tell us about the direction of causality?

4. Regression analysis has many applications in finance. One common application is in calculating the "beta coefficient." This term can be interpreted as an index of undiversifiable risk, and it can be identified as the slope coefficient obtained by regressing the rate of return associated with some asset on the rate of return associated with some broad based portfolio or market index. Suppose the quarterly rates of return from XYZ Corporation stock and those associated with the S and P 500 over a three–year period are as follows:

Quarter	XYZ	S&P 500
1	5.50%	6.25%
2	10.25%	8.5%
3	3.10%	4.20%
4	-1.20%	-1.00%
1	-4.50%	-4.00%
2	8.00%	-5.25%
3	1.50%	1.25%
4	6.25%	4.50%
1	4.20%	5.50%
2	-3.50%	-2.25%
3	1.30%	2.50%
4	8.50%	6.50%

Calculate the associated "beta coefficient." What does this result indicate about the performance of the XYZ stock as compared to the broader market? How would you interpret the sum of the intercept and error term in this regression?

Note

1. Actually, since the sample size in this case, is relatively small (10 − 2 = 8 degrees of freedom), the tabled t value is 2.31.

References

Bain, L. J. and M. Engelhardt, *Introduction to Probability and Mathematical Statistics*, Boston: Duxbury Press, 1987.

Dudewicz, E. J. and S. N. Mishra, *Modern Mathematical Statistics*, New York: John Wiley and Sons, 1988.

Freund, J. E. and R. E. Walpole, *Mathematical Statistics*, Englewood Cliffs, NJ: Prentice-Hall, 1987.

Hogg, R. V. and E. A. Tanis, *Probability and Statistical Inference*, New York: Macmillan Publishing Co., Inc., 1977.

Solutions to Exercises

Chapter 1

Exercise Set–Page 15

1. a) Disagree. This is a matter of degree. All models are abstractions from reality to some extent in order to make the model manageable.

   b) Disagree. In order to be testable, a model must lend itself to the possibility of falsification. This is impossible if all potential outcomes are possibilities.

   c) Disagree. A model may explain well, in that it properly isolates the impacts due to the included causal or independent variables. However, it may not predict well because there may be many additional factors, not included, which may affect the performance of the predicted variable. On the other hand, a more comprehensive model, which includes many factors, may predict well but not provide a good explanation of the relevant phenomena. This might occur if the effects of the independent variables become intertwined.

2. a) These are variables that are used to explain the behavior of other variables.

   b) These are variables for which the behavior is to be explained.

   c) A relationship such that, for every admissible value assigned to the independent variable or variables, there will exist a unique value corresponding to the dependent variable.

3. a) This is the fallacy of false cause or the post hoc fallacy. The error is to believe that because two events occur together or in sequence, the first caused the second.

    b) This is the fallacy of division. The error is to believe that what is true for the whole is also true for all of the parts.

    c) This is the fallacy of composition. The error is to believe that what is true for the parts is also true for the whole.

4. False. If two variables are correlated they move together in some type of pattern. This, however, says nothing about causality. The two variables in question may be related due to a common relationship with some omitted variable.

Chapter 2

Exercise Set 2.1–Page 41

1. a) This is a linear function. The independent variable is raised to the first degree and it has a constant slope positively.

    b) $\dfrac{\Delta y}{\Delta x} = 5 \qquad y = 20$

    A slope value of 5 indicates that a one unit change in x will result in a 5 unit change in y, in the same direction. The intercept value of 20 represents the value of y when x = 0.

c) Graphed answer.

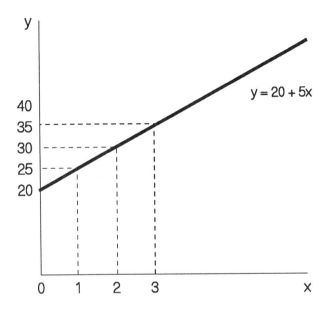

$y = 20 + 5x$

2. a) The variables x and y are inversely related.

b) Graphed answer.

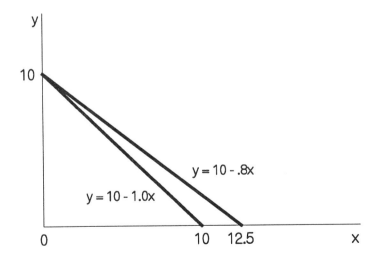

$y = 10 - .8x$

$y = 10 - 1.0x$

c) The second curve has a steeper slope.

3. a) The Q intercept = 6, which is the value when P = 0. The slope = -2, which is the rate at which the quantity demanded decreases as price increases or increases as price decreases.

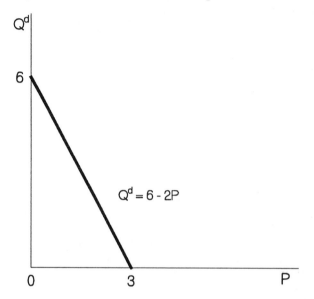

$Q^d = 6 - 2P$

b) $P = 3 - \dfrac{Q^d}{2}$

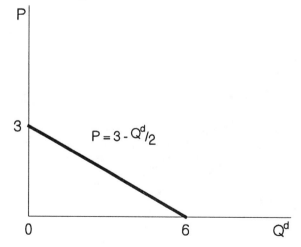

$P = 3 - Q^d/2$

4. a) $2x + 3y = 10$

$$y = \frac{10}{3} - \frac{2x}{3}$$

$y = 3.33 - .67x$

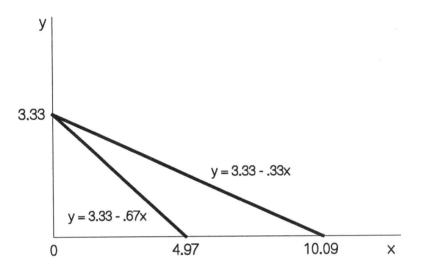

b) $x + 3y = 10$

$10 - x = 3y$

$$y = \frac{10}{3} - \frac{1}{3}x$$

or $y = 3.33 - .33x$

The new curve is flatter and has a higher x intercept.

c) $2x + 3y = 20$

$3y = 20 - 2x$

$$y = \frac{20}{3} - \frac{2x}{3}$$

$$y = 6.67 - .67x$$

The two intercepts have increased.

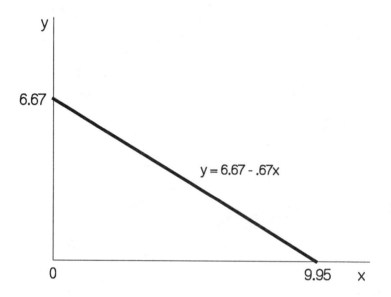

Exercise Set 2.2—Page 63

1. a) Intercept = 0

    b) This is a nonlinear function.

c and d) Graphed answer. The slope of $y = 2x^{1/2}$ changes continuously over the course of the entire function.

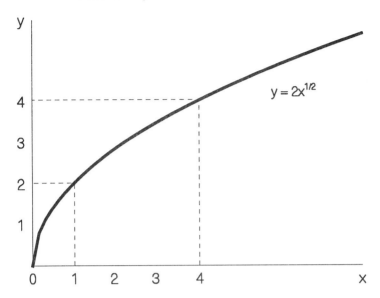

2. a) $\dfrac{\Delta y}{\Delta x} = \dfrac{2 - 0}{1 - 0} = \dfrac{2}{1} = 2.0$　　　　$1/\sqrt{1} = 1$

   b) $\dfrac{\Delta y}{\Delta x} = \dfrac{2.83 - 2}{2 - 1} = \dfrac{.83}{1} = .83$　　　　$1/\sqrt{2} = .71$

   c) $\dfrac{\Delta y}{\Delta x} = \dfrac{3.46 - 2.83}{3 - 2} = \dfrac{.63}{1} = .63$　　　　$1/\sqrt{3} = .58$

   d) $\dfrac{\Delta y}{\Delta x} = \dfrac{4 - 3.46}{4 - 3} = \dfrac{.54}{1} = .54$　　　　$1/\sqrt{4} = .5$

They are somewhat smaller, because they represent the slopes at each chosen point on the curve. The average slopes, in Part a, pertain to the slopes of secants connecting each point.

3. a) This is a quadratic function.

   b) x and y are inversely related.

c) Graphed answer. It is a downward sloping curve, convex away from the origin.

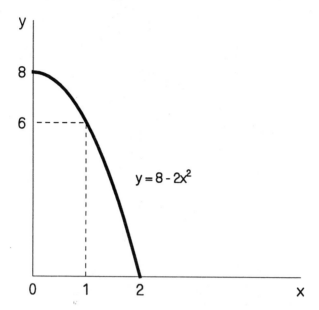

d) $y = 8$, $x = 2$

e)

$$\frac{\Delta y}{\Delta x} = \frac{6 - 8}{1 - 0} = \frac{-2}{1} = -2$$

$$= \frac{0 - 6}{2 - 1} = \frac{-6}{1} = -6$$

The amount of y foregone, in order to choose more units of x, increases as more x is chosen.

4. a) Graphed answer.

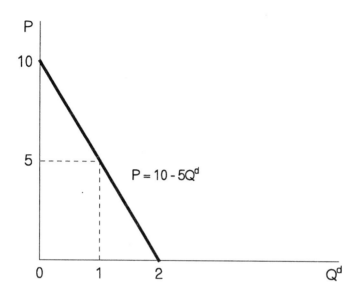

$P = 10 - 5Q^d$

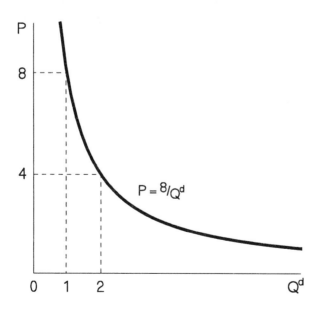

$P = 8/Q^d$

b) The first is a linear function of the form $y = b_0 + b_1x$. This has a constant slope of -5.

The second is a rectangular hyperbola. It has a slope of $-8Q^{d-2}$ which changes over the entire function.

c)

P	Q^d	TE	P	Q^d	TE
7.5	.5	3.75	8	1	8
5	1	5	4	2	8
2.5	1.5	3.75	2	4	8

For the linear case, total expenditures vary along the curve, rising then declining for movements down the curve. For the rectangular hyperbola, total expenditures remain constant for movements along the curve.

5. Graphed answer. The intercept represents fixed costs. As a result, the function represents a short run total cost function. The cubic shape of the function reflects the law of diminishing marginal productivity. Costs increase at a decreasing rate up to the inflection point A, and then increase at an increasing rate. It becomes increasingly expensive to produce more units of a product varying only some inputs while holding others constant.

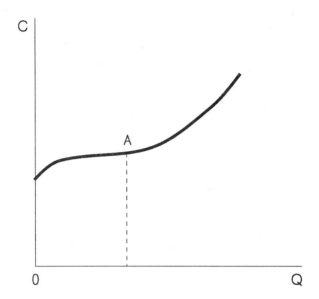

6. At time 0, which is the current time period, the interest rate would be:

$$R = 10 + T^{1/2}$$
$$R = 10 + 0^{1/2}$$
$$R = 10$$

The general form of this yield curve is quadratic.

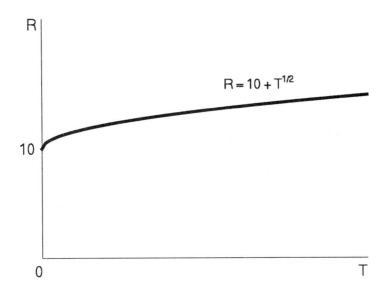

$$R = 10 + T^{1/2}$$

R

10

0   T

Long term rates, in this case, are greater than short term rates, because investors expect short term rates to rise in the future.

Chapter 3

Exercise Set 3.1—Page 74

1.   a)

$$\frac{\Delta y}{\Delta x_1} \Big| x_{2,0} = 2$$

$$\frac{\Delta y}{\Delta x_2} \Big| x_{1,0} = 4$$

b) $y = 5 + 2x_1 + 4x_2$
$y = 5 + 2x_1 + 4(1)$
$y = 9 + 2x_1$
y intercept $= 9$

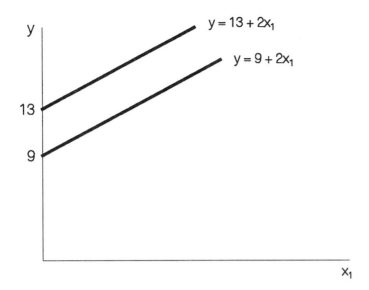

c) $y = 5 + 2x_1 + 4x_2$
   $y = 5 + 2x_1 + 4(2)$
   $y = 13 + 2x_1$
   y intercept = 13
   The y intercept value increases from 9 to 13.

2. $y = 5 + 2x_1 + 4x_2$
   $y = 5 + 2(1) + 4x_2$
   $y = 7 + 4x_2$
   y intercept = 7
   $y = 5 + 2x_1 + 4x_2$
   $y = 5 + 2(2) + 4x_2$
   $y = 9 + 4x_2$
   y intercept = 9

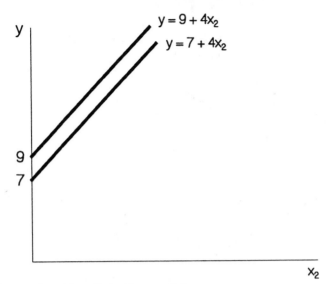

Exercise Set 3.2–Page 84

1. a) $Q^d = 5000 - 50P + .1(20) + 80(200)$
   $= 5000 - 50P + 2 + 16000$
   $Q^d = 21,002 - 50P$

   b) slope $= \dfrac{\Delta Q^d}{\Delta P} = -50$ intercept $= 21,002$

   For every \$1 increase in price, quantity demanded will decrease by 50,000 units. If $P = 0$, $Q^d = 21,002$ units.

   c)

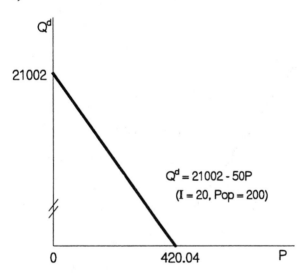

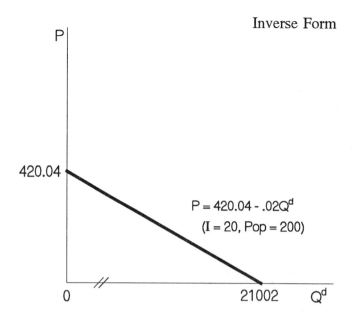

Inverse Form

P = 420.04 - .02Q^d
(I = 20, Pop = 200)

2. $Q^d = 5000 - 50P + .1(40) + 80(200)$
    $= 5000 - 50P + 4 + 16000$
    $Q^d = 21,004 - 50P$

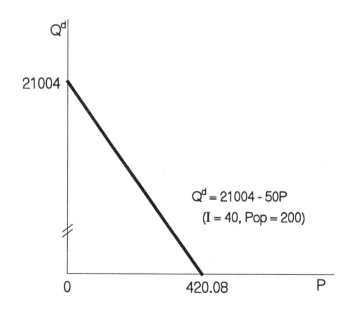

$Q^d = 21004 - 50P$
(I = 40, Pop = 200)

or

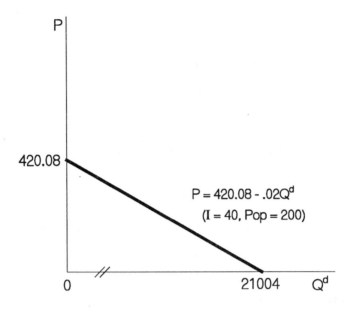

$$P = 420.08 - .02Q^d$$
$$(I = 40, Pop = 200)$$

Many textbooks will say that the curve has "shifted" to the right. Actually we have taken a two-dimensional cross section, which is located further to the right.

3. $Q^d = 5000 - 50(50) + .1I + 80(200)$
    $= 5000 - 2500 + .1I + 16000$
    $Q^d = 18500 + .1I$

    $slope = \dfrac{\Delta Q^d}{\Delta I} = .1$

    intercept $= 18500$
    $Q^d = 5000 - 50(75) + .1I + 80(200)$
    $= 5000 - 3750 + .1I + 16000$
    $Q^d = 17250 + .1I$

The Q^d intercept is now lower. When plotted, the Engel curve will appear to have shifted down.

4. a) $Q^s = -500 + 20P - 5W$
    $Q^s = -500 + 20P - 5(25)$

$Q^s = -500 + 20P - 125$

$Q^s = -625 + 20P$

Anything above a price of \$312.50 will yield some quantity, Q, which will be supplied. The negative Q^s intercept is meaningless.

b) $Q^s = -500 + 20(P) - 5(W)$ $Q^s = -500 + 20P - 5W$
     $= -500 + 20(50) - 5(25)$ $Q^s = -500 + 20(60) - 5(25)$
     $= -500 + 1000 - 125$ $= -500 + 1200 - 125$
   $Q^s = 375$ $Q^s = 575$

Since this was due to a change in price from \$50 to \$60, this would represent a change in quantity supplied. This change represents a movement along the supply curve.

5. $C = 600 + .8(1 - t)y$
    $C = 600 + (.8 - .8t)y$

a) The $(.8 - .8t)$ term represents the slope which, in economic terms, is the MPC (Marginal Propensity to Consume out of income). The intercept = 600 and represents the value of autonomous consumption.

b) Graphed answer.
    $C = 600 + .8y$ $(t = 0)$
    $C = 600 + [.8 - .8(.10)]y$ $(t = .10)$
      $= 600 + .8y - .08y$
    $C = 600 + .72y$
    $C = 600 + [.8 - .8(.20)]y$ $(t = .20)$
      $= 600 + .8y - .16y$
    $C = 600 + .64y$

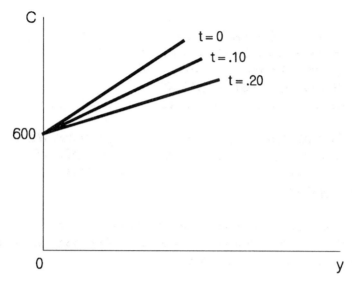

c) The intercept is unaffected. The higher t values, however, cause the slope to decrease. Changes in this factor cause the curve to "rotate" rather than "shift."

6. Graphed answer. No, this curve is parallel to the one presented in Chapter 2. It has simply "shifted up."

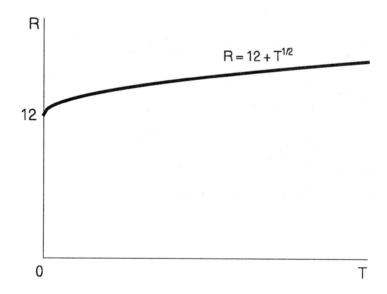

7. $C_2 = Y_2 + (Y_1 - C_1) + R(Y_1 - C_1)$
    $C_2 = 20,000 + (10,000 - C_1) + .10(10,000 - C_1)$
    $ = 20,000 + 10,000 - C_1 + 1000 - .1C_1$
    $ = 30,000 - C_1 + 1000 - .1C_1$
    $C_2 = 31,000 - 1.1C_1$

$C_2 = 31,000 - 1.1C_1$	$C_2 = 31,000 - 1.1C_1$
$0 = 31,000 - 1.1C_1$	$C_2 = 31,000 - 1.1(0)$
$31,000 = 1.1C_1$	$C_2 = 31,000$
$C_1 = 28,181.81$	

The C_1 intercept represents the maximum level of consumption in period one ($C_2 = 0$). It is equal to the income in period one plus the present value of the income from period two or:

$$C_1 = Y_1 + \frac{Y_2}{1 + R}$$

The C_2 intercept represents the maximum level of consumption in period two ($C_1 = 0$). It is equal to the income from period two plus the future value of the income from period one or:

$$C_2 = Y_2 + (1 + R)Y_1$$

If R increases to 20%, both the slope and two intercepts will be affected. The new slope is $(1 + .20) = 1.20$.

$C_2 = 20,000 + (10,000 - C_1) + .20(10,000 - C_1)$
$ = 20,000 + 10,000 - C_1 + 2000 - .20C_1$
$C_2 = 32,000 - 1.2C_1$
C_2 intercept = 32,000
C_1 intercept = $\dfrac{32,000}{1.2}$ = 26,666.67

The constraint has rotated clockwise.

Chapter 4

Exercise Set 4.1–Page 99

1. a) The identity relation, $Y_d = S + C$, can be rewritten as $C = Y_d - S$. Replicating the table adjacent to Figure 4.1 gives:

Y_d	S	$C = Y_d - S$	C
0	−100	0−(−100)	100
100	−80	100−(−80)	180
500	0	500−(0)	500
700	40	700−(40)	660
1000	100	1000−(100)	900
5000	900	5000−(900)	4100

b) The Saving function was given as $S = -100 + .2Y_d$. Substituting this function into the identity $C = Y_d - S$ yields $C = Y_d - (-100 + .2Y_d) = Y_d + 100 - .2Y_d = 100 + .8Y_d$.

c) Graphed answer. The slope of this function $= \dfrac{\Delta C}{\Delta Y_d} = .8$, which is the marginal propensity to consume (out of disposable income), or the MPC. It represents the rate at which consumption expenditures increases for each dollar increase in disposable income. In this example, consumption expenditures would increase $.80 (80 cents) for each additional dollar in disposable income. This result was noted in the text.

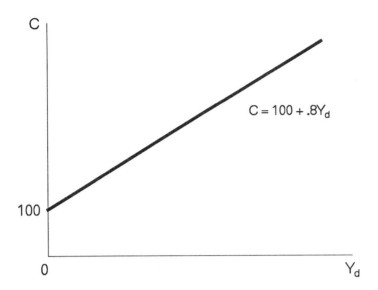

C

100

0

$C = 100 + .8Y_d$

Y_d

2. Graphed answer. The slope of this function is $\Delta I/\Delta Y$ = .05. It represents the rate that investment expenditures would change (increase) for every additional dollar in national income. This rate of change is known as the **marginal propensity to invest** (out of national income), or **MPI**. The MPI in this example = .05, meaning that investment expenditures will increase by $.05 for each additional dollar in national income. The constant term in this function (100) represents the level of investment expenditures that is not affected by Y. This is referred to as **autonomous investment**.

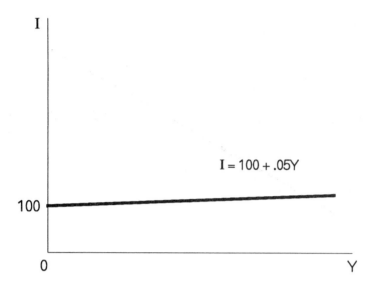

I = 100 + .05Y

100

0   Y

3.   Graphed answer. The slope of the consumption function is the MPC or marginal propensity to consume.

In this example, \$.75 out of each additional dollar of disposable income will be spent on consumption expenditures. The Saving function is $S = Y_d - C = Y_d - (1000 + .75Y_d) = - 1000 + .25Y_d$.

The slope of the saving function is $+.25$, which is the marginal propensity to save, or MPS.

By definition, each dollar of disposable income must be spent (C) or saved (S), since $Y_d = C + S$. Similarly, any change in Y_d (ΔY_d) must be either spent (resulting in ΔC) or saved (resulting in ΔS). This can be written as $\Delta Y_d \equiv \Delta C + \Delta S$. Assume that initially $Y_d = Y_{d0}$, $C = C_0$, and $S = S_0$. If Y_d changes and is equal to Y_{d1}, where $Y_{d1} - Y_{d0} = \Delta Y_d$, then the corresponding levels of C and S, C_1 and S_1, are $C_1 = C_0 + \Delta C$ and $S_1 = S_0 + \Delta S$. Both before and after the change $Y_d = C + S$ so $Y_{d0} = C_0 + S_0$ and $Y_{d1}, = C_1 + S_1$. This latter equation can be rewritten as $Y_{d1} = Y_{d0} + \Delta Y_d = C_0 + \Delta C + S_0 + \Delta S = (C_0 + S_0) + \Delta C + \Delta S = Y_{d0} + \Delta C + \Delta S$. Subtracting Y_{d0} from both sides yields $Y_{d1} - Y_{d0} = \Delta Y_d = \Delta C + \Delta S$. Dividing through by ΔY_d yields:

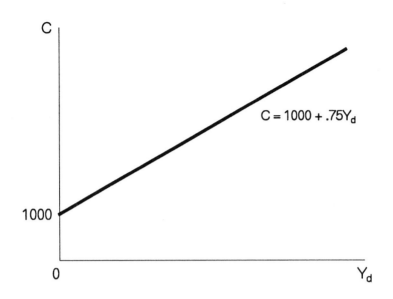

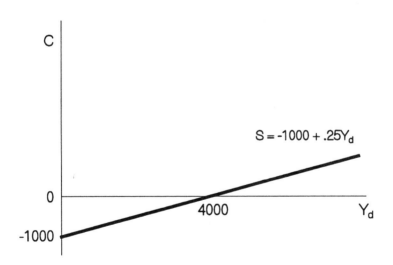

$$\frac{\Delta Y_d}{\Delta Y_d} = \frac{\Delta C}{\Delta Y_d} + \frac{\Delta S}{\Delta Y_d}$$

However, $\Delta Y_d/\Delta Y_d = 1$, $\Delta C/\Delta Y_d = MPC$, and $\Delta S/\Delta Y_d = MPS$. Therefore, $1 = MPC + MPS$, which implies that the slopes of the saving and consumption functions (with respect to Y_d) must sum to unity. The logic underlying this result is as follows: Assume Y_d goes up by 1 dollar, and consumers respond by increasing consumption by some amount (say $.80). The part of that increase in Y_d that is not spent must be saved (by definition of Y_d). Therefore, when consumers increase C by $.8 for each additional dollar of Y_d, they must increase S by the remainder or $.2. In that event, the MPC = .8 and MPS = .2 and, of course, MPC + MPS = 1.

4. Total profits, (π), by definition are equal to total revenue (R) minus total cost (C) or $\pi \equiv R-C$. Since $R = R(Q)$ and $C = C(Q)$, π must also be a function of Q, i.e., $\pi(Q)$. When $Q = Q_0$, unique values of π, R, and C will result (by definition of a function), those being π_0, R_0, and C_0. Similarly, when $Q = Q_1$ the resulting values are π_1, R_1, and C_1. By virtue of the profit identity we have at both levels of Q, $\pi \equiv R - C$ so, $\pi_0 = R_0 - C_0$ and $\pi_1 = R_1 - C_1$. As Q changes from Q_0 to Q_1, π changes from π_0 to π_1, and similarly for R and C. As Q changes from Q_0 to Q_1 the change in profits $\Delta\pi = \pi_1 - \pi_0$, $\Delta R = R_1 - R_0$, and $\Delta C = C_1 - C_0$. $\pi_1 = \pi_0 + \Delta\pi$, $R_1 = R_0 + \Delta R$, and $C_1 = C_0 + \Delta C$. Therefore, $\pi_1 = \pi_0 + \Delta\pi = (R_0 + \Delta R) - (C_0 + \Delta C) = (R_0 - C_0) + (\Delta R - \Delta C) = \pi_0 + (\Delta R - \Delta C)$. Subtracting π_0 from both sides yields $\Delta\pi = \Delta R - \Delta C$. In other words, the change in profit equals the change in total revenue minus the change in total cost. Dividing through by ΔQ (the change in $Q = Q_1 - Q_0$) yields $\Delta\pi/\Delta Q = \Delta R/\Delta Q - \Delta C/\Delta Q$ or more familiarly $M\pi = MR - MC$. $M\pi$ is the rate that profits change per unit change in Q, while MR and MC are analogously defined. Intuitively, if Q increases by 1, total revenue and total cost will adjust by some amounts. Assume that R increases by $5/unit and C increased by $3/unit. In that event, π will increase by $5/unit - $3/unit or $2/unit. This would be the marginal profit rate, $M\pi$.

5. (a–c)

Q	$10 + Q^2$	C	Average Slope $MC = \Delta C/\Delta Q$	Instantaneous Slope $MC = 2Q$
0	$10 + (0)^2$	10		$2(0) = 0$
			$(11-10)(1-0) = 1$	
1	$10 + (1)^2$	11		$2(1) = 2$
			$(14-11)(2-1) = 3$	
2	$10 + (2)^2$	14		$2(2) = 4$
			$(19-14)(3-2) = 5$	
3	$10 + (3)^2$	19		$2(3) = 6$
			$(26-19)(4-3) = 7$	
4	$10 + (4)^2$	26		$2(4) = 8$
			$(35-26)(5-4) = 9$	
5	$10 + (5)^2$	35		$2(5) = 10$
			$(46-35)(6-5) = 11$	
6	$10 + (6)^2$	46		$2(6) = 12$
			$(59-46)(7-6) = 13$	
7	$10 + (7)^2$	59		$2(7) = 14$
			$(74-59)(8-7) = 15$	
8	$10 + (8)^2$	74		$2(8) = 16$
			$(91-74)(9-8) = 17$	
9	$10 + (9)^2$	91		$2(9) = 18$
			$(110-91)(10-9) = 19$	
10	$10 + (10)^2$	110		$2(10) = 20$

d) The cost curve is quadratic and therefore nonlinear. Consequently, its slope is not constant but varies at each point on the curve. It is therefore not surprising that the slope of a chord between two points on the curve (the average slope over that interval) differs from the tangent to the curve (the instantaneous slope) at the beginning or end of the interval. In this example (but not in general), the average slope method (using 1 unit changes in Q) equals the instantaneous slope method if the midpoint is used. For example, in going from Q = 3 to Q = 4, the midpoint is 3.5. The instantaneous slope at Q = 3.5 = 2(3.5) = 7, which is the average slope result.

6. a) $\pi = R - C$
   $R = 100Q - 10Q^2$ (from Example 4.2)
   $C = 10 + Q^2$ (from Problem 5)
   $\pi = (100Q - 10Q^2) - (10 + Q^2) = 100Q - 10Q^2 - 10 - Q^2$
   $\quad = -10 + 100Q - 11Q^2$

b) $M\pi = MR - MC$
     $MR = 100-20Q$
     $MC = 2Q$
     $M\pi = (100-20Q) -2Q = 100 -22Q$
c) Graphed answer.
    For $Q < 4.5\overline{45}$, $M\pi > 0$
    For $Q = 4.5\overline{45}$, $M\pi = 0$
    For $Q > 4.5\overline{45}$, $M\pi < 0$

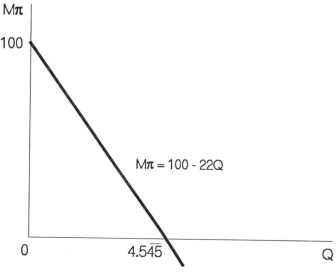

When $M\pi > 0$, $(Q < 4.5\overline{45})$, i.e., π and Q are directly related, increases in Q cause π to increase. When $M\pi < 0$, $(Q > 4.5\overline{45})$, π and Q are inversely related and increases in Q cause π to decrease. When $Q = 4.5\overline{45}$, π is stationary with respect to Q, i.e., it is neither increasing or decreasing. In other words, the tangent to the total profit function is flat at that point. Since total profits increased (as Q increased) for $Q < 4.5\overline{45}$ and decrease for Q greater than that, total profits must be at their maximum at that point $(Q = 4.5\overline{45})$. As will be discussed later, a necessary condition for profits to be maximized is that $MR = MC$ or, equivalently, $M\pi = 0$.

Exercise Set 4.2–Page 142

1.   The budget constraint in general is $I = P_xX + P_yY$. Expressing Y as a function of X, it can be written as:

$$Y = \frac{I}{P_y} - \frac{P_x X}{P_x}$$

where I, P_y, and P_x are usually constants. Therefore, Y is a linear function of X, with I/P_y being the Y intercept and $-P_x/P_y$ being the slope. The X intercept = I/P_x. The Y and X intercepts represent quantities (per some unit of time) of the two goods respectively that could be purchased if all income were devoted to that good and none of the other good were purchased. As such, it represents the maximum amount of that good that can be purchased with the available income, given these prices. The slope, $-P_x/P_y$, represents the change in Y caused by a change in X, while using up all of the income. It is negative because, in order to increase X consumed, some amount of Y must be given up (with income and prices constant). The ratio P_x/P_y is the **relative price of good X** (in terms of foregone Y) and is also the **opportunity cost** of an additional unit of good X.

a) Graphed answer.
   Y = (100/5) – (10/5)X = 20 – 2X
   Y intercept = 20, X intercept = 10, slope = –2

If all income went to purchase Yy (at $5/unit) and no X was purchased, 20 units could be purchased. Similarly, when all income goes for good X, 10 units could be purchased. Additionally, in order to purchase 1 additional unit of X (at $10/ unit), we have to give up 2 units of good Y (at $5/unit).

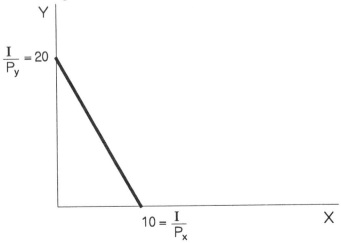

b) Graphed answer.

$Y = (200/10) - (2/10)X =$
$Y = 20 - .2X$
Y intercept = 20
X intercept = 100

Each additional unit costs 1/5 or .2 units of y.

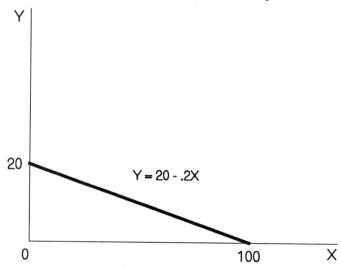

c) Graphed answer.

$Y = (126/3) - (21/3)X =$
$Y = 42 - 7X.$
Y intercept = 42
X intercept = 6

Each additional unit of X costs 7 units of y.

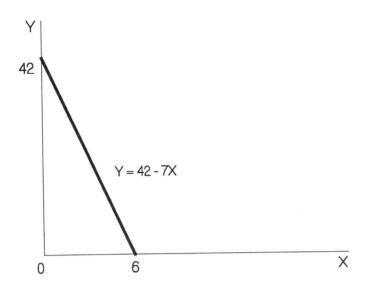

Y = 42 - 7X

2. The MR function is linear and has a slope of -10. The slope of the MR function is the M' of this chapter. So M is decreasing as Q increases over any interval. For $0 \le Q < 50$, MR > 0, therefore R is increasing at a decreasing rate over this interval. For Q > 50, MR < 0, so that R and Q are inversely related over this interval and in fact R is decreasing at an increasing rate. At Q = 50, MR = 0, and since M' < 0, R is at a maximum at this point. The R function is **strictly concave** (and, therefore, concave) over the whole domain. The MR function is linear and is, therefore, concave and convex though strictly neither. In order to keep $R \ge 0$, $0 \le Q \le 100$. The sufficient condition for a maximum is that MR = 0 and is decreasing (M' < 0) at that point. It is satisfied at Q = 50. Substituting into the total revenue function yields:

$R = 500(50) - 5(50)^2 = 25,000 - 5(2500) = 25,000 - 12,500$
$= 12,500$

When Q = 0, and when Q = 100, R = 0.

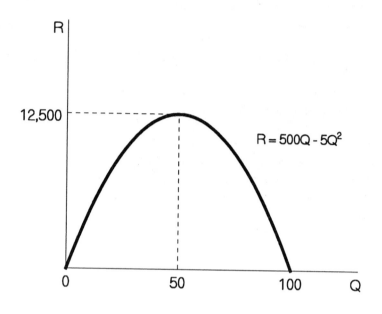

$R = 500Q - 5Q^2$

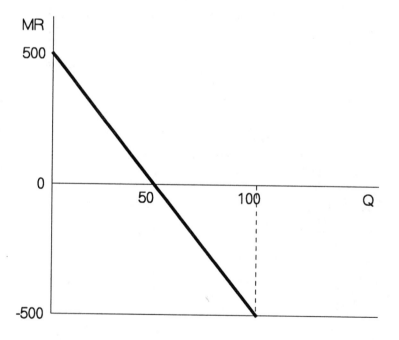

3. Graphed answer. For $0 \leq L < 15$ the production function is strictly convex, and for $L > 15$ the function is strictly concave. At $L = 15$, an inflection point exists as the function switches from convex to concave. At $L = 25$, Q is at its maximum as $M = 0$ and is decreasing as $M' < 0$.

The value of MP_L in this problem is M, and its slope $= M'$. It therefore starts at 0 and rises until $L = 15$ after which it continously falls. It has its maximum at $L = 15$. For $0 \leq L < 15$, output is rising at an increasing rate as L increases, i.e., $MP_L > 0$ and increasing. For $15 < L < 25$ output rises at a decreasing rate ($MP_L > 0$ and decreasing). Q is at its maximum at $L = 25$ ($MP_L = 0$ and decreasing) and after that output starts to fall at an increasing rate ($MP_L < 0$ and decreasing).

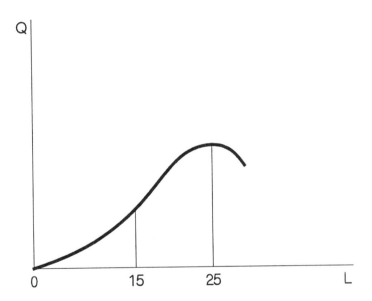

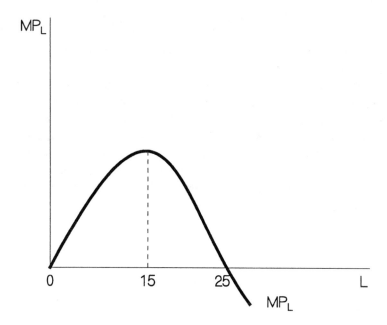

4. Graphed answer. For Q < 25, C is increasing at a decreasing rate and the total cost function is strictly concave. For Q > 25, C is increasing at an increasing rate and the function is strictly convex. At Q = 25, the function switches from concave to convex and therefore is an inflection point. At Q = 0, C = 50, therefore, fixed costs, FC = 50. Fixed cost by definition does not change as Q changes and, therefore, the FC function is a horizontal line at C = 50. While MC is positive throughout (M > 0), it decreases until Q = 25 and increases thereafter. Consequently, it must be at its minimum at Q = 25.

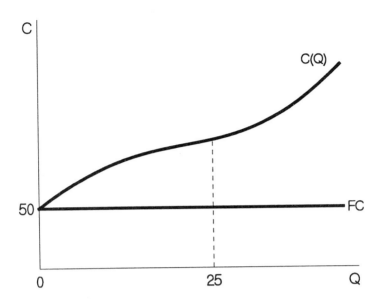

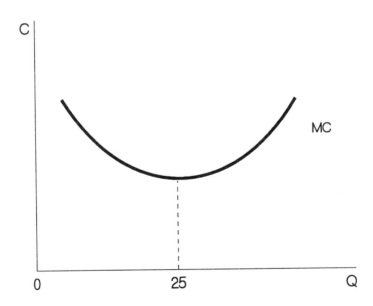

5. Graphed answer. Total π has two points at which M = 0, those being Q = 5 and Q = 20. However, at Q = 5 the function is strictly convex (M' > 0), while at Q = 20 the function is strictly concave (M' < 0). Therefore, Q = 5 is a profit minimum, while Q = 20 is the profit maximum. Mπ increases until Q = 10 at which point it is stationary and then declines thereafter. Consequently, at Q = 10 it is at its maximum value.

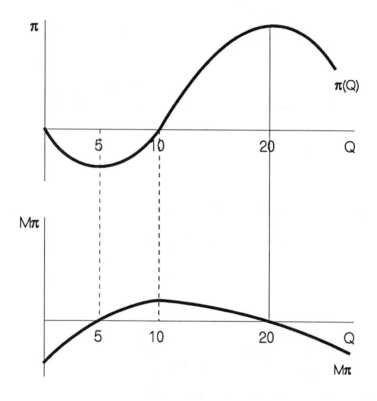

6. a) Graphed answer. R is strictly convex as is UR (the vertical difference between R and SR). SR is a horizontal line and is therefore concave and convex, but strictly neither.

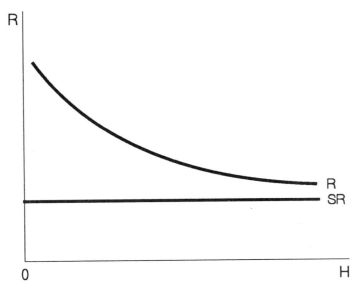

b) Graphed answer. When YTM = 6%, the curve is strictly concave, while when YTM = 10%, the curve is strictly convex. When YTM = 8%, the curve is a horizontal line (see graph above). At M = 0 all 3 curves must pass through P = 1000.

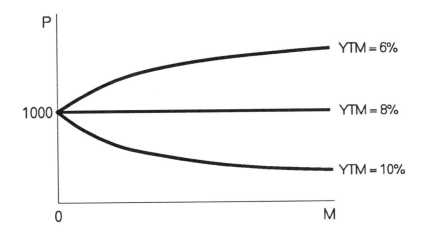

Chapter 5

Exercise Set 5.1–Page 167

1. a) Graphed answer.

$$AR = \frac{R}{Q} = 25/Q$$

$$AR = \frac{2Q}{Q} = 2$$

$$AR = \frac{10Q - Q^2}{Q} = 10 - Q$$

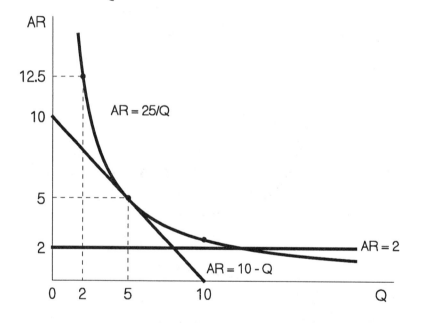

b) AR = 25/Q hyperbolic
    AR = 2 constant
    AR = 10 – Q linear

c)

AR = 25/Q	AR = 2	AR = 10 − Q
f(0) = 0	f(0) = 2	f(0) = 10
f(1) = 1	f(1) = 2	f(1) = 9
f(2) = 25/2	f(2) = 2	f(2) = 8
f(3) = 25/3	f(3) = 2	f(3) = 7
.	.	.
.	.	.
.	.	.
f(10) = 25/10	f(10) = 2	f(10) = 0

2. a) Graphed answer.

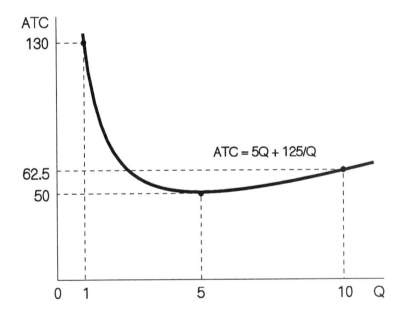

$$
\begin{array}{ll}
TC & = AC \times Q \\
130(1) & = 130 \\
72.50(2) & = 145 \\
56.67(3) & = 170.01 \\
51.25(4) & = 205 \\
50(5) & = 250 \\
50.83(6) & = 304.98 \\
52.86(7) & = 370.02 \\
55.63(8) & = 445 \\
58.89(9) & = 530.01 \\
62.50(10) & = 625
\end{array}
$$

b) $TC = 5Q^2 + 125$

TC in dollars

3. a) $TC = 4200 + 145Q - 18Q^2 + 3Q^3$
    $FC = 4200$
    $VC = 145Q - 18Q^2 + 3Q^3$

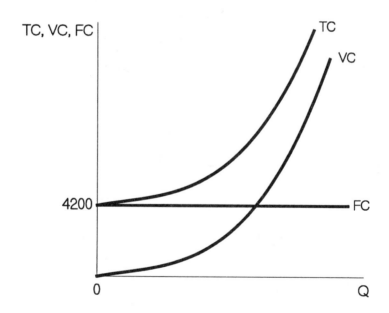

Quantity	FC	VC	TC
0	4200	0	4200
1	4200	130	4330
2	4200	242	4442
3	4200	354	4554
4	4200	484	4684
5	4200	650	4850
6	4200	870	5070
7	4200	1162	5362
8	4200	1544	5744
9	4200	2034	6234
10	4200	2650	6850
11	4200	3410	7610
12	4200	4332	8532
13	4200	5434	9634
14	4200	6734	10934
15	4200	8250	12450
16	4200	10000	14200
17	4200	12002	16202
18	4200	14274	18474
19	4200	16834	21034
20	4200	19700	23900

b) $ATC = \dfrac{4200}{Q} + 145 - 18Q + 3Q^2$

$AFC = \dfrac{4200}{Q}$

$AVC = 145 - 18Q + 3Q^2$

Quantity	FC	VC	TC	ATC	AFC	AVC
0	4200	0	4200	undef	undef	undef
1	4200	130	4330	4330.00	4200.00	130.00
2	4200	242	4442	2221.00	2100.00	121.00
3	4200	354	4554	1518.00	1400.00	118.00
4	4200	484	4684	1171.00	1050.00	121.00
5	4200	650	4850	970.00	840.00	130.00
6	4200	870	5070	845.00	700.00	145.00
7	4200	162	5362	766.00	600.00	166.00
8	4200	544	5744	718.00	525.00	193.00
9	4200	034	6234	692.67	466.67	226.00
10	4200	650	6850	685.00	420.00	265.00
11	4200	410	7610	691.82	381.82	310.00
12	4200	332	8532	711.00	350.00	361.00
13	4200	434	9634	741.08	323.08	418.00
14	4200	734	10934	781.00	300.00	481.00
15	4200	250	12450	830.00	280.00	550.00
16	4200	0000	14200	887.50	262.50	625.00
17	4200	2002	16202	953.06	247.06	706.00
18	4200	4274	18474	1026.33	233.33	793.00
19	4200	6834	21034	1107.05	221.05	886.00
20	4200	9700	23900	1195.00	210.00	985.00

c)   The ray drawn from the origin to the curve is flatter when the ATC is at its minimum.

$Q = 3$, $AVC = 118 = MC$
$Q = 10$, $ATC = 685 = MC$

d)   MC > AVC when AVC is rising, therefore, MC > AVC for Q > 3.
MC < AVC when AVC is falling, therefore, MC < AVC for Q < 3.

4. $AP_L = \dfrac{Q}{L} = \dfrac{100K^{1/2}L^{1/2}}{L} = 100K^{1/2}L^{-1/2}$

a)   If $K = 4$, $AP_L = 100(4^{1/2})L^{-1/2}$
$AP_L = 200L^{-1/2}$
If $K = 9$, $AP_L = 100(9^{1/2})L^{-1/2}$
$AP_L = 300L^{-1/2}$

b)   As L increases, AP_L decreases. This implies that the MP_L is less than the AP_L.

c) $AP_K = \dfrac{100K^{1/2}L^{1/2}}{K} = 100K^{-1/2}L^{1/2}$

a)   If $L = 25$, $AP_K = 100K^{-1/2}(25)^{1/2}$
$= 500K^{-1/2}$

If $L = 100$, $AP_K = 100K^{-1/2}(100)^{1/2}$
$= 1000K^{-1/2}(100)^{1/2}$

5. $Y_d = C + S$

$\dfrac{Y_d}{Y_d} = \dfrac{C}{Y_d} + \dfrac{S}{Y_d}$
$1 = APC + APS$

Exercise Set 5.2–Page 188

1.   a) $APC = \dfrac{C}{Y_d} = \dfrac{b_0 + b_1 Y_d}{Y_d} = \dfrac{b_0}{Y_d} + b_1$
As Y_d increases, APC will decrease.
If $b_0 = 0$, $APC = b_1 = MPC$.

b) $E_{C,Y_d} = \dfrac{\Delta C}{\Delta Y_d} \times \dfrac{Y_d}{C} = \dfrac{b_1 Y_d}{b_0 + b_1 Y_d}$

If $b_0 = 0$, $E_{C,Y_d} = \dfrac{b_1 Y_d}{b_1 Y_d} = 1.0$

$E_{C,Y_d} = \dfrac{b_1}{\dfrac{b_0}{Y_d} + b_1}$

If $b_0 > 0$, E_{C,Y_d} decreases as Y_d increases.

If $b_0 = 0$, E_{C,Y_d} does not vary as Y_d varies.

E_{C,Y_d} is in the inelastic range for the first case and of unitary elasticity for the second case.

2. $E_{L,Y} = 1.0$ indicates that the demand for money with respect to income is of unitary elasticity. This means a 1% increase in income results in a 1% increase in the demand for money. $E_{L,i} = -.2$ indicates that the demand for money with respect to the interest rate is inelastic. This means a 1% increase in the interest rate results in a .2% decrease in the demand for money.

3. a) $Q^d = 1000 - 4P + 5(20) + .2(100)$
      $= 1000 - 4P + 100 + 20$
      $Q^d = 1120 - 4P$

   b) $Q^d = 1120 - 4(150)$
      $Q^d = 520$

   $E_{Q^d,P}^d = \dfrac{\Delta Q^d}{\Delta P} \times \dfrac{P}{Q^d} = (-4)\left(\dfrac{150}{520}\right) = -1.15$

   If $P = 130$, $Q^d = 1120 - 4(130) = 600$

   $E_{Q^d,P}^d = (-4)\left(\dfrac{130}{600}\right) = -.87$

   If $P = 140$, $Q^d = 1120 - 4(140) = 560$

   $E_{Q^d,P}^d = (-4)\left(\dfrac{140}{560}\right) = -1.0$

c) $E_{Q^d,P} = \dfrac{\Delta Q^d}{\Delta P} \dfrac{(P_1 + P_2)/2}{(Q_1 + Q_2)/2} = \dfrac{560 - 600}{140 - 130} \dfrac{(130 + 140)/2}{(600 + 560)/2}$

$\qquad = \dfrac{-40}{10} \dfrac{135}{580} = -.93 \quad \text{inelastic}$

$E_{Q^d,P} = \dfrac{520 - 600}{150 - 130} \dfrac{(130 + 150)/2}{(520 + 600)/2} = \dfrac{-80}{20} \dfrac{140}{560}$

$\qquad = -1.0 \quad \text{unitary elastic}$

d)

$E_{Q^d,I} = \dfrac{\Delta Q^d}{\Delta I} \dfrac{I}{Q^d}$

$\qquad = (5)\left(\dfrac{20}{560}\right) = .18 \text{ Normal good}$

$E_{Q^d,P_z} = \dfrac{\Delta Q}{\Delta P_z} \dfrac{P_z}{Q^d} \qquad\qquad \dfrac{\Delta Q}{\Delta P_z} = .2$

$E_{Q^d,P_z} + \left(.2\right)\dfrac{100}{560} = .036 \text{ Substitutes}$

4. a) Yes, slope $= -100P^{-2}$

$\qquad E_{Q^d,P} = (-100P^{-2})\left(\dfrac{P}{100P^{-1}}\right) = -1.0$

b) Graphed answer.

Q^d	P
10	10
11.1	9
12.5	8
14.3	7
16.7	6
20	5
25	4
33.3	3
50	2
100	1

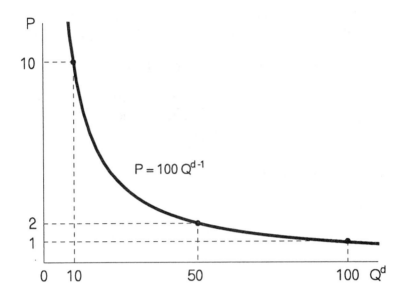

P = 100 Q^{d-1}

c) For $P = 10$ and $P = 9$
   $Q^d = 10$ and $Q^d = 11.1$

$$E_{Q^d,P} = \frac{11.1 - 10}{9 - 10} \frac{(10 + 9)/2}{(10 + 11.1)/2} = -1.0$$

For $P = 9$ and $P = 8$
   $Q^d = 11.1$ and $Q^d = 12.5$

$$E_{Q^d,P} = \frac{12.5 - 11.1}{8 - 9} \frac{(9 + 8)/2}{(11.1 + 12.5)/2} = -1.0$$

d) $R = P \times Q^d = 100$ for all P, Q^d points
   $R = P \times Q^d = P(100P^{-1}) = 100$

Constant function

$$Q^s = 2P \quad E = (2)\left(\frac{P}{Q^s}\right) = 2\left(\frac{P}{2P}\right) = 1.0$$

5. A demand curve parallel to the price axis. $E = 0$. Q^d does not vary as P varies.

    A demand curve parallel to the quantity axis. $E \to \infty$. As P_d varies, the resulting change in Q^d is infinite.

    $$Q^d = 250P^{-2}, \quad E = -500P^{-3} \; \frac{P}{250P^{-2}} = -2$$

    The demand is elastic over the entire demand curve.

6. a) If $A(x)$ is directly related to x, then $M(x) > A(x)$. Therefore:

    $$E_{T,x} = \frac{M(x)}{A(x)} > 1$$

    $E_{T,x}$ is in the elastic range.

    b) If $A(x)$ is inversely related to x, then $M(x) < A(x)$. Therefore:

    $$E_{T,x} = \frac{M(x)}{A(x)} < 1$$

    c) If $A(x)$ is stationary, then $M(x) = A(x)$. Therefore:

    $$E_{T,x} = \frac{M(x)}{A(x)} = 1$$

    $E_{T,x}$ is unitary.

7. Initial price = PV = \$5,000
    Coupon = $(.05)(5000)$ = \$250/year at R = 10%.

    $$PV = \frac{250}{1 + .10} + \frac{250 + 5,000}{(1 + .10)^2} = \frac{250}{1.10} + \frac{5250}{1.21}$$
    $$= 227.27 + 4338.84 = 4566.11$$

    $$E_{P_B, Y_M} = \frac{\% \Delta P_B}{\% \Delta (1 + Y_M)} = \frac{\Delta P_B}{\Delta (1 + Y_M)} \times \frac{1 + Y_M}{P_B}$$
    $$= \frac{(4566.11 - 5,000)}{(1.10 - 1.05)} \frac{(1.05)}{(5,000)} = -1.82\%$$

    The interest rate risk is relatively low. Since the percent change in $Y_M = .05/1.05 = .0476$, a change in Y_M of 4.76% yields a change in the bond price of 1.82 times as much.

8. Let $R_2 = -R_1$. Then $V = X(1 + R_1)(1 - R_1) = X(1 - R^2) = X - XR_1^2$. Notice that $R_1^2 > 0$ independent of whether $R_1 > 0$ or < 0. Therefore, $X - XR_1^2 < X$ for $X > 0$. This implies that the value of your portfolio decreased over the year. The rate of return $= R = (1 - R_1^2) - 1 = -R_1^2$. Not only is the rate of return negative but, as R_1 increases in absolute value, your rate of return worsens (negative and larger in absolute value). While the arithmetic average rate of return is 0 since $R_1 + R_2 = 0$, it is clear that your actual R must be negative if the value of your portfolio declines. The difference arises because the percentage increase in your portfolio uses a smaller base than the decrease does, and this is true independent of the order of occurrence. For example, assume $X = \$1,000$, $R_1 = 10\%$, $R_2 = -10\%$. The 10% increase in value is relative to $1,000 and brings the total value to $1,000 (1 + .1) = \$1,100$. The 10% decrease in value is from $1,100 or -$110, leaving the value of the portfolio at $1,100 [1 + (-.1)] = \$1,100(.9) = 990$. Similarly, if $R_1 = -10\%$ and $R_2 = +10\%$, the percentage increase uses a smaller base and therefore results in a smaller dollar increase than an equiproportionate loss. At the end of the first period, 10% of the initial $1,000 is lost leaving .9(1000) = 900 (a $100 loss). Then the 10% increase is relative to only $900 or 1.1(900) = 990 (a $90 gain), again leaving 990. In general, arithmetic average returns will always exceed the compound average returns (as long as returns are not constant), due to this factor.

Chapter 6

Exercise Set 6.1–Page 214

1. a) $Q^d = Q^s$. There is no excess demand or excess supply, thus there are no forces operating to change the prevailing, or equilibrium, price pertaining to this situation.

   b) P, Q^d, and Q^s are dependent variables. I and P_A are independent variables.

   c) $1000 - 5P + 50I = -100 + 10P - 5P_A$
   $15P = 1000 + 100 + 50I + 5P_A$
   $P_e = (1100 + 50I + 5P_A)/15 = (220 + 10I + P_A)/3$
   $Q_e = Q^s = Q^d = 1000 - 5P + 50I$
   $P = 200 + 10I - .2Q$

$$Q^s = -100 + 10(200 + 10I - .2Q) - 5P_A$$
$$= -100 + 2000 + 100I - 2Q - 5P_A$$
$$Q_e = Q^s = (1900 + 100I - 5P_A)/3$$

d) $P_e = [220 + 10(30) + 9]/3 = 176.33$
   $Q_e = [1900 + 100(30) - 5(9)]/3 = 1618.33$
   $P_e = [220 + 10(24) + 12]/3 = 157.33$
   $Q_e = [1900 + 100(24) - 5(12)]/3 = 1413.33$

e) $\dfrac{\Delta P_e}{\Delta I} \Big| \bar{P}_A = 3.33$

   A \$1 increase in P_A will result in a \$.33 increase in P_e.

   $\dfrac{\Delta P_e}{\Delta P_A} \Big| \bar{I} = .33$

   A one thousand dollar increase in I will result in a \$3.33 increase in P_e.

   $\dfrac{\Delta Q_e}{\Delta I} \Big| \bar{P}_A = 33.33$

   A one thousand dollar increase in I will result in a 33.33 increase in Q_e.

   $\dfrac{\Delta Q_e}{\Delta P_A} \Big| \bar{I} = -1.67$

   A \$1 increase in P_A will result in a 1.67 decrease in Q_e.

2. a) MR = MC
   $50 - .2Q = 2$
   $Q = 240 = Q^d$
   $MR = 50 - .2(240) = 2$
   $C = 25 + 2(240) = 505$
   $Q^d = 500 - 10P$
   $P = 50 - .1Q^d = 50 - .1(240) = 26$
   $R = 50(240) - .1(240)^2 = 6240$
   $\pi = 6240 - 505 = 5735$

b) Graphed answer.

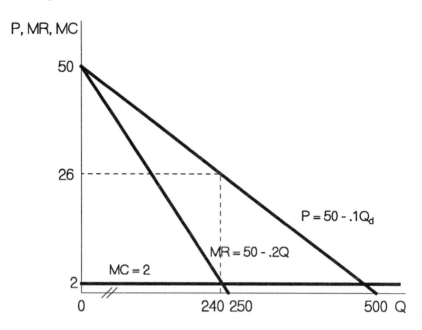

3. a) $C = b_0 + b_1 Y_d$, $I = I_0 + a_1 Y$, $G = G_0$, and $T = T_0$ are behavioral. $Y_d = Y - T$ and $AE = C + I + G$ are identities. $AE = Y$ is an equilibrium condition.

b) $Y = AE = C + I + G$
$Y = b_0 + b_1 Y_d + I_0 + a_1 Y + G_0$
$Y = b_0 + b_1 (Y - T_0) + I_0 + G_0$
$Y = b_0 + b_1 Y - b_1 T_0 + I_0 + G_0$
$Y(1 - b_1) = b_0 - b_1 T_0 + I_0 + G_0$
$$Y = \frac{1}{1 - b_1}(b_0 - b_1 T_0 + I_0 + G_0)$$

c) $Y = b_0 + b_1 (Y - T_0) + I_0 + a_1 Y + G_0$
$Y = b_0 + b_1 Y - b_1 T_0 + I_0 + a_1 Y + G_0$
$Y(1 - b_1 - a_1) = b_0 - b_1 T_0 + I_0 + G_0$
$$Y = \frac{1}{1 - b_1 - a_1}(b_0 - b_1 T_0 + I_0 + G_0)$$
A nonzero a_1 leads to a higher level of income.

d) The government expenditure and autonomous investment multipliers, for $a_1 = 0$, are both $\dfrac{1}{1 - b_1}$

For $a_1 > 0$ they are $\dfrac{1}{1 - b_1 - a_1}$

The autonomous tax multiplier for $a_1 = 0$, is $\dfrac{b_1}{1 - b_1}$

For $a_1 > 0$, it is $\dfrac{b_1}{1 - b_1 - a_1}$

e) $Y = \dfrac{1}{1 - .8}[600 - .8(100) + 50 + 150]$

$Y = 3600 = AE$

$Y_d = 3600 - 100 = 3500$

$C = 600 + .8(3500) = 3400$

$I = 50$

f) $Y = \dfrac{1}{1 - .8 - .1}[600 - .8(100) + 50 + 150]$

$Y = 7200 = AE$

$Y_d = 7200 - 100 = 7100$

$C = 600 + .8(7100) = 6280$

$I = 50 + .1(7200) = 770$

4. a) $E(R_i) = [E(P_{i1}) - P_{i0} + E(D_{i1})]/P_{i0}$

$E(RR_i) = RF + \beta_i(RP_M)$

$E(RR_i) = E(R_i)$ equilibrium condition

$RF + \beta_i(RP_M) = [E(P_{i1}) - P_{i0} + E(D_{i1})]/P_{i0}$

$P_{i0}[RF + \beta_i(RP_M)] = [E(P_{i1}) - P_{i0} + E(D_{i1})]$
    (multiply both sides by P_{i0})

$P_{i0}[RF + \beta_i(RP_M)] + P_{i0} = [E(P_{i1}) + E(D_{i1})]$
    (add P_{i0} to both sides)

$P_{i0}[1 + RF + \beta_i(RP_M)] = [E(P_{i1}) + E(D_{i1})]$

$P_{i0}^* = \dfrac{[E(P_{i1}) + E(D_{i1})]}{[1 + RF + \beta_i(RP_M)]}$

b) $E(RR_i) = 4\% + 1(6\%) = 10\%$ or $.1$

$E(R_i) = [50 - 45 + 2.80]/45 = 7.80/45 = 17\ 1/3\%$ or $.17\overline{33}$.

Since $E(R_i) > E(RR_i)$, $.45$ is not an equilibrium price. Given that the security is expected to have a return greater than required, its price should be higher. In fact, using the result from Part a, $P_{io}{}^*$ = $(50 + 2.80)/[1+ .04 + 1(.06)] = (52.80/1.1) = \$48$.

Chapter 7

Exercise Set 7.1–Page 252

1. $C = 300 + .9Y_d$

$S = Y_d - C$

$S = Y_d - (300 + .9Y_d)$

$S = -300 + (1 - .9)Y_d$

$S = -300 + .1Y_d$

$MPS = \dfrac{dS}{dY_d} = .1$

2. a) $MR = \dfrac{dR}{dQ} = 1000 - 20Q$

b) $MR > 0$ for $Q < 50$

$MR < 0$ for $Q > 50$

$MR = 0$ for $Q = 50$

c) $AR = R/Q = (1000Q - 10Q^2)/Q = 1000 - 10Q$

d) Graphed answer.

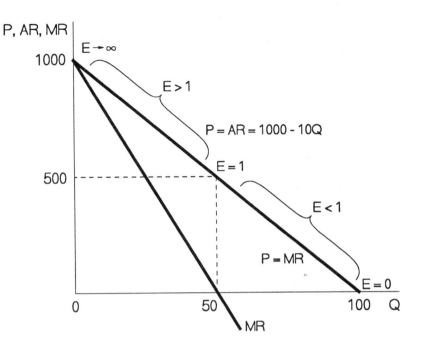

3. a) $MC = \dfrac{dC}{dQ} = 30Q$

b) $ATC = C/Q = (15Q^2 + 60)/Q$
   $= 15Q + 60/Q = 15Q + 60Q^{-1}$

c) $\dfrac{dATC}{dQ} = 15 - \dfrac{60}{Q^2}$
   Positive slope for $Q > 2$
   Negative slope for $Q < 2$

4. a) $U = 100X^{.5}Y^{.5}$
   $800 = 100X^{.5}Y^{.5}$
   $Y^{.5} = 800/100X^{.5} = 8/X^{.5}$
   $(Y^{.5})^2 = Y = (8/X^{.5})^2 = 64/X = 64X^{-1}$

b) $\dfrac{dU}{dX} = 100[.5X^{.5}\,Y^{-.5}\,\dfrac{dY}{dX} + .5X^{-.5}Y^{.5}] = 0$

$.5X^{.5}Y^{-.5}\,\dfrac{dY}{dX} + .5X^{-.5}Y^{.5} = 0$

$\dfrac{dY}{dX} = \dfrac{-.5X^{-.5}\,Y^{.5}}{.5X^{.5}\,Y^{-.5}} = \dfrac{-Y}{X}$

or MRS = Y/X

$\text{MRS} = \dfrac{16}{4} = 4$

c) from Part a.

$Y = \dfrac{64}{X} = 64X^{-1}$

$\dfrac{dY}{dX} = -64X^{-2}$

when $X = 4$, $\dfrac{dY}{dX} = -\dfrac{64}{4^2} = -\dfrac{64}{16} = -4$

or MRS $= \dfrac{-dY}{dX} = 4$

5. a) $C = C\,[f(L)]$

$\text{MFC}_L = \dfrac{dC}{dL} = \dfrac{dC}{df} \times \dfrac{df}{dL}$

$\dfrac{df}{dL} = \dfrac{dQ}{dL}$ represents the extra output per extra unit of labor (marginal product)

$\dfrac{dC}{df} = \dfrac{dC}{dQ}$ represents the extra cost per extra unit of output (i.e., marginal cost, MC). Therefore, $\text{MFC}_L = \text{MC} \times \text{MP}_L$

b) $\text{MFC}_L = \dfrac{dC}{dL} = W = \text{MC} \times \text{MP}_L$ (from Part a).

$\text{MC} = \dfrac{W}{\text{MP}_L}$

$$E_{Q,P} = \frac{dQ}{dP} \times \frac{P}{Q}$$

$$= -1.5(50)P^{-2.5} \times \frac{P}{Q}$$

$$= -75P^{-2.5}\frac{P}{50P^{-1.5}} = \frac{-75}{50} = -1.5$$

6. a)
No, it is not dependent on Q.

b) The good in question is elastic in that a 1 percent change in price yields a 1.5 percent change in quantity demanded in the opposite direction.

c) $MR = P(1 + \frac{1}{E_{Q,P}})$

$MR = P(1 - \frac{1}{1.5}) = P(1 - .67) = .33P$
MR is always positive.

Exercise Set 7.2–Page 272

1. a) $\pi = R - C = 1000Q - 10Q^2 - 15Q^2 - 60$
   $\pi' = \frac{d\pi}{dQ} = 1000 - 20Q - 30Q$
   $= 1000 - 50Q$

b) $1000 - 50Q = 0$
   $Q = 20$

c) $MR = \frac{dR}{dQ} = 1000 - 20Q$

   $MC = \frac{dC}{dQ} = 30Q$
   $MR = MC$
   $1000 - 20Q = 30Q$
   $1000 = 50Q$
   $Q = 20$

d) $\dfrac{d\left(\dfrac{d\pi}{dQ}\right)}{dQ} = \pi'' = -50 < 0$

It is a maximum, and the total profit function is concave.

$MR' = \dfrac{dMR}{dQ} = -20$

therefore, the R function is concave.

$MC' = \dfrac{dMC}{dQ} = 30$

therefore, the C function is convex.

2.　$\pi = R(f(L)) - C(f(L))$

$\dfrac{d\pi}{dL} = \dfrac{dR}{dQ} \times \dfrac{dQ}{dL} - \dfrac{dC}{dQ} \times \dfrac{dQ}{dL} = 0$

$\dfrac{d\pi}{dL} = MR \times MP_L - MC \times MP_L = 0$

$MR \times MP_L = MC \times MP_L$ or

$MRP_L = MFC_L$

Dividing both sides by MP_L yields:

$MR = MC$

3.　a) $AP_L = \dfrac{Q}{L}$

$\dfrac{dAP_L}{dL} = \dfrac{L\dfrac{dQ}{dL} - Q\dfrac{dL}{dL}}{L^2} = 0$

$L\dfrac{dQ}{dL} - Q = 0$

$\dfrac{dQ}{dL} = \dfrac{Q}{L}$

$MP_L = AP_L$

b) $\dfrac{d\left(\dfrac{dAP_L}{dL}\right)}{dL} < 0$

4. a) $\dfrac{dATC}{dQ} = 4(Q - 2)^3 \dfrac{dQ}{dQ} = 4(Q - 2)^3$

$4(Q - 2)^3 = 0$

$Q = 2$

b) $C = (ATC) \times Q$

$= Q \times (Q - 2)^4 + 10Q$

$MC = \dfrac{dC}{dQ} = 4Q(Q - 2)^3 + (Q - 2)^4 + 10$

c) It occurs where ATC is at its minimum, i.e., where $Q = 2$.

d) $ATC'' = d\ \dfrac{\left(\dfrac{dATC}{dQ} \right)}{dQ} = 12\,(Q - 2)^2$

when $Q = 2$, $12(Q - 2)^2 = 0$

$ATC''' = 24(Q - 2)$

when $Q = 2$, $24(Q - 2) = 0$

$ATC'''' = 24 > 0$

Since this is the fourth derivative, which is even, $Q = 2$ is a minimum.

5. 7.4 $Q = 20L^{.75}$

$MP_L = \dfrac{dQ}{dL} = 15L^{-.25}$

$\dfrac{d\left(\dfrac{dQ}{dL} \right)}{dL} = -3.75L^{-1.25} < 0$

Concave

7.5 $C = 50 + 2Q + Q^2$

$MC = \dfrac{dC}{dQ} = 2 + 2Q$

$\dfrac{d\left(\dfrac{dC}{dQ} \right)}{dQ} = 2 > 0$

Convex

7.6 $R = 98Q - 2Q^2$

$$MR = \frac{dR}{dQ} = 98 - 4Q$$

$$\frac{d\left(\frac{dR}{dQ}\right)}{dQ} = -4 < 0$$
$$\text{Concave}$$

6. a) Let $E(P_1) + E(D_1) = C_1 =$ a constant, and
$1 + RF = C_2 =$ another constant, and
$RP_M = C_3 =$ another constant.
Then $P_0^* = C_1/(C_2 + C_3\beta_i)$.

$$\frac{dP_0^*}{d\beta_i} = \left[\frac{dC_1}{d\beta_i}(C_2 + C_3\beta_i) - \left(\frac{dC_2}{d\beta_i} + C_3 \right)(C_1) \right] / [C_2 + C_3\beta_i]^2$$

$$= -(C_1C_3)/(C_2 + C_3\beta_i)^2. \quad \left(\text{Since } \frac{dC_1}{d\beta_i} = \frac{dC_2}{d\beta_i} = 0. \right)$$

Since C_1, C_2, $C_3 > 0$ and the denominator is squared, this derivative must be negative. Therefore, for given values of the other variables, the equilibrium price and β are inversely related. (Since a higher β implies a riskier security, it requires a higher expected rate of return. For a given ending period price, a lower equilibrium price implies greater price appreciation and, therefore, a higher expected rate of return). However, if the counter assumptions C_1 or $C_3 = 0$, the derivative is 0.

The second derivative $d^2P_0^*/d\beta_i^2$, by again using the quotient rule on $dP_0^*/d\beta_i$, is:

$$\frac{d^2P_0^*}{d\beta_i^2} = [-2(C_2 + C_3\beta_i)C_3(-C_1C_3)]/(C_2 + C_3\beta_i)^4$$

$$= 2C_1C_3^2/(C_2 + C_3\beta_i)^3 = 2P_0^* \cdot C_3^2/(C_2 + C_3\beta_i)^2 > 0$$

Therefore, the equilibrium price decreases at a decreasing rate as β increases. The curve is downward sloping and strictly convex.

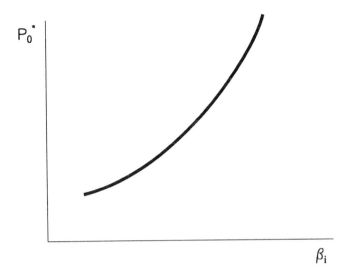

$$P_0^*$$

$$\beta_i$$

b) The equation can be rewritten as:

$$P^*_0 = [E(P_1) + 2.80]/1.1 = \left(\frac{2.8}{1.1}\right) + \left(\frac{1}{1.1}\right) E(P_1)$$

which is clearly a linear function with intercept = (2.8/1.1) and slope (first derivative) = 1/1.1. Since it is linear, the second derivative = 0. For each (and every) dollar increase in $E(P_1)$, P_0^* increases by 1/1.1 ≅ 91¢. Since the required rate of return is 10 percent, this represents the present discounted value of $1, 1 period from now. This rate is independent of the actual value of $E(P_1)$, since each dollar appreciation in $E(P_1)$ increases the period's dollar return by 1. A dollar more 1 period from now discounted at a 10 percent rate is worth approximately 91¢ now.

Chapter 8

Exercise Set 8.1–Page 295

1. a) $$MU_X = \frac{\partial u}{\partial x} = 10xy^3$$
$$= 10(2)(3)^3 = 540$$

b) $MU_y = \dfrac{\partial u}{\partial y} = 15x^2y^2$

$\qquad = 15(2)^2(3)^2 = 540$

c) MU_x increases as x increases.

MU_y increases as y increases.

They violate the law of diminishing marginal utility.

2. a) $MP_K = \dfrac{\partial Q}{\partial K} = 16KL^2 - 6K^2L^3$

$\quad MP_L = \dfrac{\partial Q}{\partial L} = 16K^2L - 6K^3L^2$

b) Graphed answer.

$MP_K = 16K(1)^2 - 6K^2(1)^3$

$\qquad = 16K - 6K^2 \quad$ Yes, for K > 1.33.

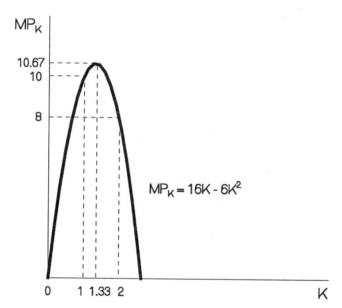

c) $MP_K = 16(2)(1)^2 - 6(2)^2(1)^3$

$\qquad = 32 - 24 = 8$

$\quad MP_L = 16(2)^2(1) - 6(2)^3(1)^2$

$\qquad = 64 - 48 = 16$

d) $\dfrac{dQ}{dL} = 8\left(2K^2L\dfrac{dL}{dL} + 2L^2K\dfrac{dK}{dL}\right) - 2\left(3K^3L^2\dfrac{dL}{dL} + 3L^3K^2\dfrac{dK}{dL}\right) = 0$

$= 16K^2L + 16KL^2\dfrac{dK}{dL} - 6K^3L^2 - 6K^2L^3\dfrac{dK}{dL} = 0$

$6K^2L^3\dfrac{dK}{dL} - 16KL^2\dfrac{dK}{dL} = 16K^2L - 6K^3L^2$

$\dfrac{dK}{dL}[6K^2L^3 - 16KL^2] = 16K^2L - 6K^3L^2$

$\dfrac{dK}{dL} = \dfrac{16K^2L - 6K^3L^2}{6K^2L^3 - 16KL^2} = \dfrac{2K^2L(8 - 3KL)}{2KL^2(3KL - 8)}$

$\quad = \dfrac{-K(8 - 3KL)}{L(8 - 3KL)} = -\dfrac{K}{L}$

This is the marginal rate of technical substitution, which is defined as the rate at which capital can be substituted for labor while still producing the same level of output.

3. a) $Q^d_x = 400 - 40(10) + 50(6) + .005(20{,}000)$

$\quad = 400 - 400 + 300 + 100 = 400$

b) $E_{Qx^d,Px} = \dfrac{\partial Q^d_x}{\partial P_x} \times \dfrac{P_x}{Q^d_x} = (-40)\left(\dfrac{10}{400}\right) = -1.0$

$E_{Qx^d,Py} = \dfrac{\partial Q^d_x}{\partial P_y} \times \dfrac{P_y}{Q^d_x} = (50)\left(\dfrac{6}{400}\right) = .75$

$E_{Q^d x,I} = \dfrac{\partial Q^d_x}{\partial I} \times \dfrac{I}{Q^d_x} = (.005)\left(\dfrac{20{,}000}{400}\right) = .25$

c) The own-price demand is of unitary elasticity. A 1 percent rise in own-price results in a 1 percent decline in quantity demanded of good x.

   A 1 percent rise in the price of good y results in a .75 percent rise in quantity demanded of good x.

   A 1 percent rise in income results in a .25 percent rise in

quantity demanded of good x.

d) Substitutes

e) Normal

4. $\dfrac{dQ}{dt} = \dfrac{2}{3} K^{1/3} L^{-1/3} \dfrac{dL}{dt} + \dfrac{1}{3} K^{-2/3} L^{2/3} \dfrac{dK}{dt}$

$\dfrac{dK}{dt} = 2$ $\qquad\qquad$ $\dfrac{dL}{dt} = 4$

$\dfrac{dQ}{dt} = \dfrac{2}{3} \left(\dfrac{K}{L} \right)^{1/3} (4) + \dfrac{1}{3} \left(\dfrac{L}{K} \right)^{2/3} (2)$

$\qquad = \dfrac{8}{3} \left(\dfrac{1}{8} \right)^{1/3} + \dfrac{2}{3} \left(\dfrac{8}{1} \right)^{2/3} = \dfrac{8}{3} \left(\dfrac{1}{2} \right) + \dfrac{2}{3} (4)$

$\qquad = \dfrac{4}{3} + \dfrac{8}{3} = \dfrac{12}{3} = 4$

$Q = (1)^{1/3} (8)^{2/3} = (1)(4) = 4$

growth rate $= \dfrac{\dfrac{dQ}{dt}}{Q} = 4/4 = 1\%$

Exercise Set 8.2–Page 316

1. $\mathcal{L} = X^{1/2} + Y^{1/2} + \lambda (I - P_X X - P_Y Y)$

$\dfrac{\partial \mathcal{L}}{\partial X} = \dfrac{1}{2} X^{-1/2} - \lambda P_X = 0$

$\dfrac{\partial \mathcal{L}}{\partial Y} = \dfrac{1}{2} Y^{-1/2} - \lambda P_Y = 0$

$\dfrac{\partial \mathcal{L}}{\partial X} = I - P_X X - P_Y Y = 0$

$\dfrac{(1/2) X^{-1/2}}{(1/2) Y^{-1/2}} = \dfrac{\lambda P_X}{\lambda P_Y}$

$$\frac{Y^{1/2}}{X^{1/2}} = \frac{P_X}{P_Y}$$

$$Y^{1/2} = \frac{P_X}{P_Y} X^{1/2}$$

$$Y = \frac{P_x^2}{P_y^2} X$$

$$I - P_X X - P_Y \left(\frac{P_x^2}{P_y^2} \right) X = 0$$

$$I - (1)X - 2\left(\frac{1}{4} \right) X = 0$$

$$I - \frac{3}{2} X = 0$$

$$X = \frac{2}{3} I = \frac{2}{3}(300) = 200 \text{ units}$$

$$Y = \frac{1}{4} X = \frac{1}{4}(200) = 50 \text{ units}$$

2. $$K = \frac{C}{P_K} - \frac{P_L L}{P_K}$$

$$\frac{dK}{dL} = \frac{-P_L}{P_K}$$

$$\frac{dQ}{dL} = 2K^{1/4}\left(\frac{3}{4} \right) L^{-1/4} + 2L^{3/4}\left(\frac{1}{4} \right) K^{-3/4} \frac{dK}{dL} = 0$$

$$\frac{3}{2} K^{1/4} L^{-1/4} + \frac{1}{2} K^{-3/4} L^{3/4} \left(\frac{-P_L}{P_K} \right) = 0$$

$$\frac{3K}{L} = \frac{P_L}{P_K} = \frac{10}{100} = \frac{1}{10}$$

$$L = 30K$$

$$K = \frac{100,000}{100} - \frac{10}{100}(30K)$$

$$K = 1000 - 3K$$

4K = 1000
K = 250   L = 30(250) = 7500

3. $\mathcal{L} = Q + \lambda(C - P_K K - P_L L)$

   $= 2K^{1/4} L^{3/4} + \lambda(C - P_K K - P_L L)$

   $\dfrac{\partial \mathcal{L}}{\partial K} = \dfrac{1}{2} K^{-3/4} L^{3/4} - \lambda P_K = 0$

   $\dfrac{\partial \mathcal{L}}{\partial L} = \dfrac{3}{2} K^{1/4} L^{-1/4} - \lambda P_L = 0$

   $\dfrac{\partial \mathcal{L}}{\partial \lambda} = C - P_K K \ P_L L = 0$

   $\dfrac{\dfrac{3}{2} K^{1/4} L^{-1/4}}{\dfrac{1}{2} K^{-3/4} L^{3/4}} = \dfrac{\lambda P_L}{\lambda P_K}$

   $\dfrac{3K}{L} = \dfrac{P_L}{P_K} = \dfrac{10}{100} = .1$

   L = 30K
   100,000 − 100K − 10(30K) = 0
   100,000 − 100K − 300K = 0
   K = 250
   L = 30K = 30(250) = 7500
   λ represents the extra output associated with an extra dollar of expenditure outlay.
   $Q = 2(250)^{1/4}(7500)^{3/4} = 6410$

   Constrained Cost Minimization Approach
   $\mathcal{L} = C + \lambda[Q - 2K^{1/4} L^{3/4}]$
   $\mathcal{L} = P_K K + P_L L + \lambda[Q - 2K^{1/4} L^{3/4}]$

   $\dfrac{\partial \mathcal{L}}{\partial K} = P_K - \dfrac{1}{2} \lambda K^{-3/4} L^{3/4} = 0$

   $\dfrac{\partial \mathcal{L}}{\partial L} = P_L - \dfrac{3}{2} \lambda K^{1/4} L^{-1/4} = 0$

   $\dfrac{\partial \mathcal{L}}{\partial \lambda} = Q - 2K^{1/4} L^{3/4} = 0$

$$\frac{\frac{3}{2}\lambda K^{1/4}L^{-1/4}}{\frac{1}{2}\lambda K^{-3/4}L^{3/4}} = \frac{P_L}{P_K}$$

$$\frac{3K}{L} = \frac{P_L}{P_K} = \frac{10}{100} = .1$$

$L = 30K$

$6410 - 2K^{1/4}(30K)^{3/4} = 0$

$6410 - 2(30)^{3/4}K = 0$

$K = 250 \qquad L = 30(250) = 7500$

$C = 100(250) + 10(7500) = 100,000$

4. $\mathscr{L} = C + \lambda[Q - K^{1/2}L^{1/2}]$

$\mathscr{L} = P_K K + P_L L + \lambda[Q - K^{1/2}L^{1/2}]$

$\frac{\partial\mathscr{L}}{\partial K} = P_K - \frac{1}{2}\lambda K^{-1/2}L^{1/2} = 0$

$\frac{\partial\mathscr{L}}{\partial L} = P_L - \frac{1}{2}\lambda K^{1/2}L^{-1/2} = 0$

$\frac{\partial\mathscr{L}}{\partial\lambda} = Q - K^{1/2}L^{1/2} = 0$

$$\frac{\frac{1}{2}\lambda K^{1/2}L^{-1/2}}{\frac{1}{2}\lambda K^{-1/2}L^{1/2}} = \frac{P_L}{P_K}$$

$$\frac{K}{L} = \frac{P_L}{P_K} = \frac{4}{1}$$

$K = 4L$

$100 - (4L)^{1/2}L^{1/2} = 0$

$100 - 2L = 0$

$L = 50 \qquad K = 4(50) = 200$

5. $u = f(C_1, C_2)$ where $u = C_1^{1/2}C_2^{1/2}$

$\mathscr{L} = C_1^{1/2}C_2^{1/2} + \lambda[31,000 - 1.1C_1 - C_2]$

$\quad = C_1^{1/2}C_2^{1/2} + \lambda 31,000 - \lambda 1.1 C_1 - \lambda C_2$

$$\frac{2\mathcal{L}}{2C_1} = \frac{1}{2}C_1^{-\frac{1}{2}}C_2^{-\frac{1}{2}} - \lambda 1.1 = 0$$

$$\frac{2\mathcal{L}}{2C_2} = (\frac{1}{2})C_1^{\frac{1}{2}}C_2^{-\frac{1}{2}} - \lambda = 0$$

$$\frac{2\mathcal{L}}{2\lambda} = 31{,}000 - 1.1C - C_2 = 0$$

$$\frac{\frac{2\mathcal{L}}{2C_1}}{\frac{2\mathcal{L}}{2C_2}} = \frac{\left(\frac{1}{2}\right)C_1^{-\frac{1}{2}}C_2^{\frac{1}{2}} - \lambda 1.1}{\left(\frac{1}{2}\right)C_1^{\frac{1}{2}}C_2^{-\frac{1}{2}} - \lambda} = 0$$

$$\frac{1/2\,C_1^{-1/2}C_2^{1/2}}{1/2\,C_1^{1/2}C_2^{-1/2}} = \frac{\lambda 1.1}{\lambda}$$

$$\frac{C_2}{C_1} = 1.1$$

$$C_2 = 1.1\,C_1$$

$$31{,}000 - 1.1C_1 - 1.1C_1 = 0$$

$$31{,}000 - 2.2C_1 = 0$$

$$C_1 = 14{,}091$$

$$C_2 = (14{,}091)\,1.1$$

$$C_2 = 15{,}500$$

Borrowing, since the individual's consumption exceeds his or her income for the first period.

Chapter 9

Exercise Set 9.1–Page 329

1. A deterministic relationship is one for which the value of the dependent variable is uniquely determined by the value(s) taken on by the independent variable(s). In a stochastic relationship, the dependent variable can take on more than one value for each set of value(s) of the independent variable(s). An error term is included in

a stochastic relationship to account for the fact that the actual values of a dependent variable may be different from the average values predicted by the rest of the function.

2. a)

Outcome				Probability
1	$\left(\dfrac{1}{2}\right)$	$\left(\dfrac{1}{2}\right)$	=	$\left(\dfrac{1}{4}\right)$
2	$\left(\dfrac{1}{2}\right)$	$\left(\dfrac{1}{2}\right)$	=	$\left(\dfrac{1}{4}\right)$
3	$\left(\dfrac{1}{2}\right)$	$\left(\dfrac{1}{2}\right)$	=	$\left(\dfrac{1}{4}\right)$
4	$\left(\dfrac{1}{2}\right)$	$\left(\dfrac{1}{2}\right)$	=	$\left(\dfrac{1}{4}\right)$

b) $\dfrac{1}{4}(0) + \dfrac{1}{4}(1) + \dfrac{1}{4}(1) + \dfrac{1}{4}(2) = 1.0$

c)

Outcome	Probability
3	$\dfrac{1}{2}$
4	$\dfrac{1}{2}$

$\dfrac{1}{2}(1) + \dfrac{1}{2}(2) = 1.5$

This is a conditional mean. Yes, the mean has been increased.

3. a) Class 1 $\bar{X} = \displaystyle\sum_{i=1}^{N} \dfrac{Xi}{N} = \dfrac{715}{10} = 71.5$

$$\text{Class 2} \quad \bar{X} = \sum_{i=1}^{N} \frac{Xi}{N} = \frac{715}{10} = 71.5$$

b)

Class 1 $(X_1 - X)^2$	Class 2 $(X_1 - X)^2$
342.25	552.25
132.25	272.25
272.25	210.25
992.25	1122.25
182.25	72.25
420.25	380.25
.25	30.25
12.25	20.25
12.25	182.25
42.25	272.25
2408.5	3114.5

Class 1: $\quad \text{Var} = \dfrac{2408.5}{10} = 240.85$

$\text{Std. Dev.} = \sqrt{240.85} = 15.52$

Class 2: $\quad \text{Var} = \dfrac{3114.5}{10} = 311.45$

$\text{Std. Dev.} = \sqrt{311.45} = 17.65$

There is a wider dispersion of test performance in the second class.

4. a) The sum of the rates of return $= 12 + 5 + (-20) + \ldots + (-5) = 60$. Since the number of observations, $N = 10$, the arithmetic mean rate of return $= 60/10 = 6\%$.

    b) The sum of squared deviations $= (12 - 6)^2 + (5 - 6)^2 + \ldots + (-5 - 6)^2 = 1624$. Since $N = 10$, the standard deviation of returns $= \sqrt{(1624)/10} = \sqrt{162.4} = 12.74$.

Exercise Set 9.2–Page 362

1. a) Graphed answer.

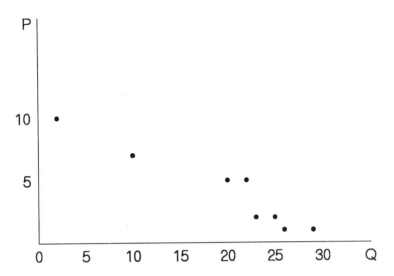

b) $\bar{P} = \sum\limits_{i=1}^{8} P_i/8 = 4.125$

$\bar{Q} = \sum\limits_{i=1}^{8} Q_i/8 = 19.625$

N	Q	P	$P_i-\bar{P}$	$Q_i-\bar{Q}$	$(P_i-\bar{P})^2$	$(P_i-\bar{P})(Q_i-\bar{Q})$	$\hat{Q}_i$	$Q_i-\hat{Q}_i$	$(Q_i-\hat{Q}_i)^2$	$(Q_i-\bar{Q}_i)^2$
1	20	5	.875	.375	.766	.328	17.264	2.736	7.486	.141
2	23	2	-2.125	3.375	4.516	-7.172	25.358	-2.358	5.560	11.391
3	26	1	-3.125	6.375	9.766	-19.922	28.056	-2.056	4.227	40.641
4	10	7	2.875	-9.625	8.266	-27.672	11.868	-1.868	3.489	92.641
5	25	2	-2.125	5.375	4.516	-11.422	25.358	-.358	.128	28.891
6	2	10	5.875	-17.625	34.516	-103.547	3.774	-1.774	3.147	310.641
7	22	5	.875	2.375	.766	2.078	17.264	4.736	22.430	5.641
8	29	1	-3.125	9.375	9.766	-29.297	28.056	.944	.891	87.891
Σ	157	33			72.878	-196.626			47.358	577.878

c) $\hat{b}_1 = \dfrac{-196.626}{72.878} = -2.698$

$\hat{b}_0 = 19.625 - (-2.698)(4.125) = 30.754$

d) Standard error of independent var P:

$$\left(\frac{72.878}{8}\right)^{\frac{1}{2}} = 3.018$$

Standard error of estimate:

$$\left(\frac{47.358}{6}\right)^{\frac{1}{2}} = 2.809$$

Standard error of $\hat{b}_1$:

$$\frac{2.809}{(3.018)\sqrt{8}} = .329$$

e) H_0: $b_1 = 0$

H_a: $b_1 \neq 0$

$t_{tab,6} = 2.45$

$$t = \frac{-2.698 - 0}{.329} = -8.201 > 2.45$$

Reject H_0 that $b_1 = 0$.

f) $R^2 = 1 - \dfrac{47.358}{577.878} = .918$

91.8% of the variation in Q is explained by the independent variable in the repression equation.

$$F_{1, 10-2} = \frac{RSS/1}{ESS/-2}$$

$$RSS = TSS - ESS$$

$$= 577.878 - 47.358$$

$$= 530.528$$

g) $F = \dfrac{530.528}{47.35816/6} = \dfrac{530.52}{7.893} = 67.214$

$F_{1,8-2} = 5.99$ for .05 level

Since $67.21 > 5.99$, we can reject H_0 that $b_1 = 0$.

2. a) The intercept represents the estimated value of Q^d when price and income have no influence. The partial slope coefficient,

   -4, estimates $\frac{\Delta Q}{\Delta P} \mid \bar{I}$,

   and

   $+2$, estimates $\frac{\Delta Q}{\Delta I} \mid \bar{P}$.

   b) Since the intercept accounts for factors not explicitly included in a regression equation, omitting I would increase the estimated intercept.

   c) The independent variables together, as a package, explain a significantly high percent of the variation in the dependent variable. This is indicated by the significant F statistic. However, the insignificant t statistics indicate that the independent variables, taken separately, do not significantly influence the dependent variable. There is likely some interaction or colinearity between the independent variables.

3. a) The intercept, 1000, indicates that national income would be 1000 billion dollars when G = 0. The slope coefficient, 20, indicates that for every 1 billion increase in G, there will be a 20 billion increase in national income. These are predicted values.

   b) No, not necessarily. There may be omitted variables influencing both Y and G, which if included would provide a better explanation for the variation in Y.

   c) Nothing. The results of the model indicate that there is a relationship between Y and G, not that changes in G necessarily cause changes in Y. The direction of causality might even be reversed.

4. Dependent variable Y = XYZ rate of return
   Independent variable X = S and P 500 rate of return

OBS	Y_1	X_1	$Y_i - \bar{Y}$	$X_i - \bar{X}$	$(X_i - \bar{X})^2$	$(X_i - \bar{X})(Y_i - \bar{Y})$	$\hat{Y}_i$	$Y_1 - \hat{Y}_i$	$(Y_1 - \hat{Y}_i)^2$
1	0.0550	0.0625	0.0355	0.0403	0.001620	0.001428	0.0677	-0.0127	0.00016128
2	0.1025	0.0850	0.0830	0.0628	0.003937	0.005208	0.0946	0.0079	0.00006173
3	0.0310	0.0420	0.0115	0.0198	0.000390	0.000227	0.0432	-0.0122	0.00014764
4	-0.0120	-0.0100	-0.0315	-0.0323	0.001040	0.001015	-0.0191	0.0071	0.00005069
5	-0.0450	-0.0400	-0.0645	-0.0623	0.003875	0.004015	-0.0550	0.0100	0.00010089
6	-0.0800	-0.0525	-0.0995	-0.0748	0.005587	0.007437	-0.0700	-0.0100	0.00009974
7	0.0150	0.0125	-0.0045	-0.0098	0.000095	0.000043	0.0078	0.0072	0.00005149
8	0.0625	0.0450	0.0430	0.0227	0.000517	0.000978	0.0467	0.0158	0.00024828
9	0.0420	0.0550	0.0225	0.0328	0.001072	0.000736	0.0587	-0.0167	0.00027950
10	-0.0350	-0.0225	-0.0545	-0.0448	0.002002	0.002438	-0.0341	-0.0009	0.00000083
11	0.0130	0.0250	-0.0065	0.0027	0.000007	-0.000010	0.0228	-0.0098	0.00009591
	0.0850	0.0650	0.0655	0.0428	0.001827	0.002800	0.0707	0.0143	0.00020468
Σ					0.021973	0.026313			0.00150264

$\bar{Y} = 0.0195$

$\bar{X} = 0.02225$

$$\hat{B}_1 = \frac{\sum(X_i - \bar{X})(Y - \bar{Y}_i)}{\sum(X_i - \bar{X})^2} = \frac{.026313}{.021973} = 1.20$$

$$\hat{B}_0 = \bar{Y} - \hat{B}_1\bar{X} = .0195 - 1.20(.0225) = -.0071$$

Therefore, $\hat{Y} = -.0071 + 1.20X$

For any one unit change in the market index (X), there would be a 1.20 unit change in the return on asset Y, in the same direction.

$$\hat{S}^2_{u_i} = \frac{\sum\limits_{i=1}^{N} (Y_i - \hat{Y}_i)^2}{N - 2} = \frac{.0015}{10} = .00015$$

$$S^2_{\hat{b}_1} = \frac{\hat{S}^2_{u_i}}{\sum\limits_{i=1}^{N} (X_i - \bar{X})^2} = \frac{.00015}{.022} = .0068$$

$$S_{\hat{b}_1} = .0825$$

H_0: $b_1 = 0$
H_a: $b_1 \neq 0$

$$t = \frac{1.20 - 0}{.0825} = 14.54$$

Since $t_{cal} = 14.54 > t_{crit} = 2.23$, we can reject H_0 that $b_1 = 0$.

The sum of the intercept and the error term can be interpreted as the diversifiable return.